Studies in Latin American
Ethnohistory & Archaeology

Joyce Marcus
General Editor

Volume I   *A Fuego y Sangre: Early Zapotec Imperialism in the Cuicatlán Cañada, Oaxaca*, by Elsa Redmond, Memoirs of the Museum of Anthropology, University of Michigan, No. 16. 1983.

Volume II   *Irrigation and the Cuicatec Ecosystem: A Study of Agriculture and Civilization in North Central Oaxaca*, by Joseph W. Hopkins, Memoirs of the Museum of Anthropology, University of Michigan, No. 17. 1984.

Volume III   *Aztec City-States*, by Mary G. Hodge, Memoirs of the Museum of Anthropology, University of Michigan, No. 18. 1984.

Volume IV   *Conflicts over Coca Fields in Sixteenth-Century Peru*, by María Rostworowski de Díez Canseco, Memoirs of the Museum of Anthropology, University of Michigan, No. 21. 1988.

Volume V   *Tribal and Chiefly Warfare in South America*, by Elsa Redmond, Memoirs of the Museum of Anthropology, University of Michigan, No. 28. 1994.

Volume VI   *Imperial Transformations in Sixteenth-Century Yucay, Peru*, transcribed and edited by R. Alan Covey and Donato Amado González, Memoirs of the Museum of Anthropology, University of Michigan, No. 44. 2008.

Volume VII   *Domestic Life in Prehispanic Capitals: A Study of Specialization, Hierarchy, and Ethnicity*, edited by Linda R. Manzanilla and Claude Chapdelaine, Memoirs of the Museum of Anthropology, University of Michigan, No. 46. 2009.

Volume VIII   *Yuthu: Community and Ritual in an Early Andean Village*, by Allison R. Davis, Memoirs of the Museum of Anthropology, University of Michigan, No. 50. 2011.

Volume IX   *Advances in Titicaca Basin Archaeology–III*, edited by Alexei Vranich, Elizabeth A. Klarich, and Charles Stanish, Memoirs of the Museum of Anthropology, University of Michigan, No. 51. 2012.

Volume X   *Regional Archaeology in the Inca Heartland: The Hanan Cuzco Surveys*, edited by R. Alan Covey, Memoirs of the Museum of Anthropology, University of Michigan, No. 55. 2014.

Memoirs of the Museum of Anthropology
University of Michigan
Number 55

Studies in Latin American Ethnohistory & Archaeology
Joyce Marcus, General Editor
Volume X

Regional Archaeology in the Inca Heartland

The Hanan Cuzco Surveys

edited by R. Alan Covey

Ann Arbor, Michigan
2014

©2014 by the Regents of the University of Michigan
The Museum of Anthropology
All rights reserved

Printed in the United States of America
ISBN 978-0-915703-83-8

Cover design by Katherine Clahassey

The University of Michigan Museum of Anthropology currently publishes two monograph series:
Anthropological Papers and Memoirs. For permissions, questions, or catalogs, contact Museum of
Anthropology Publications: 1109 Geddes Avenue, Ann Arbor, MI 48109-1079;
umma-pubs@umich.edu; www.lsa.umich.edu/umma/

Library of Congress Cataloging-in-Publication Data

Regional archaeology in the Inca heartland: the Hanan Cuzco surveys / edited by R. Alan Covey.
    pages cm. -- (Memoirs of the museum of anthropology, University of Michigan ; number 55)
(Studies in Latin American ethnohistory & archaeology ; volume X)
 Includes bibliographical references.
 ISBN 978-0-915703-83-8 (alk. paper)
 1. Incas--Peru--Cuzco Region--Antiquities. 2. Archaeological surveying--Peru--Cuzco Region. 3.
Cuzco Region (Peru)--Antiquities. I. Covey, R. Alan, 1974- editor, author.
 F3429.1.C9R44 2014
 985.'3701--dc23
                        2014000867

The paper used in this publication meets the requirements of the ANSI Standard Z39.48-1984
(Permanence of Paper).

Front cover: Photo of a dance group from Pisac gathering at the Inca ruins above their town to
make reverence to Pachatusan (background) before descending to take part in an annual saint's
day festival. Photo: A. Covey.

Contents

Illustrations

Tables

Foreword

Settlement Patterns in the Inca Heartland

by Joyce Marcus

The Inca are known mainly from written documents, a record that began with the arrival of Francisco Pizarro in A.D. 1532. Pizarro captured Atahuallpa, the Inca ruler, and held him hostage in Cajamarca for more than 8 months. To free him, the Inca assembled a ransom that consisted of 10 tons of gold and 70 tons of silver (Rostworowski and Morris 1999:771). After filling entire rooms from floor to ceiling with gold and silver, Atahuallpa's loyal subjects fully expected their ruler to be released. Instead, Pizarro had Atahuallpa killed in July of 1533.

The conquistadors' lust for gold was surprising to the Inca because the latter measured their wealth in fine textiles, herds of alpacas and llamas, and well-stocked storehouses at way-stations along the roads of their empire. In their relentless pursuit of precious metals, Pizarro's men traveled to Cuzco to strip the Inca capital of its treasures. They removed gold sheets from the walls of Cuzco's Sun Temple, the "Golden Enclosure" or Coricancha. From other buildings they took sheets of gold alloy, gold benches, gold vessels, and gold fountains. In another building, the Spaniards discovered so many silver vessels that they could not transport them all to Cajamarca; instead they sealed the door, placed guards there, and claimed the silver in the name of King Charles I and Pizarro. After spending 8 days sacking Cuzco, Pizarro's men carried as much of the treasure as they could to Cajamarca on the backs of 700 native porters.

Having such dramatic and detailed accounts—including the names, dates, and deeds of specific protagonists—it is no wonder that so many scholars prefer to rely on Colonial documents. A good example would be the writings of Juan de Betanzos ([1557] 1987), who spent years in Cuzco as an interpreter for the viceroyalty of Peru (Betanzos had intimate knowledge of royal life because he was married to a former wife of Atahuallpa). By relying almost exclusively on such documents, however, we have put off learning about Cuzco's deep history, the millennia preceding the Inca Empire. Our knowledge of the communities surrounding Cuzco has also been limited by an over-reliance on documents concerning the capital.

To learn about the deep history of Cuzco and its hinterland, we must turn to the archaeological record. Early explorers and archaeologists focused on the well-preserved Inca stonework at Saqsaywaman, Machu Picchu, and Cuzco. They were drawn to Inca sites with spectacular architecture, rather than to the smaller towns and villages in Cuzco's hinterland. Such monumental works were the focus of Ephraim George Squier (who also mapped the earthworks at Newark, Ohio, and elsewhere in North America), Hiram Bingham (who excavated at Machu Picchu), and Luis Valcárcel (excavator of Saqsaywaman) (see Squier [1877] 1973; Bingham 1913, 1915, 1922; Valcárcel 1934, 1935, 1946). Although monumental buildings tell us much about the vision of Inca nobles, they provide little information about the rise of the Inca and the lives of the farmers and herders who supported them.

The Spaniards did, of course, record the Incas' own myths of their origins (Bauer 1991, 1992, 2004; Kosiba 2010). One of these relates the story of the four mythical Ayar brothers (Rostworowski 1970). All four emerged from the cave of Tampu T'oqo at Pakariq Tampu (Pacariqtambo) in search of good agricultural land. The first brother was Ayar Kachi, "ancestor salt." The second brother was Ayar Uchu, "ancestor chile pepper"; he later transformed himself into a stone on the mountain called Huanacauri, where he became a sacred shrine or *wak'a*. The third brother, Ayar Awka or "ancestor enemy or outsider," was the first to arrive at what would become Cuzco. He, too, was turned into stone. The fourth brother was Ayar Manqu, "first ancestor"; he became known as Manqu Khapaq (Manco Capac), the first Inca king. He allegedly lived in the Temple of the Sun in Hurin (or lower) Cuzco.

This Volume

In this volume, R. Alan Covey and his collaborators demonstrate that a narrow focus on monumental stonework and Inca royalty have limited the development of Inca and pre-Inca archaeology in the Cuzco region. To document the rise of the Inca, we need to combine ethnohistory with systematic surveys and expansive horizontal excavations. From documents, we know that the atmosphere before the early Inca state arose was competitive. There was increasing rivalry among ethnic groups and polities. The Inca state was born out of that regional competition.

For example, the chroniclers tell us that Manco Capac, founder of the Inca dynasty, had two rivals that used the title of *qhapaq*, or king. The most powerful was Tocay Capac of the Ayarmaca, a group lying northwest of Cuzco in the Maras area. Tocay Capac used not only the title "king" but also *sinchi*, or war leader, and in that latter role he was able to consolidate his power. At the height of his power, Tocay Capac forged marriage alliances to elite families in the Sacred Valley and Xaquixaguana Valley. As the Inca dynasty grew more powerful, former Ayarmaca subordinates established marriage alliances with Inca nobles, and the Ayarmaca became tribute-paying subjects of the growing Inca state.

We might therefore expect settlement patterns northwest of Cuzco, home of the Ayarmaca, to reflect disruption or abandonment as the Inca took control. As this volume shows, settlement in the Maras area does indeed reveal major reorganization prior to the development of the Inca imperial ceramic style.

One of the principal goals of the Hanan Cuzco surveys was to expand our knowledge of the full range of settlements surrounding the Inca capital. In the past, some archaeologists shied away from doing full-coverage survey because they were most interested in what happened after Pachacuti and they assumed that survey data would add few details. They also were drawn to the monumental stonework, and only recently extended their interest to include much less impressive archaeological remains.

Even though conducting full-coverage surveys in mountainous terrain was exhausting and difficult, Covey et al.'s dedicated efforts have yielded settlement pattern data that are altering our understanding of the Inca and all the societies that preceded them. It has become increasingly clear that one must utilize this kind of regional framework and conduct both extensive excavations and large-scale settlement surveys.

This volume reports on the systematic survey of four areas in Hanan (or upper) Cuzco, which together constitute a survey area of 1200 km². That 1200 km² area was occupied for millennia, culminating with the remains of country estates, irrigation canals, and pasturelands that once belonged to Inca rulers of the Hanan Cuzco moiety (Covey 2006; Covey, Aráoz Silva, and Bauer 2008; Niles 2004). Although preceramic occupation was once thought to be missing from the Cuzco region, Brian Bauer et al. have shown it was there (Bauer, Jones, and Klink 2004; Bauer 2007). The identification of Early Archaic (9500–7000 B.C.) projectile points has pushed back the date of human occupation to the end of the Pleistocene. Excavations by Allison Davis (2010, 2011, this volume) and Véronique Bélisle (2011, this volume) have documented the presence of Formative villages in the region.

Hanan Cuzco Surveys

John H. Rowe (1944, 1945) was the first to publish an artifact sequence and ceramic chronology for the later periods around Cuzco. Subsequent excavations have refined his definition of particular pottery types and styles, and stratified deposits have allowed those styles to be given absolute dates. One of Rowe's doctoral students, Edward Dwyer (1971), conducted fieldwork on the pre-Inca occupation of Cuzco. Rowe and Dwyer noted that the Inca (Late Horizon) ceramics were preceded by Late Intermediate wares that were usually decorated with geometric designs in black and red. The most widely distributed Late Intermediate style throughout the Cuzco region is called Killke (Rowe 1944; Dwyer 1971; Rivera Dorado 1971a, 1971b; Bauer 1999). Killke pottery was the dominant style in Cuzco and within 20 km of the Cuzco Basin, suggesting that it was locally manufactured.

Thanks to Miguel Rivera Dorado, Gordon McEwan, Bauer, Covey, and others, we now know that there were indeed a number of different ceramic styles in the region during the Late Intermediate. To the south of the Cuzco Valley, Bauer (1999) identified the Colcha style in the Paruro region. To the southeast of Cuzco, McEwan, Chatfield, and Gibaja (2002) found the Lucre style, also known from the Cuzco Valley and Sacred Valley. North of the Vilcanota-Urubamba River, Covey (2006) identified a local style called Cuyo in the Chongo Basin. To the west and northwest of Cuzco, there seem to be two local Late Intermediate styles—one centered on Chinchero (Rivera Dorado 1972) and another in the Maras area (Maqque Azorsa and Haquehua Huaman 1993; Haquehua Huaman and Maqque Azorsa 1996). These multiple styles reinforce our impression that the Inca had to overcome numerous rival polities.

Clearly, the 400-year period we call Late Intermediate is much more complex than we formerly assumed (Covey 2008). In addition to the variety of local styles, the settlement pattern data show significant discontinuity, with many new villages appearing for the first time in the Late Intermediate. Many are situated on ridgetops that lacked occupation during the preceding Middle Horizon; and later, many Middle Horizon sites were simply abandoned.

A fascinating topic that has emerged over the last couple of decades is the degree of overlap of Killke and Inca pottery styles. Excavations indicate that the Inca "imperial" style actually originated prior to A.D. 1400, and that some Late Intermediate pottery types continued to be used during the Inca period (Covey 2006:90–91; Dwyer 1971; Kendall 1985; Lunt 1988). This ceramic overlap creates a challenge for surveyors who are trying to specify when Late Intermediate sites were abandoned, when new Inca sites were founded, and when sites were continuously occupied throughout both periods. Some areas lack Cuzco polychrome pottery despite not having been completely abandoned around A.D. 1400.

Following the pioneering work of Rowe and Dwyer, Ann Kendall (1985) carried out a study of Inca and pre-Inca architectural remains in the Cuzco region. Kendall later directed the Cusichaca Project, a reconnaissance and excavation program in the Urubamba Valley, situated between Ollantaytambo and Machu Picchu (Kendall 1994). As a member of Kendall's project, Bauer got his introduction to Cuzco archaeology. In turn, Covey got his start as a member of Bauer's Cuzco Valley Archaeological Project.

In the late 1980s, Bauer conducted the first systematic full-coverage survey in the area. His survey in the Paruro region covered 600 km² to the south of the Cuzco Valley. Bauer reconstructed regional settlement patterns from the first millennium B.C. to the era of the Inca Empire. Significantly, Bauer also conducted excavations at 15 of those sites to clarify the Paruro sequence. He was ultimately able to tie particular ceramic types found in stratigraphically meaningful contexts to radiocarbon dates (Bauer 1999). Having demonstrated the value of conducting full-coverage systematic survey south of the Cuzco Valley, Bauer then turned to the Cuzco Valley to conduct a survey in the early 1990s, and from 1997 to 1999 he set about surveying the Cuzco and Oropesa Basins. By extending systematic survey coverage into the Lucre Basin in 2006, Bauer and Aráoz Silva finished the survey of the greater Cuzco Valley.

Covey directed the first Hanan Cuzco survey in the Sacred Valley in 2000. That survey covered 400 km² in the Vilcanota-Urubamba Valley and its tributary basins. That Sacred Valley Project entailed a full-coverage survey of sites below 4000 m. Higher terrain between 4000 and 4500 m was systematically surveyed by the Qoricocha Puna Survey. The surveys documented in the present volume retain the survey methods developed by Bauer and add improvements to show period-by-period distributions of ceramic styles at large multicomponent sites.

Covey and his colleagues present their hard-won results from four surveys, united here in this volume. By doing so, we see significant differences from survey to survey, from subregion to subregion. This diversity in settlement history is important, showing that we cannot take data from one subregion and assume that they apply to all the other subregions. This volume shows that the four regional surveys in Hanan Cuzco—those conducted in the Sacred Valley, the Xaquixaguana Plain, the Calca-Yanahuara area, and the Qoricocha Puna Survey—are not isomorphic. Each subregion displays distinctive patterns, all of which need to be understood to reconstruct the whole region's history.

It is important that a uniform set of methods was used to survey the entire Hanan Cuzco region. As a result, when we see contrasts among the four survey areas, we know that they are genuine cultural differences, rather than a byproduct of differences in survey methods. The data presented in this volume were retrieved after covering thousands of kilometers, hiking up and down steep mountain slopes. By implementing such a systematic approach, Covey et al. have generated a great deal of information about the settlement patterns of Hanan Cuzco. In turn, they have transformed the Cuzco region into a laboratory for understanding long-term social change.

References

Bauer, Brian S.
1991   Pacariqtambo and the mythical origins of the Inca. *Latin American Antiquity* 2(1):7–26.
1992   *The Development of the Inca State*. Austin: University of Texas Press.
1999   *The Early Ceramics of the Inca Heartland*. Fieldiana Anthropology, New Series no. 31. Chicago: Field Museum of Natural History.
2004   *Ancient Cuzco: Heartland of the Inca*. Austin: University of Texas Press.
2007   *Kasapata and the Archaic Period of the Cuzco Valley*. Cotsen Institute Monograph 57. University of California, Los Angeles: Cotsen Institute of Archaeology.

Bauer, Brian S., Bradford Jones, and Cindy Klink
2004   The Archaic period and the first people of the Cuzco Valley (9500–2200 BC). In *Ancient Cuzco: Heartland of the Inca*, edited by Brian S. Bauer, pp. 31–37. Austin: University of Texas Press.

Bélisle, Véronique
2011   Ak'awillay: Wari State Expansion and Household Change in Cusco, Peru (AD 600–1000). PhD dissertation, Department of Anthropology, University of Michigan, Ann Arbor.

Betanzos, Juan de
[1557] 1987   *Suma y narración de los Incas*, transcribed and edited by María del Carmen Rubio. Madrid, Spain: Ediciones Atlas.

Bingham, Hiram
1913   The discovery of Machu Picchu. *Harper's Magazine* 127:709–19.
1915   Types of Machu Picchu pottery. *American Anthropologist* 17:257–71.
1922   *Inca Land: Explorations in the Highlands of Peru*. Cambridge, MA: Riverside Press.

Covey, R. Alan
2006   *How the Incas Built Their Heartland: State Formation and the Innovation of Imperial
       Strategies in the Sacred Valley, Peru*. Ann Arbor: University of Michigan Press.
2008   Multiregional perspectives on the archaeology of the Andes during the Late Intermediate period
       (ca. AD 1000–1400). *Journal of Archaeological Research* 16(3):287–338.

Covey, R. Alan, Miriam Aráoz Silva, and Brian S. Bauer
2008   Settlement patterns in the Yucay Valley and neighboring areas. In *Imperial Transformations
       in Sixteenth-Century Yucay, Peru*, edited by R. Alan Covey and Donato Amado González, pp.
       3–17. Memoirs, no. 44. Ann Arbor: Museum of Anthropology, University of Michigan.

Davis, Allison R.
2010   Excavations at Yuthu: A Community Study of an Early Village in Cusco, Peru (400–100 BC).
       PhD dissertation, Department of Anthropology, University of Michigan, Ann Arbor.
2011   *Yuthu: Community and Ritual in an Early Andean Village*. Memoirs, no. 50. Ann Arbor:
       Museum of Anthropology, University of Michigan.

Dwyer, Edward B.
1971   The Early Inca Occupation of the Valley of Cuzco, Peru. PhD dissertation, Department of
       Anthropology, University of California, Berkeley.

Haquehua Huaman, Wilbert, and Rubén Maqque Azorsa
1996   Cerámica de Cueva Moqo-Maras. Tesis, Facultad de Ciencias Sociales, Universidad Nacional
       de San Antonio Abad del Cusco.

Kendall, Ann
1985   *Aspects of Inca Architecture: Description, Function and Chronology*, parts 1 and 2. BAR
       International Series 242. Oxford: British Archaeological Reports.
1994   *Proyecto Arqueológico Cusichaca, Cusco: Investigaciones arqueológicas y de rehabilitación
       agrícola*. Tomo I. Lima: Southern Peru Copper Corporation.

Kosiba, Steven B.
2010   Becoming Inca: The Transformation of Political Place and Practice during Inca State Formation
       (Cusco, Peru). PhD dissertation, Department of Anthropology, University of Chicago.

Lunt, Sarah
1988   The manufacture of the Inca aryballus. In *Recent Studies in Pre-Columbian Archaeology, Part
       2*, edited by Nicholas J. Saunders and Olivier de Montmollin, pp. 489–511. BAR International
       Series 421(ii). Oxford: British Archaeological Reports.

McEwan, Gordon F., Melissa Chatfield, and Arminda Gibaja
2002   The archaeology of Inca origins: Excavations at Chokepukio, Cuzco, Peru. In *Andean
       Archaeology I: Variations in Sociopolitical Organization*, edited by William H. Isbell and
       Helaine Silverman, pp. 287–301. New York: Kluwer Academic/Plenum Press.

Maqque Azorsa, Rubén, and Wilbert Haquehua Huaman
1993   Prospección arqueológica de Cueva Moqo-Maras. Informe de prácticas preprofesionales,
       Facultad de Ciencias Sociales, Universidad Nacional de San Antonio Abad del Cusco.

Niles, Susan A.
2004　The nature of Inca royal estates. In *Machu Picchu: Unveiling the Mystery of the Incas*, edited by Richard L. Burger and Lucy C. Salazar, pp. 48–68. New Haven, CT: Yale University Press.

Rivera Dorado, Miguel
1971a　La cerámica killke y la arqueología de Cuzco (Perú). *Revista Española de Antropología Americana* 6:85–124.
1971b　Diseños decorativos en la cerámica killke. *Revista del Museo Nacional* 37:106–15.
1972　La cerámica de Cancha-Cancha, Cuzco, Perú. *Revista Dominicana de Arqueología y Antropología* 2(2–3):36–49.

Rostworowski, María
1970　Los ayarmaca. *Revista del Museo Nacional* 36:58–101.

Rostworowski, María, and Craig Morris
1999　The fourfold domain: Inca power and its social foundations. In *The Cambridge History of the Native Peoples of the Americas, Volume III, Part I: South America*, edited by Frank Salomon and Stuart B. Schwartz, pp. 769–863. Cambridge, UK: Cambridge University Press.

Rowe, John H.
1944　*An Introduction to the Archaeology of Cuzco*. Papers of the Peabody Museum of American Archaeology and Ethnology 27(2). Cambridge, MA: Harvard University.
1945　Absolute chronology in the Andean area. *American Antiquity* 10(3):265–84.

Squier, Ephraim George
[1877] 1973　*Peru: Incidents of Travel and Exploration in the Land of the Incas*. New York: Henry Holt.

Valcárcel, Luis E.
1934　Los trabajos arqueológicos en el Departamento del Cusco. Sajsawaman redescubierto II. *Revista del Museo Nacional* 3:3–36, 211–33.
1935　Los trabajos arqueológicos en el Departamento del Cusco. Sajsawaman redescubierto III–IV. *Revista del Museo Nacional* 4:1–24, 161–203.
1946　Cuzco Archaeology. In *Handbook of South American Indians, Volume 2: The Andean Civilizations*, edited by Julian H. Steward, pp. 177–82. Bulletin of the Bureau of American Ethnology, no. 143. Washington, D.C.: United States Government Printing Office.

Acknowledgments

by R. Alan Covey

Regional surveys are labor intensive, and the collection of data requires crews who are tough, patient, and committed to the research even in adverse conditions. The data presented in this volume represent thousands of miles of hiking, some of it in rain or hail, across dangerous mountain slopes, or around the paths of angry dogs, livestock, and people. None of these projects could have been successfully brought to completion without the collaborative efforts of every member of the research team. Wilfredo Yépez Valdez deserves special mention as the co-director of most of the survey research reported here (Miriam Aráoz Silva co-directed the Calca-Yanahuara survey with Brian Bauer and me). Although he was unable to join us in the field, Wilfredo was a supportive presence in the project administration, and he treated me as a member of his family during my time in Cuzco. Several members of the Yépez family worked with us in the laboratory, helping to wash, label, and organize field collections.

The survey crew for the Sacred Valley Archaeological Project consisted of Ricardo Huayllani, Rene Pilco, Herberth Reynaga, and Werner Delgado. Amelia Pérez and Christina Elson joined the crew for short stints, and Kenny Sims directed mapping at several of the larger Late Intermediate period sites at the end of the survey work.

The Xaquixaguana project was a larger and more intensive undertaking, and Allison Davis and Véronique Bélisle worked as crew chiefs for both seasons. Our Peruvian colleagues included Luz Apaza, Viky Galiano, Yolanda Paucar, Naty Menacho, Natalie Vicuña, and Belén Olivera. After the first season in the Xaquixaguana region, Carlo Socualaya and Jorge Flores joined us in the field in the Qoricocha survey, and Karina Yager helped to supervise one of the two crews that worked there. In 2005 the crew from the first season was joined by Kristina Garcia, Nicholas Griffis, Catherine Covey, and Michael Trapp. Steve Kosiba joined us briefly in the field during a phase of intensive collections at large sites. Following fieldwork, Maeve Skidmore and Kylie Quave worked with Viky Galiano to conduct a regional toponym survey, while Donato Amado directed local archival work. Melissa Clark conducted a supervised landcover analysis of satellite imagery from the Xaquixaguana region, and Lia Tsesmeli developed a DEM for the region and has been responsible for generating most of the maps presented in this volume.

The small Calca-Yanahuara survey crew comprised three co-directors (Aráoz Silva, Bauer, and Covey), as well as three local archaeology students—Geaneth Guzmán, Benigno Zamalloa, and Jorge Flores. Brad Jones had conducted preliminary reconnaissance in this region and generously offered the results of his work as we engaged in systematic surveys.

The Hanan Cuzco survey projects received generous research support from several sources. Reconnaissance work in the Cuzco region was funded by a National Science Foundation Graduate Research Fellowship (1998–2002), as well as various sources at the University of Michigan, including the Rackham Graduate School, the Latin American and Caribbean Studies program, and the James B. Griffin Fund at the Museum of Anthropology. The 2000 survey research of the Sacred Valley Archaeological Project received support from a Fulbright-Hays Doctoral Dissertation Research Abroad Fellowship; excavations at Pukara Pantillijlla were supported by the Wenner-Gren Foundation (Individual Grant #6604), and a National Science Foundation Dissertation Improvement Grant (BCS-0135913; PI: Joyce Marcus) funded radiocarbon dates from excavations and standing architecture. The Xaquixaguana Plain Archaeological Survey (2004–2006) received support from the National Science Foundation (BCS-0342381), which was supplemented by internal research grants from the American Museum of Natural History and Southern Methodist University. The National Geographic Society (#7661-04) supported the high-elevation survey of the Qoricocha region, and the Heinz Grant Program for Latin American Archaeology provided funding for the Calca-Yanahuara Archaeological Project. A Collaborative Research Grant (RZ-50818-07) from the National Endowment for the Humanities permitted additional archival research and a formal toponym survey and mapping work in the Xaquixaguana region following the completion of the survey research. Support for recent GIS analysis and preparation of maps has been provided by Dartmouth College.

Beyond the field and the laboratory, many people have been generous supporters of this research. Joyce Marcus has been a patient and generous editor, which made the journey from data to monograph much less intimidating. Jill Rheinheimer kept the editorial ship afloat when I was distracted with teaching and other research responsibilities, and she helped to identify and correct lingering flaws in the manuscript. Kay Clahassey designed the cover art. Finally, Dartmouth College provided research funds to support publication costs, including the editorial assistance of Emily Neely.

Introduction

by R. Alan Covey

In 1534, European readers began to devour published accounts of the Spanish invasion of the Inca empire, the most powerful indigenous civilization in the Americas. Eyewitnesses described the Spanish penetration of the Andean realm of the Incas in 1532, including the fateful encounter between Francisco Pizarro and Atahuallpa (the last independent Inca ruler) at Cajamarca, a highland city on the royal Inca road from Cuzco, the Inca capital, to the northern frontier in what is today Ecuador and southern Colombia. The capture, ransom, and execution of the Inca monarch kept the Spaniards at Cajamarca for nine months, and it was not until November 15, 1533, that the Pizarro expedition reached the Inca capital. What they saw in Cuzco overwhelmed them, and the eyewitness description of Pizarro's secretary, Pedro Sancho, compares the city favorably with European centers and the most impressive Roman ruins on the Iberian peninsula.

Sancho's account of Cuzco and its surrounding hinterland established the Inca city in the European mind, setting the tone for how historians and archaeologists have approached the region until very recently. To Sancho, Cuzco's wealth and monumentality made it a city that would be noteworthy in Spain, and its countryside was dominated by rural palaces and estates for the pleasure of Inca nobles (Fig. 1). Although much of Cuzco burned in an Inca uprising that was already underway by the time Sancho's chronicle was published in Europe, many of the monumental remains of Inca architecture survive to this day. These marvels drew explorers and naturalists to the Cuzco region in the late eighteenth and nineteenth centuries, men like E. George Squier who pioneered the description of ancient indigenous monuments in the United States. The archaeology of Cuzco was born from a fascination with these ruins—from the rediscovery of Machu Picchu by Hiram Bingham in 1911 to Luis Valcárcel's excavations at the Inca "fortress" of Saqsaywaman to commemorate the 400th anniversary of the Spanish founding of Cuzco (Fig. 2) (Bingham 1922; Valcárcel 1934, 1935).

Figure 1. Woodcut from a 1554 edition of Pedro de Cieza de León's *Crónica del Perú*, showing a Spaniard and an Inca at Cuzco, which is depicted as a European city.

Figure 2. Aerial view of the Inca monumental site of Saqsaywaman, taken by the Shippee-Johnson expedition in 1931, just before Valcárcel's excavations commenced. Courtesy Department of Library Services, American Museum of Natural History (neg. no. 334794).

Moving beyond Monuments

Inca palaces and other constructed remains have served for centuries as mnemonics for historical narratives that were told by Inca nobles and put to paper only in the generations following the European invasion. They buttress a historicist reading of Colonial narratives as they promote a royal geography for the Inca capital and surrounding areas. Unfortunately, the stories they present are incomplete, and often far from factual. Together, the monuments and early chronicles tell us a great deal about noble life on the eve of the European invasion, but they do not offer a reliable portrayal of the lives of ordinary people living in the Inca heartland, and they fail to provide plausible accounts of the Cuzco region before the rise of the Inca empire. The chronicles focus on the heroic exploits of male Inca paramounts, deploying an Inca concept of civilization that is centered on royal networks in and around Cuzco—people living at a temporal, geographic, or social distance from the monarch are portrayed as wild and ungoverned (Covey 2011).

The longstanding focus on noble Incas and their monumental remains has limited the advance of archaeology in the Cuzco region. One has only to compare maps of the region over time

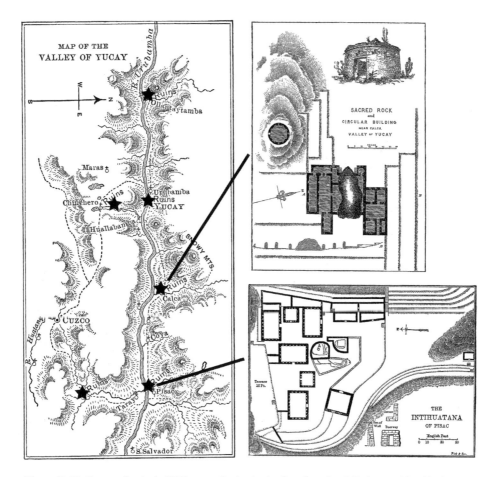

Figure 3. E. George Squier's 1877 map of ruins in the Inca heartland. Ruins are identified at just a handful of imperial Inca sites, marked with stars. Most of these, like Urco and Pisac, are imperial Inca sites.

to understand the slow accretion of knowledge. Squier (1877:483) identifies Inca ruins in six locations in the region to the north and west of Cuzco (Fig. 3), and Valcárcel (1946:177) states that the descriptions of Squier and other nineteenth-century explorers (such as Markham [1856], Wiener [1880], and Middendorf [1893–1895]) remained authoritative until the 1930s (cf. Rowe 1944:8). Eighty years after Squier, Pardo (1957) discusses a few dozen sites outside Cuzco, of which only Pikillacta is a pre-Inca site. By the 1980s, the number of published archaeological sites remained fewer than 100—for example, Kendall (1985:393) provides the most comprehensive map of that time, which locates 36 Inca and pre-Inca sites across the broader Cuzco region (cf. Rowe 1944; McEwan 1984). In the absence of a representative depiction of the archaeological history of the Inca heartland, it was possible until quite recently for historians to construct the pre-Inca landscape using Inca mythology alone (e.g., Julien 2000:242). In 2002, Terence D'Altroy (2002:55) noted that "[t]he archaeological origins of Inca society are almost as sketchy as the historical record."

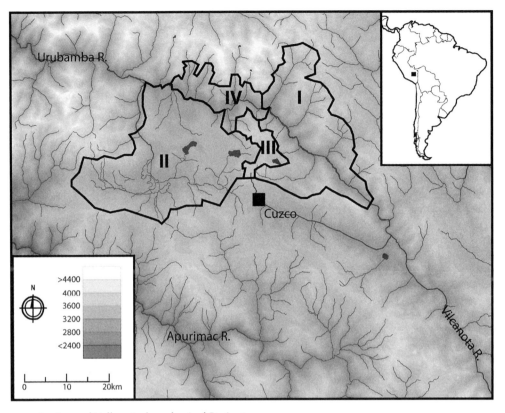

I. Sacred Valley Archaeological Project
II. Xaquixaguana Plain Archaeological Survey
III. Qoricocha Puna Survey
IV. Calca-Yanahuara Archaeological Survey

Figure 4. Map of Cuzco region showing Hanan Cuzco survey boundaries.

Today, more than 3000 archaeological sites across the Cuzco region have been registered. The vast majority of these are scatters of ancient pottery and stone tools collected in a series of systematic full-coverage regional surveys conducted from the mid-1980s to the present (Fig. 4). Systematic regional research using a consistent field methodology has done more than simply populate the Inca imperial heartland with the towns and villages of non-royal populations—it has transformed the region from an ancillary illustration of Colonial narratives into a laboratory for understanding human social change over millennia. As Cuzco has become one of the largest continuously surveyed regions in South America, settlement pattern data are beginning to contribute to scientific reconstructions of Andean prehistory, from the time of human colonization to the period of Spanish colonialism.

Contemporary Cuzco and the Hanan Cuzco Survey Region

This volume presents the results of four regional survey projects conducted by the editor and his North American and Peruvian colleagues from 2000 to 2007. The chapters that follow discuss key developments over time across a region to the north and west of Cuzco that is referred to here as the Hanan Cuzco region. This region contains much of the environmental diversity found around Cuzco today, but unique local characteristics influence occupational histories and the results of archaeological survey work. In Chapter 1, Covey, Bélisle, and Davis offer a detailed description of the Hanan Cuzco region, with an emphasis on environmental characteristics and ethnographic evidence for subsistence practices in the late twentieth and early twenty-first centuries. This discussion includes a brief consideration of how rural Cuzco in the ethnographic present differs from prehistoric conditions, including the ways in which climate and seasonality presented challenges and opportunities for subsistence at different times in the past.

In Chapter 2, Covey and Skidmore place the Hanan Cuzco region in a research context. After a brief discussion of the development of the regional artifact sequence and the introduction of the common survey methodology used by all Hanan Cuzco projects, this chapter discusses specific methods employed by each project in the field and laboratory.

Transitions to Sedentism

Having discussed some of the interpretive opportunities and challenges of working with the Hanan Cuzco survey data, the monograph turns to a number of thematic chapters that present data from different periods in the prehistory of Cuzco. The first of these is the question of the initial human colonization of Cuzco, and the processes through which sedentary villages eventually became established in the region. As Americanist archaeology came of age in the mid-twentieth century, many researchers embraced the concept of a "formative" period in which sedentism, agriculture, pottery, and other cultural innovations appeared together (e.g., Willey and Phillips 1958). The transition from hunter-gatherer lifeways to agriculture was initially linked to the spread of Chavín-style pottery and iconography, considered to be a cultural "horizon" of widespread influence. In recent decades, Andean archaeologists have come to recognize a more complex relationship between subsistence, sedentism, and the technologies of everyday life. Sedentary communities first appeared in the Andes long before the appearance of agriculture, among societies that exploited the rich fisheries of the Pacific coast (e.g., Sandweiss 2008) or hunted wild camelids in high grassland areas (e.g., Aldenderfer 2008). Some groups exploited a wide range of wild plant resources as they settled into local landscapes and reduced their mobility, and there is evidence that these groups began to intensify their relationships with domesticated plants thousands of years before the first appearance of pottery (e.g., Dillehay et al. 2005; Pearsall 2008). Monumental construction and the advent of irrigation-based maize agriculture appeared on the north coast by 5000 years ago, a thousand years before the first known pottery in the central Andes.

In the Cuzco region, regional survey work in the past 15 years has begun to disentangle processes of sedentism, the increasing commitment to agricultural production, and the appearance of new settlement patterns and social practices suggesting social complexity. The identification of Early Archaic (9500–7000 BC) projectile points has pushed back the earliest entry by humans to the Terminal Pleistocene, and excavations at Kasapata, a Late Archaic open-air site to the southeast of Cuzco, demonstrate a more intensive occupation than was expected in the years before systematic survey work commenced (Bauer 2007; Bauer et al. 2004). Although the Hanan Cuzco surveys were designed to collect evidence on sedentary societies, research crews encountered evidence of a preceramic occupation of some parts of the region, which Covey and Griffis present in Chapter 3. The regional survey data indicate that Cuzco was first settled by hunter-gatherers, and their transition to sedentism and their growing commitment to agriculture and herding occurred over a long period of time. In this light, the chapters on early ceramic societies emerge out of an uncertainty that calls for new problem-oriented excavation work. Davis (2011) has already made great advances through her horizontal excavations at Yuthu, and she presents the regional evidence from the Formative period in the Xaquixaguana region in Chapter 4. This chapter identifies some of the chronological challenges that remain to be resolved regarding the earliest ceramic production in the Cuzco region, the organization of village societies, and the extent to which the current evidence substantiates interpretations of political hierarchies in the region by around 2000 years ago. Chapter 5 (Covey) presents complementary data from the neighboring Sacred Valley for the same time period.

Dispersals of Maize, Polychrome Pottery, and Early States

Maize has been excavated in Formative contexts in the Cuzco region (Davis 2011:14) and maize pollen is present in lake cores that date to circa 3000 BP (Mosblech et al. 2012:1367–69). Some scholars link the proliferation of this cultigen with the spread of the Chavín horizon (but see Burger 2012), whereas others implicate another horizon culture—the Wari state of the central highlands (ca. AD 600–1000)—as the society that introduced irrigation-supported maize agriculture as part of an imperial dominion that spread across the Andean highlands. The Hanan Cuzco settlement pattern data offer a critical perspective on the chronological and geographic context of Wari state colonization in the Cuzco region, speaking to questions of subsistence and social organization. Bélisle (Chapter 6) describes continuity and change in the Xaquixaguana region, from Formative settlement patterns into the Middle Horizon. She discusses how the introduction of polychrome pottery and settlement shifts to farmlands more suitable for maize cultivation occurred well before the Wari occupation of other parts of the Cuzco region, persisting for centuries with relatively little evidence of outside influence. In Chapter 7, Covey presents the settlement pattern evidence from the Sacred Valley, a region with excellent valley-bottom farming resources located close to Pikillacta, a massive Wari administrative center under construction to the southeast of Cuzco. The Sacred Valley data indicate a similar settlement shift before the arrival of Wari settlers, which was followed by continuity until the time that the Wari colonies were abandoned.

Risk Management Strategies in the Late Intermediate Period (AD 1000–1400)

The centuries that preceded the rise of the Inca empire, today known as the Late Intermediate period, have been characterized as a period of political decentralization and widespread warfare. This has been in part due to a loose correlation between indigenous Colonial accounts of the pre-Inca Andes and the long-acknowledged hiatus in state integration across most highland regions following the collapse of the Wari and Tiwanaku states (Covey 2008). Many archaeologists have overlooked the fact that the ethnohistoric descriptions describe a time *before*—rather than *between*—eras of widespread state influence across the Andean highlands. Inca accounts of universal conflict do not discuss early highland states, nor do they mention the existence of wealthy urban societies on the Pacific coast during the period of widespread balkanization in the highlands. Inca informants omitted the story of statecraft in other times and places to present their ancestors as the founders of the only Andean civilization, and yet they also conjure up states in highland regions such as Andahuaylas and the Lake Titicaca Basin, where archaeology shows them not to have existed during the Late Intermediate period (Arkush 2011; Bauer et al. 2010).

Archaeologists have long recognized that parts of the Cuzco region diverge from the picture of isolated, warring, hilltop villages. Edward Dwyer (1971) drew on his regional reconnaissance work to portray the Cuzco Valley as a place relatively untouched by the fractious and violent world that surrounded it, an impression that has been borne out in Brian Bauer's systematic surveys (1992, 2004). The Hanan Cuzco surveys do more than replicate evidence for stable valley-bottom settlements focused on intensive agriculture—they demonstrate that while some parts of the Cuzco region held onto such lifeways after AD 1000, other areas experienced widespread settlement reorganizations that suggest major changes in social organization and subsistence strategies. Chapter 8 (Covey) presents data from the Xaquixaguana region, showing the persistence of large valley-bottom communities, as well as the expansion of hierarchically-organized societies into new parts of the region. By contrast, data from the Sacred Valley presented in Chapter 9 (Covey) indicate widespread abandonment of low-elevation areas in favor of high ridges and mountaintops where mixed horticultural and herding practices could be pursued (see Covey 2006a). These variable settlement patterns offer important perspectives for reconstructing early Inca expansion using archaeology as the primary source of evidence.

The Creation and Destruction of an Imperial Heartland

Indigenous Andean chroniclers described the creation of the Inca heartland as an act of Manco Capac, the founding Inca ancestor, who spread his dominion over the peoples of the Cuzco region (Covey 2006a:26; cf. Rowe 1945). This presents a portrait of the Inca imperial core as being of great antiquity and geographic consistency—a center of power that required peripheral subjects rather than a place still in the process of being created at the time of the European invasion. Archaeologists should be critical of the content of narratives that emerged during the early Colonial debates over Inca imperialism (Covey 2006b); we should not be surprised to find that a large regional settlement database offers a more complicated picture of the development of the imperial heartland. The two chapters (Chapters 10 and 11, both authored by Covey) on the Inca transformation of the Hanan Cuzco region discuss how pre-Inca social hierarchies and subsistence practices correlate with imperial-era patterns. These chapters discuss some of the challenges of using survey data to evaluate late prehispanic settlement chronology and Inca influence.

The discussion of the Hanan Cuzco data indicates the central role of royal estate construction practices in altering the balance of social and economic life in rural Cuzco. The development of settlement hierarchies and the discussion of regional organization of the Inca heartland are hampered by the monumental Inca sites that served for centuries as the symbols of Inca order. Sites with extensive architectural remains, or where archaeologists have conducted repeated surface collections and excavations prior to survey work, cannot always be investigated using regional survey methods, and it is difficult to use excavation reports to establish the size of many sites over time. This is true not only for dozens of archaeological sites across the Hanan Cuzco region, but also for prehispanic settlements occupied intensively since the fall of the Inca empire. Many of the largest contemporary towns and cities in the study region were *reducción* settlements where Spanish administrators aggregated indigenous communities in the 1570s, and documentary and archaeological evidence indicates prehispanic occupations of unknown size at many locations.

The Hanan Cuzco data begin with one kind of colonization—the first human settlement of the region during the Terminal Pleistocene—and they end with the implementation of Spanish colonial government. Much of the Spanish destruction of the Inca imperial heartland occurred before easily identifiable Colonial glazed pottery began to be produced or commonly distributed in Peru (e.g., Jamieson 2001)—so that Colonial settlement patterns represent long-term responses to the disruptive implementation of Spanish colonial rule rather than changes occurring upon the arrival of the first Europeans in the 1530s. In Chapter 12, Quave presents a statistical analysis of Colonial settlement patterns from the Xaquixaguana region and nearby areas, a study that identifies some of the challenges for developing a regional archaeology for the Colonial period.

The work of the Hanan Cuzco projects represents a step forward in reconstructing the human occupation of the Cuzco region. The settlement pattern data presented in this volume clarify some important issues, but they complicate many others, calling for problem-based horizontal excavations, specialized laboratory analyses, and closer collaborations between archaeologists and climate scientists. The completion of multiple regional surveys marks an exciting—and vexing—milestone for the archaeology of Cuzco. The overall inventory of known archaeological sites is already diminishing in the face of population growth, urbanization, and looting—for the first time, professional archaeologists are beginning to understand what is being lost even as they explore new frontiers for explaining Cuzco's prehistoric past.

References

Aldenderfer, Mark S.
2008   High elevation foraging societies. In *Handbook of South American Archaeology*, edited by Helaine Silverman and William H. Isbell, pp. 131–44. New York: Springer.

Arkush, Elizabeth N.
2011   *Hillforts of the Ancient Andes: Colla Warfare, Society, and Landscape*. Gainesville: University Press of Florida.

Bauer, Brian S.
1992   *The Development of the Inca State*. Austin: University of Texas Press.
2004   *Ancient Cuzco: Heartland of the Inca*. Austin: University of Texas Press.

Bauer, Brian S. (editor)
2007   *Kasapata and the Archaic Period of the Cuzco Valley*. Cotsen Institute Monograph 57. University of California, Los Angeles: Cotsen Institute of Archaeology.

Bauer, Brian S., Bradford Jones, and Cindy Klink
2004   The Archaic period and the first people of the Cuzco Valley (9500–2200 BC). In *Ancient Cuzco: Heartland of the Inca*, edited by Brian S. Bauer, pp. 31–37. Austin: University of Texas Press.

Bauer, Brian S., Lucas C. Kellett, and Miriam Aráoz Silva
2010   *The Chanka: Archaeological Research in Andahuaylas (Apurimac), Peru*. Cotsen Institute Monograph 68. University of California, Los Angeles: Cotsen Institute of Archaeology.

Bingham, Hiram
1922   *Inca Land: Explorations in the Highlands of Peru.* Cambridge, MA: Riverside Press.

Burger, Richard L.
2012   Central Andean language expansion and the Chavín sphere of interaction. In *Archaeology and Language in the Andes: A Cross-Disciplinary Exploration of Prehistory*, edited by Paul Heggarty and David Beresford-Jones, pp. 135–61. Oxford: Oxford University Press.

Covey, R. Alan
2006a   *How the Incas Built Their Heartland: State Formation and the Innovation of Imperial Strategies in the Sacred Valley, Peru.* Ann Arbor: University of Michigan Press.
2006b   Chronology, succession, and sovereignty: The politics of Inka historiography and its modern interpretation. *Comparative Studies in Society and History* 48(1):166–99.
2008   Multiregional perspectives on the archaeology of the Andes during the Late Intermediate period (ca. AD 1000–1400). *Journal of Archaeological Research* 16(3):287–338.
2011   Landscapes and languages of power in the Inca imperial heartland (Cuzco, Peru). *SAA Archaeological Record* 11(4):29–32, 47.

D'Altroy, Terence N.
2002   *The Incas.* New York: Blackwell.

Davis, Allison R.
2011   *Yuthu: Community and Ritual in an Early Andean Village.* Memoirs, no. 50. Ann Arbor: Museum of Anthropology, University of Michigan.

Dillehay, Tom D., Herbert H. Eling Jr., and Jack Rossen
2005   Preceramic irrigation canals in the Peruvian Andes. *Proceedings of the National Academy of Sciences* 102(47):17241–44.

Dwyer, Edward B.
1971   The Early Inca Occupation of the Valley of Cuzco, Peru. PhD dissertation, Department of Anthropology, University of California, Berkeley.

Jamieson, Ross W.
2001   Majolica in the early Colonial Andes: The role of Panamanian wares. *Latin American Antiquity* 12(1):45–58.

Julien, Catherine
2000   *Reading Inca History.* Iowa City: University of Iowa Press.

Kendall, Ann
1985   *Aspects of Inca Architecture*, parts 1 and 2. BAR International Series 242–243. Oxford: British Archaeological Reports.

Markham, Clements Robert
1856   *Cuzco: A Journey to the Ancient Capital of Peru: With an Account of the History, Language, Literature, and Antiquities of the Incas. And Lima: A Visit to the Capital and Provinces of Modern Peru; With a Sketch of the Viceregal Government, History of the Republic, and a Review of the Literature and Society of Peru.* London: Chapman and Hall.

McEwan, Gordon F.
1984   The Middle Horizon in the Valley of Cuzco, Peru: The Impact of the Wari Occupation of Pikillacta in the Lucre Basin. PhD dissertation, Department of Anthropology, University of Texas.

Middendorf, Ernst W.
1893–1895   *Peru: Beobachtungen und Studien über das Land und seine Bewohner.* Berlin: Robert
            Oppenheim (Gustav Schmidt).

Mosblech, Nicole A. Sublette, Alex Chepstow-Lusty, Bryan G. Valencia, and Mark B. Bush
2012   Anthropogenic control of Late-Holocene landscapes in the Cuzco region, Peru. *The Holocene*
       22(12):1361–72.

Pardo, Luis A.
1957   *Historia y arqueología del Cuzco*, tomos I and II. Callao, Peru: Imprenta del Colegio Militar
       Leoncio Prado.

Pearsall, Deborah M.
2008   Plant domestication and the shift to agriculture in the Andes. In *Handbook of South American
       Archaeology*, edited by Helaine Silverman and William H. Isbell, pp. 105–20. New York:
       Springer.

Rowe, John H.
1944   *An Introduction to the Archaeology of Cuzco.* Papers of the Peabody Museum of American
       Archaeology and Ethnology 27(2). Cambridge, MA: Harvard University.
1945   Absolute chronology in the Andean area. *American Antiquity* 10(3):265–84.

Sancho de la Hoz, Pedro
[1534] 1962   *Relación de la conquista del Perú.* Madrid: Ediciones J. Porrúa Turanzas.

Sandweiss, Daniel H.
2008   Early fishing societies in western South America. In *Handbook of South American Archaeology*,
       edited by Helaine Silverman and William H. Isbell, pp. 145–56. New York: Springer.

Squier, E. George
1877   *Peru: Incidents of Travel and Exploration in the Land of the Incas.* New York: Henry Holt.

Valcárcel, Luis E.
1934   Los trabajos arqueológicos en el Departamento del Cusco. Sajsawaman redescubierto II. *Revista
       del Museo Nacional* 3:3–36, 211–33.
1935   Los trabajos arqueológicos en el Departamento del Cusco. Sajsawaman redescubierto III–IV.
       Revista del Museo Nacional 4:1–24, 161–203.
1946   Cuzco archaeology. In *Handbook of South American Indians, Volume 2: The Andean
       Civilizations*, edited by Julian H. Steward, pp. 177–82. Washington, D.C.: United States
       Government Printing Office.

Wiener, Charles
1880   *Pérou et Bolivie: Récit de voyage suivi d'études archéologiques et ethnographiques et de notes
       sur l'écriture et les langues des populations indiennes.* Paris: Hatchette et Cie.

Willey, Gordon R., and Philip Phillips
1958   *Method and Theory in American Archaeology.* Chicago: University of Chicago Press.

PART I

Regions and Research

Chapter 1: Research Projects and Field and Laboratory Methods

R. Alan Covey, Véronique Bélisle, and Allison R. Davis

The Hanan Cuzco region comprises four systematic regional surveys directed by the editor and colleagues from 2000 to 2007. The name "Hanan Cuzco" is used to refer to the combined area of approximately 1200 km² because these studies correspond more or less to Inca designations of the Hanan (Upper) divisions surrounding Cuzco, the imperial capital (Zuidema and Poole 1982). Additionally, the study region contains the remains of country palaces, improved farmlands, and pasture areas belonging to almost all the later Inca rulers, who belonged to the Hanan Cuzco moiety (Covey 2006; Covey, Aráoz Silva, and Bauer 2008; Niles 2004) (Fig. 1.1). It is appropriate to treat the Hanan Cuzco region as a single region for some aspects of discussion, given that it was surveyed using the same basic field methodology and laboratory protocols. At the same time, the various projects in the region made certain methodological adjustments that encourage separate regional discussions for some time periods. In this chapter, we describe the various projects that make up the Hanan Cuzco region, as well as the artifact sequence used to analyze surface collections in the laboratory.

Regional Archaeology in Cuzco before 2000

Hanan Cuzco research builds on previous archaeological studies in the Cuzco region, relying on earlier research for its basic field methodology and relative ceramic chronology. John H. Rowe (1944) presented the earliest published artifact sequence for Cuzco, and subsequent excavation work has improved the definition of particular styles and added absolute dates to the sequence (for example, see the table of radiocarbon dates presented in Bauer 2004, 2008) (Fig. 1.2). The refinement of the Cuzco ceramic sequences and its application in Hanan Cuzco laboratory analyses are discussed in greater detail later in this chapter, but it is important to note the intellectual debt that this monograph owes to previous researchers, particularly Brian Bauer.

Bauer's influence in the present monograph extends beyond stylistic definition to the methods used to conduct full-coverage survey work and systematically identify sites. All Hanan Cuzco projects used a basic field methodology that was first introduced to the Cuzco region by Bauer in his Paruro regional survey

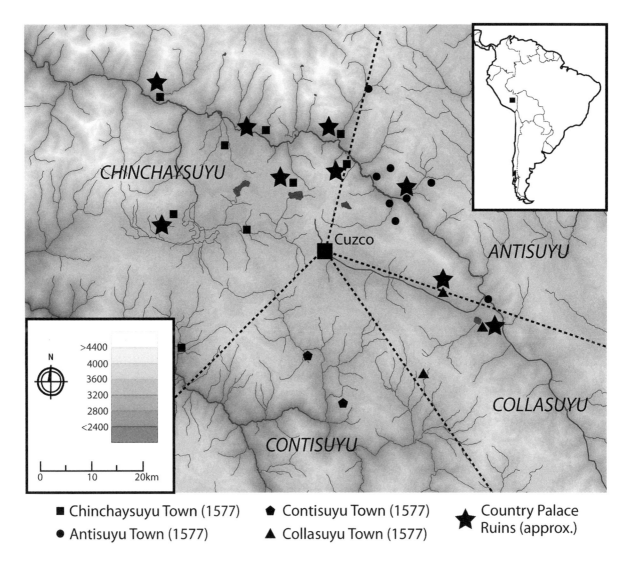

Figure 1.1. Map of Hanan Cuzco region with *suyu* boundaries and remains of estates of later Inca rulers.

(Bauer 1992, 1999). To attain full coverage of a naturally defined region, survey crews of 3–5 traversed all safely passable parts of a region in parallel lines, maintaining a target interval of 50 m to the extent possible (Fig. 1.3). In practice, survey lines might narrow or widen to traverse planted agricultural fields or natural boundaries, or to visit flat or prominent locations where sites would be likely. Sites were identified by the presence of artifacts on the surface, which were sampled purposively in general collections and analyzed in the laboratory. Site locations were recorded on maps, and the characteristics of the location and the artifact scatter were recorded.

This methodology was modified from the one introduced to the Andean highlands by Jeffrey Parsons and colleagues (2000) in their Tarama-Chinchaycocha survey in the 1970s, a regional approach that has its ultimate origins in the survey work that

Parsons conducted with William Sanders and colleagues in the Basin of Mexico in the 1960s (Sanders, Parsons, and Santley 1979). Bauer's survey work was not the first archaeological investigation conducted at a regional scale, although it was the first project to implement a full-coverage approach that registered surface artifacts.

In the late 1960s, Edward Dwyer (1971) conducted dissertation work on the pre-Inca occupation of Cuzco that attempted to assess the organization of the region in the centuries prior to Inca imperial expansion. A few years later, Ann Kendall (1985) carried out an extensive investigation of known Inca and pre-Inca architectural remains in the Cuzco region. Kendall later directed the Cusichaca Project, a regional program of reconnaissance and excavations in the Urubamba Valley between Ollantaytambo and Machu Picchu (Kendall 1994)—a project that brought Bauer to

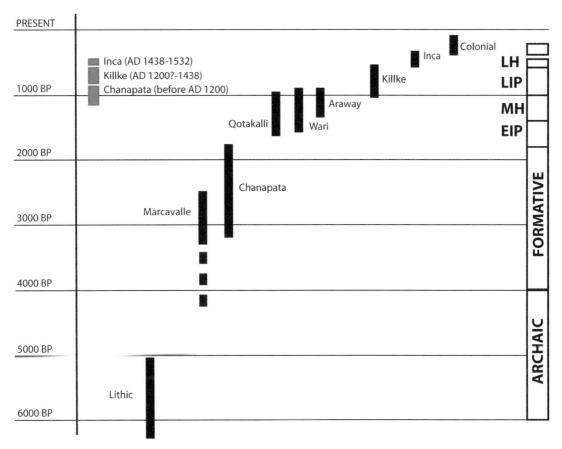

Figure 1.2. The relative ceramic sequence developed by Rowe (1944) (*left, gray bars*), compared with radiocarbon-dated artifacts compiled by Bauer (2008). Stylistic dates show the current range of dates at 95% confidence levels, excluding samples with error ranges larger than ±100 years. At right is the conventional phasing of Horizon and Intermediate periods used in the Cuzco region.

Figure 1.3. Hanan Cuzco field crew conducting survey work in the Qoricocha puna, fall 2004.

the Cuzco region for the first time (Bauer, pers. comm.). Studies that were oriented toward standing architecture tended to emphasize only certain parts of the Cuzco region, with a focus on settlements after circa AD 1000, although Gordon McEwan's (1984, 1991) reconnaissance work around the Middle Horizon (ca. AD 600–1000) Wari site of Pikillacta generated descriptions of occupations of that time period in the Lucre Basin.

In the late 1980s, Bauer conducted a full-coverage regional survey just to the south of the Cuzco Valley, which registered several hundred stylistic components from a region of approximately 600 km². Where architecture-oriented projects had investigated an extremely limited number of sites in the region, Bauer was able to reconstruct regional settlement patterns from the first millennium BC through the Inca period. This work identified local ceramic traditions that were not well known at previously excavated sites, and Bauer conducted small-scale excavations at 15 sites to clarify the local and regional artifact sequence and to add radiocarbon dates of materials found in stratigraphic contexts with a particular style (Bauer 1999). Having demonstrated the efficacy of conducting full-coverage pedestrian survey in the

Cuzco region, Bauer turned to the Cuzco Valley itself, conducting a pilot survey within the Cuzco Basin in the early 1990s and returning for a survey of the Cuzco and Oropesa Basins from 1997 to 1999. (Bauer and Aráoz Silva later surveyed the Lucre Basin in 2006, completing the survey of the entire Cuzco Valley.) The Cuzco Valley Archaeological Project provided the training for a number of American and Peruvian archaeology students including Alan Covey, who subsequently directed the first Hanan Cuzco survey project in the Sacred Valley in 2000.

The Sacred Valley Archaeological Project (2000)

The Sacred Valley Archaeological Project (SVAP) studied a 400 km² region in the Vilcanota-Urubamba Valley and its tributary basins (Fig. 1.4). Drainage patterns determined the north and south boundaries of the survey region, while the eastern and western limits were arbitrarily designated a narrowing of the valley above the modern town of San Salvador and below the town of Calca, respectively. SVAP research focused on prehistoric

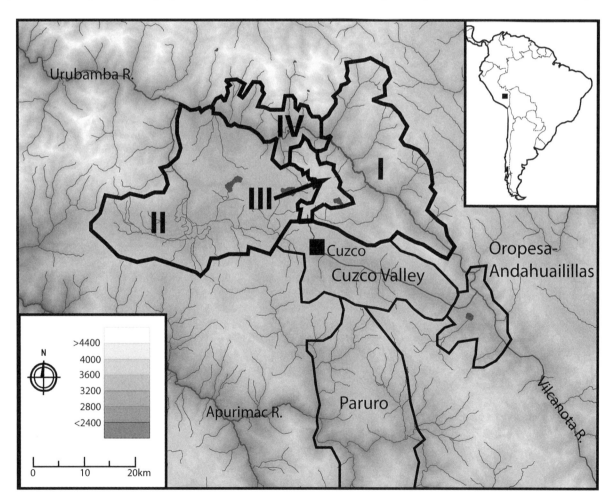

Figure 1.4. Map of Cuzco region survey projects directed by Bauer and Covey. The Hanan Cuzco projects, outlined in bold, comprise the Sacred Valley Archaeological Project (I), the Xaquixaguana Plain Archaeological Survey (II), the Qoricocha Puna Survey (III), and the Calca-Yanahuara Archaeological Project (IV).

agricultural communities, with full-coverage survey below 4000 m. All passable ridges were walked to 4500 m, while hillslopes between 4000 and 4500 m were purposively traversed—much of this upper-elevation area was later systematically surveyed in 2004 by the Qoricocha Puna Survey. With an elevation range of 2900–4500 m, the SVAP region included valley-bottom maize lands (*kichwa*), hillside dry-farmed plots (*suni*), and limited expanses of high-elevation grassland (*puna*).

The 2000 field research was designed to retain the survey methodology developed by Bauer while establishing expedient improvements to artifact collection techniques. Earlier projects had made purposive samples of diagnostic surface artifacts, and the Cuzco Valley Archaeological Survey included second visits to multicomponent sites in order to clarify period-by-period distribution areas (Bauer 2004). SVAP research attempted a more complex set of collection protocols that would combine grab samples with purposively placed ~50 m² intensive collection units (circular units with a radius of 4 m). Upon identifying an artifact scatter of sufficient density to register (for pottery, more than 5 sherds in a 2500 m² area), a crew member would reconnoiter the area to determine the size and density of the scatter. For small scatters (less than 2500 m²) and larger sites of low artifact density, purposive collections of diagnostic material would be collected, up to 25 samples of each identified style. For large and dense sites, one intensive collection unit would be placed in a high-density part of the scatter for every 2500 m² of estimated area, and all materials in the unit would be collected. For sites with extensive architectural remains, surface materials were to be observed, but collections were left for a second visit that involved mapping.

Implementing the more intensive collection protocols proved impractical at the outset of field research. Not only did they paralyze the progress of the survey crew, but intensive collections generated large quantities of surface artifacts that had to be carried throughout the day. After attempting an alternative approach—using pin flags to mark the distribution of different styles prior to collecting them—the project reverted to purposive sampling, with second visits to multicomponent sites. Large sites with significant architectural components (e.g., Pukara Pantillijlla, Ancasmarca) were collected more intensively in separate visits. Because the intensity of SVAP collection techniques yielded less precise results than did the Xaquixaguana Plain survey, the data from these projects are presented separately in this volume.

SVAP research introduced the use of a field coding manual and standard code sheet for recording sites. Each crew member carried a copy of the manual, which described the objectives of the research, the parameters for site identification, and the procedures for registering and collecting a site. The code sheet also provided space for sketching a map of the site locale, and for writing out pertinent notes. The use of an open coding system permitted the consistent recording of data between fieldworkers, although some aspects of field analysis (e.g., current land use) were subject to interobserver error. The basic coding system introduced in the Sacred Valley project proved useful in subsequent projects, with minor modifications.

The Xaquixaguana Plain Archaeological Survey (2004–2006)

The Xaquixaguana Plain Archaeological Survey (XPAS) built on results of the Sacred Valley research (Fig. 1.4). The study area of approximately 600 km² has natural boundaries on its southern and western sides, but abuts five other survey areas: Bauer's CVAP, SVAP, the Qoricocha Puna Survey, the Calca-Yanahuara Archaeological Project, and Kosiba's (2010) Wat'a Archaeological Project. XPAS research was in many ways less challenging than the Sacred Valley project. The terrain was less vertical and broken, and the incorporation of hand radios permitted continuous communication between crew members. The SVAP coding system was employed with only limited modifications that reflected local ecological variations. Site registration was carried out collaboratively by at least two crew members, which helped to reduce interobserver error (Fig. 1.5). Data were recorded directly into hand-held personal digital assistant (PDA) devices, which were downloaded and checked regularly in the laboratory; each crew member also maintained a notebook of notes and sketches.

The open landscape and overall lack of standing architecture encouraged a more intensive collection strategy than had been carried out in the Sacred Valley. Rather than attempt intensive collections when large sites were encountered, XPAS crews made purposive collections at sites smaller than one hectare, but only observed surface pottery at larger sites. A substantial part of each field season was dedicated to second visits to these larger sites to conduct a formal series of intensive collections. During a second collection, crews checked the size and density of the scatter to determine whether intensive collections were appropriate. They then selected a site datum and used a Brunton and laser distance meter to place an orthogonal grid of ~50 m² collection units at 50 m intervals (a 2% sample of site area). Within each unit, crew members collected all materials within 4 m of a central nail or rod, recorded the count of decorated and undecorated pottery and other artifacts, and carried all diagnostic material back to the laboratory for analysis.

The introduction of second collections permitted the XPAS to collect more robust data on the size of different components at large sites, but it presented new logistical challenges. Second collection crews moved directly from one site to another, generating a much larger mass of pottery than other survey crews. Transporting equipment and collections between sites and back to Cuzco was difficult much of the time, and the influx of large amounts of pottery created backlogs in the laboratory. In total, XPAS collected nearly 1000 (*n* = 982) intensive units, recording more than 120,000 objects in the field, of which more than 22,000 were brought to the laboratory for analysis.

The intensive collection data from the XPAS research make it possible to reconstruct more accurate site size hierarchies for all time periods, and they offer a systematic perspective on the distribution of different styles across the large sites in the region. The use of purposive sampling in other projects limited the analytical power of survey collections to identifying the

Figure 1.5. Site registration by a survey crew in the Xaquixaguana region, summer 2004.

presence or absence of a style in a given sample, and relative abundance and spatial distribution were recorded based on visual estimates during site visits (rather than spatially isolated collection locations). This improved interpretive power, but imposed some interpretive dilemmas that are still difficult to reconcile. The most obvious is that site size estimates for large sites in different survey regions cannot simply be combined and treated as compatible data. This is also true for small and large sites within the XPAS sample. Despite some reduction to data comparability, the results of the intensive collections help to establish a more rigorous measure of settlement area, especially for earlier periods.

The Qoricocha Puna Survey (2004)

Complementing the existing research focus on agricultural settlement patterns, the 2004 Qoricocha Puna Survey (QPS) introduced systematic survey to an area of high-elevation grassland (~4000–4600 m) lying between three archaeological survey regions (the Cuzco Valley Archaeological Project, SVAP,

and XPAS) (Fig. 1.4). Field crews employed standard survey techniques to all areas above 4000 m in the study area, which yielded continuous survey coverage between existing projects. Since the Sacred Valley project had traversed ridges in parts of the area, there was some overlapping survey coverage. Because QPS research targeted herding areas, field crews registered all corral features in the study area, regardless of whether ceramics were present on the surface. Colonial and contemporary ceramics were collected along with the rare instances of prehispanic materials, and GPS points were also taken for ridgetop boundary markers (*apachetas*) maintained by contemporary communities, some of which show evidence of Colonial and Inca ritual activities (Fig. 1.6). The intensive collection techniques employed in XPAS research were found to be impractical in the puna. Not only were few village sites encountered by the survey, but there was also an overall paucity of surface material for making meaningful collection grids. The survey of the Qoricocha Basin was logistically challenging and encountered few prehispanic sites, but it generated valuable perspectives on the economic use of the region in pre-Inca, Inca, and Colonial times.

Figure 1.6. Ridgetop boundary marker (*apacheta*) registered during the Qoricocha Puna Survey, fall 2004.

Calca-Yanahuara Archaeological Project (2007)

The Calca-Yanahuara Archaeological Project (CYAP) was designed to fill a small (~120 km²) gap lying between the SVAP and XPAS study regions and Kosiba's Wat'a Archaeological Project (Fig. 1.4). High glaciated peaks bound this study region to the north, and although the 4000 m elevation mark was originally designated as an arbitrary limit for survey work, field crews encountered marginal environmental conditions (broken, steep landscape with tundra vegetation) much lower, and survey limits were adjusted accordingly. All accessible ridges were walked within the survey boundaries. In many areas the valley sides were too steep to negotiate safely, and were bypassed or crossed along existing trails.

Survey techniques that had been effective in other parts of the Hanan Cuzco region met with difficulties in many valley-bottom areas. This was due to the walling off of private property on fertile alluvial fans with abundant irrigation water, as well as urbanization in the valley, especially in the Urubamba area. Survey crews attempted to walk straight lines where possible, and to negotiate ad hoc access to land when owners were pres-

ent, but many survey days involved scrambling over walls and then attempting to climb out of an enclosed field or dooryard in a productive direction (or without disturbing a sleeping dog). Central parts of Urubamba have been completely urbanized and could not be surveyed (Fig. 1.7).

Of all areas in the broader Hanan Cuzco region, the Calca-Yanahuara project offered the greatest constraints to collecting systematic settlement pattern data. There are locales in which our survey results must be considered incomplete, but the completion of full-coverage survey also ensured that we collected systematic data from areas surrounding these. Even if some very large sites once existed that can no longer be discerned through survey, large and hierarchical settlement systems would have left traces in smaller communities and outlying agricultural fields. An overview of results of the Calca-Yanahuara survey has been presented elsewhere (Covey, Aráoz Silva, and Bauer 2008). Because the project made purposive samples of surface artifacts, results correspond more closely with those of the Sacred Valley project, and the Calca-Yanahuara data are discussed alongside those from immediately upstream.

Figure 1.7. The Urubamba area in the Calca-Yanahuara survey region. The 2007 survey of this region encountered challenges of work in an urbanized context.

Ceramic Typology in the Hanan Cuzco Region

As discussed above, the four Hanan Cuzco projects targeted regions characterized by different terrain, environmental characteristics, and intensity of contemporary settlement. Slight modifications to survey methods and collection strategies have implications for the interpretations of results, as do the minor differences in laboratory work between campaigns of analysis in 2000, 2004–2006, and 2007. All Hanan Cuzco projects used the regional ceramic sequence developed by Bauer (1999, 2002) to conduct type-variety analysis of diagnostic pottery to identify the presence or absence of different components in a particular collection. Differences in collection strategy influenced additional studies of these collections, and these are discussed following a review of the Cuzco sequence.

Formative (ca. 1200 BC–AD 300)

Formative period pottery in the Hanan Cuzco region is very similar to well-known contemporary styles from the Cuzco Basin and neighboring areas (Bauer 1999, 2004). At present, the Formative period ceramic styles in the Xaquixaguana study area do not allow fine-grained temporal analysis. Chanapata and Chanapata-

related pottery was prevalent (Fig. 1.8, *right*). The most common vessel forms are globular closed vessels with and without necks and large open vessels. The pottery is coil built and the rims of open vessels and closed vessels without a neck are often thickened as a result of folding the clay over and smoothing the seam (Fig. 1.9). Most vessels are reddish-orange as a result of firing in an oxidizing environment, though some are dark as a result of firing in reducing conditions. Most decoration is located on the exterior rim of closed vessels and the interior rim of open vessels. Vessels may be burnished to form a thick shiny line around the rim and thinner vertical lines descending the body. Decorated vessels may be painted with red, cream, and sparkly hematite pigments. Occasionally, deeply incised lines delimit painted zones.

Chanapata pottery is often divided into subtypes based primarily on surface treatment and firing conditions. For example, Rowe (1944:15–20) divided the pottery at the site of Chanapata into ten types.[1] Based on his system, Davis (2010:29) divided

---

1. Eight of Rowe's subtypes can be considered variations of Chanapata-style pottery (Chanapata Plain, Chanapata Incised Plain, Chanapata Pattern Burnished, Chanapata Polished Black, Chanapata Polished Red, Chanapata Incised Red, Pacalla-mocco White on Red, and Pacalla-mocco Red on Buff). Chanapata Punctate and Chanapata Incised Black are a distinct style similar to Marcavalle pottery. Carmenca Red on White is a later style.

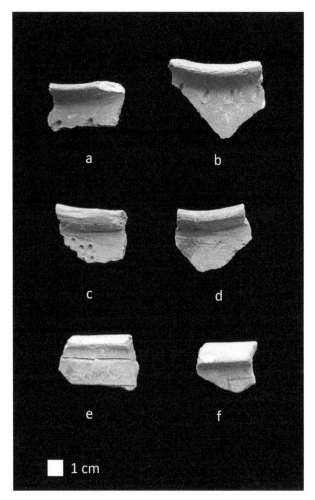

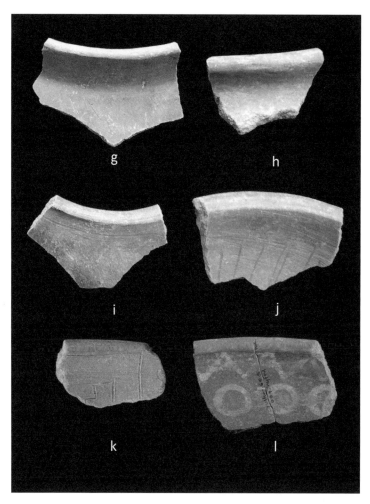

Earlier pottery similar to Marcavalle style
(tentative date 1200 - 400 BC)

Later Chanapata-style pottery
(750 BC - AD 300)

Figure 1.8. Two distinct Formative period pottery styles were found during the Xaquixaguana Plain Archaeological Survey. The style on the left is similar to Marcavalle pottery from the Cuzco Basin. It includes short-rimmed closed vessels with punctation decoration around the shoulder (*a, b, c, d*) and straight-walled bowls with incised exterior decoration (*e, f*). Chanapata-style pottery (*right*) is common throughout the Cuzco region. It includes closed vessels with necks (*g, h*), closed vessels without necks (*i*), and open flaring bowls that are decorated on the interior rim with patterned burnishing (*j*), painting and incision (*k*), or polychrome paint (*l*).

Ideal cross sections of Chanapata-style rim sherds

closed vessel without a neck   open vessel

5 cm

Figure 1.9. Thickened rims of Chanapata open vessels and closed vessels without a neck were created by folding the clay and smoothing the seam. This manufacturing technique can be used to identify Chanapata pottery even if the surface finish has been destroyed.

Chanapata-style pottery into five subtypes. Given that two of Rowe's subtypes were named for the type site of Pacallamoqo in the XPAS study region (X-047), it seems that it should have been possible to identify these subtypes in surface collections. In practice, the identification of distinct subtypes was not possible because the pottery collected rarely had preserved surface paint or burnishing. Chanapata pottery was frequently identified by forming technique rather than decorative treatment. The folded clay used to create a fattened rim was visible in sherds from open vessels and closed vessels without a neck. Since closed vessels with a neck were not built this way, it was often impossible to distinguish them from similar vessels from other time periods.

Chanapata pottery is well understood as a style, but the date range during which it was used is still under question. The style is frequently associated with the Late Formative period (500 BC–AD 200 following Bauer's 2004 chronology). Yet, radiocarbon dates associated with the style range from 750 BC to AD 300 (94.5%) (for a complete list of Formative period dates, see Davis 2011:161, Table B). In addition, recent excavations of houses at Ak'awillay in the XPAS study region have found "Formative-like" cooking and storage vessels mixed with Qotakalli-style pottery that typically dates from AD 200 to 600 and Middle Horizon Muyu Urqu and Araway-style pottery that dates from AD 600 to 1000 (Bélisle 2011). This suggests that (1) Chanapata-style pottery may have been used alongside Marcavalle-style pottery for up to 250 years (Marcavalle pottery dates as late as 400 BC; see below), and (2) Chanapata-style pottery may have continued to be used in some contexts for 400 to 800 years alongside later styles.

A rare type of pottery found in the study region is probably an earlier Formative period style. This pottery is distinct from Chanapata pottery in form and decoration. The closed vessels have very short necks and pointed rim profiles that are sometimes decorated on the shoulder with punctation. Open vessels have straight walls that meet the base at an approximately right angle and may be decorated on the exterior with incisions (Fig. 1.8). These vessels were usually fired in an oxidizing environment, creating a light tan color.

This pottery has never been found in excavations in the Xaquixaguana study area. As a result, no radiocarbon dates are available to assign the style to an absolute date range. Based on comparison with pottery from the Cuzco Basin, it is likely that this style predates Chanapata-style pottery. Rowe (1944) found very similar sherds in the lowest excavation levels of the site of Chanapata, below levels containing Chanapata-style pottery. He called this style "Chanapata Punctate" and "Chanapata Incised Black" (Rowe 1944:15–20); however, after excavations at Marcavalle found larger concentrations of similar pottery, "Marcavalle" became the accepted name in archaeological publications and discussions since the 1970s (see Chávez 1977, 1980, 1981a, 1981b). The style is typically associated with the Middle Formative period (1500–500 BC following Bauer's 2004 chronology), but associated radiocarbon dates from excavations at Marcavalle range from 1250 to 400 BC (95.4%). In the Xaquixaguana study area, this pottery has been tentatively assigned

a date range from 1200 to 400 BC. Unfortunately, this temporal assignment is tentative and only future excavations will be able to confirm or reject it.

Early Intermediate Period/Middle Horizon (ca. AD 200–1000)

The end of the long Formative period appears to have coincided with some disruptions to local settlement patterns in parts of the Cuzco region, although the question of temporal continuity of the Formative style raises questions that will require more intensive study. The periods that follow the Formative—the Early Intermediate period (ca. AD 200–600) and Middle Horizon (ca. AD 600–1000)—also present some chronological and interpretive challenges (see Bauer 1999, 2004; Bauer and Jones 2003; Bélisle 2011; Covey 2006; Covey et al. 2013, for some discussions; cf. Glowacki 2005). Several styles that first appear in the Early Intermediate period (EIP) continued to be produced during the Middle Horizon (MH), and there are local imitations of some of the more common styles at local sites across the Hanan Cuzco region. Excavation work is needed to continue to clarify and subdivide this part of the sequence.

Qotakalli (Fig. 1.10) is the most common pottery style throughout the Cuzco region during the EIP and MH (Barreda Murillo 1982; Bauer and Jones 2003:45; Bauer 1999:70–75, 2004:47–54; Espinoza Martínez 1983; Torres Poblete 1989). It has also been found in Wari contexts at Pikillakta (Glowacki 1996:212–16, 2005:106–7) and Chokepukio (McEwan, Gibaja, and Chatfield 1995), and in Wari burials at Batan Urqu in Huaro (Zapata 1997; see Bauer 1999:73). Qotakalli pottery appears to have been associated with a complex pre-state polity that dominated the Cuzco Basin and nearby areas during both the EIP and MH. It was produced in the Cuzco Basin and its production was not halted or interrupted with the arrival of the Wari. Geometric motifs are painted in black, black and red, or red on a cream surface.

Muyu Urqu (Fig. 1.11) is a fine polychrome ceramic style that has been identified throughout the Cuzco region (Bauer 1989, 1999:78–81; Bauer and Jones 2003:63–65; Espinoza Martínez 1983; Torres Poblete 1989; Zapata 1997, 1998). It was produced at the end of the EIP until sometime during the Middle Horizon. Bauer (1999:84–85) believes that Muyu Urqu is a locally made (i.e., Cuzco region) pottery style related to late Tiwanaku. Black, white, and orange geometric motifs are painted on a dark red background. Surfaces are highly polished, which gives a shiny look to the pottery.

Waru (Fig. 1.12) is a little-known pottery style that Rowe (1944:19–20) first identified at the site of Chanapata in the Cuzco Basin and named "Carmenca Red-on-White." Waru pottery was later found at Batan Urqu (Rowe 1956:142; Zapata 1997), Pikillacta (Glowacki 1996:247–50), and at various sites in the Paruro region (Bauer 1999:151–53). Waru was first produced in the EIP and continued to be used during the Middle Horizon. Simple geometric motifs are painted in red on a white-slipped surface.

Araway (Fig. 1.13) is a Middle Horizon pottery style that was influenced by Wari pottery (Bauer 1999:69–70; Bauer and Jones

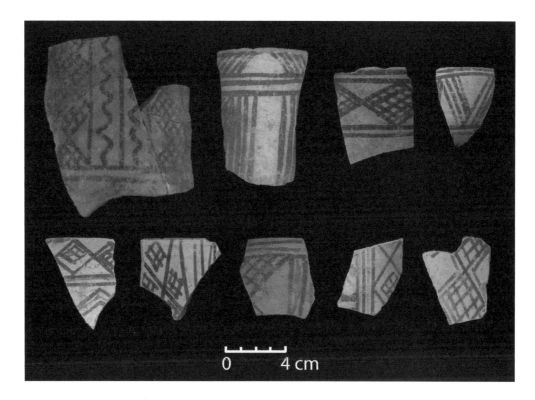

Figure 1.10. Qotakalli-style pottery, dated to the Early Intermediate and Middle Horizon periods. Many local sites at a distance from the Cuzco Basin have imitations of this style.

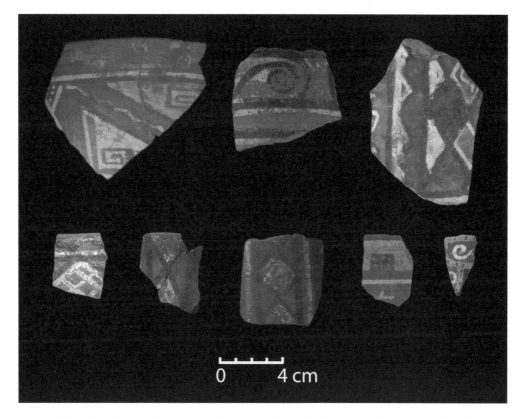

Figure 1.11. Muyu Urqu-style pottery, produced from the late Early Intermediate period and used during the Middle Horizon.

2003:38). Its production started after the Wari state established colonies in Cuzco. Araway pottery has been found in many parts surrounding the Cuzco Basin (Bauer 1999, 2004; Covey 2006:74–78; Espinoza Martínez 1983; Glowacki 1996:199–207, 2002, 2005; Torres Poblete 1989; Zapata 1997), although with a somewhat more restricted distribution than Qotakalli (Covey et al. 2013). Geochemical analyses and systematic regional surveys suggest that it was produced in the Cuzco Basin and exchanged with neighboring areas (Bauer 1999:70; Covey 2006:77; Covey et al. 2013; Delgado et al. 2007; Montoya et al. 2009). Black and red geometric motifs are painted on a cream or buff background.

Late Intermediate Period (ca. AD 1000–1400)

The ceramics of the Late Intermediate period (LIP) are typical of the south-central Andes in the centuries following the collapse of the Wari and Tiwanaku states—simple wares decorated with geometric designs in black and red. The most widely distributed LIP style in the Cuzco region is Killke, first identified by Rowe (1944:60–62) and elaborated on by subsequent researchers (Dwyer 1971; Bauer 1999). Like Bauer's survey projects, all Hanan Cuzco surveys have employed a strict definition of Killke as one of many local LIP styles in the Cuzco region that can be distinguished based on differences in paste/temper, vessel forms, and decoration (Fig. 1.14). Some excavators treat Killke as a broader term for Cuzco region LIP pottery (Rivera Dorado 1971a, 1971b, 1972), or as a class of material that deviates from Inca imperial pottery (Chatfield 2007). Such approaches contribute to confusion regarding the definition of LIP styles in space and time (e.g., Chatfield 2010).

Distribution patterns of Killke suggest that its production location was in the Cuzco Basin, and it is the predominant style within about 20 km of the basin. Beyond that, there are a number of other local LIP styles that have been formally identified to varying degrees. To the south, Bauer (1999) has identified the Colcha style in the Paruro region, which has limited distribution in the Cuzco Valley and other parts of the region. To the southeast of Cuzco, McEwan and colleagues (2002) find the Lucre style, which was distributed in nearby parts of the Cuzco Valley and Sacred Valley. North of the Vilcanota-Urubamba River, a local style called Cuyo (or Kuyu) has been identified in the Chongo Basin and nearby areas (Covey 2006) (Fig. 1.15). To the west and northwest of Cuzco, there may be two distinct local LIP styles— one centered around Chinchero (Rivera Dorado 1972) and one in the Maras area (Maqque and Haquehua 1993; Haquehua and Maqque 1996)—although additional research needs to be done to define these styles formally.

The treatment of the LIP as an undifferentiated 400-year period presents some important interpretive issues. As discussed in later chapters, there is significant settlement discontinuity in some parts of the Hanan Cuzco region in the MH–LIP transition—that is, many sites that have Qotakalli and Araway ceramics on the surface lack a component of LIP pottery, and many of the ridgetop villages that proliferated in parts of the region after AD 1000 lack the EIP/MH styles. Evidence of settlement shifts at that transition raises the question of additional resettlements during the LIP, which would affect the reconstruction of population sizes and regional rank-size measures. A second important issue to consider is the demonstrated overlap of the Killke and Inca styles. As noted elsewhere (e.g., Covey 2006:90–91), excavation evidence indicates that the Inca imperial style originated prior to AD 1400, and that "LIP" pottery continued to be used in some local contexts during the imperial period (e.g., Dwyer 1971; Kendall 1985; Lunt 1988). This means that the interpretation of Inca imperial settlement patterns must consider that some areas lacking Cuzco polychrome pottery were not necessarily completely abandoned around AD 1400.

Figure 1.12. Waru-style pottery, once treated as an Early Intermediate period style, and now known to be used from the late Early Intermediate period into the Middle Horizon.

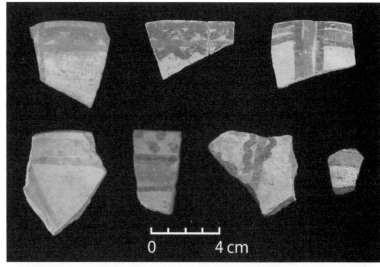

Figure 1.13.

Araway pottery is a Wari-influenced style from the Middle Horizon that was produced in the Cuzco Basin. Imitations of this style occur in many local sites at a distance from the basin.

Figure 1.14.

Late Intermediate period pottery styles from across the Hanan Cuzco region. Killke is the predominant style within about 20 km of Cuzco.

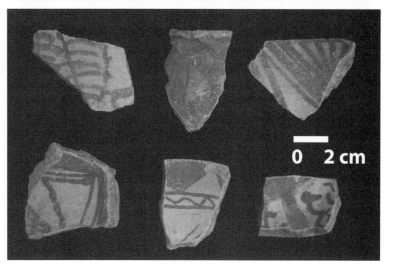

Figure 1.15.

Cuyo pottery, a local Late Intermediate period style found in the Chongo Basin to the north of the Sacred Valley.

The Inca ceramic style presents wares, vessel forms, and iconography that differ from other Cuzco region styles (Fig. 1.16). These have been studied by many researchers (e.g., Bingham 1915; Baca Cosío 1974, 1989; Rowe 1944), and the Hanan Cuzco projects have used the same diagnostics laid out by Bauer (1999:8–10, 2004:91–93). Even though many non-diagnostic sherds could be reliably classified as Inca based on their paste/temper, wall thickness, and/or rim form, these observations were separated into a category of "Inca-related" pottery, which was never used as the sole basis for identifying an Inca component.

As noted above, the overlap of LIP and Inca pottery presents some chronological challenges in the interpretation of settlement pattern data from different surveys. Survey collections often included material that seemed "Inca-like" in many respects, but which was not canonically faithful. Some of this material reflects the transition between the Killke and Inca styles (e.g., Dwyer 1971), but other sherds could be local imitations or hybrid styles, or examples of provincial Inca styles brought to the imperial heartland (Fig. 1.17). More work needs to be done with excavated samples to address the stylistic variability that falls under the rubric "Inca."

Colonial and Contemporary
(Late Sixteenth Century to Present)

The first Cuzco regional surveys targeted prehispanic settlement patterns only, in part because Colonial ceramics were not well classified or dated—they remain so to this day (see Chapter 12 by Quave). In the Sacred Valley survey, crews noted the presence of glazed Colonial pottery, but did not make consistent collections of post-Conquest materials. The SVAP identified about 20 sites with a Colonial component, but these observations were opportunistic and were not substantiated with surface collections. It is likely that significantly more Colonial sites are present in the SVAP region. Subsequent survey projects included Colonial materials in the collection strategy, and some interesting patterns emerge in the comparison of survey results and the distribution of early Colonial *reducción* settlements (see Chapter 12). There were many instances where new crew members were training, or where unknown materials were collected when sites were registered, and all projects processed some pottery that was identified in the laboratory as "contemporary," and not included in settlement pattern analysis.

When discussing the distribution of surface collections of Colonial pottery, we do not treat the attributes of the post-Conquest period (glazed vessels, some with green decorations; evidence of the use of a potter's wheel; and new paste recipes and vessel forms) as representative of the mid-sixteenth century. The distribution of glazed wares—the most easily identifiable Colonial material—would not have been common before the late sixteenth century, making our surface collections more appropriately linked to long-term local responses to Spanish Colonial settlement

policies. This leaves our regional picture of settlement with an uncomfortable lacuna between the Inca imperial period and the late sixteenth or early seventeenth century. This can be partly filled with analysis of documents from the intervening period, although these offer a less-than-complete perspective on the disruptions of the European invasion, the Inca uprising, multiple waves of civil conflict, and the effects of epidemic disease and spontaneous migration.

Analytical Methods in the Laboratory

Having presented an overview of the ceramic chronology used by the Hanan Cuzco surveys, it is important to draw attention to some differences in the analytical protocols used by the survey projects. SVAP analysis focused on LIP and Inca pottery, and the relatively modest survey sample of these styles was overshadowed by the quantity of excavated materials from Pukara Pantillijlla, which included more than 40,000 fragments of pottery. Ceramic analysis for SVAP survey materials used a type-variety analysis to identify the presence or absence of different styles in survey collections, but a more intensive analysis of LIP pottery was undertaken. This consisted of a two-step coding process after the completion of type-variety analysis to determine the presence of LIP components. Working with the entire excavated assemblage from Pukara Pantillijlla and the LIP components from the regional survey, one analytical team first classified sherds by past and temper, using a typology developed specifically for the Sacred Valley sample (Covey, n.d.). This classification included non-diagnostic pottery from Pukara Pantillijlla, which was sorted, counted, and weighed. Fragments of vessel rims were coded using an open system that assigned a numeric code based on conformance to a coded rim profile (if a sherd did not conform to a profile, its profile was drawn and assigned a code number). Once preliminary ware and vessel form information had been coded, data on slipping and decoration were coded by the project director. Decoration involved an open coding of key motifs on a sherd, and up to 3 separate motifs were coded for each decorated fragment. More than 200 distinct motifs were eventually added to the coding system for decoration. The end result of this coding was a database of more than 10,000 decorated sherds in which paste/temper, vessel form, slipping, and iconography were recorded for the regional collection and the excavated sample from Pukara Pantillijlla.

Laboratory analysis of the XPAS collections was also grounded in a type-variety sort of ceramic collections, which was conducted by the project director (Qoricocha collections were analyzed at the same time). During this analysis each component was separated from the remainder of the collection and placed in a color-coded bag—Formative pottery went in blue bags, EIP/MH into green, LIP into yellow, and Inca into red. With the overall sample bagged in uncolored clear bags, it was possible to work quickly with collections in a sample that included more than 1500 separate site and collection proveniences. After the

Figure 1.16.

Inca imperial pottery from surface collections in the Sacred Valley.

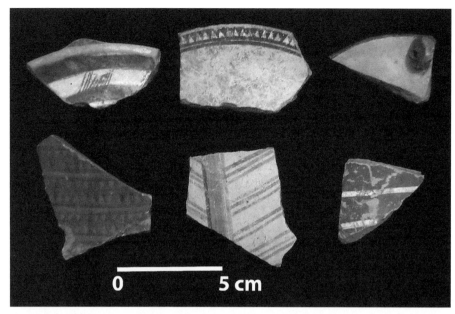

Figure 1.17.

Inca pottery that deviates from the imperial canon. This may represent local production, earlier examples of the style, or both.

preliminary presence-absence designation, a second phase of analysis was conducted for Formative and EIP/MH samples. Allison Davis analyzed all Formative components, and Véronique Bélisle worked with the EIP/MH components. These researchers were engaged in their own excavation projects related to the respective time periods, and their analysis was considered definitive—some materials were reclassified during the second analysis. Unlike the SVAP, there was no intensive coding of LIP pottery from the Xaquixaguana region. The full interpretation of production and distribution of pottery across the Hanan Cuzco region remains an unanswered research question that calls for

geochemical analysis of stratigraphically isolated samples from sites across the region.

The Calca-Yanahuara survey was co-directed by Covey, Bauer, and Miriam Aráoz Silva, and all three directors collaborated in the analysis of surface collections. The general surface collections and compromised site contexts that were identified in many parts of the survey discouraged more intensive analysis beyond the basic type-variety identification of all diagnostics. This was carried out using the same typology employed by other projects, and the survey results yielded less stylistic diversity (especially for the EIP/MH), making for fairly straightforward assessments of presence or absence of a given component.

The Hanan Cuzco surveys represent a methodologically unified study region that can reconstruct human settlement patterns to the extent that site preservation, field methods, and analytical protocols permit. This chapter has discussed some of the contemporary conditions that affected survey work, as well as the modest variations in collection strategies and analytical intensity that permitted each project to target specific archaeological questions beyond the broader goal of reconstructing settlement patterns. The chapters that follow present the data from the various Hanan Cuzco projects, attempting to develop broad regional patterns while remaining mindful of the ways that some project data were distinctive.

References

Baca Cosío, Jenaro F.
1974   *Motivos de ornamentación de la cerámica inca Cusco*, t. 1. Camaná, Peru: Librería Studium S.A.
1989   *Motivos de ornamentación de la cerámica inca Cusco*, t. 2. Camaná, Peru: Librería Studium S.A.

Barreda Murillo, Luis
1982   Asentamiento humano de los Qotakalli del Cuzco. In *Arqueología del Cuzco*, edited by I. Oberti Rodríguez, pp. 13–21. Cusco: Instituto Nacional de Cultura.

Bauer, Brian S.
1989   Muyu Orqo y Ccoipa: Dos nuevos tipos de cerámica para la región del Cuzco. *Revista Andina* 7(2):537–42.
1992   *The Development of the Inca State*. Austin: University of Texas Press.
1999   *The Early Ceramics of the Inca Heartland*. Fieldiana Anthropology, n.s., 31. Chicago: Field Museum of Natural History.
2002   *Las antiguas tradiciones alfareras de la región del Cuzco*. Cuzco: Centro de Estudios Rurales Andinos "Bartolomé de Las Casas."
2004   *Ancient Cuzco: Heartland of the Inca*. Austin: University of Texas Press.
2008   *Cuzco antiguo: Tierra natal de los incas*. Cuzco: Centro de Estudios Rurales Andinos "Bartolomé de Las Casas."

Bauer, Brian S., and Bradford M. Jones
2003   *Early Intermediate and Middle Horizon Ceramic Styles of the Cuzco Valley*, pp. 1–65. Fieldiana Anthropology, n.s., 34. Chicago: Field Museum of Natural History.

Bélisle, Véronique
2011   Ak'awillay: Wari State Expansion and Household Change in Cusco, Peru (AD 600–1000). PhD dissertation, Department of Anthropology, University of Michigan.

Bingham, Hiram
1915   Types of Machu Picchu pottery. *American Anthropologist* 17:257–71.

Chatfield, Melissa
2007   From Inca to Spanish Colonial: Transitions in Ceramic Technology. PhD dissertation, Department of Anthropology, University of California, Santa Barbara.
2010   Tracing firing technology through clay properties in Cuzco, Peru. *Journal of Archaeological Science* 37(4):727–36.

Chávez, Karen L. Mohr
1977   Marcavalle: The Ceramics from an Early Horizon Site in the Valley of Cusco, Peru, and Implications for South Highland Socio-Economic Interaction. PhD dissertation, Department of Anthropology, University of Pennsylvania.
1980   The archaeology of Marcavalle, an Early Horizon site in the Valley of Cusco, Peru: Part I. *Baessler-Archiv* n.f. 28(2):203–329.
1981a The archaeology of Marcavalle, an Early Horizon site in the Valley of Cusco, Peru: Part II. *Baessler-Archiv* n.f. 29(1):107–25.
1981b The archaeology of Marcavalle, an Early Horizon site in the Valley of Cusco, Peru: Part III (decorated ceramics). *Baessler-Archiv* n.f. 29(1):241–386.

Covey, R. Alan
2006   *How the Incas Built Their Heartland: State Formation and the Innovation of Imperial Strategies in the Sacred Valley, Peru*. Ann Arbor: University of Michigan Press.
n.d.   A Multiscalar Investigation of Early Inka State Expansion. Manuscript in preparation.

Covey, R. Alan, Miriam Aráoz Silva, and Brian S. Bauer
2008   Settlement patterns in the Yucay Valley and neighboring areas. In *Imperial Transformations in Sixteenth-Century Yucay, Peru*, edited by R. Alan Covey and Donato Amado González, pp. 3–17. Memoirs, no. 44. Ann Arbor: Museum of Anthropology, University of Michigan.

Covey, R. Alan, Brian S. Bauer, Véronique Bélisle, and Lia Tsesmeli
2013   Regional perspectives on Wari state influence in Cusco, Peru (c. AD 600–1000). *Journal of Anthropological Archaeology* 32(4):538–52.

Davis, Allison R.
2010   Excavations at Yuthu: A Community Study of an Early Village in Cusco, Peru (400–100 BC). PhD dissertation, Department of Anthropology, University of Michigan.
2011   *Yuthu: Community and Ritual in an Early Andean Village*. Memoirs, no. 50. Ann Arbor: Museum of Anthropology, University of Michigan.

Delgado, M., P. Olivera, E. Montoya, and A. Bustamante
2007   Building a bridge to the past: Archaeometry at the IPEN reactor. *Archaeometry* 49(2):403–12.

Dwyer, Edward B.
1971   The Early Inca Occupation of the Valley of Cuzco, Peru. PhD dissertation, Department of Anthropology, University of California, Berkeley.

Espinoza Martínez, Hector
1983   Evidencia cultural del Horizonte Medio (Wari) Aqomoqo-Cusco. In *Arqueología Andina*, edited by Arminda M. Gibaja Oviedo, pp. 16–22. Cusco, Peru: Instituto Nacional de Cultura.

Glowacki, Mary
1996 The Wari Occupation of the Southern Highlands of Peru: A Ceramic Perspective from the Site of Pikillacta. PhD dissertation, Department of Anthropology, Brandeis University, MA.
2002 The Huaro archaeological site complex: Rethinking the Huari occupation of Cuzco. In *Andean Archaeology I: Variations in Sociopolitical Organization*, edited by W. H. Isbell and H. Silverman, pp. 267–85. New York: Kluwer Academic/Plenum Publishers.
2005 Pottery from Pikillacta. In *Pikillacta: The Wari Empire in Cuzco*, edited by Gordon F. McEwan, pp. 101–14. Iowa City: University of Iowa Press.

Haquehua Huaman, Wilbert, and Rubén Maqque Azorsa
1996 Cerámica de Cueva Moqo-Maras. Tesis, Facultad de Ciencias Sociales, Universidad Nacional de San Antonio Abad del Cusco.

Kendall, Ann
1985 *Aspects of Inca Architecture: Description, Function and Chronology*, pts. 1 and 2. BAR International Series 242. Oxford: British Archaeological Reports.
1994 *Proyecto Arqueológico Cusichaca, Cusco: Investigaciones arqueológicas y de rehabilitación agrícola, tomo I*. Lima: Southern Peru Copper Corporation.

Kosiba, Steven B.
2010 Becoming Inka: The Transformation of Political Place and Practice during Inka State Formation (Cusco, Peru). PhD dissertation, Department of Anthropology, University of Chicago.

Lunt, Sarah
1988 The manufacture of the Inca aryballus. In *Recent Studies in Pre-Columbian Archaeology, Part ii*, edited by Nicholas J. Saunders and Olivier de Montmollin, pp. 489–511. BAR International Series 421(ii). Oxford: British Archaeological Reports.

Maqque Azorsa, Rubén, and Wilbert Haquehua Huaman
1993 Prospección arqueológica de Cueva Moqo-Maras. Informe de prácticas preprofesionales. Facultad de Ciencias Sociales, Universidad Nacional de San Antonio Abad del Cusco.

McEwan, Gordon F.
1984 The Middle Horizon in the Valley of Cuzco, Peru: The Impact of the Wari Occupation of Pikillacta in the Lucre Basin. PhD dissertation, Department of Anthropology, University of Texas.
1991 Investigations at the Pikillacta site: A provincial Huari center in the Valley of Cuzco. In *Huari Administrative Structures: Prehistoric Monumental Architecture and State Government*, edited by William H. Isbell and Gordon F. McEwan, pp. 93–119. Washington, D.C.: Dumbarton Oaks Research Library and Collection.

McEwan, Gordon F., Melissa Chatfield, and Arminda Gibaja
2002 The archaeology of Inca origins: Excavations at Chokepukio, Cuzco, Peru. In *Andean Archaeology I: Variations in Sociopolitical Organization*, edited by William H. Isbell and Helaine Silverman, pp. 287–301. New York: Kluwer Academic/Plenum Press.

McEwan, Gordon F., Arminda M. Gibaja, and Melissa Chatfield
1995 Archaeology of the Chokepukio site: An investigation of the origin of the Inca civilisation in the Valley of Cuzco, Peru. A report on the 1994 field season. *Tawantinsuyu* 1:11–17.

Montoya, E., M. Glowacki, J. Zapata, and P. Mendoza
2009 Caracterización de cerámicos wari mediante análisis por activación neutrónica. *Revista de la Sociedad Química del Perú* 75(4):473–78.

Niles, Susan A.
2004 The nature of Inca royal estates. In *Machu Picchu: Unveiling the Mystery of the Incas*, edited by Richard L. Burger and Lucy C. Salazar, pp. 49–68. New Haven, CT: Yale University Press.

Parsons, Jeffrey R., Charles M. Hastings, and Ramiro Matos M.
2000 *Prehispanic Settlement Patterns in the Upper Mantaro and Tarma Drainages, Junín, Peru. Volume 1: The Tarama-Chinchaycocha Region, Part 1*. Memoirs, no. 34. Ann Arbor: Museum of Anthropology, University of Michigan.

Rivera Dorado, Miguel
1971a La cerámica killke y la arqueología de Cuzco (Perú). *Revista Española de Antropología Americana* 6:85–124.
1971b Diseños decorativos en la cerámica killke. *Revista del Museo Nacional* 37:106–15.
1972 La cerámica de Cancha-Cancha, Cuzco, Peru. *Revista Dominicana de Arqueología y Antropología* 2(2–3):36–49.

Rowe, John H.
1944 *An Introduction to the Archaeology of Cuzco*. Papers of the Peabody Museum of American Archaeology and Ethnology 27(2). Cambridge, MA.
1956 Archaeological explorations in southern Peru, 1954–1955. *American Antiquity* 22(2):135–50.

Sanders, William T., Jeffrey R. Parsons, and Robert S. Santley
1979 *The Basin of Mexico: Ecological Processes in the Evolution of a Civilization*. New York: Academic Press.

Torres Poblete, Nilo
1989 Sondeo arqueológico en Araway. Licenciatura thesis, Social Sciences Faculty, Universidad Nacional de San Antonio Abad del Cusco, Cusco, Peru.

Zapata Rodríguez, Julinho
1997 Arquitectura y contextos funerarios Wari en Batan Urqu, Cusco. *Boletín de Arqueología PUCP* 1:165–206.
1998 Los cerros sagrados: Panorama del período Formativo en la cuenca del Vilcanota, Cusco. *Boletín de Arqueología PUCP* 2:307–36.

Zuidema, Reiner Tom, and Deborah Poole
1982 Los límites de los cuatro suyus incaicos en el Cuzco. *Bulletin de l'Institut Français des Études Andines* 11(1–2):83–89.

Chapter 2: Environment and Ecology in the Hanan Cuzco Region

R. Alan Covey and Maeve Skidmore

The four regional surveys that comprise the Hanan Cuzco region span a range of ecological zones typical of the area surrounding the city of Cuzco (Fig. 2.1). Environmental characteristics of the contemporary landscape vary from one locale to another, and the symbolic conceptualization and economic exploitation of local landscapes is correspondingly diverse. Quechua speakers identify a few broad ecozones based on differences in elevation, micro-environmental conditions, and agricultural potential across a landscape, such as *kichwa* (warm valley bottom), *suni* (upper hillslope agricultural lands), and *puna* (high grassland pasture). Such categories are heuristically useful, although they should be employed with caution. Even though it is the most readily available source of geographic information, elevation alone is not a straightforward predictor of ecology and each ecozone may contain significant internal heterogeneity. For example, puna lands begin around 3800 masl or so between Calca and Pisac in the Sacred Valley, but comparable landscapes appear in the Urubamba area at around 3500 masl. Additionally, human use of diverse landscapes cuts across ecozones. The surveyed landscapes of the Hanan Cuzco region are not timeless environments that inform us unambiguously about human settlement and subsistence in the past, so settlement pattern data cannot necessarily be regarded as a full or straightforward representation of subsistence practices of the past. This chapter presents a "contemporary" introduction to the environments and subsistence practices seen across the Hanan Cuzco region, to frame the archaeological discussions that follow in subsequent chapters. Climatic fluctuations in the short and long term are also reviewed in consideration of risk reduction strategies employed in the region today and how environmental factors of the same landscape varied in the past. Where pertinent, the text also addresses how the modern landscape influenced regional survey work.

The Hanan Cuzco Landscape as a Dynamic Region

Leaving the bustle of Cuzco for the tranquility of the countryside, it is easy to forget that the landscape of the Hanan Cuzco region is a modern one. The social practices and environmental characteristics described in this chapter are specific to the ethnographic present—indeed, many of the conditions described in the ethnographic record prior to the 1969 land reform are unrecognizable today (e.g., Núñez del Prado 1973). The strong focus on the indigenous village in the ethnographic literature of the late twentieth century belies the overall distribution of resources before the land reform—in the Department of Cuzco in the early 1960s, just a quarter of agropastoral units were communally held, and private property represented more than 85% of the total area being worked (CONESTCAR 1964:10–11). There is an ideology of rural timelessness that pervades some of the

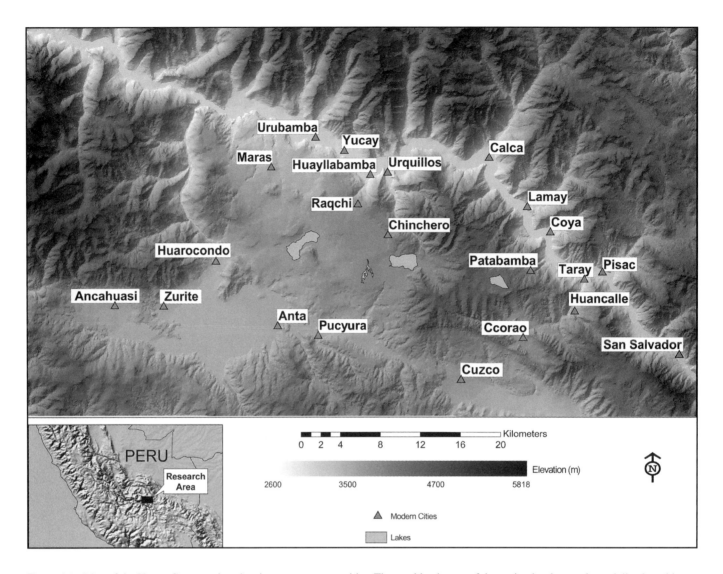

Figure 2.1. Map of the Hanan Cuzco region showing contemporary cities. The rural landscape of the region has been substantially altered in recent decades. Courtesy of L. Tsesmeli.

ethnographic literature, which manages to overlook the structures of the *hacienda* system, as well as land invasion practices that reallocated resources in the years prior to the land reform (Neira 1964). Even the policies of the reform maintain a sense of deep history regarding indigenous farming communities. Some of the most detailed documents that we encountered during the Hanan Cuzco research were 1590s titles for indigenous communities that were found in the archive of the land reform, which had treated these documents as evidence of just claim to the same lands in the late twentieth century.

The land reform attempted to undo the hacienda-oriented encroachment on indigenous communities, but initially only replaced *hacendados* with government officials and cooperatives intent on maintaining centralized agricultural production.

As cooperatives later were dissolved, large numbers of new communities were forged across the landscape, sometimes converting unused lands or pastures into agricultural fields. For example, of the 95 indigenous communities in the province of Calca, 45 were established after the land reform (Gobierno Regional del Cusco 2012). Funds aiding in the purchase of land, fertilizer, and machinery to amplify production were made available by numerous national and international organizations concerned with the plight of local farmers who had suffered economically, first under the hacendados and later under the cooperatives (CENCIRA 1979; Boada 1991). Today, such costs fall largely to individual families or communities, and many of the communities forged in the wake of land reform have proven unsustainable.

Figure 2.2. Aerial photograph of the Cuzco Basin taken by the Shippee-Johnson expedition, circa 1930. Today, virtually the entire valley-bottom area shown in the photo is covered by the urban occupation of Cuzco, which is now a city of several hundred thousand residents. Courtesy of Department of Library Services, American Museum of Natural History (neg. no. 334756).

Population growth in the mid-twentieth century contributed to social unrest that led to the agrarian reform, but the prohibition of indirect usufruct encouraged return migration to rural communities, raising growth rates and stimulating new cycles of migration (see Guillet 1976). In the most recent national census (2007), the Department of Cuzco had a population of just over 1.2 million, a figure that has more than doubled since 1940 (INEI). Decades of sustained annual growth rates above 1% reflect a demographic transformation of the region that is a significant departure from earlier times. Not only are populations larger in the region, but they are more urbanized—the 2007 census was the first in which the urban population of the Department of Cuzco outnumbered rural population, and the first census in which rural populations declined (Fig. 2.2). Urbanization and population growth have had variable impacts in the Hanan Cuzco region. Whereas the Sacred Valley provinces (Calca and Urubamba) experienced average annual growth rates of 1.1% and 1.2% from 1993 to

2007, the neighboring province of Anta saw the average annual population decline by 0.2% (INEI).

Urbanization has occurred within a context of rural transformation. Migration from rural areas has driven the growth of urban areas and changed the economic organization of the region, in turn presenting new pressures on, and opportunities for, rural areas that produce the food consumed by city dwellers. Perversely, urban expansion has consumed some of the most productive farmland of the Cuzco region, most notably in the Cuzco Basin and the Urubamba area in the Sacred Valley. Population growth has imposed greater food demands, which are satisfied by more intensive production and reliance on a broader sustaining region. With regard to the former, during our survey work in the Xaquixaguana region, many of the farmers we met told us that they produced food for their own subsistence, as well as staples that could be sold in regional markets. The continuous cultivation of many lands requires the use of chemical fertilizers, pesticides, and herbicides, and only certain crops can be produced as commodities. The broadening of Cuzco's urban sustaining area has been achieved through improvements in transportation infrastructure, especially roads and railways, allowing areas as distant as Quillabamba to play a significant role in provisioning the city.

The improved transportation infrastructure in the Cuzco region has occurred in the context of development programs aimed at stimulating the tourist economy (Fig. 2.3). Rail access down the Sacred Valley has linked Cuzco and Machu Picchu for decades, and the construction of paved highways links Cuzco to other parts of the highlands, also creating a touristic loop that connects the city with major archaeological sites in the Sacred Valley. Tourism has exploded in Cuzco in recent decades, especially with the cessation of Shining Path violence in the 1990s, and more than 2 million tourists visited the region in 2011 (*El Comercio* 3/29/12). These temporary visitors represent an economic force that influences agriculture and landscape management as outsiders place new demands on food, lodging, and tourist destinations. In addition to the direct effects of the tourist industry, there are secondary effects on local economies. For example, road construction has reduced the role of llamas in transporting staple goods from farm to market; this reduced role and the concomitant demand for meat in Cuzco's restaurants has encouraged shifts in herding patterns from Andean camelids to European herd animals (sheep and cattle) that leave a different footprint on the landscape. A new airport is being planned for construction in the Hanan Cuzco region, to bring an ever-increasing flow of tourists—this will ensure that the transformation of rural landscapes continues into the future.

Even though the landscape of the Hanan Cuzco is a modern one subject to contemporary political and economic forces, the strategies that private landowners and indigenous communities have used to reap profits and reduce subsistence risks offer a window into some of the ecological parameters of the region. We offer a description of environment and subsistence across the Hanan Cuzco region as a point of departure into discussion of the diverse ways that earlier populations approached this landscape as it changed over time.

Environment and Agriculture in the Sacred Valley Region

The Sacred Valley region is environmentally diverse, and the discussion below highlights that diversity through description of the valley proper as well as a selection of side valleys to the north and south, sampling a range of elevations and a broad array of microclimates. Five subregions can be identified based on variations in local environment, and the discussion of these below draws on field observations, published literature, and survey data.

Figure 2.3. Tourists at the Inca ruins of Pisac in the Sacred Valley. The booming tourist industry has enormous influence on the Cuzco region.

Site registration included observations regarding land use at the site location, permitting the generation of a coarse-grained map of land use across the region.[1] For the purpose of the present introduction, the Sacred Valley is discussed first, and then the four main transverse valley areas surveyed in 2000.

Sacred Valley

The moniker "Sacred Valley of the Incas" is commonly used to refer to the stretch of the Vilcanota-Urubamba River between Pisac and Ollantaytambo, largely due to the presence of monumental Inca sites and the tourist infrastructure for visiting them. This stretch of the valley floor lies below 3000 masl, and its frost-free climate makes it an ideal location for maize cultivation. However, although temperatures encourage maize agriculture, water constrains such production in several regards. Water for agriculture must come either from rainfall or from irrigation works that draw from tributaries of the river. Annual rainfall averages 400–600 mm or so (Morlon et al. 1996), but it is highly variable and falls unevenly across the valley (Winterhalder 1994:40–41) (Table 2.1). In many parts of the main valley, insufficient precipitation and poor soils make the steep, rocky valley sides too marginal for continuous farming. Survey crews found many areas to be too dangerous to traverse at the project survey interval, so these were sampled by following established trails and visiting areas of lower gradients wherever possible (Fig. 2.4).

The Vilcanota-Urubamba River is not used as a source of irrigation water, probably due to the significant seasonal fluctuations in its depth (Gade 1975:6). Irrigation systems are supported by tributary rivers that have distinct distribution on the north and south sides of the main valley. To the north of the Sacred Valley are several tributary valleys that bring considerable amounts of water to the main river, and between Calca and Ollantaytambo there are several glaciated peaks that contribute meltwater throughout the year. There are only three tributaries that drain into the valley from the south: the Huatanay River (from the Cuzco Basin), the Huancalle River (from the Chit'apampa Basin), and the Huarocondo River (from the Xaquixaguana Plain). Aside from these sources, there is limited irrigation potential on the south side of the Sacred Valley. The Hanan Cuzco research crew surveyed almost the entire length of the main valley between these key confluences; work began just upstream from San Salvador (about 10 km below the Huatanay confluence) to around the Huarocondo River confluence.

Soils along the main valley vary due to natural and anthropogenic factors (Gade 1975:9–10). Sandy soils filled with gravel and cobble predominate along parts of the river channel where canal and terrace construction has not taken place, and the river floods and meanders seasonally. These stretches of valley bottom remain uncultivated, whereas improved valley-bottom lands represent incredibly productive farmland. Irrigation works are found in proximity to tributary valleys offering permanent water, and the transportation of soil to artificial terraces protects such lands from erosion processes that wash away the thin soils of the valley sides. As Farrington (1983) has discussed, much of the valley-bottom agricultural infrastructure is associated with Inca-era projects by ruling elites.

The elite association with valley-bottom lands in the Sacred Valley can be traced forward from Inca times, through the institution of the hacienda system, to contemporary patterns of land ownership and agricultural production (e.g., Gade 1975:30–33). Private property predominates at the valley floor—which presented challenges for conducting archaeological survey in some locations—and economic production focuses on commodities rather than subsistence. Maize is the most prominent crop in the valley, and Gade (1975:120) estimated that 85% of irrigated land is used for maize, predominantly a high-yield variety (*parakay*) and a variety that can be used for multiple purposes (*uwina*), including brewing. Within the Sacred Valley, the irrigated lands between Calca and Yanahuara are particularly productive—they have fertile soils that can be used to grow early varieties (*miska*) of maize (Gade 1975:118), and commercial yields. The lands that made up the estate of the Inca ruler Wayna Qhapaq are used not only for maize, but for vegetables and fruit trees, a practice that dates at least to the early Colonial period, when leading citizens of Cuzco sought lands for country homes and gardens (see Covey and Amado 2008; Villanueva 1970).

The economy of the kichwa zone of the Sacred Valley emphasizes continuous cropping of low-diversity cultigens that can yield large surpluses that are sold in market towns and in Cuzco. The economic power of massive haciendas and other private landholdings at the valley floor contrasts starkly with that of indigenous communities holding corporate title to less productive lands on the steep valley slopes, where families have access to less than a hectare of arable land (e.g., Molinié-Fioravanti 1982; cf. Manya 1971; Mayta Medina 1971).

Chit'apampa Basin

The Chit'apampa Basin is the only significant side valley to the south of the Sacred Valley. It borders the Cuzco Valley to the south, and as such, it is a natural corridor between Cuzco and the Sacred Valley. The upper part of the basin is used for mixed farming, and the 2000 survey encountered potatoes, quinoa, and beans in higher-elevation areas where dry farming was possible (Fig. 2.5). In lower elevations where local populations have irrigation systems, maize is a prominent crop. The upper part of the basin was logistically easy to survey—the hillsides were safe to traverse and the distance from ridgetops to valley floor tended to be modest. Below the community of Rayanniyoc, however, the confluence of several streams creates broken terrain dominated by a canyon that drops abruptly into the Sacred Valley.

---

1. The results of land use identifications must be taken with due caution, as they are contingent upon local crop rotations, the agricultural knowledge of different crew members, and the season of site identification. As research progressed and crops were harvested, it was more likely that a site would be registered as "not in use."

Table 2.1. Multiyear precipitation and temperature data from Cuzco region weather stations.

Station	Precip. Avg (mm)	Precip. Max. (mm)	Precip. Min. (mm)	Avg Temp. Max. (°C)	Avg Temp. Min. (°C)
Cuzco	745.0	982.1	389.5	19.7	4.3
Granja Kayra	676.7	923.2	477.7	24.8	4.3
Anta	742.0	887.7	591.3	18.0	3.4
Chinchero	799.9	1113.8	420.5	20.4	6.8
Pisac	669.5	1414.3	219.8	N/A	N/A
Calca	514.3	668.5	357.3	22.1	5.6
Yucay	512.7	601.9	397.5	23.1	6.8
Urubamba	391.4	592.4	70.6	22.2	6.2
Machu Picchu	1996.3	2381.3	1571.3	22.3	9.9

Source: Winterhalder 1994: Tables 2.5, 2.6. Data represent at least a decade of observation.

Figure 2.4.

The Sacred Valley at Pisac, facing upriver toward San Salvador and the peak of Pachatusan. Rocky valley sides could not be effectively surveyed in parts of the region.

Figure 2.5. The upper Chit'apampa Basin, with the town of Ccorao in the center. The Cuzco region lies beyond the ridge in the upper center of the picture.

Ethnographic research has been conducted in the Chit'apampa Basin at the eponymous village (de la Cadena 1992) and in the community of Kallarayan (Radcliffe 1986). Families in Chit'apampa, which is located on the floor of the basin, cultivate vegetables, potatoes, and maize, with a minor component of cow and sheep herding (de la Cadena 1992). In Kallarayan, which is situated in a small tributary valley at 3700 masl, residents pursue suni zone mixed agriculture with a focus on potatoes and other Andean tubers, barley, and maize, with a limited pursuit of animal husbandry (Radcliffe 1986). Irrigated land constituted just 1% of the community lands of Kallarayan in the 1980s, and most lands were farmed using a lengthy rotation cycle (*laymi*) (Radcliffe 1986:32). Across the basin from Kallarayan, in Matinga and other nearby communities, agronomical research has documented the cultivation of *añu*, *oca*, *olluco*, potatoes, and other indigenous Andean cultigens (Ortega et al., n.d.).

Chongo Basin

The Chongo Basin lies to the north of the Vilcanota-Urubamba River, and its waters drain into the larger river at Pisac. A prominent ridge divides the upper and lower basins. The lower landforms in the valley represent an overthrust wedge of the Paucartambo formation prone to large-scale landslide activity (López-Zapana, Carreño, and Kalafatovich C. 2005) (Fig. 2.6). In the lower basin, there are several small agricultural villages that occupy the kichwa and suni zones; these have traditionally been dominated by *mestizo* elites in Pisac (Núñez del Prado 1973:15). Núñez del Prado (1973) conducted a long-term applied anthropology project in the lower basin village of Kuyo Chico and describes aspects of the local agrarian economy in the 1950s. More than 90% of the lands of Kuyo Chico were dry farmed at that time, with just 9.44% of lands supported by irrigation (Núñez del Prado 1973:23). Maize was the primary crop produced on village lands (53.9% of land use), followed by wheat (27.5%), barley (16.2%), and very small areas of peas, quinoa, and beans (Núñez del Prado 1973:25). Modest numbers of cattle, sheep, guinea pigs, and chickens were kept in the village.

The upper basin consists of suni lands that transition into rolling grasslands beyond the boundaries of the Sacred Valley survey (Fig. 2.7). There communities were larger than those of the lower basin, and in the mid-twentieth century were governed

Figure 2.6. The lower Chongo Basin occupies a range of ecozones from the maize-producing kichwa to upper tuber lands near the ridgelines.

Figure 2.7. Communities in the upper Chongo Basin have united to established the Parque de la Papa, an indigenous effort to manage local landscapes and biodiversity.

by local officials who had more autonomy than was observed in lower basin villages. The four villages of the upper basin possess small amounts of farmland below 3600 masl, which is used to cultivate small areas of irrigated and terraced maize plots (Cosio et al. 1981:14). These lands represent a small part of each community's territory, and maize was cultivated on less than 9% of agricultural lands in use in 1981 (Cosio et al. 1981:45). Simple irrigation networks were used to the extent possible, and each community farmed hundreds of small plots annually, maintaining soil fertility using animal dung and a careful crop rotation system. Barley was a common crop (and wheat less so), but Andean cultigens represent a prominent part of rotation-based dry-farming practices. Tubers including potato, oca, olluco, and añu represent about 40% of agricultural land use, and quinoa and *tarwi* are other autochthonous crops still used in the upper basin at that time (Cosio et al. 1981:45). With a complex system of intercropping, crop rotation, and fallowing, the upper basin communities spread risk across a wide range of resources. Herding in the upper pasturelands constituted a substantial part of this diverse agricultural economy, and Cosio et al. (1981:49) report more than 16,000 sheep, nearly 2000 cattle, and more than 1000 camelids in the local herds. Domestic animal husbandry included pigs, chickens, and guinea pigs.

As with other upper valley areas in the Sacred Valley, diversity and social interconnection figure prominently in the local econo-mies of the upper Chongo Basin. From 2000 to 2003, the four basin towns (Amaru, Cuyo Grande, Paru Paru, Sacaca) worked with two neighboring ones (Chawaytire and Pampallaqta) to establish the Parque de la Papa (Potato Park), a protected landscape in which an estimated 1200 varieties of native tubers are maintained by local cultivators. A similar project is being developed to rebuild camelid populations in the high grasslands nearby.

Huaynapata, Carmen, and Huancohuayco Quebradas

Downstream from Pisac are three smaller basins on the north side of the Sacred Valley. Above Lamay, Quebrada Carmen is the only one of these that extends more than a few kilometers from the main valley, and this small drainage possesses characteristics that are intermediate to the Chongo and Qochoc Valleys—it is narrower than the former, and wider than the latter, with a distinct lower basin (near Lamay) and an upper basin with multiple tributaries and small communities that practice diverse tuber-based horticulture and small-scale herding (e.g., Ortega et al. 2007) (Fig. 2.8). Genetic similarities in ocas cultivated in communities above Lamay and Pisac have been interpreted as evidence of tuber seed flow among the upvalley communities living to the north of the Sacred Valley (Ortega et al., n.d.), and it is worth noting that this area is mentioned as a single cultural zone in some early Colonial period myths (e.g., Molina 2011 [1570s]:12–13).

Figure 2.8. The Poques area in the mid-valley area above Lamay. Colonial mythology and contemporary agrarian exchanges link this area with the upper valleys between Pisac and Calca.

Qochoc Valley

The Qochoc River runs through a narrow and steep side valley that drains into the Vilcanota-Urubamba River at Calca (Fig. 2.9). The river drops approximately 1000 m vertically in about 10 km, from high-elevation puna lands to warm valley-bottom maize lands in the Sacred Valley proper. The Qochoc Valley represents an important conduit between the Sacred Valley and the warm Lares Valley, which has a tropical climate suitable for cultivating crops that cannot be produced closer to Cuzco (e.g., cacao, coca leaf, manioc, citrus fruits) (Flores Ochoa 1986:271). The valley has abundant water flowing from multiple tributary streams, including water that comes from the melt of the glacier peak of Ccolque Cruz (5818 masl) (Fig. 2.10). The steep and narrow nature of this valley made it particularly challenging to survey intensively, and many areas were strategically sampled to avoid places that were unsafe to walk, or logistically difficult to reach.

Maize agriculture is dominant in the lower part of the Qochoc Valley, giving way quickly to potatoes, barley, and beans with increasing elevation. In the upper valley, communities like Pampallaqta engage in a mix of tuber cultivation and herding. Sánchez Farfán (1983) describes agricultural production in Pampallaqta, an upvalley community lying 18 km from Calca. The community lies just below the archaeological site of Ankasmarka, on the suni-puna ecotone at about 3850 masl. Whereas communities lower in the valley cultivate maize, the people of Pampallaqta focus on the cultivation of sweet and bitter potatoes,

with a small component of other tubers, such as oca and olluco (Sánchez Farfán 1983:165). Extended families labor together to reduce risks to their food supply by planting early (*maway*) tuber varieties that can be harvested before other crops are ready, and they process bitter potatoes into *chuño* and *moraya*, which can be stored for periods when other food supplies are less abundant. As Sánchez Farfán describes (1983:166), local producers also address risk by observing natural signs, such as the movement of ants and foxes, to predict whether a year will be rainy or dry and to adjust their plot locations and emphasis on appropriate cultivars. The observation of the Pleiades in August is another predictive practice (see Cuba de Nordt 1971; Urton 1981:98).

In addition to tuber cultivation, families in Pampallaqta herd sheep and camelids, frequently engaging in seasonal journeys during the rainy season to neighboring communities with better pasturelands, where they shear the herds (Sánchez Farfán 1983). Camelids provide a source of labor for bearing harvests from field to village, and corrals near the community offer a source of natural fertilizer that can be applied to fields to enhance soil fertility. The households of Pampallaqta engage in interzone exchanges, trading seed potatoes for agricultural produce that cannot be cultivated locally (e.g., quinoa, wheat, beans, maize) and other desired products (e.g., sugar, salt, coca leaf, alcohol) (Sánchez Farfán 1983:172–73). These exchanges link the town not only with communities in the Sacred Valley, but also with more distant areas.

Figure 2.9. The confluence of the Qochoc and Vilcanota-Urubamba Rivers at Calca.

Figure 2.10. The mid-valley area of the Qochoc Valley. Glacier melt provides abundant irrigation water for terraced fields in the lower valley, carried by the Inca-era canals shown in the picture.

Flores Ochoa (1986:267–73) offers a broader perspective on herding in the upper valley above Pampallaqta, reporting the presence of hacienda and community herds of alpacas (4000), llamas (8360), horses (3000), and sheep (27,000). Some cattle are also raised in this area. Family-based herds of 30–50 alpacas and some other animals seek out moist pasturelands in narrow puna valleys where glacier melt creates ideal conditions for the animals. Until good roads were constructed between Calca and Lares, llama caravans provided key labor for transporting agricultural goods and maintaining regional commerce at larger market towns. Alpacas are raised for their wool, and the pastures of this area are some of the last where forage quality has been sufficiently maintained for herding these animals.

Environment and Agriculture in the Xaquixaguana Region

The Xaquixaguana region consists of the eastern districts of the province of Urubamba, including Maras and Chinchero, as well as several districts of the Anta province, including Anta, Huarocondo, Zurite, and Ancahuasi. The region is distinct from its surroundings in that it represents a vast expanse of land with relatively modest topographic relief, in contrast to the more rugged and steeply ascending terrain west of the region and in the Sacred Valley to the north. Survey of Xaquixaguana was followed up by a 2008 project that talked with local residents of communities across the region to collect information about local agriculture and economy, as well as other aspects of community life. Those exchanges inform the discussion below concerning use of the land today.

In exploring the ecology and economic potential of the region, literature on Xaquixaguana classifies different landscape zones in varied ways (e.g., Boada 1991; CENCIRA 1979; Guillet 1979). Here, three zones will be considered. Two of these are distinguished by differences in elevation, topography, availability of water, and humidity; the third represents a transitional zone between these. The Xaquixaguana Plain proper, the higher and hillier districts of Chinchero and Maras, and the transitional zone (between the plain and the rolling hills districts, but also including southern and western edges of the plain where the land rises) are considered below. While maintaining these distinctions, the discussion, at times, considers other salient characteristics of the land, such as water features, and ecological differences that condition vegetation and land use.

The Xaquixaguana Plain

The plain is a unique geographical feature in the region, notable for its size (approximately 6000 ha) and the relative evenness of its topography (Fig. 2.11). Most of the plain lies at around 3400 masl, though to the west the land rises in elevation gradually as it tapers and approaches Ancahuasi. The plain widens in its central eastern portions before it narrows again around Anta, where a small pass allows access to the Cuzco Basin further east. At one time the plain was home to a large lake whose banks reached Huarocondo (Cebrecos Revilla 1968:20), and parts of the valley bottom are still quite wet today. The Xaquixaguana (also called the Anta or Izcuchaca) and Katañiray (also called the Pitumayo) Rivers flow through the plain, draining water from hills that flank it. These rivers converge near the center of the

Figure 2.11. The Xaquixaguana (or Anta) Plain presents abundant well-watered farmland at elevations where maize thrives. The floor of the valley was inundated at times in the past.

plain and from there carry water to Huarocondo, and from there through a steep pass into the Sacred Valley.

The Xaquixaguana Plain collects water year-round from numerous small streams that flow down from the hillsides surrounding it, as well as from natural springs, making it a particularly humid area in the region (Cebrecos Revilla 1968; Guillet 1979). Horizontally extensive deposits of fine mud and clay in the bottom of the ancient lakebed inhibit drainage, and today, various sub-basins of the ancient lake may accumulate standing water even in the dry season. Poor soil drainage can be a problem for those who seek to use the land for agriculture. Tuber crops are particularly at risk in the lower, wetter portions of the plain because too much water in the soil causes root rot. Maize manages such conditions better, but in general, local communities utilize the swampiest areas mostly as pastureland. Despite these limitations, most of the plain supports crop cultivation.

Today, fields in the plain constitute prime agricultural land—in terms of variability in what may be produced and in the number of growing seasons that are possible. Multiple growing seasons are limited to certain communities and rely on access to irrigation. For example, the community of Rahuanki can produce two harvests a year because it receives sufficient water year-round from canals and local springs. Residents of the plain consistently produce maize, wheat, potatoes, fava beans, and other produce. Crops vary from one field to the next and from community to community but there is a general emphasis on maize agriculture: residents interviewed in 2008 frequently reported that maize was the most important crop grown, sometimes representing up to 80% of a community's production. According to locals, aside from maize and potatoes, native cultigens were not among the principal crops grown on the plain.

Large livestock are more prevalent in communities on the plain than elsewhere in the Xaquixaguana region. Cattle in particular are maintained in higher numbers, though pigs, sheep, chickens, and guinea pigs are raised as well. In 2008, a resident of Tambo Real estimated that 80% of community land was devoted to the bovine industry. A resident of Markju similarly reported that raising cattle was extremely important to the local economy because of unpredictable harvests. Cows are raised both for their sale and for the production and sale of dairy products, such as cheese. This is usually a supplementary activity to—rather than the focus of—other family agricultural pursuits.

Rolling Hills in the Maras and Chinchero Districts

South of the Sacred Valley, the landscape around Maras and Chinchero represents a large undulating plateau, approximately 29,000 ha in size, dotted with a number of large protruding hills and small to large depressions (Figs. 2.12, 2.13). To the east of Chinchero the rolling hills give rise to the Qoricocha puna (discussed below), and the western edge of the plateau is defined by the steep canyon that drains water from Huarocondo down to the Vilcanota-Urubamba River. Many of the depressions accumulate water, forming temporary pools and a few more permanent lakes

and ponds. Some of the more famous of the depressions in this region can be found at Moray, where concentric agricultural terraces were fashioned in natural hollows by the Inca. On the southwestern side of the plateau, undulations intensify slightly, lending a hillier quality to the landscape, before it descends to the Xaquixaguana Plain.

The climate in this region is generally temperate but it is slightly colder than on the plain so that frost more frequently falls upon the land (CBCR 1974:2). Less water is available for fields in the hilly districts year-round because of runoff. Although many communities maintain canals, very few of them are able to successfully irrigate lands and instead they rely on rain-fed agriculture. Numerous small and large lakes exist in the region but few communities utilize their waters for irrigation or cultivate lakeside land. The two largest lakes are Lake Piuray, which lies on the eastern edge of Chinchero, and Lake Huaypo, located a few kilometers west of this (Fig. 2.14). In recent decades, shrinking shore levels in these lakes have caused problems for surrounding communities that utilize lake resources (Huallpa Ccahuantico 1995:62). The land around Lake Huaypo is heavily salinized, and land near Lake Piuray has large quantities of calcium carbonate on its surface (Contreras Hernández 1985:15). This inhibits the growth of plants in the area immediately adjacent to the lakes and limits the capacity to irrigate lands with lake waters because the water has farther to travel and local people do not wish to further deplete the lakes.

A unique productive feature of the rolling hills district are the salt pans (or *salineras*) located on hillsides that descend to the Yucay Valley, between the communities of Yunkaray and Yanahuara. When water from rain and nearby springs flows through the salineras, subterranean gem salt deposits are dissolved and redeposited on the hillslopes (Fig. 2.15). By controlling water flow through a series of canals, apportioning water to the reservoirs and periodically allowing it to evaporate, salt remains in the pans can periodically be collected for sale (Beltrán Costa 1988). Local inhabitants have exploited the saline streams of the salineras since prehistoric times.

The agricultural potential of the hills district is highly variable. The hillier quality of the region makes some areas particularly subject to erosional processes. Soil near rock outcrops and on hillsides may be fairly rocky, with negative repercussions for agriculture. Conversely, some have noted that increased relief can be beneficial to some areas by sheltering plots of land from temperature variation and harsh wind (Guillet 1979:50). In general, agriculture in the rolling hills is more limited than on the plain because most of the land lies in the suni ecozone, where warm-weather crops fare less well. Maize is cultivated in some communities in the hills district, but it typically does not thrive; maize plants may be stunted in growth and produce smaller cobs but, according to interviews and observations, this does not keep all farmers from cultivating them. Informants from communities in the rolling hills districts emphasized the importance of *ayni* (reciprocal labor) to planting and harvesting crops because they do not make sufficient revenue from the sale of their crops to

Figure 2.12. Rolling hills in the Chinchero area. While suitable for dry farming of high-elevation crops in many parts, there are swampy low-lying areas that are less productive for farming.

Figure 2.13. Rolling hills near Amantuy in the district of Maras. The plain drops several hundred meters into the fertile Sacred Valley.

Figure 2.14. View of Lake Piuray, near Chinchero. The prominent hill on the left in the middle distance is Cerro Huanacaure, which overlooks Lake Huaypo.

Figure 2.15. The Maras salt pans (salineras). Note the ruins of Inca structures in the foreground on the right. Colonial documents associate the facility with specialized salt production affiliated with the royal estate of Huayna Capac.

pay assistants for their labor. This stands in contrast with some communities at lower elevation, such as Inquillpata and Cconchakalla, that are transitioning away from this traditional practice in favor of wage labor.

Potatoes and other native tubers such as olluco, *mashua*, and oca are important crops for communities in the hills district, sometimes representing 50–80% of community crop production. Other native crops such as quinoa and tarwi are cultivated in this region with frequency, though they are not generally considered a primary crop. Barley has a special place in production for this area; the district of Maras once yielded some of the highest barley returns in the country (Hopkins Larrea 1978) though many local residents noted that this had diminished in recent years. In some communities it continues to be particularly important: for example, in K'aqllaraccay, informants reported that barley represents 60% of crops produced.

Livestock in the hills district is more diverse than on the plain, with camelids, goats, and donkeys kept in addition to the cattle, pigs, sheep, and yard animals (chickens and guinea pigs) more typical of the plain. Camelids and goats are not very common, however, and the communities in which they continue to be raised are mainly those where the land is rugged and high. In general, large animals are kept in small numbers in the rolling hills districts. Cattle are an important resource but they do not play as big a role in local economies as they do for some communities on the plain. Donkeys are kept in some communities to facilitate transportation of crops and other materials across long distances.

Between the Plain and Rolling Hills

At the northern and southern edges of the Xaquixaguana Plain, the land rises fairly gradually, whereas in the west, the ascent is somewhat sharper or the land transitions to higher peaks. Numerous communities are located in these transitional zones, and these benefit from the ability to exploit multiple ecological floors and from the varied products characteristic of each. They do not often rely on a primary crop, such as maize or potatoes, but engage in a diverse subsistence strategy, concentrating maize in the lower kichwa zone, and growing potato, wheat, barley, tarwi, quinoa, and other crops in suni fields at higher elevations. Communities in the transition zone raise a variety of livestock including cows, pigs, donkeys, chickens, and guinea pigs. At Zurite, large Inca terraces have been restored and are now managed by the Peruvian Ministry of Agriculture, which uses them to various ends, including the development of new varieties of cultigens (Fig. 2.16).

The kichwa lands at the edges of the plain that these communities hold are usually better drained than some others in the more central and wetter zones of the plain, providing good growing conditions. Erosion places some limitations on agriculture, and communities often deal with this by occupying the lands where this is most a problem or by cultivating forested areas there (Boada 1991:11). Access to water is provided through canal systems; some communities, where water is particularly abundant, support multiple growing seasons in a year. For example, Huarocondo benefits from the natural channeling of water from the Xaquixaguana Plain in its direction, and Chamancalla (which is located around the convergence of numerous minor streams that drain surrounding hills) similarly has sufficient access to water to harvest twice a year.

Herding on the Qoricocha Puna

The Qoricocha puna lies between the Cuzco and Sacred Valleys, and is flanked to the east and west by the Chit'apampa Basin and the Lake Piuray areas, respectively. At 4050 masl, Lake Qoricocha is the central feature of this high basin, surrounded by rolling puna that drops down to the surrounding valleys (Fig. 2.17). Numerous corral complexes are found throughout the Qoricocha area, the largest of which are in the main basin (Fig. 2.18). Small corrals were encountered in side valleys, which we suspect were used seasonally by herders from nearby communities. As discussed in Chapter 12, there was a strong Colonial presence in the basin, with little evidence of pre-Columbian habitation.

Herding constitutes a primary economic activity in the Qoricocha puna, although the large-scale introduction of sheep has degraded pasture there. In addition to the herding of sheep and llamas, high-elevation cultivation, presumably of bitter potatoes, was observed at elevations up to 4200 masl. During the 2004 survey of the basin, grass height was minimal throughout the basin, and there were areas of extensive erosion around Quenco, the village that herded within the basin. Boundary markers between Quenco and neighboring communities were well maintained, and individuals from neighboring communities from the Chit'apampa Basin, such as Huilcarpata, were observed at the frontiers, presumably to protect the much better maintained pasture on the other side of the boundary. As Radcliffe (1990) describes for the village of Kallarayan, the annual tracing of community boundaries occurs as part of corporate celebrations of community during the Carnival period, and some of the markers (*hitos*) are stone piles that may date to the sixteenth century or earlier.

Overall, the Qoricocha Basin appears never to have been a populated center, although its extensive pasturelands undoubtedly have served as a resource for nearby farming communities.

Climate Variation over Time

The preceding discussion has identified some important geographic patterns in the Hanan Cuzco region that influence human settlement and subsistence patterns. Ancient populations of the region addressed the perceived risks presented by a particular landscape through a number of social strategies, including mobility, crop diversity, animal husbandry, and surplus production and storage. These strategies targeted risk in both geographic and temporal dimensions, so it is important to discuss some of the time-related aspects of climatic variations in the region.

Figure 2.16. Rehabilitated Inca terraces at Zurite in the Xaquixaguana area.

Figure 2.17. Lake Qoricocha dominates a high puna basin lying between the Cuzco Valley and Sacred Valley.

Figure 2.18. Large corral complex located near Lake Qoricocha.

Seasonal Variations

The most proximate scale to consider is seasonal. The Cuzco highlands experience two principal seasons: a dry season from April to October and a rainy season from November to March. The arrival of the summer rains is essential to all human subsistence practices (Chepstow-Lusty et al. 2003). High-elevation snowfall replenishes the glaciers that provide irrigation water to valley-bottom lands, and the rain nourishes high puna grasses, creating temporary swampy areas (*bofedales*) preferred by the Andean camelids (Fig. 2.19). Varying levels of rainfall reach the slopes and valley bottoms across the region, providing the only source of water for cultivating many of the hillside plots used by local farmers. The cessation of the rains is also important for human subsistence strategies. As the high puna areas dry out and their grasses are consumed, herds must be moved, and wild animals migrate to other sources of water and food. Unseasonal precipitation—often in the form of hail—can damage plants in the field, or destroy harvested crops that are left in the field to dry before being transported and processed. Excessive water is unwelcome in the valley bottom, where terraced areas can be difficult to drain.

The seasonality of the Andean highlands is strongly influenced by the South American summer monsoon regime (Bird et al. 2011), and it encourages the basic scheduling of subsistence labor, as well as risk reduction strategies aimed at maintaining a reliable food supply throughout the year. This would have been true for early hunting and gathering groups in Cuzco, as it is for farming communities today. The harvest season is a complex and extended period in which labor groups from multiple households work on numerous small plots as different crops ripen. The practice of providing food for the laborers on one's plot—especially by building the *wathiya* (or *pachamanca*), an earth oven for roasting potatoes—ensures that large amounts of fresh food are eaten in the fields, so that labor networks eating across hundreds of plots at harvest time even out some of the field-by-field differences in crop yield. After the harvest has ended, households subsist on dried surplus staples, and many communities with high-elevation lands cultivate bitter potatoes that can be freeze-dried as chuño and moraya. These, as well as dried meat (*charki*) and other stored food, can be important food sources in the time before the next harvest is available

The diverse horticulture of upvalley communities ideally schedules in tandem with the productive calendars of valley-

Figure 2.19. Seasonally inundated areas of puna grassland in the Qoricocha area are used during the rainy season.

bottom monocrop agriculture and high-elevation herders. When villages conduct small-scale transhumant herding in the puna and limited maize production on small kichwa plots, they are able to harness the risk reduction potential of these zones. Animal labor can reduce some production costs (e.g., transport), and animals can store food energy against unpredictable shortfalls; their manure can improve the yields of a household's plots. As noted above, many communities cultivate early varieties of potato (maway) and maize (miska) to reduce the length of time between harvests, and these tend to be in lower-elevation areas that are less prone to frost or other climatic fluctuations. As discussed in the last chapters of this monograph, however, the economic shift to state-controlled agriculture at the valley floor has the potential to compromise the ability of ordinary households to schedule labor and to maintain the diverse suite of risk reduction mechanisms necessary to ensure a stable food supply. This could be mitigated to a certain extent by participation in regional market systems and festivals, although the evidence from ethnohistory and ethnography suggests negative outcomes have been the norm at least since the sixteenth century.

Interannual Fluctuations

Colonial Quechua dictionaries link seasonal concepts of dry/ warm (*chakiy/ruphay*) and wet/cold (*paray/chiri*), and there is a pronounced sense that these conditions should co-occur in their proper sequence (Covey, n.d.). As Winterhalder (1994; see Table 2.1) has observed, there are extreme precipitation fluctuations in contemporary Cuzco, and precipitation does not always come at the times when it is needed, especially in the transition between seasons when young plants and harvests are most vulnerable. The El Niño/Southern Oscillation (ENSO) is best known for the devastation it wreaks on the Pacific coast, but extreme ENSO events also block the summer monsoon rains, leading to drought conditions (Thompson 1993). Insufficient rainfall can destroy crops, although the use of irrigated plots mitigates this danger. Too much rain is perhaps a greater concern across the region, as it can erode the thin soils of the hillsides or wash away an entire slope in landslides (*llokllay*), overflowing the riverbanks at the valley floor and inundating or sweeping away improved farmland.

Local farming communities confront precipitation uncertainty by forecasting prevailing conditions at the outset of the planting season in August. The Pleiades constellation returns to view in the region around this time, and its aspect low on the horizon can be affected by atmospheric humidity, a visual indication of the advent of monsoon rains (Orlove, Chang, and Cane 2000; Urton 1981). Local farmers also observe the behavior of animals as an indication of prevailing conditions. Local forecasting leads horticulturalists to tailor their plot and cultigen selection to expected conditions, which requires coordination of land use by residential groups (*ayllus*), and probably accounts for some of the evidence of seed exchange between communities in different valleys. Valley-bottom agriculture is less affected by drought conditions, and there seems to be more emphasis on observing locally significant dates in the ritual calendar (Inca or Catholic).

Long-Term Climate Changes

The onset of Holocene conditions in the Andean highlands established a regional climate that was warm and characterized by extended arid periods between 9000 and 4400 cal yr BP (Mosblech et al. 2012). The first hunter-gatherers may have entered the Cuzco region under such conditions, and presumably would have found more pronounced seasonal patterns of water availability influencing the migration patterns of prey species that they hunted. Precipitation appears to have increased after 4800 BP, and lake core evidence from Lake Huaypo in the Hanan Cuzco region indicates accumulations of water starting around 4500 BP (Mosblech et al. 2012:1367; cf. Chepstow-Lusty et al. 2003:498–99). Stroup et al. (2011) have identified moraine advances at the Quelccaya glacier that date to circa 3000 BP, indicating a period of wetter and cooler conditions. This general climate regime persisted until about 1850 BP, although there is evidence of multiple periods of severe drought that might be correlated with an observed intensification of ENSO events, especially after 3200–2800 BP (Chepstow-Lusty 2011; Mosblech et al. 2012; Sandweiss et al. 2001).

Lake core data indicate trends toward more arid conditions after 1850 BP, with evidence for major droughts inferred from lake and ice cores (Mosblech et al. 2012:1369; Thompson et al. 1985). Chepstow-Lusty and colleagues (2003:499) suggest a decline in temperatures from 1900 to 1340 BP, followed by an increase in temperatures. Warmer temperatures with frequent drought continued until Inca times, when the onset of the Little Ice Age introduced a wetter and cooler climate. As Stroup and colleagues (2011) have recently noted, moraine distributions and lake sediments around Quelccaya indicate periods of glacial advance at 480 ± 60 and 340 ± 10 BP. These dates indicate that the onset of cooler and wetter conditions associated elsewhere with the Little Ice Age occurred during the time of Inca imperial expansion and the Spanish Conquest.

The conditions of the Little Ice Age persisted through much of the Colonial period, when European plants (e.g., wheat, barley, beans) and animals (e.g., sheep, cattle, chickens) came to play a significant role in both the political economy and domestic subsistence strategies. The introduction of new domesticates altered the costs and benefits of farming and herding in the region, as did the arrival of new technologies for producing and processing staple goods (Covey, Childs, and Kippen 2011). The agrarian transformation of rural Cuzco was probably more transformative than climate fluctuations during the early Colonial period. Evidence from the Quelccaya glacier suggests that the wet conditions seen after AD 1500 shifted to more arid patterns from 1720 to 1860, when ice cores show accumulations more than 20% below the mean (Thompson et al. 1985). This pattern changed again to one of increased precipitation from 1870 until 1984, when the cores were taken; this shift accompanied a period of rapid warming that has continued to the present.

Today, the Cuzco region is experiencing strong annual fluctuations in temperature and precipitation that many farmers attribute to global warming and the impacts of economic activities in the nearby Amazonian slope. In a broader context, the climate today is warmer than it has been in earlier recorded times, and it has until recently been wetter as well — ideal conditions for the spread of farming that was encouraged by the land reform and the rapid urbanization of the region, but certainly not representative of conditions in prehistory.

References

Beltrán Costa, O.
1988   La producción de sal en el distrito de Maras: Procedimiento técnico y economía campesina. Manuscript at the Centro Bartolomé de las Casas, Cusco, Peru.

Bird, Broxton W., Mark B. Abbott, Mathias Vuille, Donald T. Rodbell, Nathan D. Stansell, and Michael F. Rosenmeier
2011   A 2,300-year-long annually resolved record of the South American summer monsoon from the Peruvian Andes. *Proceedings of the National Academy of Sciences* 108(21):8583–88.

Boada, Hugo
1991   *Acciones de Desarrollo y Cambios en Anta.* Cusco: PRODERM.

CBCR (Centro Básico de Capacitación Rural)
1974   Investigación de 8 comunidades de los sectores de Anta y Urubamba. Centro Básico de Capacitación Rural. Manuscript at the Centro Bartolomé de las Casas, Cusco, Peru.

Cebrecos Revilla, Félix
1968   Drenaje de la Pampa de Anta–Cuzco. Tesis de Licenciatura, Facultad de Ingeniero, Pontifica Universidad Católica del Perú.

CENCIRA (Centro Nacional de Capacitación y Investigación para la Reforma Agraria)
1979   *Plan de desarrollo de Antapampa: Diagnóstico.* Lima: CENCIRA.

Chepstow-Lusty, Alex
2011   Agro-pastoralism and social change in the Cuzco heartland of Peru. A brief history using environmental proxies. *Antiquity* 85:570–82.

Chepstow-Lusty, Alex, Michael R. Frogley, Brian S. Bauer, Mark B. Bush, and Alfredo Tupayachi Herrera
2003   A Late Holocene record of arid events from the Cuzco region, Peru. *Journal of Quaternary Science* 18(6):491–502.

CONESTCAR
1964   *Primer muestreo agropecuario nacional, 1964: Resultados preliminares. Zona Sur: Apurímac, Arequipa, Ayacucho, Cuzco, Madre de Díos, Moquegua, Puno, Tacna.* CONEST-CAR.

Contreras Hernández, Jesús
1985   *Subsistencia, Ritual, y Poder en los Andes.* Barcelona: Editorial Mitre.

Cosio C., P., A. Peña P., M. Tapia N., O. Blanco G., and S. Torres F.
1981   *Diagnóstico: Técnico agropecuario y socio-económico de las comunidades de Amaru, Paru-Paru, Sacaca, y Cuyo Grande.* Cusco: IICA-CIID.

Covey, R. Alan
n.d.   Inca Imperial Responses to Environmental Hazards and Catastrophic Events. Manuscript in preparation.

Covey, R. Alan, and Donato Amado González (editors)
2008   *Imperial Transformations in Sixteenth-Century Yucay, Peru.* Memoirs, no. 44. Ann Arbor: Museum of Anthropology, University of Michigan.

Covey, R. Alan, Geoff Childs, and Rebecca Kippen
2011   Dynamics of indigenous demographic fluctuations: Lessons from sixteenth-century Cuzco, Peru. *Current Anthropology* 52(3):335–60.

Cuba de Nordt, Carmela
1971   Las Cabañuelas. *Allpanchis Phuturinga* 3:45–46.

de la Cadena, Marisol
1992   Las mujeres son más indias: Etnicidad y género en una comunidad del Cuzco. *Revista Isis Internacional* 16:25–43.

El Comercio
2012   Cusco fue visitado por más de 2 millones de turistas el año pasado. March 29, 2012.

Farrington, Ian S.
1983   Prehistoric intensive agriculture: Preliminary notes on river canalization in the Sacred Valley of the Incas. In *Drained Field Agriculture in Central and South America*, edited by J. P. Darch, pp. 221–35. BAR International Series 189. Oxford: British Archaeological Reports.

Flores Ochoa, Jorge
1986   Interaction and complementarity in three zones of Cuzco. In *Andean Ecology and Civilization: An Interdisciplinary Perspective on Andean Ecological Complementarity*, edited by Shozo Masuda, Izumi Shimada, and Craig Morris, pp. 251–76. Tokyo: University of Tokyo Press.

Gade, Daniel W.
1975   *Plants, Man and Land in the Vilcanota Valley of Peru.* The Hague: Dr. W. Junk B.V.

Gobierno Regional del Cusco
2012   Expediente técnico comunal provincia Calca. Report, edited by Ramiro Francisco Samaniego Díaz, in author's possession.

Guillet, David
1976   Migration, agrarian reform, and structural change in rural Peru. *Human Organization* 35(3):295–302.
1979   *Agrarian Reform and Peasant Economy in Southern Peru.* Columbia: University of Missouri Press.

Hopkins Larrea, Raúl
1978   La agroindustria cervecera y la agricultura de cebada en el sur del Perú. Thesis, Department of Economics, Pontificia Universidad Católica del Perú.

Huallpa Ccahuantico, Pedro
1995   Estudio Geológico y Geohidrológico de la Cuenca de Piuray, Chinchero, Urubamba, Cusco. Tesis de Licenciatura en la Facultad de Geología, Universidad Nacional de San Antonio Abad de Cusco.

López-Zapana, Ronald, Raúl Carreño, and Susana Kalafatovich C.
2005   Large scale landslides in overthrust wedges: Genetic and paleomorphological relations in the Calca area, Cusco, Peru. In *6th International Symposium on Andean Geodynamics (ISAG 2005, Barcelona), Extended Abstracts*, pp. 450–53. Institut de recherche pour le développement, Universitat de Barcelona, Instituto Geológico y Minero de España.

Manya, Juan Antonio
1971   Sara tarpuy. Siembra del maíz. *Allpanchis Phuturinga* 3:47–55.

Mayta Medina, Faustino
1971   La cosecha del maíz en Yucay. *Allpanchis Phuturinga* 3:101–12.

Molina, Cristóbal de
2011 [1570s]   *Account of the Fables and Rites of the Incas*, translated by Brian S. Bauer, Vania Smith-Oka, and Gabriel E. Cantarutti. Austin: University of Texas Press.

Molinié-Fioravanti, Antoinette
1982   *La Vallée Sacrée des Andes.* Recherches Américaines 4. Paris: Société d'Ethnographie.

Morlon, P., A. Hibon, D. Horton, M. Tapia, and F. Tardieu
1996   ¿Que tipos de mediciones e qué criterios para la evaluación? In *Comprender la agricultura campesina en los Andes Centrales: Perú–Bolivia*, edited by Pierre Morlon, pp. 276–312. Cusco: Centro Bartolomé de las Casas.

Mosblech, Nicole A. Sublette, Alex Chepstow-Lusty, Bryan G. Valencia, and Mark B. Bush
2012   Anthropogenic control of Late-Holocene landscapes in the Cuzco region, Peru. *The Holocene* 22(12):1361–72.

Neira Samanez, Hugo
1964   *Cuzco: Tierra y muerte.* Lima: Problemas de Hoy.

Núñez del Prado, Oscar
1973   *Kuyo Chico: Applied Anthropology in an Indian Community.* Chicago: University of Chicago Press.

Orlove, Benjamin S., John C. H. Chang, and Mark A. Cane
2000   Forecasting Andean rainfall and crop yield from the influence
        of El Niño on Pleiades visibility. *Nature* 403:68–71.

Ortega, O. R., E. Duran, C. Arbizu, R. Ortega, W. Roca, D. Potter, and
C. F. Quiros
2007   Pattern of genetic diversity of cultivated and non-cultivated
        mashua, *Tropaeolum tuberosum*, in the Cusco region of Perú.
        Genetic Resources and Crop Evolution 54:807–21.

Ortega, Ramiro, Carlos Quiros, Carlos Arbizu, et al.
n.d.   Collaborative Crop Research Program. The McKnight
        Foundation Collaborative Crop Research Program. Research
        and Training Progress Report: December 1, 2004–November
        30, 2005. http://mcknight.ccrp.cornell.edu/program_docs/
        project_documents/AND/AND_01-1563/01-1563_yr4_04-
        05_vweb.pdf.

Radcliffe, Sarah A.
1986   Gender relations, peasant livelihood strategies and migration:
        A case study from Cuzco, Peru. *Bulletin of Latin American
        Research* 5(2):29–47.
1990   Marking the boundaries between the community, the state,
        and history in the Andes. *Journal of Latin American Studies*
        22(3):575–94.

Sánchez Farfán, Jorge
1983   Pampallaqta, centro productor de semilla de papa. In
        Evolución y tecnología de la agricultura andina, edited by
        Ana María Fries, pp. 163–75. Cuzco: IICA/CIID.

Sandweiss, Daniel H., Kirk A. Maasch, Richard L. Burger, James B.
Richardson III, Harold B. Rollins, and Amy Clement
2001   Variation in Holocene El Niño frequencies: Climate
        records and cultural consequences in ancient Peru. *Geology*
        29(7):603–6.

Stroup, J. S., M. A. Kelly, T. V. Lowell, S. A. Beall, C. Smith, and H.
E. Baranes
2011   A record of Late-Holocene fluctuations of Quelccaya
        ice cap, Peru, based on glacial moraines and lake sedi-
        ments. *American Geophysical Union, Fall Meeting
        2011, Abstract #PP51A-1827*. http://adsabs.harvard.edu/
        abs/2011AGUFMPP51A1827S.

Thompson, Lonnie G.
1993   Reconstructing the Paleo ENSO records from tropical and
        subtropical ice cores. *Bulletin de l'Institut Français d'Études
        Andines* 22(1):65–83.

Thompson, L. G., E. Mosley-Thompson, J. F. Bolzan, and B. R. Koci
1985   A 1500-year record of tropical precipitation in ice cores from
        the Quelccaya ice cap, Peru. *Science* 229:971–73.

Urton, Gary
1981   *At the Crossroads of the Earth and the Sky: An Andean
        Cosmology*. Austin: University of Texas Press.

Villanueva Urteaga, Horacio H.
1970   Documento sobre Yucay en el siglo XVI. *Revista del Archivo
        Histórico del Cuzco* 13:1–148.

Winterhalder, Bruce
1994   The ecological basis of water management in the central
        Andes: Rainfall and temperature in southern Peru. In
        *Irrigation at High Altitudes: The Social Organization of Water
        Control Systems in the Andes*, edited by William P. Mitchell
        and David Guillet, pp. 21–67. Society for Latin American
        Anthropology Publication Series 12. Washington, D.C.:
        American Anthropological Association.

PART II

Transitions toward Sedentism and Agriculture

Chapter 3: The Preceramic Occupation of the Hanan Cuzco Region

R. Alan Covey and Nicholas Griffis

The initial peopling of the Cuzco region stands out as one of the most significant—and poorly understood—research questions for archaeologists working in this part of the central Andes. Until recently, there was little known evidence for a preceramic occupation in the area surrounding the city of Cuzco, and many researchers assumed that colonization by early horticultural communities established the first permanent human occupation of the Cuzco Valley and surrounding areas (see Bauer et al. 2004, 2007). Undated aceramic sites were first registered in the Department of Cuzco during the 1960s, particularly in the remote grasslands of Espinar, about 150 km southeast of Cuzco (Barreda 1983:11). As archaeologists identified caves and rock art in this general area, there were reports of similar sites in the high grasslands lying to the north of Calca and Pisac in the Sacred Valley (Barreda 1983:12; Sánchez Farfán 1983:164).

During the field research of Bauer's Cuzco Valley Archaeological Project (1997–1999), the identification of diagnostic bifacial tools (especially projectile points) and scatters of aceramic lithic debitage demonstrated a much earlier human presence within the Cuzco Valley (Bauer, Jones, and Klink 2004), and subsequent excavations at the open-air site of Kasapata have yielded evidence for a sustained occupation of the region at least as early as the Late Archaic, with occupation dates that begin after 4700 BC (Bauer 2007). As Jones and Bauer (2007:2) note, the archaeological reconstruction of this period remains tentative and incomplete, but it is clear that mobile hunter-gatherer groups began to exploit wild plant and animal resources in the Cuzco region thousands of years before the first agricultural villages were established. The Late Archaic strata at Kasapata indicate a population already well established on the Cuzco landscape, with evidence of domestic architecture, burials, and a broad toolkit made primarily from local andesite sources (Bauer et al. 2007:123). Evidence of the Archaic occupation of the Hanan Cuzco region adds to this picture of local collector societies.

Site Identification

The Hanan Cuzco survey projects maintained the research protocols developed by the Cuzco Valley Archaeological Project for investigating aceramic sites, identifying several categories of material remains potentially affiliated with the Archaic period. The most significant of these are (1) stone tools, (2) scatters of lithic debitage, and (3) rock paintings or carvings stylistically similar to Archaic remains from other parts of the south-central Andes.

Stone Tools

The lithic sequence and typology for the Cuzco region is still developing, but some temporal markers have been identified, especially among bifaces (see Klink 2007). Projectile points provide the clearest temporal markers for identifying and subdividing the Archaic period, although this interpretive aid skews the overall sample of aceramic sites identified, as other classes of tools (e.g., awls, scrapers) were less likely to be registered as artifacts and identified as diagnostics of a particular time period (Fig. 3.1). In many cases, projectile points were registered as isolated finds with no additional evidence of associated human occupation. Such finds demonstrate the presence of humans in an area for certain activities (especially hunting), but provide limited aid in the reconstruction of residence and mobility patterns of early nomadic groups.

Lithic Scatters

The process of stone tool production left areas of debitage scattered across the landscape, some of them associated with other residential activities. Many of these have been destroyed by subsequent human subsistence activities and settlement, and the identification of lithic sites has occurred largely in areas with limited agricultural utility, potentially contributing to a flawed window into Archaic lifeways. When encountered, lithic scatters fell into three basic categories, each of which presented interpretive problems for developing regional perspectives on Archaic hunter-gatherers: (1) debitage scatters without finished tools present lacked a diagnostic temporal marker and were treated as aceramic rather than preceramic; (2) non-diagnostic lithic material found in association with surface pottery could not be recorded as preceramic sites, and had to be considered as possible components of ceramic occupations; and (3) aceramic lithic scatters with diagnostic tools were treated as preceramic sites. The co-occurrence of pottery and lithic materials led to the exclusion of most of this material from consideration of the Archaic, which imposed serious limitations for developing regional patterns.

Rock Art

Carved and painted rock outcrops have been identified in the Cuzco region (e.g., Bauer, Jones, and Klink 2004:36; Covey, Aráoz Silva, and Bauer 2008; cf. Hostnig 2007) (Fig. 3.2). The tentative identification of these features as Archaic is based on stylistic similarity with rock art known from other parts of the Andes, but this is admittedly not grounded in a sophisticated chronology, and rock art from the present study region is not considered to be definitively dated to the Archaic period. There is no evidence that caves and rock shelters ceased to be used following the introduction of pottery, or that agriculture completely supplanted hunting and gathering agriculture around that time. Indeed, Hostnig (2007) has cataloged rock art with iconography that suggests a late prehispanic date.

Interpretive Limitations for Archaic Survey Data

The principal diagnostic markers of the preceramic occupation of the Cuzco region are all hindered by interpretive ambiguities and biases. It is also important to note that field methods used in the Hanan Cuzco survey projects were not designed for the systematic study of collecting and foraging practices of early nomadic groups (see Chapter 1 of this volume). The intensity of all settlement surveys targeted sedentary agropastoral settlements—survey intervals of 50 meters or more could expect to register all sites settlements of about 0.25 ha and larger, but smaller sites were only encountered opportunistically and even though hundreds were recorded, the sample cannot be considered to be representative. Even if survey intensity had been adjusted to an interval better suited to the study of small nomadic groups, which would have increased the necessary labor input by 300–500%, the use and modification of the region by agropastoral groups has biased the likelihood of site identification and precluded the collection of robust data on the activities and seasonal movements of hunter-gatherers. Terrace construction and contemporary village settlement have irrevocably altered most valley-bottom areas, so that most "preceramic" identifications were made in marginal areas, especially in places undergoing higher rates of soil erosion.

A related and equally serious issue is that the widespread presence of settlements with surface pottery makes the identification of Archaic sites dependent on diagnostic tools, especially projectile points. Scatters of lithic debris with or without pottery present are most appropriately identified as aceramic rather than Archaic. The bias toward conclusively identifying projectile points in marginal areas skews site identification toward specific kinds of activity areas, such as hunting. Other kinds of sites were found only where the right conditions favored their discovery, while some kinds of activity areas have been obliterated by agricultural landscape modification.

Identification and Intensive Study of Lithic Sites

Field researchers identified a lithic component at more than 300 sites in the Xaquixaguana Plain and Sacred Valley study regions, but the vast majority of these designations consisted of debitage at sites with a ceramic component and no further study was made. The discussion that follows focuses on finds of biface tools and lithic scatters in the Sacred Valley, and then turns to the data collected at a cluster of aceramic and Archaic sites near Lake Huaypo in the Xaquixaguana study region (Fig. 3.3).

Sacred Valley Sites

Archaic period stone tools were rare finds in the Sacred Valley. Fieldworkers registered isolated projectile points at four locations, most of them located at high elevations in remote areas. These consisted of (1) an andesite point fragment found near Ccorao in the Ch'itapampa Basin (VS-022), (2) an obsidian

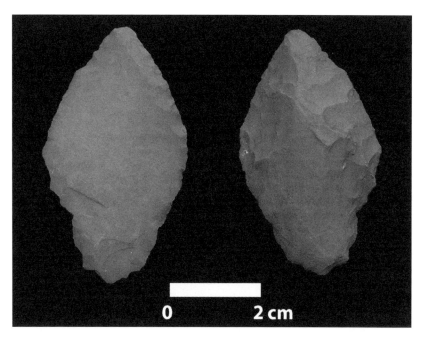

Figure 3.1. Projectile point from the Xaquixaguana study region. Biface tools like this one are easiest to place into a temporal sequence, but they overstate the importance of hunting in Archaic subsistence practices.

Figure 3.2. Small panel of painted designs on a cliff wall at Site 139 in the Calca-Yanahuara study region, showing camelids and possible celestial bodies.

Figure 3.3. Lake Huaypo area in the Xaquixaguana study region. The dashed line marks a concentration of lithic sites in an area with no significant ceramic-era settlements.

point fragment found near Qotataki in the upper Chongo Basin (VS-220), (3) a collection of 17 obsidian points and other tools found near Patabamba on the south side of the Vilcanota Valley (Q-042), and (4) a sandstone point found near Urubamba in the Urubamba Valley (CY-18). From their forms, the obsidian points are most likely from the Formative period, while the others appear to be Archaic.

In addition to these finds, three aceramic debitage scatters were identified in the Sacred Valley. One (VS-074) was a small (400 m²) lithic scatter containing andesite, diorite, and obsidian flakes, but lacking diagnostic materials. Of the other two scatters, one (VS-022) was a small (2500 m²) dispersion that included ground slate tools and an andesite point that did not appear to date to the Archaic period. The other (VS-225) was a low density 3 ha debitage scatter (mostly andesite) on an eroded hillslope in the lower Chongo Basin where 2 Late Archaic andesite projectile points were found on the surface (Fig. 3.4).

Overall, survey research in the Sacred Valley encountered occasional evidence of Late Archaic human activities, including procurement of stone for tools, production of projectile points, and retouching of tools. The presence of projectile points suggests that hunting activities took place at higher elevations throughout the valley (especially above 3500 m). Other activities and residential sites were not identified in the valley, but this is likely due to the extremely disturbed archaeological record. Andesite appears to have been the Archaic material of choice in the upper part of the Sacred Valley region, whereas sandstone predominates

in the lower Sacred Valley and Xaquixaguana regions. This suggests that the evidence of limited mobility seen at Kasapata might be representative of other parts of the Cuzco region.

Xaquixaguana Plain Sites

The Xaquixaguana Plain study region yielded a number of isolated projectile point finds and lithic scatters (Fig. 3.5). In particular, field crews encountered a concentration of sites in the hills above Lake Huaypo during the 2004 field season. Following the identification of 23 aceramic/preceramic sites in the northern part of the Xaquixaguana Plain study region, a second phase of study was initiated by the second author and two Peruvian colleagues during the 2005 field season (Griffis 2007). Each site was revisited for a preliminary assessment, and additional surface collections were made at 16 sites. Collections included intensive collection units of 2 × 2 m, placed in high-density scatters at different parts of each site. General collections of tools and tool fragments were made across the entire site surface. The results of this research are discussed in greater detail below.

Second visits to preceramic sites confirmed two clusters of sites located near Lake Huaypo, as well as a small number of isolated sites. The first site cluster comprises 9 sites (X-085, X-088, X-092, X-100, X-105, X-111, X-131, X-164, and X-165) located in a 6 km² area in the hills above the lake, between 3625 and 3750 m (lake level is 3542 m). The second cluster of sites consists of 4 sites (X-124, X-125, X-127, X-128) located about

Figure 3.4. Lower Chongo Basin in the Sacred Valley. The dashed line marks the location of an eroded hillside site (VS-225) with a scatter of lithic materials, including andesite projectile points.

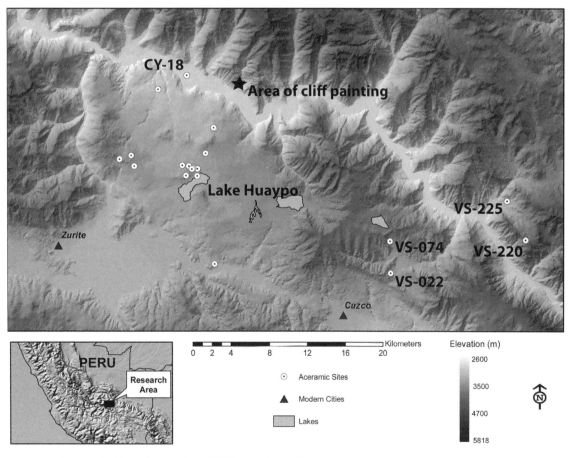

Figure 3.5. Map of aceramic and lithic sites in the Hanan Cuzco region. Courtesy of L. Tsesmeli.

Figure 3.6. Small rockshelter in the Xaquixaguana region. Lithic material was present on the talus slope in front of the overhang.

5 km to the northeast of the first cluster, distributed around a hilltop. Site sizes ranged from small scatters (60 m²) to a dense 5 ha scatter at X-165, with 2 other sites larger than 1 ha. The range of site sizes, locations, and surface artifacts suggests different activities, including base camps and primary tool production, as well as ambush hunting and the retouching of projectile points (Fig. 3.6). While these identified site distributions should not be considered as representative of Archaic settlement patterns, they do provide the clearest evidence of Archaic period site clustering and activity areas identified to date in the Cuzco region (cf. Bauer, Jones, and Klink 2004; Bauer 2007).

The collections made at Xaquixaguana lithic sites provide some systematic data on site size and lithic materials present on the surface. These data represent a first phase of analysis of materials from the region, which involved a visual inspection of stone tools to identify function and material. A more intensive study of the Xaquixaguana collections is critically needed, and additional survey and excavation work would undoubtedly yield valuable data for expanding our understanding of Late Archaic hunter-gatherer lifeways in the Cuzco region. Although counts and weights of materials from intensive collection units were generated in the laboratory (Griffis 2007), the present discussion focuses on the analysis of tools and tool fragments.

A total of 519 artifacts were recovered in surface collections and photographed. These were inspected visually and assigned to one of five forms: complete tools, fragmentary tools, flakes,

Table 3.1. Classes and categories used in tool analysis.

Class	Categories
uniface	expedient, formed, retouched
biface	undifferentiated, bifacial
blade	undifferentiated, retouched
debitage	undifferentiated, retouched
core piece	worked, unworked
ground stone	undifferentiated, retouched
unclear	undifferentiated, retouched

knapped block pieces, and unidentifiable pieces. These forms were subdivided into classes of artifacts (unifacial, bifacial, debitage, blade, ground stone, core piece, or unclear), which were in turn separated based on production stage or condition of the artifact (Table 3.1).

Within the overall artifact sample, 72 tool fragments were identifiable by class, whereas 187 completed tools were recovered in surface collections. Unifacial tools ($n = 68$) included perforators (2), projectile points (3), cutting tools (13), and scraping tools (21). Bifacial tools ($n = 154$) were more common in our collection, and included cutting tools (27) and projectile points (96). Griffis (2007:41–68) presents a more detailed description and illustration of tool types collected from the cluster of XPAS lithic sites (Fig. 3.7).

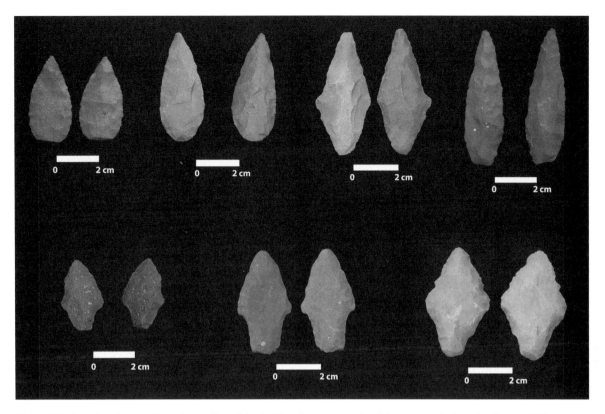

Figure 3.7. Sample of projectile points collected in the Xaquixaguana region. Most are made from locally available stone, including sandstone and quartzite.

In terms of raw material, XPAS collections encountered igneous (andesite, rhyolite, obsidian, and granite), sedimentary (sandstone and slate), and metamorphic (quartzite, slate, and limestone) material. Within the artifact assemblage, quartzite ($n = 264$) and sandstone ($n = 176$) accounted for most artifacts, with much less frequent examples of chert ($n = 21$), andesite ($n = 12$), jasper ($n = 12$), slate ($n = 11$), rhyolite ($n = 5$), obsidian ($n = 3$), and granite ($n = 1$) (Griffis 2007:70). The most common materials were available in the immediate vicinity of sites, and the reliance on lower-quality materials such as quartzite and sandstone contrasts with the predominance of andesite identified in excavations at Kasapata (Klink 2007:33). This reflects the local geology, which is dominated by the Formación Huancané, a sedimentary layer composed primarily of quartzite and sandstone (Carlotto Caillaux et al. 1996).

Discussion

The results of the Hanan Cuzco survey projects add to the emerging perspectives on the Archaic period occupation of the Cuzco region, although excavation work is necessary to understand changes over time and how hunter-gatherers exploited the environmental diversity of the region. As with the neighboring Cuzco Valley, the earliest evidence of a human presence in the Xaquixaguana Plain region comes from isolated projectile point finds dating to the Early Archaic period (ca. 11,500–9000 BP).

This suggests that humans entered the region at least seasonally shortly after the retreat of glaciers at the end of the Pleistocene. The presence of early tools made with nonlocal materials (such as obsidian) (Burger and Glascock 2007) suggests that the first nomadic groups in the region ranged broadly throughout the year, maintained periodic contact with other foraging bands, or both.

Projectile points and scrapers from the XPAS region indicate continued activity in the area during the Middle Archaic. Even though we lack a representative picture of Archaic mobility patterns, it appears that people returned repeatedly to exploit sources of stone and to carry out subsistence activities around Lake Huaypo. Some small sites were located in strategic locations for monitoring movement in and out of the lake basin, suggesting ambush hunting of game that might have had seasonal patterns. The recent publication of cores from Lake Huaypo (Mosblech et al. 2012) suggests that ponding did not commence until about 4500 BP. Prior to this time, conditions were more arid and punctuated by severe droughts, and some of the resources that cluster around the lake today would not have been present. Pollen from the earliest strata in the Huaypo core include abundant grasses, with very low incidence of tree species (Mosblech et al. 2012), suggesting the kind of *puna* environment that might have been seasonally favored by wild camelids and other mammals.

Our current chronology does not permit a detailed assessment of changes in seasonal movement over time, but the picture emerging for the Late Archaic period (7000–4200 BP) is one of groups engaged in much more localized resource exploitation. Bauer's excavations at Kasapata indicate the use of more specialized lithic toolkits and reliance on nearby stone sources (Klink 2007). The survey evidence from the Xaquixaguana region does not contradict this, and it is tempting to see the predominance of sandstone and quartzite tools as evidence of procurement patterns consistent with populations engaged in low mobility collecting lifeways. The overall absence of ground stone tools represents a key difference between the central cluster of sites in the Xaquixaguana region and the excavated assemblage from Kasapata (Klink 2007). The predominance of locally available materials and prevalence of debitage suggest that the largest and densest sites were associated with lithic procurement and the primary production of a wide range of tools.

The excavation data from Kasapata reveal mortuary treatment and increased investment in dwellings that suggest less frequent movement across the region (Bauer et al. 2007). Klink (2007) notes that the appearance of grinding stones and other tools indicates more intensive processing of plant foods, which eventually could have led to the adoption of domesticated plants as a risk reduction strategy. The transition from transhumant collecting to sedentary horticulture is an important research question that will require extensive excavations at multiple sites to resolve satisfactorily.

The evidence of Late Archaic settlement in the Hanan Cuzco region accords with the conclusions of Bauer and colleagues (2007) at Kasapata. The sites found to the north of Lake Huaypo show a heavy emphasis on procuring local (and often low quality) tool materials for a broad range of daily activities, while a greater diversity of projectile point materials indicates social relationships that crossed large regions. The cluster of Archaic sites in the Xaquixaguana region shows internal variations consistent with a broad range of local activities, including hunting.

As the preliminary description of the Archaic occupation of the Cuzco region advances, the question of its relationship to the subsequent agropastoral societies of the region looms. Only future archaeological research can determine whether hunter-gatherer groups in the Cuzco region gradually incorporated domesticated plants and animals into their increasingly localized subsistence strategies, or whether farming groups from other parts of the Andean highlands colonized the region and pushed nomadic groups to marginal parts of the region.

Works Cited

Barreda, Luis
1983 Evolución del pastoreo y de la agricultura en el área de Cusco, vista desde la arqueología. In *Evolución y tecnología de la agricultura andina*, edited by Ana María Fries, pp. 11–16. Cuzco: IICA/CIID.

Bauer, Brian S. (editor)
2007 *Kasapata and the Archaic Period of the Cuzco Valley.* University of California, Los Angeles: Cotsen Institute of Archaeology.

Bauer, Brian S., Bradford Jones, and Cindy Klink
2004 The Archaic period and the first people of the Cuzco Valley (9500–2200 BC). In *Ancient Cuzco: Heartland of the Inca*, edited by Brian S. Bauer, pp. 31–37. Austin: University of Texas Press.

Bauer, Brian S., Bradford Jones, Cynthia Klink, Richard C. Sutter, Susan D. deFrance, and Richard L. Burger
2007 The Archaic period of the Cuzco Valley. In *Kasapata and the Archaic Period of the Cuzco Valley*, edited by Brian S. Bauer, pp. 122–24. University of California, Los Angeles: Cotsen Institute of Archaeology.

Burger, Richard L., and Michael D. Glascock
2007 The sourcing of Archaic obsidian from Kasapata, Department of Cuzco. In *Kasapata and the Archaic Period of the Cuzco Valley*, edited by Brian S. Bauer, pp. 118–21. University of California, Los Angeles: Cotsen Institute of Archaeology.

Carlotto Caillaux, Víctor Santiago, Willy Fernando Gil Rodríguez, José Dionicio Cárdenas Roque, and Richard Chávez
1996 *Geología de los cuadrángulos de Urubamba y Calca, 27-r, 27-s–[Boletín A 65].* Lima: INGEMMET.

Covey, R. Alan, Miriam Aráoz Silva, and Brian S. Bauer
2008 Settlement patterns in the Yucay Valley and neighboring areas. In *Imperial Transformations in Sixteenth-Century Yucay, Peru*, edited by R. Alan Covey and Donato Amado González, pp. 3–17. Memoirs, no. 44. Ann Arbor: Museum of Anthropology, University of Michigan.

Griffis, Nicholas
2007 Preceramic Occupation of the Xaquixaguana Plain: Site Distribution and Lithic Analysis. Master's thesis, Department of Anthropology, Columbia University.

Hostnig, Rainer
2007 Hallazgos recientes en el Valle de Vilcanota, Cusco, refuerzan la hipótesis sobre la existencia de arte rupestre inca. *Boletín SIARB* 21:68–75.

Jones, Bradford, and Brian S. Bauer
2007 Research at the site of Kasapata. In *Kasapata and the Archaic Period of the Cuzco Valley*, edited by Brian S. Bauer, pp. 1–30. University of California, Los Angeles: Cotsen Institute of Archaeology.

Klink, Cynthia
2007 The lithic assemblage at Kasapata. In *Kasapata and the Archaic Period of the Cuzco Valley*, edited by Brian S. Bauer, pp. 31–77. University of California, Los Angeles: Cotsen Institute of Archaeology.

Mosblech, Nicole A. Sublette, Alex Chepstow-Lusty, Bryan G. Valencia, and Mark B. Bush
2012 Anthropogenic control of Late-Holocene landscapes in the Cuzco region, Peru. *The Holocene* 22(12):1361–72.

Sánchez Farfán, Jorge
1983 Pampallaqta, centro productor de semilla de papa. In *Evolución y tecnología de la agricultura andina*, edited by Ana María Fries, pp. 163–75. Cuzco: IICA/CIID.

Chapter 4: Formative Period Settlement Patterns in the Xaquixaguana Region

Allison R. Davis

The Formative period in the Andean highlands encompasses two and a half millennia remembered best for the intensification of agropastoral lifeways, elaboration of ritual systems, emergence of inequalities, and loss of village autonomy as political systems grew in size and complexity. Compared with other parts of the Andes, and with later periods in Cuzco, very few excavations of Formative period sites have been carried out and relatively little is known about life at that time. Archaeologists have established that people living in and around Cuzco were herders and farmers who, for the first time, formed single large settlements among increasingly dense scatters of neighboring small sites. Yet we know very little about the agropastoral strategies employed in the alpine landscape, and we do not yet understand why or how the large archaeological sites formed.

This chapter examines distributions of Marcavalle-related and Chanapata-style pottery scatters to address these questions on a regional scale. Analysis of site sizes establishes that a transition from a one- to three-tier settlement hierarchy took place in this region, but poorly refined ceramic chronology makes it difficult to interpret this pattern in terms of a lived experience of settlement reorganization. A consideration of site location in relationship to agropastoral ecozones suggests that early farmers and herders prioritized access to good quinoa, potato, maize, and herding lands that allowed them to minimize risk, to space out labor demands to increase productivity, and to have fresh foods more often. Following a drought around 500 BC, greater value was placed on quick access to a larger variety of ecological zones and to wetter areas. The significant social and political transitions that took place in Cuzco during this period must be understood within a framework of daily choices made by agropastoralists adjusting their strategies to take advantage of the ecological diversity of the local landscape.

The Formative Period in Cuzco, Peru

Throughout the Americas, archaeologists have used the term "Formative" to refer to periods when people quit relying on wild resources, gave up high mobility, began to make pottery, and settled down into agricultural or agropastoral villages. In anthropological terms, Formative periods ended when egalitarian societies were transformed into multi-village polities with inherited social and economic inequalities. In terms of archaeological material evidence, Formative periods typically end with the appearance of a new pottery style that co-occurs with a two- or three-tier site size hierarchy and wealth differences in households and burials.

This definition is generally applicable in the Cuzco region, where the Formative period is conventionally dated from 2200 BC to AD 200. The earliest known pottery style in Cuzco—Marcavalle-style ceramics—appears during the Formative period. In addition, faunal and botanical evidence indicate that people relied primarily on farming and herding. At the site of Marcavalle, for example, camelid herding was an important economic activity by 1000 BC (Chávez 1980; Miller 1979). People kept domesticated guinea pigs, and wild animals were a very minor component of the faunal assemblage (Chávez 1980). Beans were present at the site by 800 BC and corn by 200 BC, providing evidence for a complete and diversified agropastoral system (Chávez 1980).

Later Formative sites with Chanapata pottery show similar evidence for domestic plant and animal use. At Yuthu (400–100 BC), villagers relied heavily on quinoa. Maize was a smaller, but significant, portion of the diet. There were no preserved remains of potato, a species that is very difficult to identify archaeologically. However, the presence of *Solanum* sp. seeds and a potato-shaped *illa* (figurine) suggest that root crops were important. In addition, villagers herded both llamas and alpacas and kept guinea pigs in their houses. They used almost no wild animal resources (Davis 2011; Vásquez Sánchez and Rosales Tham 2009).

Many scholars have suggested that multivillage polities emerged in the region during the later Formative period, around 500 BC. The Wimpillay/Muyu Orqo site complex in the Cuzco Valley, Batan Urqu in the Lucre Basin, and Ak'awillay on the Anta Plain may have been the first regional centers in Cuzco, based on their large size and the presence of ceremonial platforms (Bauer 2004; Davis and Delgado 2009; Zapata 1998). Thus far, archaeologists have not found evidence of wealth differentiation in burials or households. This chapter examines the context for the emergence of Ak'awillay as a possible regional center in a changing agropastoral social landscape.

Formative Period Ceramics in the XPAS Study Region

The analyses in this chapter are based on surface scatters of two pottery styles in the XPAS study region: Chanapata and Marcavalle-related ceramics. *Chanapata-style* pottery is common throughout the Cuzco region. Radiocarbon dates associated with the style range from 750 BC to AD 300 (Davis 2011: Table B). Most Chanapata vessels are coil-built and reddish-orange in color due to firing in oxidizing conditions. Typical forms include (1) globular ollas with or without necks that may be decorated on the neck or shoulder, and (2) open, flaring bowls sometimes decorated on the interior rim. Decorated vessels are often burnished in patterned lines or painted red, cream, or sparkly hematite. Pottery similar to *Marcavalle-style* pottery from the Cuzco region was rare in the XPAS study area. Although this pottery has never been identified in excavations in the region, it has been tentatively assigned an earlier date than Chanapata-style pottery based on similarities with sherds associated with radiocarbon dates ranging from 1200 to 400 BC in the Cuzco Basin (see Chapter 1 for a complete description of these styles and a critical discussion of the ceramic chronology).

Vessel form and style were recorded for each pottery fragment recovered during opportunistic and systematic collections (see Tables 4.1, 4.2). The following sections examine differences between the distributions of Marcavalle-related and Chanapata pottery in order to understand (1) changes in site size hierarchies and (2) site placement in relationship to agropastoral ecozones.

Site Size Hierarchies

There is a pronounced difference between the size and number of surface scatters of earlier Marcavalle-related pottery and later Chanapata-style pottery (Figs. 4.1, 4.2). The survey identified only 9 sites with the earlier pottery style; all of those surface scatters were smaller than 1 ha (see Table 4.1). In contrast, the survey identified 67 sites with Chanapata-style pottery. Surface scatters ranged in

Table 4.1. Sites with Marcavalle-related pottery.

Site	Name	Elevation (masl)	Latitude	Longitude	Surface Scatter Size (ha)
X-30	Cruz Muqu	3251	0807830	8526806	0.21
X-32		3255	0807705	8526666	0.5
X-55		3546	0810814	8519890	0.06
X-93		3586	0808145	8519656	0.75
X-133		3625	0812574	8519340	0.56
X-206		3513	0814310	8509254	0.9
X-299	Labracuntu	3359	0803208	8514258	0.32
X-310		3452	0793942	8508528	0.49
X-358		3841	0814464	8502346	0.08

Table 4.2. Sites with Chanapata-style pottery.

Site	Name	Elevation (masl)	Latitude	Longitude	Surface Scatter Size (ha)	Chanapata Vessel Forms Collected				
						open vessel with flaring walls	open vessel with vertical walls	closed vessel with a neck	closed vessel without a neck	lid
X-1	Cruzpata	3317	0810655	8524858	0.15	X		X	X	
X-14		3529	0811186	8521270	0.8				X	
X-15		3566	0810689	8521916	0.3	X				
X-20	Naqway	3249	0808021	8526470	0.25			X		
X-31	Nawpakanchun	3230	0807656	8526224	0.3	X		X		
X-32		3255	0807705	8526666	1.5		X	X	X	
X-47	Paqayamuqu	3540	0805024	8524226	0.12				X	
X-67		3584	0808563	8522530	3	X		X	X	
X-68*		3540	0808489	8521304	0.09	unknown	unknown	unknown	unknown	unknown
X-71		3492	0808912	8521246	0.06			X	X	
X-72	Villaqua	3531	0809350	8519964	0.04				X	
X-75	Cheq'oq	3533	0809350	8519964	2	X		X	X	X
X-82		3519	0807556	8519952	0.04	X		X		
X 86		3669	0808847	8518100	0.09	X		X		
X-87*		3700	0810003	8518512	0.12	unknown	unknown	unknown	unknown	unknown
X-89		3655	0808354	8517858	0.09			X	X	
X-90	Wallpakunka	3703	0808939	8517772	0.09			X		X
X-93		3586	0808145	8519656	0.75	X		X	X	
X-107*	Wamantiyanapata	3748	0805747	8519854	1.8	unknown	unknown	unknown	unknown	unknown
X-113		3629	0804842	8521564	0.35	X		X		X
X-118		3410	0812426	8524208	0.48			X		
X-129		3583	0812047	8519298	3.75	X		X		
X-132		3552	0812739	8516284	0.2	X		X	X	
X-147		3718	0814485	8517664	0.7	X		X		
X-154		3816	0819995	8516674	0.9					
X-156	Wankapata	3791	0819939	8516432	0.25	X				
X-168	Yuthu	3590	0810913	8517430	4.5	X		X	X	X
X-170		3644	0808189	8517142	9	X		X	X	X
X-171		3627	0808208	8516940	0.15	X		X	X	X
X-172		3585	0811052	8515398	0.16	X		X	X	X
X-173		3542	0810872	8515760	3.75	X		X	X	X
X-209	Muqk'arumi	3435	0812280	8509540	0.9	X		X		X
X-210*	Pillkupaqcha	3459	0812121	8509624	1.2	unknown	unknown	unknown	unknown	unknown
X-212	Muqk'arumi	3490	0812415	8509818	0.72					
X-213	Muqk'arumi	3484	0812422	8509772	1.8	X		X	X	X
X-215		3509	0812616	8509312	0.56			X		
X-222	Bandojan	3380	0809143	8510852	0.5	X		X	X	
X-223		3431	0809836	8510918	0.24			X		
X-224		3473	0810058	8510728	0.3	X		X		
X-225		3425	0809491	8510828	0.5	X		X	X	X

Table 4.2 cont.

Site	Name	Elevation (masl)	Latitude	Longitude	Surface Scatter Size (ha)	Chanapata Vessel Forms Collected				
						open vessel with flaring walls	open vessel with vertical walls	closed vessel with a neck	closed vessel without a neck	lid
X-226		3419	0810340	8510432	1.5	X				
X-227		3388	0807878	8511644	1.65	X		X	X	
X-228	Ak'awillay	3499	0806966	8511830	33.75 (10)**	X		X	X	X
X-234		3655	0812506	8513360	0.5			X	X	X
X-241	Urquillos	2924	0820337	8520337	0.15			X		
X-244	Mosoqllaqta	3372	0806564	8510802	0.25				X	
X-245	Capillapata	3442	0808303	8512816	0.54				X	
X-251	Chaqepay	3550	0803950	8517478	0.72			X		X
X-268	Rumikancha	3666	0806622	8514238	0.5	X	X			
X-270	Kantuq'aqa	3617	0805734	8514844	0.5	X		X	X	X
X-274	Paqpayuqpata	3420	0812289	8507898	2.25	X		X	X	X
X-289	Santa Rosa	3626	0794831	8511160	0.02			X		
X-295	Umacalle	3359	0802962	8513460	1.44	X				
X-296	Umacalle	3361	0802901	8513302	0.5	X		X		
X-305	Chakillq'asa	3499	0793257	8511078	0.12	X	X	X		
X-310		3452	0793942	8508528	0.49	X		X	X	X
X-311	Qhakyaurqu	3414	0794241	8508746	0.16	X		X	X	
X-313	Colcarada	3399	0812377	8508104	0.04			X	X	X
X-314	Sircaqaqya	3467	0793752	8508898	0.35			X		
X-320	Qhakyaurqu	3431	0793642	8508654	0.16	X				
X-338		3586	0789519	8512078	0.4	X		X	X	X
X-354	Colqe Ñustayoq	3446	0808773	8509300	0.25			X		
X-360	Sokahuara	3706	0790119	8512490	0.02			X		
X-388		3413	0808493	8507700	0.04	X		X	X	
X-390	Pacca	3370	0807907	8507878	0.04	X		X	X	
X-392	Pacca	3391	0808319	8507806	0.18	X		X	X	
X-454	Ayllu Tumibamba	3433	0800254	8506162	0.5	X		X		

*The ceramics collected at these sites were unavailable for analysis. They have been included in spatial analysis as sites with Chanapata-style pottery.
**The surface scatter of Chanapata-style pottery at Ak'awillay covers over 30 ha, but excavations carried out by Bélisle suggest that the Formative period occupation may be no larger than 10 ha (pers. comm.).

Figure 4.1.
Surface scatters of Chanapata pottery can be divided into three groups based on size: small (<1.8 ha), medium (1.8–9 ha), and large (33 ha). It is possible that the appearance of a single large site may signal the first concentration of population and power in a single settlement.

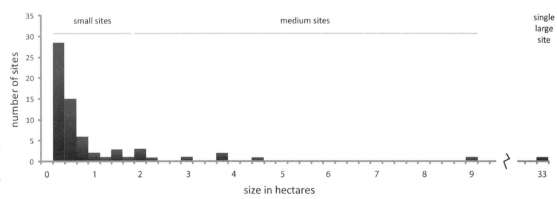

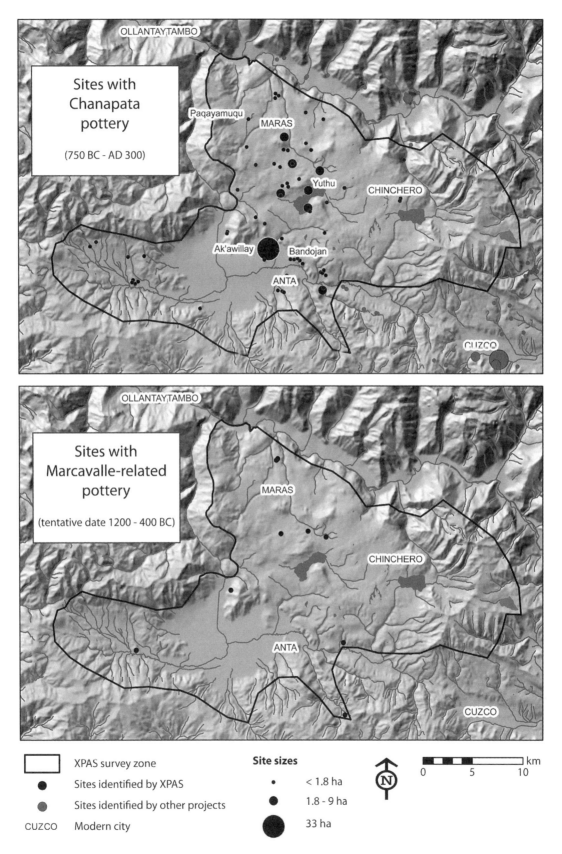

Figure 4.2. Surface scatters of Marcavalle-related pottery were found at 9 sites smaller than 1 ha. Chanapata-style pottery was identified at 67 sites that can be divided into three size classes using natural breaks: small (<1.8 ha), medium (1.8–9 ha), and very large (33 ha).

size from very small (150 m^2) to large (about 33 ha) and they can be divided into three groups based on size[1] (see Table 4.2, Fig. 4.1). Small scatters were less than 1.8 ha and medium sites were between 1.8 and 9 ha. One very large scatter covered 33 ha, though excavations suggest that the true size of the buried site may have been closer to 10 ha (Bélisle, pers. comm.). Comparing the sizes of earlier and later settlements, two changes are apparent. First, there is a notable increase in number of sites and the size of sites. Second, whereas earlier sites were all similar in size, one scatter of Chanapata pottery was much larger than the others. While the difference between settlement patterns is very clear, it is difficult to determine what this pattern represents in anthropological terms.

Cross-culturally, the shift from a one- to a two- or three-tier settlement pattern has been associated with the shift from an autonomous village society to a multi-village polity with the seat of power located in the largest site (Bandy 2004; Bauer 2004; Johnson 1980; Parsons 1972). It is tempting to interpret the concentration of population at Ak'awillay and the emergence of a three-tiered settlement hierarchy as the material remains of the development of the first multi-village polity in the XPAS study area. In fact, Bauer (2004:45) has used similar evidence to argue that chiefdoms emerged during the Formative period in the Cuzco Basin.

This interpretation is problematic in both empirical and theoretical terms. Most troubling, changes in ceramic styles in Cuzco do not represent short or discrete time periods. When pottery styles do not change quickly and multiple styles are used at once, spatial patterns in distribution of surface scatters cannot be interpreted as representations of a single moment in the history of a region. Marcavalle-related pottery in the XPAS study region has never been associated with any absolute dates. Although stylistic similarity with pottery from Marcavalle makes it unlikely, it remains possible that this style represents a functional or social category of pottery used alongside another style. Many absolute dates exist for Chanapata-style pottery, but these dates are spread over a very long time span, demonstrating that the use of Chanapata-style pottery overlapped with the use of other pottery styles. Although the style is frequently associated with the Late Formative period (500 BC–AD 200), associated radiocarbon dates range from 750 BC to AD 300 (for a complete list of Formative period dates, see Davis 2011:162, Table B). Particularly troubling, excavations at Ak'awillay have found Chanapata cooking and storage vessels mixed with pottery styles dating from AD 200 to AD 1000. Some scatters of Chanapata pottery may have been contemporary with Marcavalle-style pottery while others represent domestic portions of later assemblages. As a result, Chanapata surface scatters probably do not represent a set of contemporary villages ordered by a single political system.

Even if the scatters were roughly contemporary, surface scatters alone would not provide sufficient evidence to reconstruct a

sociopolitical system. Currently available excavation data supply little direct evidence regarding how villages were organized, whether there were notable differences in household status or burial treatment, if value systems were related to prestige goods, whether craft specialists existed, how systems of power worked, or if there were variations in public works. It is flawed logic to assume that a complex society existed based only on the presence of a multi-tiered settlement pattern (Feinman and Neitzel 1984; Wylie 2002). At this point, we simply do not have the refined chronology or enough data about daily life to establish that a multi-village society with hereditary inequality emerged during the Formative period in this region.

Even so, the emergence of Ak'awillay as a single large site occupied by people using Chanapata pottery mirrors the contemporary developments at Muyu Orqo in the Cuzco Basin and Batan Urqu in the Lucre Basin (Bauer 2004; Zapata 1998). Both Bauer (2004) and Zapata (1998) have interpreted these large sites with significant ceremonial architecture as the material representation of significant changes in social and political organization in the Cuzco region during the Formative period. The settlement pattern in the Formative period of the XPAS survey region supports their basic interpretation, even if we do not yet understand the details of that transition.

Site Placement and Access to Ecological Zones

Leaving aside the question of political hierarchy, the survey data can be used to investigate how people who made and used Marcavalle-related and Chanapata-style pottery understood and used their landscape for agricultural and pastoral activities. In the Andes, significant changes in altitude within relatively short distances create a diverse array of microclimates within small regions. Modern subsistence strategies recognize and take advantage of this variety to manage risk, spread out labor demands, and provide a more diverse diet with fresh food available during more months of the year (Davis 2011:16–19). GIS analysis was used to consider Formative period site placement in relation to agropastoral ecozones to determine which zones were most important to early farmers and herders. Both Marcavalle-related and Chanapata-style sites had quick access to zones suitable for herding camelids and growing tubers and native grains. Lower-altitude areas where maize could grow on a slightly different agricultural schedule were the second most important agropastoral zone, but whereas Marcavalle period sites were located near dry maize zones, Chanapata sites were more often located near wetter maize zones.

To carry out this analysis, the landscape was categorized as one of four possible agropastoral ecozones: (1) dry *kichwa*, (2) wet *kichwa*, (3) *suni*, or (4) *puna* (see Fig. 4.3, Table 4.3). Classification was limited to terrestrial resources because faunal and botanical data from excavations at Yuthu indicate that the subsistence system was heavily agropastoral and used almost no wild plant or animal resources (Davis 2011:15–20). ArcMap 10 software was

---

1. Using ArcMap 10 Natural Breaks, Jenks method.

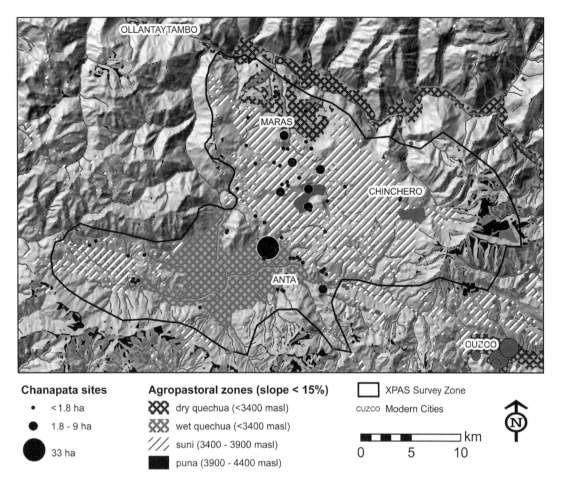

Chanapata sites
- •   < 1.8 ha
- ●   1.8 - 9 ha
- ⬤   33 ha

Agropastoral zones (slope < 15%)
- ▨   dry quechua (<3400 masl)
- ▨   wet quechua (<3400 masl)
- ▨   suni (3400 - 3900 masl)
- ■   puna (3900 - 4400 masl)

▢   XPAS Survey Zone
cuzco   Modern Cities

km
0   5   10

Figure 4.3. Prime agropastoral zones were classified according to slope, altitude, and wetness. Early and late Formative period settlements show a preference for locations with easy access to suni zones. Marcavalle-related sites often had secondary access to dry kichwa zones while Chanapata-style sites had secondary to wet kichwa zones.

Table 4.3. Access to multiple agropastoral zones.

	Within 1 km		Within 5 km	
	Marcavalle	*Chanapata*	*Marcavalle*	*Chanapata*
Two Zones				
suni, dry kichwa	0.0%	7.5%	55.6%	25.4%
suni, wet kichwa	33.3%	40.3%	0.0%	10.4%
suni, puna	11.1%	1.5%	11.1%	1.5%
Three Zones				
suni, dry kichwa, wet kichwa	0.0%	0.0%	0.0%	9.0%
suni, dry kichwa, puna	0.0%	0.0%	0.0%	9.0%
suni, wet kichwa, puna	0.0%	0.0%	22.2%	37.3%
Four Zones				
suni, dry kichwa, wet kichwa, puna	0.0%	0.0%	11.1%	6.0%
Total	44.4%	49.3%	100.0%	98.6%

used to apply a simple classification scheme similar to Kosiba's (2010:44) categorization of maize-producing terrain based on slope and altitude. Prime zones were identified as areas with a moderate slope (less than or equal to 15%). Since Andean farmers often take advantage of small fields, no minimum size was defined. The 92 × 92 m cell size of the raster data would have been a large enough area for farmers to take advantage of a small microclimate.

Suni is the most common agropastoral ecozone in the XPAS survey region (27.9%; see Table 4.4). The zone ranges in altitude from 3400 to 3900 masl and includes a small area in the western part of the survey zone as well as a large area of rolling hills with spring-fed lakes near the modern cities of Maras and Chinchero. Today most of that area is used to grow grains and potatoes and to pasture sheep. Potatoes and quinoa grown on the traditional agricultural cycle in this area are planted from October to December and are harvested in May and June. Early potatoes are planted in June and July and harvested in December and January (Kimura 2000:311). The suni is suitable for growing most crops that comprised the Formative period diet, including quinoa, tubers, beans, and kiwicha. In addition, crops can be grown on multiple cycles, providing access to fresh food during more months of the year and maximizing productivity by spacing out labor demands. Llamas may have preferred the dry pastures in these rolling hills year-round while alpacas could have been moved during the dry season to wetter pasture.

Two distinct kichwa zones lower than 3400 masl are located within the XPAS survey area. Together they comprise 16.6 % of the total area (see Fig. 4.3, Table 4.4). North of Maras, dry kichwa (4.2%) borders the Sacred Valley, an area outside the survey area and with a valley floor between 2800 and 2900 masl that is used for intensive agriculture and some fruit trees. The dry kichwa is suitable for potatoes and grains as well as some maize, though it is still rather high in elevation for optimal production. Today, spray irrigation helps to extend the growing season, but

during the Formative period, farmers would have been dependent on rainfall alone. The zone shares the same planting schedule with the surrounding suni, with regular planting for quinoa and potatoes and an early cycle for potatoes. During the Formative period, it would have provided pasture for alpacas and llamas in the wet season and llamas in the dry season.

The wet kichwa near Anta (12.4%) is distinguished from the northern section of kichwa because of marshland created by springs. Today, drainage allows intensive farming of many crops including some corn. During the Formative period, the region was likely very wet, as evidenced by the lack of Formative period sites within this zone and the ring of sites around its edges (see Fig. 4.3). This area may have been particularly attractive for grazing alpacas, animals that prefer grasses that grow in wet environments and that often have to be moved between pastures during the dry season (Bonavia 2008; Flores Ochoa 1979). This region may also have been used to collect *Scirpus*, a common aquatic grass-like plant recovered at Yuthu that can be used to make baskets, mats, ropes, boats, and thatch roofs (Davis 2011:26–27).

Compared with other agropastoral zones, the survey area contained very little puna (3900–4400 masl, 2.4%), and it was distributed in much smaller patches in clusters along the eastern section. Additional puna was located just outside the southern limit of the study region. Today, these marginal areas are used primarily as pasture for camelids. The area is not well suited for extensive farming, though some bitter tubers can be grown. During the Formative period, these pasturelands could have been used to pasture camelids, but they may have had little appeal if the suni was not overcrowded with farm fields and animal herds.

Formative site placement shows an overall preference for locations within prime agropastoral zones (n_{sites} = 65, area = 46.91%) compared with steep areas (n = 11, area = 53.1%), χ^2 = 45.51, p < .01 (see Table 4.4). Sites with Marcavalle-related

Table 4.4. Site proximity to agropastoral zones.

Zone	% Land Area	% Sites in Zone	% Sites within 1 km	% Sites within 5 km
Marcavalle-related Sites				
dry kichwa	4.2	22.2	22.2	66.7
wet kichwa	12.4	0.0	33.3	33.3
suni	27.9	66.7	77.8	100.0
puna	2.4	0.0	11.1	44.4
steep slope (>15%) or water	53.1	11.1	n/a	n/a
Chanapata Sites				
dry kichwa	4.2	7.5	11.2	49.3
wet kichwa	12.4	13.4	20.0	62.7
suni	27.9	64.2	95.8	100.0
puna	2.4	0.0	0.0	53.7
steep slope (>15%) or water	53.1	14.9	n/a	n/a

pottery were mostly located in the suni (66.7%) with just 2 sites located in the dry kichwa. Most Chanapata pottery sites were also located in the suni (64.2%), but the second most common location was the wet kichwa (13.4%) with about an equal number in steep areas (14.9%). Settlements in the dry kichwa were less common (7.5%).

Due to the vertical ecology in the region, sites located within one zone often had easy access to others. Formative period people prioritized quick access to suni and kichwa ecozones within 5 km of sites, a rough estimate of the distance walked in about 1 hour. *Every* Marcavalle-related site was within 5 km of the suni, most were within 5 km of the dry kichwa (66.7%), and one-third were within 5 km of the wet kichwa (33.3%). While none of these sites was located within the puna zone, nearly half were within 5 km of puna patches. Similarly, *all* Chanapata sites were located within 5 km of the suni, most were within 5 km of the wet kichwa (62.7%), and nearly half were within 5 km of the dry kichwa (49.3%) and the puna (53.7%). This suggests that, throughout the Formative period, inhabitants of the plain preferred quick access to land appropriate for growing tubers and grains and grazing camelids. While people using Marcavalle-related pottery favored access to dry kichwa, Chanapata pottery users preferred wet kichwa zones.

In addition to considering *which* ecozones were favored, the *number* of accessible zones may have been an important factor in site placement. Access to multiple ecozones creates opportunities for diversification, risk management, and efficient labor organization. Within 1 km, nearly half of all sites had access to two zones (Marcavalle 44.4%, Chanapata 49.3%; see Table 4.3); no sites had access to 3 or more zones. All sites located within 1 km reach of two zones had access to the suni. Most commonly, Marcavalle and Chanapata sites had secondary access to wet kichwa (33.3%, 40.3%). One Marcavalle site and 1 Chanapata site had secondary access to the puna (11.1%, 1.5%). Dry kichwa was easily reached within 1 km of 7.5% of Chanapata sites.

Every site but one had access to suni and at least one additional ecological zone within 5 km (or about 1-hour walking distance). While this pattern may primarily reflect the diversity of the ecology in the survey area, the variation in combinations of zones near Marcavalle-related versus Chanapata-style sites probably reflects conscious choice in site placement. Over half of the Marcavalle-related sites had access to only one zone in addition to the suni. Most often, dry kichwa was available nearby (55.6%), but 1 site was within reach of the puna. When three zones were accessible to Marcavalle-related sites, they were suni, wet kichwa, and puna (22.2%). One Marcavalle-related site had access to all four ecological zones. Most often, Chanapata sites were located within about 1 hour of three ecological zones: suni, wet kichwa, and puna (37.3%); suni, dry kichwa, and puna (9%); or suni, dry kichwa, and wet kichwa (9%). Many sites also had access to only suni and one other zone: dry kichwa (25.4%), wet kichwa (10.4%), or puna (1.5%).

Access to agropastoral ecozones was an important factor that influenced choices about site placement. All Marcavalle-related and Chanapata-style pottery users maintained a strong preference for locations within or very near the suni. This zone was well suited for almost all agropastoral activities practiced during the Formative period including dry-season herding of llamas; wet-season herding of alpacas and llamas; farming of quinoa, tubers, beans, and kiwicha on a normal cycle; and farming of tubers on an early cycle. The only significant portion of the botanical assemblages that could not be produced in this region was maize. Most Formative period sites had additional access to kichwa zones where maize can be grown. While more Marcavalle-related sites were close to dry kichwa areas, most Chanapata sites were close to wet kichwa areas. While either zone would have allowed farmers to grow different crops on a slightly different schedule, the wet kichwa would have provided better pastureland for alpacas during the dry season and more water for agriculture during dry years. Proximity of the puna—the zone where the least diversity of activities was possible—had little effect on site placement.

Events around 500 BC Influencing Changes in Settlement Patterns

Two events around 500 BC may help explain the shift in preferences from dry to wet kichwa: (1) increased reliance on camelids, and (2) drought. These events correspond roughly with the overlapping transition between Marcavalle and Chanapata pottery use. Although camelids were domesticated in the Andes by 2500 BC (Lavallée, Julien, and Wheeler 1984; Wheeler Pires-Ferreira, Pires-Ferreira, and Kaulicke 1976), the development of completely agropastoral systems was not immediate. When sufficient data are available, archaeologists have identified a shift from hunting wild animals to nearly exclusive herding of camelids around 500 BC. This was true at Huacaloma (Shimada 1982, 1985) and Chavín de Huántar (Miller and Burger 1995).

Although datasets from Cuzco are less complete, it is clear that between 4400 and 3100 BC, people exploited wild camelids and guinea pigs and did not keep domesticated animals (deFrance 2007). During the Formative period, that pattern changed. Considering only large mammals in the mixed Marcavalle and Chanapata period faunal assemblage from Marcavalle, camelids were most common (82.5% NISP, 79.3% MNI specimens identified to species level), but deer were also present (6.5% NISP, 13.8% MNI) (unidentified were not included in figures) (Miller 1979). At Yuthu, llamas and alpacas dominated the faunal assemblage (37.93% NISP specimens identified at any level, unidentified mammals 45.79%, NISP were probably also camelids). Deer comprised less than one percent of the entire faunal assemblage (0.48% NISP; Vásquez Sánchez and Rosales Tham 2009).

Additional evidence for increasing reliance on camelids comes from orbatid mite abundance in the Markaqocha lake sediment cores, suggesting significant pastoral activity between about 700 BC and AD 100 (Chepstow-Lusty 2011). This shift toward reliance on camelids was not only a change in subsistence strategy, it co-occurred with the appearance of high proportions of obsidian at Formative sites throughout the Andes, signaling the growing long-distance trade carried out by llama caravans (Burger, Mohr Chávez, and Chávez 2000; Chávez 1980; Davis 2011; McEwan, Gibaja, and Chatfield 1995; Rowe 1943; Yábar Moreno 1972).

At about the same time, environmental data suggest that a drought disrupted agricultural production. Data from sediment cores from Markaqocha show peaks in inorganics and Cyperaceae around 500 BC (Chepstow-Lusty 2011; Chepstow-Lusty, Bauer, and Frogley 2004). In addition, snail species recovered at Yuthu reveal a transition from a cooler and wetter climate to a drier climate during the use of the site (400–100 BC). Charopidae, gastropods that live in cool and wet climates, were replaced with *Gastrocopta* sp., which thrives in drier environments (Davis 2011; Vásquez Sánchez and Rosales Tham 2009).

Both the increased reliance on camelids and the drought may have made wet kichwa zones more attractive. In general, rainfall agriculture may have become difficult in the suni and dry kichwa. In addition, it may have become more important to move camelids to wet pasture during the dry season; this would have been especially true for alpacas. Drought may have also motivated people to place sites in areas with a greater diversity of ecological zones nearby. Access to a greater number of agropastoral zones would have helped mitigate risk in an unsure climatic situation.

The shift in the location and nature of large-scale ritual activity may be relevant for understanding changes in agropastoral zone preferences. Two sites in the XPAS survey zone with Chanapata pottery scatters had visible land modification that created platforms: Yuthu and Ak'awillay, the largest Formative site in the study region (see Figs. 4.4, 4.2). Excavations at Yuthu date occupation to 400–100 BC (Davis and Delgado 2009; Davis 2011). Although the initial date of occupation of Ak'awillay during the Formative period has not been firmly established, it is clear that the site continued to be occupied during the Early Intermediate period and Middle Horizon (Bélisle 2011: Table B.1; Bélisle and Covey 2010). Following the overall trend in site placement, Yuthu, the earlier site, was positioned to access suni and dry kichwa within 5 km, while the later site of Ak'awillay had access to suni and wet kichwa within 5 km.

The ritual system at Yuthu was related to agricultural and pastoral fertility. Ceremonial architecture on the platform was oriented with mountains, springs, and lakes. Ritual artifacts included a potato-shaped illa, probably used in rituals carried out to request a good harvest. A sunken structure originally incorporated a ceremonial canal used to perform water ritual referencing the glacier Pitusiray, probably an ideological source of water. Later, that canal was replaced with another oriented toward a different glacier, Chicón. Drought and reduced productivity may have motivated villagers to shift the focus of ritual activity away from

Figure 4.4. Two sites in the XPAS survey region with Chanapata pottery had visible land modification. Excavations at Yuthu have shown that the platform contained sunken ceremonial architecture and ritual canals dating to 400–100 BC. The platform at Ak'awillay has not yet been excavated.

Pitusiray in hopes of getting better results from rituals related to Chicón. Eventually, however, both canals and the sunken structure were purposefully buried and the village was abandoned and converted to a cemetery (Davis 2011).

In contrast with Yuthu, very little is known about the rectangular platform on the crest of the hill at Ak'awillay. Chanapata surface scatters were found near the platform, but because it has not been excavated, it is unclear when it was built and used and we do not know what types of activities took place there. Excavations of ritual architecture at Ak'awillay may help to clarify whether the failure of glacier-focused water rituals played a role in motivating people to move closer to wetter areas and to diversify subsistence strategies.

Whatever the reason for abandoning Yuthu and the ritual system there, it is likely that increasing reliance on camelids in drought conditions led to slight changes in subsistence strategies and settlement patterns during the Formative period. People using both Marcavalle-related and Chanapata-style pottery always prioritized access to suni and kichwa zones. This arrangement allowed them to carry out a diverse set of subsistence activities on a varied schedule, spreading out labor demands, maximizing production, and providing more diverse cuisine throughout the year. Further research on environmental history, faunal and botanical remains, and ritual practice should build a more detailed understanding of the transition in site location from dry to wet kichwa in terms of human action in the face of changing environmental and social circumstances.

Summary and Discussion

The lack of a refined and discrete ceramic chronology during the millennia when people used Marcavalle and Chanapata pottery makes it difficult to interpret patterns in the distributions of pottery styles as material representations of single moments in the cultural history of the region. Even so, regional settlement patterns can be used to learn about the strategies employed by people who shared common ceramic traditions, and therefore also must have shared elements of learning and knowledge systems as well as traditions in food preparation and sharing.

Early farmers and herders developed strategies that took advantage of the vertical Andean ecology to mitigate risk, spread out labor demands, diversify cuisines, and expand trade networks. These strategies played a large role in shaping daily life as people moved through the landscape tending flocks of llamas and alpacas daily and gathering in large groups periodically to plant, tend, and harvest crops. The placement of settlements or other activity sites within quick access of one or more ecological zones was one important element of these strategies. Not surprisingly, given botanical and faunal assemblages that included a variety of domesticates, most sites were located within easy access of the suni, an ecological zone that provides rich resources for herding as well as diversified farming on multiple growing schedules. In addition, many sites had access to multiple zones, including

lower-altitude kichwa that allowed further diversification of crops grown on yet another agricultural schedule. Access to multiple agropastoral zones allowed not only for a great diversity of crops, but also for maximized productivity in a landscape where production probably was limited by the availability of labor rather than the availability of land.

Settlement patterns in the XPAS study region show that some elements of the agropastoral strategy remained constant while others changed. While preference for suni zones endured, Marcavalle-related sites were more often located near dry kichwa zones compared with Chanapata sites, which were more often found near wet kichwa areas. This shift was likely part of a response to drought conditions and an increase in reliance on camelids for food and trade that roughly corresponded with the transition from principal use of Marcavalle pottery to principal use of Chanapata ceramics.

These changes in agropastoral strategies were intertwined with the social and political processes that created a single large site for the first time in this region. Ak'awillay emerged alongside the Wimpillay/Muyu Orqo site complex in the Cuzco Valley and Batan Urqu in the Lucre Basin. These developments were the local outcome of widespread transformations of Andean society representing a significant step in the development of social complexity in the region.

Works Cited

Bandy, Matthew S.
2004   Fissioning, scalar stress, and social evolution in early village societies. *American Anthropologist* 106(2):322–33.

Bauer, Brian S.
2004   *Ancient Cuzco, Heartland of the Inca.* Austin: University of Texas Press.

Bélisle, Véronique
2011   Ak'awillay: Wari State Expansion and Household Change in Cusco, Peru (AD 600–1000). PhD dissertation, Department of Anthropology, University of Michigan, Ann Arbor.

Bélisle, Véronique, and R. Alan Covey
2010   Local settlement continuity and Wari impact in Middle Horizon Cusco. In *Beyond Wari Walls: Regional Perspectives on Middle Horizon Peru*, edited by Justin Jennings, pp. 78–95. Albuquerque: University of New Mexico Press.

Bonavia, Duccio
2008   *The South American Camelids. Camélidos sudamericanos.* University of California, Los Angeles: Cotsen Institute of Archaeology.

Burger, Richard L., Karen L. Mohr Chávez, and Sergio J. Chávez
2000   Through the glass darkly: Prehispanic obsidian procurement and exchange in southern Peru and northern Bolivia. *Journal of World Prehistory* 14(3):267–362.

Chávez, Karen L. M.
1980   The archaeology of Marcavalle, an Early Horizon site in the Valley of Cuzco, Peru: Part I. *Baessler-Archiv* n.f. 28(2):203–329.

Chepstow-Lusty, Alex
2011   Agro-pastoralism and social change in the Cuzco heartland of Peru. A brief history using environmental proxies. *Antiquity* 85:570–82.

Chepstow-Lusty, Alex, Brian S. Bauer, and Michael Frogley
2004   Human impact and environmental history of the Cuzco region. In *Ancient Cuzco: Heartland of the Inca*, by Brian S. Bauer, pp. 23–29. Austin: University of Texas Press.

Davis, Allison R.
2011   *Yuthu: Community and Ritual in an Early Andean Village*. Memoirs, no. 50. Ann Arbor: Museum of Anthropology, University of Michigan.

Davis, Allison R., and Carlos Delgado
2009   Investigaciones arqueológicas en Yuthu: Nuevos datos sobre el periodo Formativo en el Cuzco, Perú (400–100 a.C.). *Boletín de Arqueología PUCP* 13:347–72.

deFrance, S. D.
2007   Faunal remains from the site of Kasapata. In *Kasapata and the Archaic Period of the Cuzco Valley*, edited by B. S. Bauer, pp. 111–17. University of California, Los Angeles: Cotsen Institute of Archaeology.

Feinman, Gary M., and Jill Neitzel
1984   Too many types: An overview of sedentary prestate societies in the Americas. In *Advances in Archaeological Method and Theory*, vol. 7, edited by Michael B. Schiffer, pp. 39–102. New York: Academic Press.

Flores Ochoa, Jorge A.
1979 [1967]   *Pastoralists of the Andes: The Alpaca Herders of Paratía*, translated by Ralph Bolton. Philadelphia: Institute for the Study of Human Issues.

Johnson, Gregory A.
1980   Rank-size convexity and system integration. *Economic Geography* 56:234–47.

Kimura, H.
2000   La tierra sin mano de obra no tiene valor: Tierra y labor en la agroganadería cuzqueña. *Senri Ethnological Reports of the National Museum of Ethnology (Osaka, Japan)* 19:295–315.

Kosiba, Steven B.
2010   Becoming Inka: The Transformation of Political Place and Practice during Inka State Formation (Cuzco, Peru). PhD dissertation, Department of Anthropology, University of Chicago.

Lavallée, D., M. Julien, and J. C. Wheeler
1984   Telarmachay: Niveles precerámicos de ocupación. *Revista del Museo Nacional* 46:55–127.

McEwan, Gordon F., Arminda Gibaja, and Melissa Chatfield
1995   Archaeology at the Chokepukio site: An investigation of the origins of the Inca civilization in the Valley of Cuzco, Peru: A report on the 1994 field season. *Tawantinsuyu* 1:11–17.

Miller, George R.
1979   An Introduction to the Ethnoarchaeology of the Andean Camelids. PhD dissertation, Department of Anthropology, University of California, Berkeley.

Miller, George R., and Richard L. Burger
1995   Ch'arki and Chavín: Ethnographic models and archaeological data. *American Antiquity* 65(3):573–76.

Parsons, Jeffrey R.
1972   Archaeological settlement patterns. *Annual Review of Anthropology* 1:127–50.

Rowe, John H.
1943   Chanapata: La cultura pre-Incaica del Cuzco. *Tupac Amaru (Cusco)* 2(2/3):41–43.

Shimada, Melody
1982   Zooarchaeology of Huacaloma: Behavioral and cultural implications. In *Excavations at Huacaloma in the Cajamarca Valley, Peru, 1979*, edited by K. Terada and Y. Onuki, pp. 303–36. Tokyo: University of Tokyo Press.
1985   Continuities and changes in patterns of faunal resource utilization: Formative through Cajamarca periods. In *The Formative Period in the Cajamarca Basin, Peru: Excavations at Huacaloma and Layzón, 1982*, edited by K. Terada and Y. Onuki, pp. 289–310. Tokyo: University of Tokyo Press.

Vásquez Sánchez, V. F., and T. E. Rosales Tham
2009   Análisis de restos de fauna y vegetales del sitio Yuthu. Centro de Investigaciones Arqueobiológicas y Paleoecológicas Andinas, Trujillo, Perú. Report submitted to Allison R. Davis.

Wheeler Pires-Ferreira, J., E. Pires-Ferreira, and P. Kaulicke
1976   Preceramic animal utilization in the central Peruvian Andes. *Science* 194:483–90.

Wylie, Allison
2002   *Thinking from Things: Essays in the Philosophy of Archaeology*. Berkeley: University of California Press.

Yábar Moreno, Jorge
1972   Época pre-Inca de Chanapata. *Revista Saqsaywaman* 2:211–33.

Zapata, J.
1998   Los cerros sagrados: Panorama del período Formativo en la cuenca del Vilcanota, Cuzco. *Boletín de Arqueología PUCP* 2:307–36.

Chapter 5: Formative Period Settlement Patterns in the Sacred Valley

R. Alan Covey

Much remains to be clarified regarding the transition to agropastoral subsistence strategies and the establishment of sedentary villages in the Cuzco region, but archaeological perspectives on early villages are beginning to emerge as settlement surveys generate patterns leading to horizontal excavation projects. Roughly 300 Formative period sites have been registered through systematic survey work in the Cuzco region (Bauer 1999, 2004; Davis 2011; Kosiba 2010; see Chapter 4), and the survey data from the Hanan Cuzco region complement those of other projects. Although the patterns reported in this chapter can be considered alongside excavations of Formative contexts in other parts of the Cuzco region (e.g., Bélisle 2011; Chávez 1980, 1981a, 1981b; Davis 2011; Valencia and Gibaja 1991; McEwan, Gibaja, and Chatfield 1995; Zapata 1998), problem-based excavations have not been conducted at Formative sites in the Sacred Valley. As noted in previous chapters, the transition to sedentism and commitment to agriculture may be a complex process involving hunter-gatherers, farmers, and herders across the Cuzco region, and excavation work is needed from sites in multiple ecological settings.

Issues of Chronology and Style

Dates for the earliest ceramic use in the Cuzco region are still unclear (Bauer 2004:39–40), but radiocarbon dates from excavated contexts show that village life was established by at least 800 BC, if not earlier. The earliest ceramic styles in the Cuzco region, first identified in the 1940s (Rowe 1944) and called Marcavalle and Chanapata, have been excavated stratigraphically and systematically described (e.g., Bauer 1999, 2002; Chapter 4). Survey research in the Sacred Valley (the Sacred Valley and Calca-Yanahuara projects) maintained consistency with earlier regional projects, lumping the Marcavalle and Chanapata styles into a single period designated "Formative" and considered to date to circa 1000 BC–AD 200 (cf. Bauer 2004:39–46). Ceramic wares and rim forms for this long time period present certain stylistic continuities, permitting reliable identification in collections of fragmented surface artifacts. At the same time, collection methods and resulting sample sizes from the Sacred Valley surveys did not yield sufficient diagnostic material to subdivide the occupation sequences of Formative sites. The average Formative component was less than 30 pottery fragments, and incised or painted material was not present at every site. The presence of specific temporal markers at a given site could provide insights into a particular occupational history, but regional data at the time of fieldwork were not fine-grained enough to develop meaningful settlement maps for different periods within the broader Formative designation.

The identification of one long, undifferentiated Formative period places constraints on the interpretation of regional settlement patterns. The appearance of settlement continuity throughout the Formative period is almost certainly exaggerated, and major changes in site occupation, subsistence practices, and social hierarchy will remain invisible until researchers can develop a more sensitive chronology that can be applied to the kinds of surface collections that can be made at early sites. An undivided Formative period cannot truly address population growth over time, or social processes such as warfare or village fissioning that might be part of the prelude to the establishment of regional settlement hierarchies. The presence of modest settlement hierarchies has already been noted in the Cuzco Valley (Bauer 2004) and the Sacred Valley (Covey 2006); although the development of large villages might reflect increases in regional political complexity, some of the apparent growth could be the result of long-term intrasite settlement shifts resulting in a palimpsest that appears to be a single contemporaneous settlement. Additionally, the designation of a temporal unit of more than a millennium makes some direct comparisons with subsequent periods problematic.

Stylistic concerns should be added to the list of interpretive caveats for the Formative period. Although burnishing and some painting are diagnostic for Formative ceramics, the most common markers for this period are globular rims. As these are not restricted to high-status vessels, there are more types of Formative pottery that are easily identifiable using surface collections than are encountered in the styles of subsequent periods.

Formative Site Counts and Sizes in the Sacred Valley

Regional projects in the Sacred Valley registered the presence of Formative pottery on the surface at more than 60 sites—54 in the SVAP region and 10 in the Calca-Yanahuara extension region (see Covey, Aráoz Silva, and Bauer 2008 for discussion of the latter) (Fig. 5.1). No standing architecture pertaining to this period was preserved, although excavations elsewhere in the Hanan Cuzco study region have encountered domestic structures, public architecture, and mortuary features (Bélisle 2011; Davis 2011). Formative sites ranged in size from small scatters (100 m^2) to village sites of 6 ha and larger. Occupations of this period were found in all parts of the Sacred Valley survey region, with an elevation range of over 1200 m (2946–4151 masl). A scatterplot of site size and elevation (Fig. 5.2) indicates that the largest villages are situated in a mosaic of mid-valley elevations and some ridgetop areas, particularly between elevations of 3700 and 4150 masl. Today, these environments are used for mixed horticulture and herding, with local variations in the relative emphasis on different crops or herding practices. Formative occupations in the Calca-Yanahuara region reflect a distinct ecological focus from what is seen in the SVAP region—sites are distributed close to the valley floor, with an elevation range of 2874 to 3293 masl. This distribution is comparable with the LIP and Inca occupations of this part of the valley.

Formative settlements occur in two modal sizes. Hamlets and small villages (settlements 3 ha and smaller) constitute more than 90% (60/64) of all registered sites, and tend to be spread across diverse farming ecozones. The remaining 4 sites (VS-94/96, VS-353, VS-175, VS-121/122) are all found in the SVAP region and range in size from 4 to 6 ha. The large village sites have very dense artifact scatters, and the common domestic pottery often appears along with fine burnished vessel fragments and sherds decorated with incised patterns and painting (see Bauer 1999; Chávez 1980; Rowe 1944). Fancy pottery tends to occur at sites that also have a greater quantity of obsidian relative to local andesite. Obsidian was observed on the surface of 16 sites, of which only 4 were under 5000 m^2; this nonlocal stone was found in association with decorated pottery at 5 sites, only 1 of which (VS-067, a 2500 m^2 site) was smaller than 1.5 ha.

Of the 4 largest Formative villages, only 1, a Chit'apampa Basin site named Muyumuyupata (VS-121/122), lacked fancy pottery (Fig. 5.3). Two small villages in the Chit'apampa Basin, Mallquikancha (VS-63) and Keser (VS-129), had fine pottery present in surface collections. This distribution might represent settlement shifts from early to late sites, proximity to Cuzco (Bauer [2004:42–43] has identified late Formative pottery at more than 80 sites), or both. Muyumuyupata might have been occupied in the early part of the Formative period, or could have had more limited relations with populations in the Cuzco Basin, where decorated pottery appears to be more common at Formative sites. Although additional excavation and geochemical analysis are needed, it appears that incised and painted Formative pottery is less common at a distance from the Cuzco Basin. A few fragments of decorated pottery were found in the upper Chongo Basin at Apu Sompechu (VS-175), but it was otherwise restricted to the Chit'apampa Basin and parts of the southern Sacred Valley rim (Fig. 5.4). This was the highest Formative village site registered in the Sacred Valley (4151 masl), and the mountaintop location offered direct access to the well-watered farmlands of the upper Chongo Basin, as well as broad expanses of pastureland in the *puna* grasslands lying above.

In general, settlement patterns suggest a stable occupation of the Sacred Valley during the Formative period, with large villages growing over time. There is some evidence for an uneven distribution of status goods such as obsidian and fancy pottery, although more work is needed to clarify this. We still lack clear evidence of hereditary political inequality, although it is possible that some of the large villages came to dominate smaller ones, forming a number of small polities with populations spread across fairly restricted territories. It appears that members of some communities in the study region had contact with groups living in the Cuzco Basin, but the stability and the clustering of

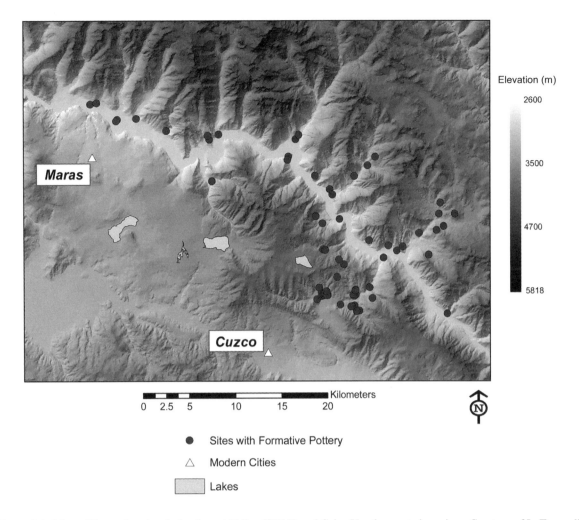

Figure 5.1. Map of Formative sites in the Sacred Valley (SVAP) and Calca-Yanahuara study regions. Courtesy of L. Tsesmeli.

settlement suggest that most areas remained autonomous at this time (cf. Bauer 2004:44–46; Covey 2006:60–63).

Mosaic Economies and the Rise of Political Inequality

Although the evidence for political complexity is ambiguous in the Sacred Valley survey data, some important inferences can be made regarding economy and settlement during this period. The mean settlement elevation for this period is 3596 masl, the highest for any period except the Late Intermediate period. The motivations for choosing high-elevation settlement locations probably were economic, as well as defensive or religious. Local management of a mosaic economy that involved horticulture (a diverse array of tubers, quinoa, and possibly some maize), village-level camelid herding, and the hunting and collecting of wild resources would tend to encourage settlement in and around elevations where a variety of ecological floors could be

accessed. It is noteworthy that the largest Formative villages are found at elevations that range from *suni* to puna, whereas small villages and hamlets are scattered across a much broader ecological range with a much lower average elevation. Formative settlement patterns from the Calca-Yanahuara region suggest a focus on *kichwa* resources, although as Davis notes in Chapter 4, the nearby Maras and Huaypo area has substantially larger settlements in suni locales.

The elevation distinctions for the settlement hierarchy can be evaluated using data registered for contemporary land use, which reveal distinctions between larger (1 ha and larger) and smaller (under 1 ha) sites in the SVAP region. Nearly half of the geomorphological designations for large sites (44%, or 7/16) were mountaintops or ridgetops, whereas small sites were found in these locations at a lower percentage (33%, or 21/63). Conversely, although nearly 20% (12/63) of smaller site designations were for alluvial terraces, valley floor, and agricultural terraces, only 6% (1/16) of large sites received this designation. Broadly

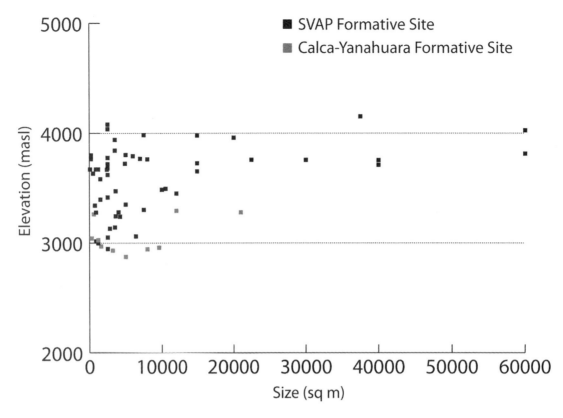

Figure 5.2. Scatterplot of elevation and site size for Formative sites in the Sacred Valley. Note that some sizes are estimated due to constraints in the field, or the availability of additional evidence.

Figure 5.3. Photograph of the middle of the Chit'apampa Basin. The site of Muyumuyupata lacks decorated Formative pottery, which is present at the ridgetop site of Raqchi. Both sites lie above 3700 meters, in areas with direct access to a wide range of natural resources.

Figure 5.4. View of the upper Chongo Basin. Although several Formative villages were found to the north of the Vilcanota-Urubamba River, only the hilltop site of Apu Sompechu (VS-175) had incised or painted pottery in surface collections.

speaking, large sites favored locations that would be visible and provide natural defense, whereas small sites were probably associated with the direct exploitation of local agricultural resources. Because the survey did not target herding areas to the north of the Sacred Valley, we cannot speculate on whether a similar pattern would be present in these areas, although it is significant that the survey of the Qoricocha puna did not encounter large Formative villages or smaller herding facilities.

This distinction becomes even more interesting when data on modern land use categories are considered. Small Formative sites are distributed nearly evenly between valley-bottom farming lands (kichwa, *maway*, and *yunlla*) (12/30, or 40%), and those designated for tuber production (suni) and herding (puna) (12/30), and sites were found in areas where maize (7), beans (8), tubers (1), quinoa (1), and European cultivars such as wheat and barley (15) were being grown in 2000. By comparison, the larger Formative sites had a similar distribution throughout the land categories, except that no sites were found in prime kichwa agricultural lands. The same modern crops were being grown on the lands where the large sites were found, but nearly half of the use designations (5/11) were for areas not currently in use (compared with 32% for the small sites).

Although these numbers offer a limited proxy for considering Formative period use of local landscapes, it is nevertheless possible to say that there are meaningful differences in the immediate catchment areas surrounding large and small sites. Larger sites appear to have been situated on the basis of nonagricultural considerations, and on average, these are situated about 200 m farther away from the nearest modern water source (506 m) than are the smaller sites (298 m). Given what is known about climate during the Formative period, the stability of large Formative villages through long-term environmental fluctuations suggests that site selection for large villages was probably grounded in cultural considerations rather than environmental advantages. Smaller sites were located closer to agricultural resources, and it might be that people living at least part-time in the larger sites would have coordinated relationships of ecological complementarity for a kin group, village, or small polity. Community members might live more or less permanently in small hamlets, but had continuing ties to the larger villages. The archaeological test of any model of ecological complementarity calls for extensive excavations at large high-elevation sites, as well as smaller ones across the subsistence spectrum.

Shrines and Refuges in the Formative Period

As seen from the discussion of geomorphology and modern land use, there is some evidence that economic considerations were not the only factors influencing settlement location of large villages, and that Formative groups chose important site locations on the basis of defensibility, visibility, and perhaps religious ideology. As mentioned already, larger Formative sites tended to be located on prominent ridges or mountaintops. For example, the site of Raqchi (VS-94/96) was located on a ridge overlooking part of the Chit'apampa Basin, and was in view of several other Formative sites in the area. The site is difficult to approach because of the mountainside's steep slopes and an area of cliffs that protect a prominent point where Formative pottery and disturbed burials were identified. Apu Sompechu (VS-175), Pukara Pantillijlla (VS-176), and Markasunay (VS-353) are also located in prominent places that require considerable effort to access (Fig. 5.5).

This does not prove that defense was a primary consideration, but modern land use and distance from water suggest that such sites did not present an immediate economic advantage for agriculturalists, although they might have been situated in part to coordinate agriculture and pastoralism. Defense, visibility, and resource management were probably concerns that influenced the siting of large villages, but it appears that some Formative sites also had a religious function.

One example of this is Pukara Pantillijlla, located on a prominent ridge that is visible throughout the Chongo Basin and from some sites in the Chit'apampa Basin. The ridge on which the site is located ends abruptly in a prominence in which numerous simple cliff tombs are located. (A comparable natural feature is present at Raqchi (VS-94) and Markasunay (VS-353) as well.) Excavations and surface reconnaissance reveal that this site was not used for large-scale permanent settlement, but there is a light Formative occupation that might be related to mortuary practices of nearby communities. More than 300 Formative sherds were identified in excavation units close to the natural prominence, including 36 rim sherds and 3 incised fragments.

Excavations in an early Inca building (Structure 6) built on the small open space on the approach to the natural prominence at Pukara Pantillijlla encountered the remains of what appear to be two small ovoid structures, as well as a covered canal running in a north-south direction (Fig. 5.6). These features underlie the architecture of the Late Intermediate period by approximately a half meter, and although they have not been dated, there were quantities of Formative pottery mixed with Late Intermediate and Inca materials in the unit. Some unidentified bone appeared in the terminal levels of each oval-shaped feature, which ended at bedrock. Small quantities of dog, camelid, guinea pig, and possible human bone appeared in the lower levels of the building interior.

The size and shape of the oval features indicates that they were not residential, and although they had been destroyed to

Figure 5.5. View of Pukara Pantillijlla. The prominent point at the center of the photograph overlooks the lower and upper Chongo Basin, and was a location for a Formative period burial, as well as a modest village.

their foundations with the Killke–Inca expansion of the site settlement, it is possible that these would have been used for burials, storage, or some special purpose. Davis (2011:108–12) identified stone-lined circular cists and oval-shaped depressions in association with ritual canals and simple human burials at Yuthu, an artificial platform that was built in the later Formative period and was oriented for ritual offerings to nearby glaciated peaks. Zapata (1998) reports stone-lined oval tombs for Late Formative burials at Batan Urqu, although excavated burials at Muyu Urqu (Zapata 1998) and Chanapata (Rowe 1944) lack such elaboration. The distinction should be made between the mortuary environment at Pukara Pantillijlla — a location where Formative populations journeyed to local landmarks to deposit their dead — and the burials found at artificial platforms near large Formative villages founded in kichwa and lower suni zones.

It appears that some Formative populations ascribed significance to prominent ridgetop locations, some of which were used as population centers, and others of which might have been conceptualized as sacred places (*wak'a*) used for burial and other ritual activities. It is possible that in addition to these economic and symbolic functions, some high places served as refuges in times of conflict, although much more work would be needed to address this potential source of social power in Formative times. Regardless of the kinds of functions that such sites might have served, there are some interesting spatial relationships between ridgetop sites and other villages. In some cases there appears to be a pairing between a ridgetop village and one located closer to the valley bottom on agricultural land. This is the case for Mallquikancha (VS-63) and VS-16, located in the Chit'apampa Basin. Whereas Mallquikancha is located near the valley bottom, VS-16 is situated along a narrow ridge about 200 m above. It is possible that the ridgetop settlement represents either a permanent defensive/ceremonial area, or a separate occupation that was paired with that of Mallquikancha. Such "pairing" might also reflect site growth over long periods of settlement, which could be accompanied by alteration to the original village center.

These issues can be considered in light of evidence from the sites of Muyu Urqu and Wimpillay in the Cuzco Valley (Fig. 5.7). This area, thought by Bauer (2004) to be the principal village of a complex polity, includes a village on the flanks of a hillside, an occupation on a prominent round hill, and a sector of disturbed burials with a high percentage of decorated pottery on the surface. Recent excavations in the hilltop have revealed what appears to be a semi-subterranean temple, indicating a ritual use of the hilltop precinct (Zapata 1998). While nothing of that level of complexity appears in the Sacred Valley, such a pairing of sites is interesting for addressing the emergence of social inequality, as well as Andean patterns of duality and community social organization.

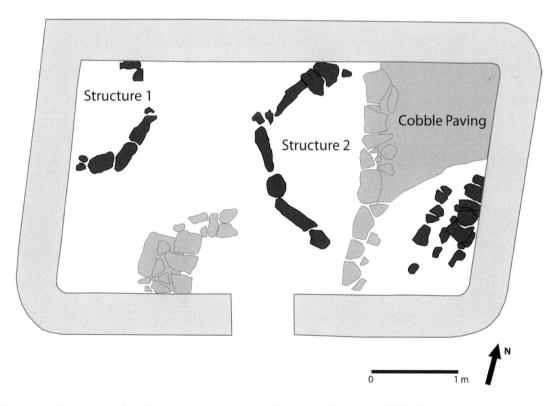

Figure 5.6. Foundations of small oval-shaped structures and a canal at Pukara Pantillijlla. The gray building outline and stones pertain to the early Inca-era use of the structure, whereas the darker stones appeared about a half meter deeper in the unit.

Figure 5.7. The site of Muyu Urqu in the Cuzco Basin has a semi-subterranean plaza built on the prominent hill, with a large Formative settlement around the hillslopes. Many of the disturbed burials contain decorated Formative pottery.

Settlement Intensity and Diachronic Change in the Formative Period

Although the existing archaeological evidence does not make possible the conclusive identification of hereditary inequality and the origins of political complexity in the study region, it does permit observations on how such processes might have occurred. It is clear that early villages in the study region were established to pursue subsistence economies that included a wide range of produced and natural resources. Such resources could be exploited efficiently through the organization and management of relationships of ecological complementarity, possibly including transhumance for some sectors of production. Internal specialization would require leadership (although not necessarily hereditary), and charismatic individuals who could manipulate the productive system might also maintain exchange ties throughout the region to acquire long-distance prestige items like obsidian. The ethnographic literature (e.g., Brush 1976) has demonstrated that the management of ecological complementarity can be achieved at the level of the kin group, or even family, depending on regional ecology—this suggests that pathways to

hereditary inequality might vary across the Cuzco region and neighboring parts of the Andes.

Without substantial excavation data, it is not possible to say whether ranked polities had emerged in the study region by AD 200. There is evidence of a simple settlement hierarchy and of economic management, but these are difficult to interpret. There are intriguing patterns in mortuary practices and the distribution of fancy pottery and obsidian that are evident by the Late Formative, but it is difficult to ascertain whether these represent the regional establishment of ascribed status inequalities. If ranking developed in the study region by the last centuries of the Formative period, it was probably only after the emergence of political complexity in the Cuzco Valley, and most areas north of the Vilcanota-Urubamba River appear to lack sufficient population or settlement hierarchy to have been considered ranked.

The one possible ranked polity in the study region would be located in the Chit'apampa Basin. Assuming that the large village of Muyumuyupata was principally an early Formative settlement (because no decorated pottery was encountered on the surface), a complex polity would have had its principal settlement at Raqchi, where related clusters of settlement would bring total occupation area to nearly 6 ha. This village would have controlled smaller hamlets surrounding it, as well as smaller villages of 1.5–2 ha at Mallquikancha (VS-63), Patakancha (VS-88), and possibly in the Patabamba area (VS-378). Raqchi includes a sector of burials on a prominent point that is visible from most of what are tentatively identified as secondary villages, and has a substantial amount of fancy pottery and obsidian (compared to other Formative sites). Although evidence that other villages had lost their autonomy to elites at Raqchi is impossible to demonstrate at present, it does appear that this site was beginning to emerge as an important settlement at the end of the Formative period, when it was abandoned.

Overview

The first villages in the Sacred Valley were organized so that communities could manage farming and herding in ways that made use of a unique set of resources in the local catchment area and beyond. Wild animals continued to be hunted during this time, and wild plant resources augmented produced food to varying degrees (e.g., Davis 2011). Larger settlements at this time were established in places that afforded defensibility, visibility, and relatively easy control over relationships of ecological complementarity. Small hamlets were established for direct access to the products of different ecozones, and large village sites were probably the locations of community rituals. Some sites may have been paired so that ridgetop locations would be used for burials and group defense. It is clear that enterprising individuals had exchange relationships outside their communities, acquiring regional prestige items such as decorated pottery and obsidian from the Cuzco Valley and beyond.

The study region was less densely populated than the Cuzco Valley, and probably followed it as ranking and political complexity emerged. As seen in Chapter 7, the Chit'apampa Basin—the most dense and possibly politically complex part of the study region—shows very strong material culture ties with the Cuzco Basin by AD 200 or so.

References

Bauer, Brian S.
1999   *The Early Ceramics of the Inca Heartland.* Fieldiana Anthropology, n.s., 31. Chicago: Field Museum of Natural History.
2002   *Las antiguas tradiciones alfareras de la región del Cuzco.* Cuzco: Centro de Estudios Rurales Andinos "Bartolomé de Las Casas."
2004   *Ancient Cuzco: Heartland of the Inca.* Austin: University of Texas Press.

Bélisle, Véronique
2011   Ak'awillay: Wari State Expansion and Household Change in Cusco, Peru (AD 600–1000). PhD dissertation, Department of Anthropology, University of Michigan.

Brush, Stephen B.
1976   Man's use of an Andean ecosystem. *Human Ecology* 4(2):147–66.

Chávez, Karen L. Mohr
1980   The archaeology of Marcavalle, an Early Horizon site in the Valley of Cuzco, Peru: Part I. *Baessler-Archiv* n.f. 28(2):203–329.
1981a   The archaeology of Marcavalle, an Early Horizon site in the Valley of Cuzco, Peru: Part II. *Baessler-Archiv* n.f. 29(1):107–25.
1981b   The archaeology of Marcavalle, an Early Horizon site in the Valley of Cuzco, Peru: Part III (decorated ceramics). *Baessler-Archiv* n.f. 29(1):241–386.

Covey, R. Alan
2006   *How the Incas Built Their Heartland: State Formation and the Innovation of Imperial Strategies in the Sacred Valley, Peru.* Ann Arbor: University of Michigan Press.

Covey, R. Alan, Miriam Aráoz Silva, and Brian S. Bauer
2008   Settlement patterns in the Yucay Valley and neighboring areas. In *Imperial Transformations in Sixteenth-Century Yucay, Peru*, edited by R. Alan Covey and Donato Amado González, pp. 3–17. Memoirs, no. 44. Ann Arbor: Museum of Anthropology, University of Michigan.

Davis, Allison R.
2011   *Yuthu: Community and Ritual in an Early Andean Village.* Memoirs, no. 50. Ann Arbor: Museum of Anthropology, University of Michigan.

Kosiba, Steven B.
2010   Becoming Inka: The Transformation of Political Place and Practice during Inka State Formation (Cusco, Peru). PhD dissertation, Department of Anthropology, University of Chicago.

McEwan, Gordon F., Arminda M. Gibaja, and Melissa Chatfield
1995   Archaeology of the Chokepukio site: An investigation of the origin of the Inca civilisation in the Valley of Cuzco, Peru. A report on the 1994 field season. *Tawantinsuyu* 1:11–17.

Rowe, John H.
1944   *An Introduction to the Archaeology of Cuzco.* Papers of the Peabody Museum of American Archaeology and Ethnology 27(2). Cambridge, MA.

Valencia, Alfredo, and Arminda Gibaja
1991   *Marcavalle: El rostro oculto del Cusco.* Cuzco: Instituto Regional de Cultura de la Región Inka.

Zapata Rodríguez, Julinho
1998   Los cerros sagrados: Panorama del período Formativo en la cuenca del Vilcanota, Cuzco. *Boletín de Arqueología PUCP* 2:307–36.

PART III

Local Societies and the Effects of Wari Colonization

Chapter 6: Early Intermediate Period and Middle Horizon Settlement Patterns in the Xaquixaguana Region

Véronique Bélisle

During the Middle Horizon (AD 600–1000), the Wari state based in Ayacucho colonized several regions of the Andes, resulting in the construction of large settlements that reproduced Wari architectural canons. Research focusing on these large Wari sites has led many scholars to conclude that the Wari state conquered widely and established direct control over several provinces during the Middle Horizon (Bergh 2012; Isbell 1987, 1989, 1997, 2001; Isbell and McEwan 1991; Isbell and Schreiber 1978; Lumbreras 1974; Matos Mendieta 1968; McEwan 1989, 1991, 2005; Menzel 1964, 1968; Nash and Williams 2009; Rowe 1956; Schaedel 1993; Schreiber 1984, 1987a, 1987b, 1992, 2001; Valdez, Bettcher, and Valdez 2002; Williams and Nash 2002).

In the Cuzco region, the Wari established a single cluster of settlements that included (1) Pikillacta and a network of irrigation canals and agricultural terraces in the Lucre Basin, 30 km southeast of the city of Cuzco; and (2) the Huaro Archaeological Complex, a group of residential sites, temples, and cemeteries in the Huaro Valley 12 km further southeast (Fig. 6.1) (Glowacki 2002; Glowacki and McEwan 2001; McEwan 2005; Zapata 1997). The impressive size of these sites has often been cited as the definitive evidence for strong and direct Wari control over the populations and resources of the Cuzco region (e.g., McEwan 2005; Schreiber 1992). Importantly, this interpretation of Wari dominance does not consider the local settlements that were presumably under Wari control to see how (and if) local populations were affected by Wari presence during the Middle Horizon.

A recent regional systematic survey in the Lucre Basin around Pikillacta identified continuity in the settlement pattern from the Early Intermediate period (EIP; AD 200–600) to the Middle Horizon (Covey et al. 2013). Large local villages that were occupied since the EIP or earlier grew in size during the Middle Horizon. Even though Wari pottery was present at several sites and Araway (a locally produced Wari-inspired pottery style) was rare, local pottery was abundant at sites in the Lucre Basin. These data suggest that Wari officials did not significantly reorganize the area during the Middle Horizon. Local populations might have participated in Wari construction projects, but the absence of change in the settlement pattern and the continuity of local material culture suggest that these communities could have remained largely autonomous during the Middle Horizon despite their proximity to Pikillacta (Covey et al. 2013).

Data from systematic survey in the Wari colony differ strongly from the interpretation of Pikillacta as a regional administrative center that imposed direct control over the region. In this chapter,

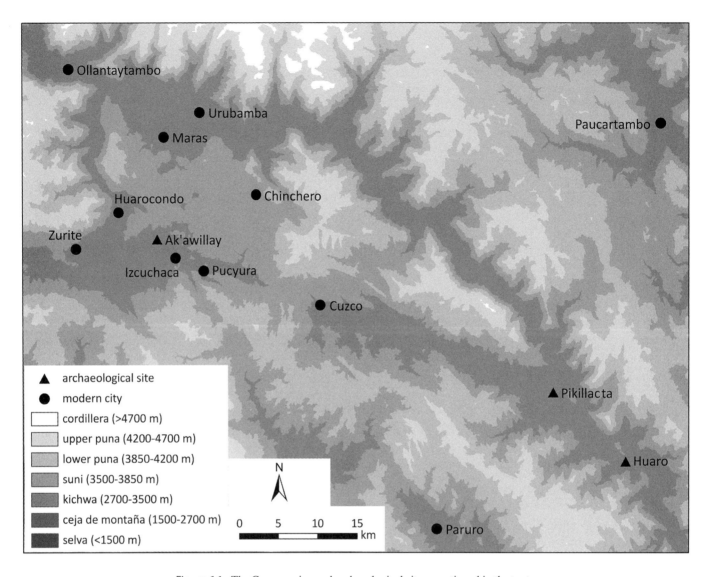

Figure 6.1. The Cuzco region and archaeological sites mentioned in the text.

I use survey data from the Xaquixaguana region to the northwest of the city of Cuzco to evaluate how Wari presence at Pikillacta and in the Huaro Valley affected the people living outside the Wari colony. Data generated by the Xaquixaguana survey provide an important tool to evaluate the impact of the Wari state at the regional level. By comparing the EIP/Middle Horizon sites and Araway components in the Xaquixaguana region, it is possible to detect Wari influence on settlement location, site clustering, settlement ecology, settlement hierarchy, and pottery style distributions. Changes in the settlement patterns that occurred *before* the arrival of the Wari (i.e., in the EIP) were not related to Wari colonization, but any changes that occurred at Araway components were contemporaneous with the Wari colony and could reveal the nature of Wari impact on local communities.

Archaeological Expectations of Wari Impact in Cuzco

As outlined by Covey (this volume) and colleagues (Covey et al. 2013), the presence of Wari colonists in Cuzco could have affected different aspects of local life. Political influence could have changed the distribution and hierarchy of settlements, and certain villages could have had a strong Wari affiliation as reflected in material culture. Economic impact could be evidenced in the procurement of Wari and Wari-managed goods (e.g., pottery, obsidian), changes in regional exchange networks, and shifts in settlement ecology and agricultural production to meet Wari demands. Local religious practices could also have been affected by Wari presence—for example, if Wari colonists imposed their ceremonial architecture and rituals on local populations, appropriated local shrines, and altered burial patterns. Military impact could be seen in the presence of defensive site locations and fortifications. While changes in everyday life could be more difficult to detect from survey data, changes in site locations and in the production of certain items could point to new subsistence and consumption practices.

Wari impact in the Xaquixaguana region could have been (1) limited to only some of these domains, (2) restricted to certain sites (e.g., villages at the top of the settlement hierarchy), or (3) ubiquitous. Before examining settlement pattern data from the Xaquixaguana region, the following sections discuss the regional chronology and the results of previous surveys in the Cuzco region.

Chronology and Ceramic Sequence

The chronology of the Cuzco region is based on a ceramic sequence developed from stratigraphic excavations and a series of radiocarbon/AMS dates (Covey et al. in this volume; see also Bauer 1989, 1999:155–56, 2004; Bauer and Jones 2003:35–37; Barreda Murillo 1982; Bélisle 2011:81–90, 254–55, Covey 2006:246–47; Davis 2011:161–62; Espinoza Martínez 1983; Glowacki 2005a, 2005b). Some ceramic styles span more than one period, showing a lack of correspondence between most local developments and the pan-Central Andean Intermediates and Horizons. Since architecture is not visible on the surface of settlements occupied before AD 1000 (except at certain Wari sites), the region's relative chronology cannot be refined by documenting architectural variations through time.

The EIP and the Middle Horizon in Cuzco shared several pottery styles, including Qotakalli, Muyu Urqu, and Waru. Two additional styles were confined to the Middle Horizon: Wari and Araway. In the Xaquixaguana survey, sites that contained Qotakalli, Muyu Urqu, or Waru pottery were interpreted as EIP/Middle Horizon components (AD 200–1000), whereas Araway and Wari pottery indicated Middle Horizon Wari influence on local settlements.

Settlement Patterns in Cuzco
outside the Xaquixaguana Region

Early Intermediate Period Settlement Shift

In the Cuzco Basin around the city of Cuzco, the EIP was a time of changing settlement patterns (Bauer 2004:52–54). In many locations, Formative (2200 BC–AD 200) hilltop sites were abandoned as new settlements were established in lower valley slopes in the southern part of the basin, where the best agricultural lands were located. This shift in site location, coupled with environmental and ecological data, suggests that local populations started to rely more heavily on the cultivation of maize and probably less on high-elevation horticulture and herding.

Settlement hierarchy indicates a regional polity centered in the western portion of the basin.

In the Sacred Valley to the north of Cuzco, during the EIP sites also shifted from hilltops to valley-bottom areas close to permanent running water (Covey 2006:60–67; see Covey in this volume). During the Formative, populations relied on a mixed agropastoral economy in the *puna* and *suni* production zones where they could have exploited tubers, quinoa, and camelids. During the EIP, large Formative villages were abandoned for smaller dispersed sites as local populations started to rely more heavily on the lower *kichwa* zone where maize could be cultivated. EIP sites were located closer to water in open and nondefensible areas, and choice of site location appears to have been based on farming needs rather than on preoccupation for defense. There was no discernible settlement hierarchy during the EIP, and the presence of Cuzco Basin pottery at many Sacred Valley sites indicates strong ties to the Cuzco Basin (Covey 2006:66–67), but the exact nature of this relationship remains to be fully understood.

In the Paruro area to the south of Cuzco, data from settlement patterns and the distribution of Qotakalli pottery indicate that the northern part of that region was under the influence of the Cuzco Basin polity (Bauer 1999:73–79). Qotakalli pottery is found at sites closest to Cuzco, and Muyu Urqu pottery is also present in Paruro. Villages and hamlets were small and there was no settlement hierarchy.

Continuity of EIP Settlement Patterns
in Middle Horizon Cuzco

Despite the arrival of Wari populations and the construction of large settlements in the Lucre and Huaro Basins, the Middle Horizon in the Cuzco region shows very limited departures from EIP settlement patterns after AD 600. In the Cuzco Basin, EIP settlement patterns continued into the Middle Horizon (Bauer 2004:55–69). Small EIP hamlets were abandoned, but the larger villages established near good maize lands during the EIP continued to be occupied. Presumably, the continuity of settlement locations and regional hierarchy indicate stability in local leadership. No Wari architecture was documented in the Cuzco Basin, although there was an overall absence of standing architecture in the region before AD 1000. Small components of Wari pottery appeared at a few dozen sites, but data from test pits and excavations indicate that Wari pottery was always associated with much larger components of local ceramic styles as well as local architecture (Bauer and Jones 2003). The Wari-influenced Araway style was produced with clays from the Cuzco Basin (Glowacki 2005a:112; Montoya et al. 2003:181, 2009), and a GIS analysis of its distribution patterns (Covey et al. 2013) suggests that Cuzco Basin populations redistributed Araway vessels to other areas of the region.

Like the Cuzco Basin, the EIP settlement patterns of the Sacred Valley continued into the Middle Horizon (Covey 2006:74–78). Small EIP hamlets were abandoned, but most villages continued to be occupied during the Middle Horizon and there was no significant change in the settlement hierarchy. Several sites that contained Araway pottery were small components at large Late Intermediate period (LIP; AD 1000–1400) sites, suggesting a late Middle Horizon settlement shift not related to the arrival of Wari in the region. In addition, if the Wari state had an economic interest in the Cuzco region, it is likely that colonization and resettlement policies would have intensively targeted valley-bottom lands in the Sacred Valley to exploit its productive, frost-free maize lands. Instead, Wari architecture was absent and Wari pottery was rare in the Sacred Valley even though the region is within a few hours' walk of Pikillacta (Covey 2006:74–78; Covey et al. 2013).

In the Paruro area, a small number of Wari fragments were recovered at only 9 sites (Bauer 1999:63–64, 67, 70–71; Covey et al. 2013). Most of these sites were around the town of Paruro closest to the Lucre Basin. One small site close to the town of Paruro, Muyu Roqo, contained a large sample of Wari pottery. Test excavations at Muyu Roqo revealed abundant Wari Okros-style pottery and camelid bones, suggesting that eating and drinking were important activities at the site. Muyu Roqo was probably a ritual site during the Middle Horizon (Bauer 1999:63–66), but its precise relationship to Pikillacta and Huaro remains to be evaluated.

The Cuzco Region through Time

Data from the regional systematic surveys conducted in the Cuzco Basin, Sacred Valley, and Paruro area indicate that the EIP was a time of change—local populations abandoned hilltop sites for lower nondefensible settlements close to maize-producing lands. A regional polity developed in the Cuzco Basin and interacted with adjacent areas in the southern part of the Sacred Valley and the northern part of Paruro. These changes in settlement locations and regional authority occurred before Wari arrival.

The Middle Horizon was not a period of drastic change but one marked by continuity—most EIP sites were still occupied, populations remained at lower altitudes to grow maize, regional exchange networks were not interrupted, and local leadership continued to be based in the Cuzco Basin. Limited amounts of Wari pottery were recovered at sites dominated by local material culture. These data suggest a more limited Wari impact in Cuzco than that indicated by research conducted at Pikillacta and Huaro. To fully evaluate the degree and nature of Wari influence in Cuzco, the following sections present survey results from Xaquixaguana.

The Xaquixaguana Region

The Xaquixaguana region to the northwest of the city of Cuzco is an important area to test Wari impact in Cuzco. The area includes the Inca road to Chinchaysuyu, and if, as suggested by earlier scholars (Hyslop 1984:270–74; Lumbreras 1974:162–63; Regal 1936:6–7; Schreiber 1984), the speed of Inca imperial expansion was due to the reuse of old Wari trails and roads for the llama caravans and the integration and consolidation of their empire, then the road passing through the Xaquixaguana region was perhaps already in use during the Middle Horizon. The Wari could have used such a route to travel to and from their capital in Ayacucho (Bélisle and Covey 2010). If this were the case, we might see more Wari influence in the Xaquixaguana region than in other parts of Cuzco. The most direct evidence for the use of this road by the Wari would be the presence of Wari material culture (and perhaps Wari architecture in the form of small administrative installations or colonies) along this route, as well as significant changes in Middle Horizon settlement patterns in Xaquixaguana.

The survey of 600 km² in the Xaquixaguana region identified 105 EIP/Middle Horizon and Araway components. Most of these sites were unknown to archaeologists because very little work had been undertaken on this period before our systematic survey. No large settlement of that era had been identified, despite unverified rumors of Wari sites in the area (e.g., Glowacki 1996:78). Some fragments of Wari pottery displayed in the museum of the Casa Garcilaso in the city of Cuzco (Bauer 1999:63) are reportedly from the Plain of Anta (the southern part of the Xaquixaguana region), but no specific information is given on the exact provenience of these vessels.

Before our survey, most known sites in Xaquixaguana were Inca, and archaeological work at those sites is still generally dedicated to reconstruction for tourism (e.g., Chinchero, Moray) (e.g., Alcina Franch et al. 1976; Wright, Wright, and Zegarra 2011). A few Formative settlements had been excavated by the National Institute of Culture—for example, the site of Bandoján excavated in 1994 (Bonnett Medina 1994)—but the EIP/Middle Horizon remained largely unknown in this region.

Disruption of Formative Settlement Patterns in the Xaquixaguana Region

We identified 71 EIP/Middle Horizon sites in Xaquixaguana based on the presence of Qotakalli, Muyu Urqu, Waru, and local pottery styles on the surface. The majority of these sites (49/71 or 69%) did not contain Formative pottery, suggesting a significant departure from the Formative period settlement pattern starting around AD 200. The adoption of new pottery styles at the beginning of the EIP coincided with new site locations and the abandonment of some areas (Figs. 6.2, 6.3). Higher-altitude areas have high abandonment rates, suggesting important economic changes among the Xaquixaguana communities at the beginning of the EIP. For example, the region around Lake Huaypo—heavily occupied during the Formative—was completely abandoned during the EIP/Middle Horizon. This left an area of 5.5 km from north to south virtually depopulated, and EIP/Middle Horizon settlements were established in two clusters to the north and south of this abandoned area (see Fig. 6.3).

The northern cluster contains 26 small sites (most are less than 1 ha) concentrated around the town of Maras (Table 6.1).

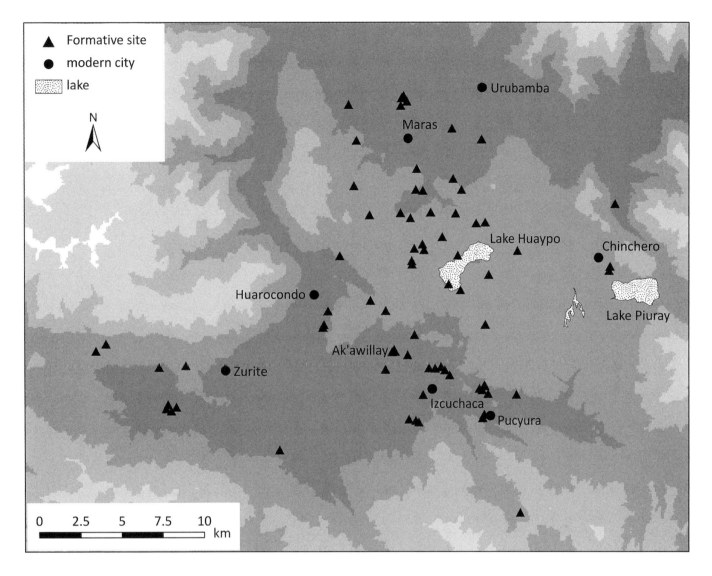

Figure 6.2. Distribution of Formative sites in the Xaquixaguana region.

This cluster represents a little over one-third of all EIP/Middle Horizon sites in Xaquixaguana, but only 19% of settled area for this period. Settlements that contained a Formative component (23%) indicate continuity of occupation at sites already established in lower areas. However, most EIP/Middle Horizon settlements contained no Formative pottery, suggesting a widespread abandonment of higher Late Formative sites.

The southern cluster lies around the towns of Pucyura, Izcuchaca, and Zurite and around Lake Piuray south of Chinchero. It contains 45 sites that comprise 81% of the total EIP/Middle Horizon settled area in Xaquixaguana. The southern cluster was more heavily occupied than the northern cluster, presumably because of longstanding villages in the Izcuchaca area that continued to grow during the EIP/Middle Horizon and whose

population established new villages on the nearby valley-bottom farming lands. Sites in the southern cluster show more settlement continuity with the Formative than those in the northern cluster; about one-third of EIP/Middle Horizon sites contained a Formative component, indicating continuity of occupation at sites established at lower altitudes.

Settlement Ecology

EIP/Middle Horizon sites were located in three ecological zones: (1) the *kichwa,* which generally includes lands below 3500 m used for maize agriculture; (2) the *suni,* comprising lands between 3500 and 3850 m where tubers, quinoa, kañiwa, kiwicha (amaranth), and tarwi (lupine) are cultivated; and (3)

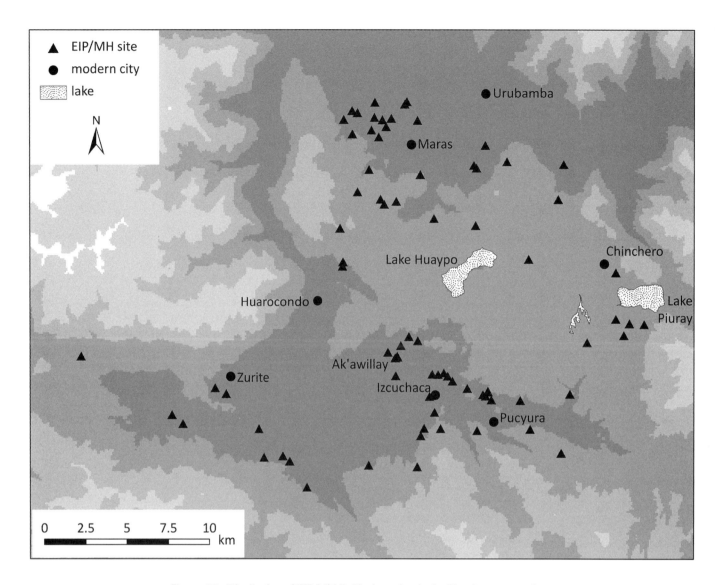

Figure 6.3. Distribution of EIP/Middle Horizon sites in the Xaquixaguana region.

the *puna,* an area of high (>3850 m) grassland typically reserved for camelid herding and limited tuber and quinoa horticulture. Only one EIP/Middle Horizon settlement was in the puna, but the suni and particularly the kichwa were more heavily occupied.

As in the Cuzco Basin and Sacred Valley, the EIP/Middle Horizon ecological pattern in the Xaquixaguana region represents a significant change from the Formative, especially in the southern cluster (Table 6.2). During the Formative, approximately half of the sites and settled area were in the kichwa and half in the suni, suggesting that populations relied on a mixed economy including maize, tubers, and quinoa. The recent analysis of botanical remains from excavated contexts at the Late Formative village of Yuthu (500–200 BC) confirms that maize, tubers, quinoa, and other suni plants were consumed, although quinoa clearly dominated the assemblage (Davis 2011:14). Sediment records from

the nearby Lake Huaypo also indicate that maize was exploited since the Middle Formative (1500–500 BC), along with quinoa (Mosblech et al. 2012).

In the EIP/Middle Horizon, more than two-thirds (69%) of settled area was in the kichwa; the suni was considerably less occupied. This trend is more apparent in the southern cluster, where 72% of EIP/Middle Horizon settled area was found in the kichwa ecological zone. Most Formative suni sites (81%) were abandoned, while many Formative sites in the kichwa (46%) remained occupied. This marked change in settlement ecology presumably represents changes in the economy, although botanical evidence from excavated contexts is needed to confirm these. Beginning in the EIP, local populations seem to have relied more heavily on maize. New vessel shapes recovered from recently excavated contexts at the large site of Ak'awillay suggest changes in consumption practices starting in the EIP; these changes likely involved increased chicha (maize beer) consumption (Bélisle 2011). The abandonment of the area around Lake Huaypo, a suni zone, was probably an effort to redirect economic activities toward maize agriculture. As has been noted in the Cuzco Basin and Sacred Valley, the settlement shift to maize-producing lands occurred *before* the Wari colonized the Cuzco region.

Site location represents another departure from the Formative period. In the EIP/Middle Horizon, less settled area in the southern cluster was on hilltops and more was on the valley floor or plain (Table 6.3). This change in site location coincides with the heavier reliance on the kichwa zone starting in the EIP. Interestingly, the northern cluster does not show this trend. The reduced proportion of settled hilltops in the southern cluster during the EIP/Middle Horizon suggests that sites were chosen for their agricultural potential rather than their visibility or defensive qualities. Like the shift to kichwa lands, movement away from hilltops in the EIP and Middle Horizon presumably reflects changes in economic priorities. Defense does not seem to have been a concern for local populations. The regional center based at the village of Ak'awillay could have mediated disputes and reduced intercommunity conflicts, contributing to a safer environment for social and economic interactions.

Some differences existed between the northern and southern clusters during the EIP/Middle Horizon, including the importance of the kichwa zone and the valley floor/plain. Another difference between the northern and southern clusters corresponded to the type of agriculture practiced. Sites in the northern cluster were farther from modern water sources—at an average distance of 330 m (median 250 m)—and agriculture probably depended on rainfall (although salinity is also a problem with water sources in the area). In the southern cluster, more sites were located in close proximity to water resources and the mean distance to water is only 140 m (median 100 m), suggesting that agriculture relied on both small irrigation works and rainfall. Such irrigation works probably supplied enough water for the cultivation of maize, permitting larger populations to rely on these maize lands than those living in the northern cluster.

Settlement Hierarchy

EIP/Middle Horizon sites in the northern cluster did not form a site size hierarchy, nor was there a single dominant site; instead, the settlement pattern is one of small, dispersed hamlets, most of them smaller than 1 ha. In contrast, the EIP/Middle Horizon sites of the southern cluster were organized in a 2-tier settlement hierarchy. At the top of this settlement hierarchy was the 10 ha village of Ak'awillay, the largest EIP/Middle Horizon site in Cuzco outside the

Lucre Basin. The remaining sites of the southern cluster were small villages and hamlets. Ak'awillay is located at an elevation of 3480 m on a low hill overlooking the Xaquixaguana Plain. The site was first settled in the Late Formative (ca. 200 BC–AD 200) and continued to be occupied through the Inca period. Because it is the largest local EIP/Middle Horizon site registered on surveys outside the Wari colony, Ak'awillay and its surrounding settlements are an excellent test case for assessing Wari state influence.

As is true for other EIP/Middle Horizon sites in the area, no architecture is exposed on the surface of Ak'awillay today. Presently, the communities of Piñanccay, Mosoq Llaqta, and Chakakurki use the lands where the site is located to grow tubers, quinoa, and Old World crops (broad beans, peas, wheat, and barley). There is no irrigation canal on the site and agriculture depends on rainfall. Once the crops are harvested, the fields are used to pasture animals. Today maize is

Table 6.1. Distribution of EIP/Middle Horizon sites by cluster.

	# Sites	% Sites	% Settled Area	% Sites with Formative Component
northern cluster	26	36.6	18.8*	23.1
southern cluster	45	63.4	81.2	35.6
total	71	100	100	–

*The size of one EIP/Middle Horizon site could not be calculated.

Table 6.2. Distribution of sites by ecological zone and period.

	Kichwa (<3500 m)		Suni (3500–3850 m)		Puna (>3850 m)	
	% sites	% area	% sites	% area	% sites	% area
Formative	50.0	49.3	50.0	50.7	0	0
EIP/MH						
northern cluster	46.2	53.8	50.0	43.0	3.8	3.2
southern cluster*	52.3	72.2	47.7	27.8	0	0
all	50	68.8	48.6	30.6	1.4	0.6

*The elevation of one site could not be calculated.

Table 6.3. Distribution of sites by location and period.

	Hilltop		Hillside		Valley Floor/Plain	
	% sites	% area	% sites	% area	% sites	% area
Formative	20.3	27.2	50.0	31.7	29.7	41.1
EIP/MH						
northern cluster	26.9	22.1	46.2	45.4	26.9	32.5
southern cluster	37.8	15.0	37.8	24.4	24.4	60.6
all	33.8	16.4	40.8	28.3	25.4	55.3

not grown on Ak'awillay because of its elevation (higher risk of freezing) and the lack of irrigation canals; it is grown around the nearby village of Piñanccay at approximately 3360–3400 m using modern and prehispanic canals.

Using data from 80 intensive collection units and various test pits throughout the site, I defined the distribution of ceramic styles and the site's approximate boundaries. My recent excavations at Ak'awillay recovered the remains of Formative, EIP, and Middle Horizon houses between one and two meters below the actual surface (Bélisle 2011; Bélisle and Covey 2010). A Middle Horizon public building, cemetery, and outdoor kitchen complete the inventory of excavated structures at the site. Preliminary evidence for social inequality during the Middle Horizon includes differences in mortuary treatment, material culture, and domestic architecture throughout the site.

Data on settlement hierarchy suggest that the southern cluster of the Xaquixaguana region was dominated by the village of Ak'awillay during the EIP and Middle Horizon. The site was surrounded by kichwa lands and valley bottoms where maize could be cultivated. Ak'awillay is also the site with the greatest ceramic diversity in the Xaquixaguana region as a whole, suggesting that people living there interacted and exchanged regularly with the people living in the nearby Cuzco Basin.

Regional Distribution of Ceramic Styles

Apart from locally produced ceramics, Qotakalli was the most common EIP/Middle Horizon pottery style in the Xaquixaguana region (Table 6.4). It was present at more sites than Muyu Urqu and Waru, and Qotakalli components were always larger than other EIP/Middle Horizon components. In the northern cluster, Muyu Urqu ceramics were completely absent while Waru was present only at a site in the southernmost part of the cluster, closest to Ak'awillay. These data suggest that people living in the northern cluster participated in a regional exchange network involving the Cuzco Basin and perhaps Ak'awillay during the EIP/Middle Horizon, although to a lesser extent than people living in the southern cluster.

There is more ceramic diversity in the southern cluster, suggesting a more lively participation in regional exchange networks by people living at and around Ak'awillay. The village of Ak'awillay included large Qotakalli, Muyu Urqu, and Waru components. The Qotakalli component at other sites was correlated with these sites' distance from Ak'awillay; in other words, the sites closest to Ak'awillay (in the southeastern part of the cluster) had more Qotakalli pottery, regardless of size (Fig. 6.4). Sites with a small Qotakalli component rarely contained other EIP/Middle Horizon styles and were dispersed throughout the cluster; settlements with a large Qotakalli component (close to Ak'awillay) often included Muyu Urqu and/or Waru pottery.

The spatial distribution of Qotakalli pottery in the southern cluster of the Xaquixaguana region and its abundance at Ak'awillay could suggest that some residents of Ak'awillay obtained Qotakalli pottery directly from the Cuzco Basin and

redistributed it throughout the area. Based on the regional settlement hierarchy and the excavations at Ak'awillay, high-status individuals from this site could also have obtained Muyu Urqu and Waru pottery that they exchanged with or offered to people living close to Ak'awillay. These data indicate that there were regular exchanges linking the Cuzco Basin to the Xaquixaguana region during the EIP and the Middle Horizon; this exchange network was well developed *before* the arrival of the Wari in Cuzco.

Wari Influence in the Xaquixaguana Region

We identified 34 Araway components in the Xaquixaguana region based on the presence of Araway pottery on the surface. The presence of this Wari-inspired pottery at Xaquixaguana sites provides a measure of Wari influence on existing settlements in the area. None of the Xaquixaguana sites have standing Wari architecture (or any architecture on the surface), and the overall paucity of Wari pottery (at only 2 sites) argues against the identification of a secondary Wari administrative center in the area.

Approximately 80% of Araway settled area was in the southern cluster (Table 6.5), echoing the heavier occupation of this area and the local preference for kichwa lands during the EIP/Middle Horizon (Fig. 6.5). The prevalence of sites in the southern cluster may also reflect proximity to the production center of Araway pottery in the Cuzco Basin, whereas sites in the northern cluster were farther away and might have procured Araway pottery less often. In the northern cluster, 6 small Araway components (40%) co-occurred with LIP components but no other EIP/Middle Horizon styles, suggesting that almost half of the sites with Araway pottery represent late Middle Horizon settlement shifts. As in the Sacred Valley, these sites were established in locations that would later hold large LIP settlements.

Settlement Ecology

Like the EIP/Middle Horizon sites, most Araway components were in the kichwa ecological zone (Table 6.6). Araway pottery was found even more often in the kichwa than other components (compare with Table 6.2). This might suggest that maize cultivated in the kichwa zone became more important through time and that sites occupied throughout the Middle Horizon were more often located close to kichwa lands than before. This trend in

Table 6.4. Distribution of EIP/Middle Horizon sites (%) by presence of pottery styles and cluster.

	Qotakalli	Muyu Urqu	Waru	Local
northern cluster	69.2	0	3.8	73.1
southern cluster	68.9	37.8	20.0	86.7

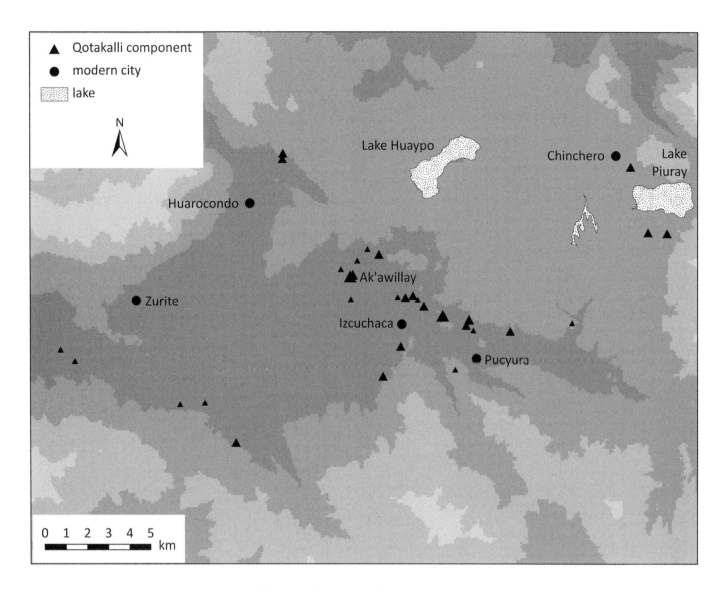

Figure 6.4. Distribution of Qotakalli components in the southern cluster of the Xaquixaguana region. The size of the triangle corresponds to the size of the Qotakalli component.

Table 6.5. Distribution of Araway components and settled area by cluster.

	# Sites	% Sites	% Settled Area
northern cluster*	15	44.1	20.2
southern cluster	19	55.9	79.8
total	34	100	100

*The size of one Araway component could not be calculated.

Table 6.6. Distribution of Araway components by ecological zone and cluster.

	Kichwa (<3500 m)		Suni (3500–3850 m)		Puna (>3850 m)	
	% sites	% area	% sites	% area	% sites	% area
northern cluster	64.3	73.3	35.7	26.7	0	0
southern cluster*	63.2	84.2	36.8	15.8	0	0

*The elevation of one site could not be calculated.

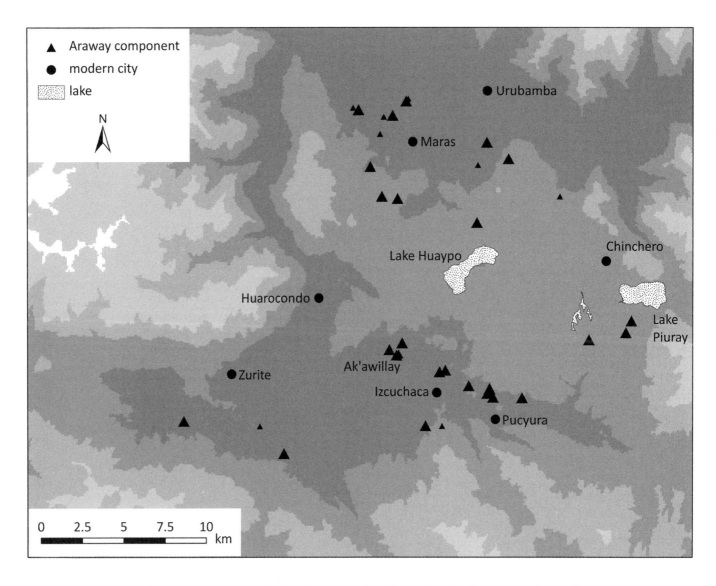

Figure 6.5. Distribution of Araway components in the Xaquixaguana region. The smaller triangles correspond to small Araway components at large LIP sites.

the increasing importance of maize through time has also been observed from excavated contexts at Ak'awillay (Bélisle 2011). There, starting in the EIP, new shapes of bowls and cups suggest new consumption practices, likely involving chicha; these bowls and cups became more popular in the Middle Horizon, which coincided with the construction of a public building where feasts could have been conducted. Interestingly, large LIP sites around the town of Maras (northern cluster) were situated in an area suitable for valley-bottom hydraulic agriculture, which may also reflect the increasing importance of maize through time (see Covey in this volume).

As with the EIP/Middle Horizon sites, Araway components were not chosen for their defensive properties (that hilltops naturally provide) but for their economic potential (Table 6.7; compare with Table 6.3). The majority of Araway components (like the other EIP/Middle Horizon components) were located on the valley floor or plain. In the northern cluster, a heavier emphasis was placed on the valley floor/plain for Araway components than for other EIP/Middle Horizon components. Instead of representing a departure from EIP settlement ecology, the importance of the valley floor for Araway components appears to represent an increasing reliance on plain agriculture during the late Middle Horizon and the LIP. In the southern cluster, the importance of the valley floor/plain is similar for Araway and other EIP/Middle Horizon components, suggesting overall stability in site location.

Table 6.7. Distribution of Araway components by location.

	Hilltop		Hillside		Valley Floor/Plain	
	% sites	% area	% sites	% area	% sites	% area
northern cluster	26.7	24.9	26.7	19.0	46.6	56.1
southern cluster	42.1	21.6	36.8	10.5	21.1	67.9

Table 6.8. Distribution of Araway components by co-occurrence of other EIP/Middle Horizon components and cluster.

	% Sites with Qotakalli Component	% Sites with Muyu Urqu Component	% Sites with Waru Component
northern cluster	46.7	0	0
southern cluster	73.7	47.4	21.1

The same variations in the type of agriculture practiced in the northern and southern clusters during the the EIP/Middle Horizon sites were observed for Araway components. Northern Araway components were farther from water sources (mean 430 m, median 300 m) than were southern Araway components (mean 150 m, median 100 m). As the other EIP/Middle Horizon components already suggested, agriculture at the northern sites probably relied on rainfall whereas it relied on both rainfall and small irrigation infrastructure in the southern cluster. It is important to note that the sites that are the farthest away from water sources are not located on hilltops but are on the valley floor, and thus proximity to water was not sacrificed for the visibility and defense of hilltops. Raiding and other conflicts do not appear to have been the primary concern for local groups during the Middle Horizon.

Settlement Hierarchy

As with the other EIP/Middle Horizon components, Araway components in the northern cluster appeared at small, dispersed settlements (most sites were less than 1 ha), suggesting overall stability of the settlement hierarchy. In the southern cluster, Araway components appeared at the large site of Ak'awillay and at a series of smaller villages and hamlets (most less than 1 ha). The emergence of a regional settlement hierarchy in the southern cluster was not a response to Wari colonization—Ak'awillay was already at the top of this hierarchy at the beginning of the EIP.

My recent excavations at Ak'awillay show significant continuity in household architecture, burial patterns, and ceramic distribution from the pre-Wari period to the Middle Horizon (Bélisle 2011; Bélisle and Covey 2010). Ak'awillay did not have a strong Wari affiliation; Wari pottery was very rare (less than 1% of the decorated pottery assemblage), Araway was present but uncommon, and Quispisisa obsidian (presumably obtained from the Wari colonists in Cuzco or from down-the-line exchange with Cuzco Basin groups in contact with Wari colonists) represented less than 10% of the sourced obsidian from Middle Horizon contexts. No defensive infrastructure was built at the site in the Middle Horizon, suggesting that residents did not interpret Wari colonization of other parts of the Cuzco region as a military threat.

Regional Distribution of Ceramic Styles

Many Araway components were found at sites with Qotakalli components, especially in the southern cluster (Table 6.8, Fig. 6.6). Close to half of the Araway components there co-occurred with Muyu Urqu and 21% with Waru. The absence of Muyu Urqu and Waru pottery at Araway components in the northern cluster reflects the quasi-absence of these latter styles in this area rather than the lack of co-occurrence of these three styles.

In the northern cluster, sites with the smallest Araway components were the farthest from the Cuzco Basin (in the northernmost part of the cluster), whereas sites with the most Araway pottery were closer to the Cuzco Basin (in the southern and eastern portions of the cluster). The only site with Wari pottery in the northern cluster is the closest to Ak'awillay, suggesting that people living at that site might have procured a Wari pot from the people of Ak'awillay rather than from the Wari colonists.

In the southern cluster, sites with the largest Araway components were close to Ak'awillay, which is the only site of the area with Wari pottery in its surface collections. As is true for Qotakalli, Muyu Urqu, and Waru pottery, the distribution of Araway ceramics in the southern cluster suggests that residents of Ak'awillay could have obtained pottery from the Cuzco Basin and then exchanged it with those living at smaller settlements in the area. Regular exchange continued between the Xaquixaguana region and the Cuzco Basin during the Middle Horizon, and the presence of Wari colonists in Lucre and Huaro did not disrupt regional exchange networks that had been in place since at least the EIP in the Cuzco region.

Impact of Wari Colonization on the Xaquixaguana Region

Settlement pattern data from the Xaquixaguana region indicate that overall Wari impact was minimal on local populations. The presence of Wari colonists in the Lucre and Huaro Basins did not affect local political life. No Wari architecture and no sites that could be interpreted as colonies, way stations, or an administrative center were identified in the region. Instead, XPAS research documented strong continuity of settlement clustering and hierarchy through time; most Araway components were

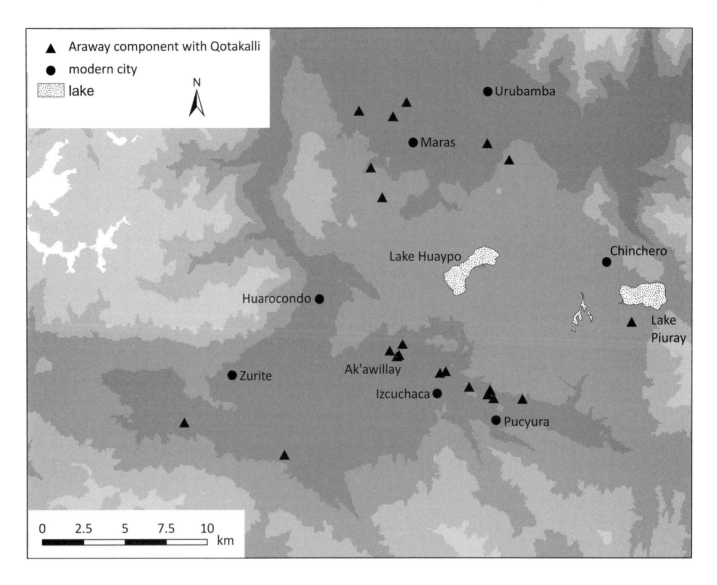

Figure 6.6. Distribution of Araway components that contain Qotakalli pottery in the Xaquixaguana region.

part of sites already occupied in the EIP and the local center of Ak'awillay did not adopt a strong Wari cultural affiliation. If the Wari had a strong impact on the Xaquixaguana region, we would expect disruptive Middle Horizon settlement patterns in the area closest to the Lucre Basin and Huaro Valley, namely, the southern cluster. Survey data show that this was not the case.

The Wari had limited economic influence on the populations in the Xaquixaguana region. There is strong continuity of settlement ecology between the EIP and later periods. The settlement shift to lower maize-producing lands occurred *before* the Wari colonized the Cuzco region, as has been reported for the Cuzco Basin and Sacred Valley. There is no evidence of intensification of agricultural production in the Middle Horizon, as would be expected if Wari colonists were regularly exacting tribute from

the populations of the Xaquixaguana region in the form of agricultural produce. Small irrigation works were probably developed in the southern part of the Xaquixaguana region to support maize cultivation in the kichwa zone, but such infrastructure was developed *before* the Wari arrived in Cuzco. Exchange networks between the Xaquixaguana region and the Cuzco Basin—that were already in place since at least the EIP—were not interrupted by the Wari. The limited distribution of Wari goods (pottery and obsidian) in Xaquixaguana is the only evidence of Wari impact on the local economy.

Everyday life and social practices are other aspects that were relatively untouched by Wari colonists. Site locations were constant through time, suggesting no major change in subsistence practices. The production, procurement, and consumption of

Qotakalli, Muyu Urqu, and Waru pottery also continued through time. Some residents at Ak'awillay obtained Araway pottery from the Cuzco Basin and possibly exchanged it with people living nearby during the Middle Horizon, but they appear to have done the same with Qotakalli, Muyu Urqu, and Waru pottery. It is difficult at the moment to evaluate whether the Wari had a religious impact on the Xaquixaguana region. Unlike Paruro and the Sacred Valley, survey in Xaquixaguana did not identify any shrine or location where the Wari could have been involved in feasts or ceremonies. Excavation data from Ak'awillay suggest continuity of local ritual practices through time (Bélisle 2011). There are no perceptible changes in local identities that can be attributed directly to Wari colonization—influence from the Cuzco Basin was much stronger in the Xaquixaguana region than was influence from the Wari colonies that lay farther to the southeast.

Defense was not a concern for local groups, indicating that Wari colonists had no military impact on the Xaquixaguana region. Local populations did not build forts or any other defensive infrastructure. The shift away from hilltops as a response to a change in economic priorities was first seen in the EIP; sites were not chosen for their defensive potential but for their proximity to maize-producing lands on valley floors or plains.

Conclusions

Survey data from the Xaquixaguana region indicate that Wari impact was minimal. Local populations continued to live at the same sites and farm the same lands as they had for centuries. Interaction with Wari colonists was limited, non-asymmetrical, and probably indirect through the elites of the Cuzco Basin. Xaquixaguana groups might have sporadically participated in Wari rituals and building projects in the Lucre Basin and Huaro Valley in exchange for food and drink, although if they did so, such participation did not alter their subsistence economies, increase their local use of Wari material culture, or lead to the adoption of Wari ideological values. Evidence from our survey indicates that the Wari state did not control the Xaquixaguana region.

For the local communities of the Xaquixaguana region, the Middle Horizon was a period of increased opportunities for exchange: in addition to products from the Cuzco Basin, they obtained new items of Wari manufacture (pottery) and objects whose distribution was managed by the Wari (Quispisisa obsidian and perhaps coca). Interactions with Wari colonists did not disrupt regional exchange networks, and the possession of Wari material culture did not alter local identities.

As evidence from systematic surveys accumulates in the Cuzco region, it becomes clearer that Wari control in Cuzco was limited to the areas immediately surrounding their major constructions in the Lucre Basin and Huaro Valley (Covey et al. 2013). A focus on Wari sites alone has led some to conclude that the Wari transformed the Cuzco region as an imperial province during the Middle Horizon (e.g., Glowacki and McEwan 2001).

The size of Pikillacta suggests that this might have been the original plan for the Wari, but the lack of occupation in many sectors of the site and survey data from outside the Lucre Basin and Huaro Valley indicate that this plan was never implemented successfully. The Wari established a small colony to the southeast of Cuzco, but failed at controlling the territory, people, and resources of the whole region. Like many other early states worldwide, the Wari appear to have established a presence in Cuzco that had little impact on local communities. The Wari colonies in the Cuzco region disintegrated at the onset of the Late Intermediate period, a time of increasing regional conflict.

References Cited

Alcina Franch, José, Miguel Rivera, Jesús Galván, María Carmen García Palacios, Balbina Martínez-Caviro, Luis J. Ramos, and Tito Varela
1976   *Arqueología de Chinchero. 2. Cerámica y otros materiales.* Madrid: Ministerio de Asuntos Exteriores.

Barreda Murillo, Luis
1982   Asentamiento Humano de los Qotakalli del Cuzco. In *Arqueología de Cuzco*, edited by Italo Oberti Rodríguez, pp. 13–21. Cusco, Peru: Instituto Nacional de Cultura.

Bauer, Brian S.
1989   Muyu Orqo y Ccoipa: Dos nuevos tipos de cerámica para la región del Cusco. *Revista Andina* 7(2):537–42.
1999   *The Early Ceramics of the Inca Heartland.* Fieldiana Anthropology, n.s., 31. Chicago: Field Museum of Natural History.
2004   *Ancient Cuzco: Heartland of the Inca.* Austin: University of Texas Press.

Bauer, Brian S., and Bradford M. Jones
2003   *Early Intermediate and Middle Horizon Ceramic Styles of the Cuzco Valley.* Fieldiana Anthropology, n.s., 34. Chicago: Field Museum of Natural History.

Bélisle, Véronique
2011   Ak'awillay: Wari State Expansion and Household Change in Cusco, Peru (AD 600–1000). PhD dissertation, Department of Anthropology, University of Michigan, Ann Arbor.

Bélisle, Véronique, and R. Alan Covey
2010   Local settlement continuity and Wari impact in Middle Horizon Cusco. In *Beyond Wari Walls: Regional Perspectives on Middle Horizon Peru*, edited by Justin Jennings, pp. 78–95. Albuquerque: University of New Mexico Press.

Bergh, Susan E. (editor)
2012   *Wari: Lords of the Ancient Andes.* New York: Thames and Hudson.

Bonnett Medina, Percy G.
1994   *Informe Final: Proyecto de Investigación Arqueológica Bandojan-Anta.* Cusco, Peru: Instituto Nacional de Cultura.

Covey, R. Alan
2006   *How the Incas Built Their Heartland: State Formation and the Innovation of Imperial Strategies in the Sacred Valley, Peru.* Ann Arbor: University of Michigan Press.

Covey, R. Alan, Brian S. Bauer, Véronique Bélisle, and Lia Tsesmeli
2013   Regional perspectives on Wari state influence in Cusco, Peru (c. AD 600–1000). *Journal of Anthropological Archaeology* 32(4):538–52.

Davis, Allison R.
2011   *Yuthu: Community and Ritual in an Early Andean Village.* Memoirs, no. 50. Ann Arbor: Museum of Anthropology, University of Michigan.

Espinoza Martínez, Hector
1983   Evidencia cultural del Horizonte Medio (Wari) Aqomoqo-Cusco. In *Arqueología Andina*, edited by Arminda M. Gibaja Oviedo, pp. 16–22. Cusco, Peru: Instituto Nacional de Cultura.

Glowacki, Mary
1996   The Wari Occupation of the Southern Highlands of Peru: A Ceramic Perspective from the Site of Pikillacta. PhD dissertation, Department of Anthropology, Brandeis University, Massachusetts.
2002   The Huaro archaeological site complex: Rethinking the Huari occupation of Cuzco. In *Andean Archaeology I: Variations of Sociopolitical Organization*, edited by William H. Isbell and Helaine Silverman, pp. 267–85. New York: Kluwer Academic/Plenum Publishers.
2005a Pottery from Pikillacta. In *Pikillacta: The Wari Empire in Cuzco*, edited by Gordon F. McEwan, pp. 101–14. Iowa City: University of Iowa Press.
2005b Dating Pikillacta. In *Pikillacta: The Wari Empire in Cuzco*, edited by Gordon F. McEwan, pp. 115–24. Iowa City: University of Iowa Press.

Glowacki, Mary, and Gordon F. McEwan
2001   Pikillacta, Huaro y la gran región del Cuzco: Nuevas interpretaciones de la ocupación wari en la sierra sur. In *Huari y Tiwanaku: Modelos vs. Evidencias*, edited by Peter Kaulicke and William H. Isbell, pp. 31–49. Boletín de Arqueología PUCP no. 5. Lima: Fondo Editorial de la Pontificia Universidad Católica del Perú.

Hyslop, John
1984   *The Inka Road System.* Orlando: Academic Press.

Isbell, William H.
1987   State origins in the Ayacucho Valley, central highlands, Peru. In *The Origins and Development of the Andean State*, edited by Jonathan Haas, Shelia Pozorski, and Thomas Pozorski, pp. 83–90. Cambridge: Cambridge University Press.
1989   Honcopampa: Was it a Huari administrative centre? In *The Nature of Wari: A Reappraisal of the Middle Horizon Period in Peru*, edited by R. Michael Czwarno, Frank M. Meddens, and Alexandra Morgan, pp. 98–114. BAR International Series 525. Oxford: British Archaeological Reports.
1997   Reconstructing Huari: A cultural chronology for the capital city. In *Emergence and Change in Early Urban Societies*, edited by Linda Manzanilla, pp. 181–227. New York: Plenum Press.
2001   Repensando el Horizonte Medio: El Caso de Conchopata, Ayacucho, Perú. In *Huari y Tiwanaku: Modelos vs. Evidencias, Primera Parte*, edited by Peter Kaulicke and William H. Isbell, pp. 9–68. Boletín de Arqueología PUCP no. 4. Lima: Fondo Editorial de la Pontificia Universidad Católica del Perú.

Isbell, William H., and Gordon F. McEwan
1991   A history of Huari studies and introduction to current interpretations. In *Huari Administrative Structure: Prehistoric Monumental Architecture and State Government*, edited by William H. Isbell and Gordon F. McEwan, pp. 1–17. Washington, D.C.: Dumbarton Oaks Research Library and Collection.

Isbell, William H., and Katharina J. Schreiber
1978   Was Huari a state? *American Antiquity* 43:372–89.

Lumbreras, Luis
1974   *The Peoples and Cultures of Ancient Peru.* Washington, D.C.: Smithsonian Institution Press.

Matos Mendieta, Ramiro
1968   Wari-Willka, Santuario Wanka en el Mantaro. *Cantuta* 2:116–27.

McEwan, Gordon F.
1989   The Wari empire in the southern Peruvian highlands: A view from the provinces. In *The Nature of Wari: A Reappraisal of the Middle Horizon Period in Peru*, edited by R. Michael Czwarno, Frank M. Meddens, and Alexandra Morgan, pp. 53–71. BAR International Series 525. Oxford: British Archaeological Reports.
1991   Investigations at the Pikillacta site: A provincial Huari center in the Valley of Cuzco. In *Huari Administrative Structure: Prehistoric Monumental Architecture and State Government*, edited by William H. Isbell and Gordon F. McEwan, pp. 93–119. Washington, D.C.: Dumbarton Oaks Research Library and Collection.

McEwan, Gordon (editor)
2005   *Pikillacta: The Wari Empire in Cuzco*. Iowa City: University
        of Iowa Press.

Menzel, Dorothy
1964   Style and time in the Middle Horizon. *Ñawpa Pacha* 2:1–105.
1968   New data on the Huari empire in Middle Horizon epoch 2A.
        Ñawpa Pacha 6:47–114.

Montoya, Eduardo, Mary Glowacki, Julinho Zapata Rodríguez, and
Pablo Mendoza
2003   *Chemical Characterization of Archaeological Ceramics Using
        K0 Based INAA: A Study in the Production and Distribution of
        Middle Horizon Pottery from Cuzco, Peru*. Nuclear Analytical
        Techniques in Archaeological Investigations, Technical
        Reports Series no. 416. Vienna: International Atomic Energy
        Agency.
2009   Caracterización de cerámicos wari mediante análisis por
        activación neutrónica. *Revista de la Sociedad Química del
        Perú* 75:473–78.

Mosblech, Nicole A. Sublette, Alex Chepstow-Lusty, Bryan G. Valencia,
and Mark B. Bush
2012   Anthropogenic control of Late-Holocene landscapes in the
        Cuzco region, Peru. *The Holocene* 22(12):1361–72.

Nash, Donna J., and P. Ryan Williams
2009   Wari political organization: The southern periphery. In *Andean
        Civilization: A Tribute to Michael E. Moseley*, edited by Joyce
        Marcus and P. Ryan Williams, pp. 257–76. University of
        California, Los Angeles: Cotsen Institute of Archaeology.

Regal, Alberto
1936   *Los caminos del Inca en el antiguo Perú*. Lima, Peru:
        Sanmarti.

Rowe, John H.
1956   Archaeological explorations in southern Peru, 1954–1955.
        American Antiquity 22(2):135–50.

Schaedel, Richard P.
1993   Congruence of Horizon with polity: Huari and the Middle
        Horizon. In *Latin American Horizons*, edited by Don Stephen
        Rice, pp. 225–61. Washington, D.C.: Dumbarton Oaks Re-
        search Library and Collection.

Schreiber, Katharina
1984   Prehistoric roads in the Carahuarazo Valley, Peru. In
        *Current Archaeological Projects in the Central Andes: Some
        Approaches and Results*, edited by Ann Kendall, pp. 75–94.
        BAR International Series 210. Oxford: British Archaeological
        Reports.

1987a   Conquest and consolidation: A comparison of Wari and Inka
        occupations of a highland Peruvian Valley. *American Antiquity*
        52:266–84.
1987b   From state to empire: The expansion of Wari outside the
        Ayacucho Basin. In *The Origins and Development of the
        Andean State*, edited by Jonathan Haas, Shelia Pozorski,
        and Thomas Pozorski, pp. 91–96. Cambridge: Cambridge
        University Press.
1992   *Wari Imperialism in Middle Horizon Peru*. Anthropological
        Papers, no. 87. Ann Arbor: Museum of Anthropology,
        University of Michigan.
2001   The Wari empire of Middle Horizon Peru: The
        epistemological challenge of documenting an empire with-
        out documentary evidence. In *Empires: Perspectives from
        Archaeology and History*, edited by Susan E. Alcock, Terence
        N. D'Altroy, Kathleen D. Morrison, and Carla Sinopoli, pp.
        70–92. Cambridge: Cambridge University Press.

Torres Poblete, Nilo
1989   Sondeo arqueológico en Araway. Licenciatura tesis in
        Archaeology, Facultad de Ciencias Sociales, Universidad
        Nacional de San Antonio Abad del Cusco, Cusco, Peru.

Valdez, Lidio M., Katrina J. Bettcher, and J. Ernesto Valdez
2002   New Wari mortuary structures in the Ayacucho Valley, Peru.
        Journal of Anthropological Research 58:389–407.

Williams, P. Ryan, and Donna J. Nash
2002   Imperial interaction in the Andes: Huari and Tiwanaku at
        Cerro Baúl. In *Andean Archaeology I: Variations in Sociopo-
        litical Organization*, edited by William H. Isbell and Helaine
        Silverman, pp. 243–65. New York: Kluwer Academic/Plenum
        Press.

Wright, Kenneth R., Ruth M. Wright, and Alfredo Valencia Zegarra
2011   *Moray: Inca Engineering Mystery*. Reston, VA: ASCE Press.

Zapata Rodríguez, Julinho
1997   Arquitectura y contextos funerarios Wari en Batan Urqu,
        Cusco. In *La Muerte en el Antiguo Perú: Contextos y
        Conceptos Funerarios*, edited by Peter Kaulicke, pp. 165–206.
        Boletín de Arqueología PUCP no. 1. Lima: Fondo Editorial de
        la Pontificia Universidad Católica del Perú.
1998   Los cerros sagrados: Panorama del periodo Formativo en la
        cuenca del Vilcanota, Cuzco. In *Perspectivas regionales del
        Periodo Formativo en el Perú*, edited by Peter Kaulicke, pp.
        307–36. Boletín de Arqueología PUCP no. 2. Lima: Fondo
        Editorial de la Pontificia Universidad Católica del Perú.

Chapter 7: Local Developments in the Sacred Valley and Responses to Wari Colonization

R. Alan Covey

As discussed previously (Chapter 5), farming and herding groups established permanent villages in the Sacred Valley by the first millennium BC, and settlement patterns suggest the gradual emergence of settlement clusters and modest site hierarchies over time. Around AD 200, subsistence strategies and social groupings that had endured for as long as a millennium began to be abandoned in the Sacred Valley, in a shift toward new economic patterns and regional networks. Some scholars have identified the spread of maize agriculture and statecraft as major drivers for the social transformation of the Andean highlands in the first millennium (e.g., Heggarty and Beresford-Jones 2010), so it is important to note that the major settlement pattern changes in the Sacred Valley occurred long after the initial introduction of maize in the Cuzco region, and well before the arrival of Wari colonists around AD 600.

Beyond alteration to subsistence practices or changes in regional social organization, climate change presents another possible explanation for the high degree of settlement discontinuity in the Sacred Valley after AD 200. There are general trends toward colder and more arid conditions in parts of the Cuzco region around this time that should be taken into consideration (Chapter 2). The transition toward a new climatic regime might have affected upvalley areas to the north of the Sacred Valley—those nearest to the glaciated peaks separating the *kichwa* lands of

the valley from the humid lowlands lying beyond—encouraging herders and horticulturalists to resettle at lower elevations, in places where irrigation-based agriculture would be an effective subsistence strategy.

This chapter considers settlement pattern changes occurring during the Formative/Early Intermediate period (EIP) transition, as well as the evidence for subsequent social and economic changes occurring after around AD 600, when Wari colonies were established in the Lucre Basin and Huaro area (Fig. 7.1).

Ceramic Styles and Measures of Continuity and Change

In the Sacred Valley, the regional break with Formative settlement patterns is seen most clearly in the appearance of Qotakalli pottery, a Cuzco Basin style with markedly different attributes from the Chanapata wares and related styles that characterized the Formative period (see Bauer 1999). Almost three-quarters (40/54) of all Formative sites have no evidence of Qotakalli pottery. This figure includes virtually all sites larger than one hectare, suggesting that the absence of Qotakalli pottery reflects settlement disruption rather than uneven distribution patterns across contemporaneous settlements. The average size for sites with Formative pottery and no Qotakalli component (1.33 ha)

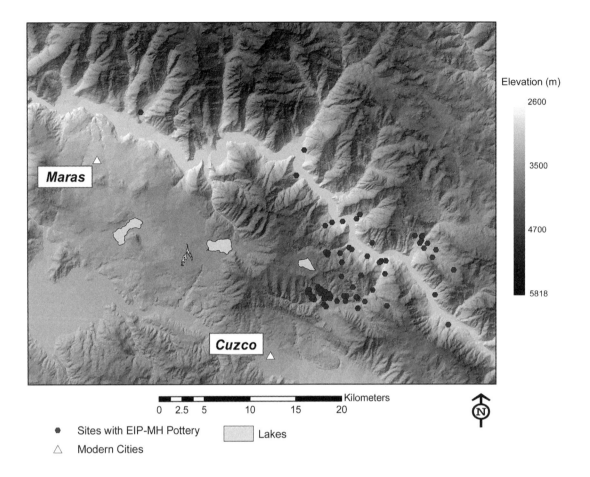

Figure 7.1. Map of Early Intermediate and Middle Horizon period (ca. AD 200–1000) sites in the Sacred Valley. Courtesy of L. Tsesmeli.

was more than twice the average for sites with both Formative and Qotakalli components (0.56 ha).

This general abandonment is more dramatic when looking only at the 20 sites that have Qotakalli pottery but no Araway, which, as discussed earlier (Chapters 1 and 6), represent our best approximation of EIP occupation. Of these, 17 (or 85%) were new sites with no previous Formative occupation. In other words, the appearance of a new decorative style in this part of the Cuzco region also corresponds closely to the regional reorganization of settlement and economy. As Bélisle's contribution to this volume demonstrates, this is not true for all parts of the Cuzco region. Because "Formative" pottery is known to continue in use in the EIP (Bélisle 2011; Bélisle and Covey 2010), what appears to be an abrupt shift may represent more gradual changes among groups to the north of the Vilcanota-Urubamba River, where interactions with Cuzco Basin populations are likely to have been less regular.

Recent excavations conducted by Bauer (Bauer 2004; Bauer and Jones 2003) and others (Bélisle and Covey 2010; Glowacki 2002; Glowacki and McEwan 2001) indicate that the Qotakalli style, which consists of black or black-and-red decorations on a white slip, was first produced in the Cuzco Basin during the

EIP, and continued to be made during the Middle Horizon (MH; AD 600–1000). Glowacki and McEwan (2001:33) speculate that the innovation of the Qotakalli style developed out of contacts between the pre-state Huarpa societies of the Ayacucho region and Cuzco populations, an interpretation that McEwan (2010) has recently broadened to account for the spread of both the Aymara and Quechua languages. Although interregional exchange relationships between Ayacucho, Nasca, Cuzco, and other regions might have intensified prior to the formation of the Wari state—and could have provided the impetus for local shifts in economic emphasis and ceramic production—it is important to remember that the Ayacucho region was not politically centralized at this time, and many neighboring areas lack Huarpa pottery (Bauer, Kellett, and Aráoz Silva 2010:57–64; Schreiber 1992:228ff; Vivanco and Valdez 1993), as is the case for the Cuzco region. It was not until after AD 600, when there was a centralized state in the Ayacucho region, that Wari populations established permanent colonies at a significant distance from their homeland.

During the period that Wari colonies occupied parts of the Cuzco region, a local Wari-influenced style called Araway was

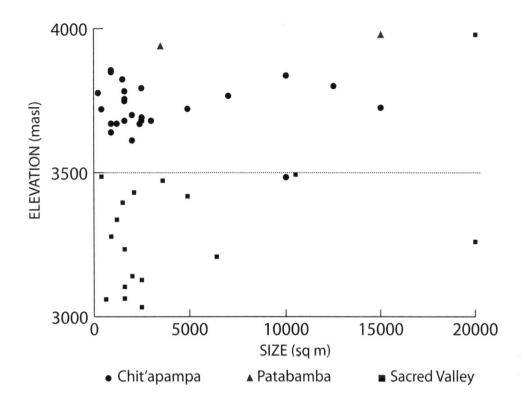

Figure 7.2. Scatterplot of estimated size and elevation for SVAP sites with Qotakalli pottery. Circles show sites lying in the Chit'apampa Basin and triangles show sites in the Patabamba area—within about a half-day's walk of the southern Cuzco Basin. These sites lie close to the lowest elevations in the Chit'apampa Basin, as do most Sacred Valley sites (*squares*), where the lowest elevations are closer to 3000 masl.

produced alongside the Qotakalli style (Bauer 2004; Covey et al. 2013; Glowacki and McEwan 2001:33). Because both styles are made on similar pastes and are coeval (Bauer 1999; Bauer and Jones 2003; Delgado et al. 2007; Montoya et al. 2003, 2009), it is often difficult to distinguish an EIP site from a MH occupation, particularly if decoration is not well preserved on the sherd. As has been noted elsewhere (Covey et al. 2013), there are characteristics regarding the regional distribution of Araway pottery that are noteworthy: (1) Araway is a relatively rare style at the monumental Wari site of Pikillacta (Glowacki 1996:201) and on the surface near other Wari colonial settlements; (2) Araway is distributed across a more restricted region than is Qotakalli; and (3) in some parts of the Hanan Cuzco region, Araway appears more frequently as a small component at large LIP sites than it does alongside Qotakalli or other MH styles. On the basis of these observations, Araway should be treated as a Wari-influenced style, but questions of Wari state hegemony or control must be tested rather than assumed. To evaluate the influence of nearby Wari settlements on the Sacred Valley, this chapter first describes the transition from Formative to EIP settlement patterns to develop a sense of existing conditions in

the SVAP region by AD 600, when the first Wari colonies were established in other parts of the Cuzco region. The evidence for Wari state influence is considered based on the distribution of state canons and changes to existing settlement patterns that can reasonably be attributed to external state policies.

Settlement Hierarchy

Qotakalli ceramics appear in the Sacred Valley at the same time as an apparent flattening of the local settlement hierarchy. Whereas the Formative period settlement pattern for the valley included areas where several small villages appear to have clustered around a nucleated village of 5 ha or more, these sites were abandoned after AD 200 in favor of a larger number of smaller sites located in a more dispersed pattern across the valley region. Figure 7.2 shows a scatterplot of elevation and estimated size for sites with Qotakalli components—these 46 sites indicate that the largest settlements were small villages of about 2 ha. More than 80% of Qotakalli sites (38/46) are smaller than a hectare, and are found near valley-bottom areas. In other parts of the central Andean highlands, regional projects have identified the

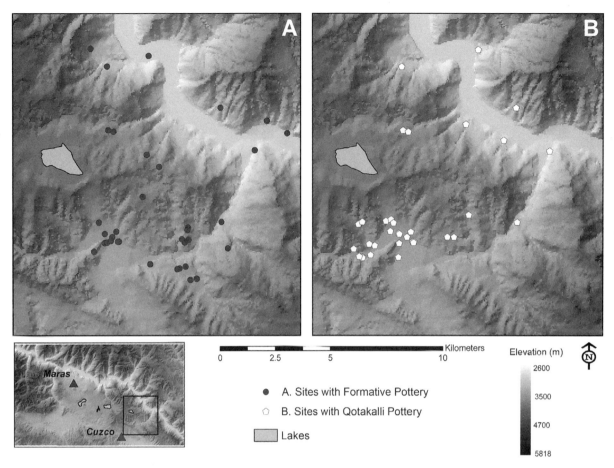

Figure 7.3. Distributions of Formative (*A*) and Qotakalli (*B*) pottery in the Chit'apampa Basin near Cuzco show the abandonment of large villages in favor of a more dispersed settlement pattern. Courtesy of L. Tsesmeli.

co-occurrence of polychrome pottery and widespread small kichwa settlements in the centuries prior to Wari state formation, with only a few larger settlements (cf. Bauer, Kellett, and Aráoz Silva 2010:57–64; Lumbreras 1974:134).

Figure 7.3 shows this shift in the Chit'apampa Basin, the part of the Sacred Valley survey closest to the Cuzco Basin. The general impression of a more dispersed settlement pattern appears to be accurate, although the sites under consideration are biased toward smaller settlements, and there were undoubtedly some larger communities established at this time. It is important to remember that comparisons of site size between the Formative and EIP are imperfect. Processes of erosion, reoccupation, and land use tend to obscure settlements occupied between AD 200 and 1000, whereas large Formative settlements can represent habitation of a millennium or more, frequently located on lands that were not heavily altered or occupied after AD 200. That is, EIP/MH sites might appear smaller based on surface remains, whereas Formative sites may appear larger, creating the impression of hierarchical differences over time.

Placing Qotakalli settlement patterns in a larger regional context, it is possible to see that the significant settlement shift seen in the Sacred Valley was not universal in the Cuzco region. In some areas, such as the Lucre Basin or the Anta Plain, prominent Formative sites located near valley-bottom farmlands have a Qotakalli component as well. The question of settlement continuity and regional hierarchy is less clear in the Cuzco Basin because of the potential for the city of Cuzco to obscure large sites (Bauer 2004:47ff; Bauer and Jones 2003), but as Bélisle notes in Chapter 6, the site of Ak'awillay is a large village on an order of size not seen in the Sacred Valley before the time of Inca territorial expansion. The site size hierarchy that is clearly in evidence in the Xaquixaguana region is absent in the Sacred Valley.

Settlement Ecology

The abandonment of the Formative village pattern in the Sacred Valley was part of an economic shift to different ecological zones, with an emphasis on new subsistence strategies (Table 7.1). Given the chronological data available for Qotakalli ceramic production, there is general consensus that this change was underway prior to AD 600 (Bauer 2004:48–50; Bauer and Jones 2003; McEwan 2010:260), when Wari colonization be-

Table 7.1. Ecological dimensions of the EIP/MH settlement shift.

Zone	Formative Sites	Settled Area	EIP/MH Sites	Settled Area
kichwa (< 3600 masl)	21	8.2 ha	31	12.2 ha
suni (3600–3800 masl)	22	20.6 ha	37	16.3 ha
puna (>3800 masl)	11	21.7 ha	15	11.3 ha

Note: Site counts include some multicomponent sites for which areas could not be calculated.

Table 7.2. Ecological designations for Qotakalli and Araway site locations.

Zone	Qotakalli	Araway
hilltop or mountain	9	10
ridge	2	4
steep valley slope	8	9
gentle valley slope	9	7
alluvial terrace	1	1
valley floor	9	7
agricultural terrace	1	0
gully	2	0
other	5	4

Table 7.3. Environmental zone and contemporary land use in the Sacred Valley.

	Qotakalli	Araway
Environmental Zone		
lower valley fields (*kichwa*)	4	3
pasture area (*yunlla*)	4	2
early planting area (*maway*)	14	8
mountain (*loma*)	8	8
tuber-producing zone (*suni*)	5	5
high grasslands (*puna*)	6	5
Crops Observed Near Sites		
none/fallow	18	18
maize	8	8
tubers	4	3
quinoa	1	2
beans	9	9
wheat	6	7
barley	4	5
other	8	6

Note: Up to three zone designations and entries for crop production could be made for each site.

gan to promote valley-bottom farming practices that relied on extensive irrigation networks (e.g., Valencia Zegarra 2005). As Table 7.1 shows, the overall site count increased for all three principal environmental zones, but the Formative focus on the *suni* and *puna* environments gave way in many areas to increased settlement in the kichwa zone. Generally, there appears to be a general shift away from mixed agropastoral resources near prominent ridge and hilltop sites toward more reliable valley-bottom resources. On average, new EIP/MH sites were found just over 200 m from the nearest water source, which was most often a small stream. By comparison, the Formative sites as a group were located at an average distance of more than 300 m from the nearest water source.

As Table 7.2 demonstrates, Qotakalli sites were infrequently found on mountaintops or ridges—roughly a quarter of sites were registered in these locations (11/46). More sites were located on the valley floor (9/46), on gentle slopes just above the valley floor (9/46), and on natural or constructed terraces (2/46). This pattern represents a significant shift from Formative site locations, but it does not necessarily represent reliance on intensive valley-bottom agriculture. Designations of indigenous environmental zones reflect a slight preference for early planting areas and kichwa agriculture, but there are still many sites in the upland tuber and herding areas (Table 7.3). Environmental and ecological designations for Qotakalli and Araway represent a

comparable diversity that appears to have been established in the EIP and continued in the MH. It should be noted that the Calca-Yanahuara survey encountered a general absence of EIP/MH components in valley-bottom areas where fertile, frost-free, and well-watered lands could be developed (Covey, Aráoz Silva, and Bauer 2008). These areas were ideal for intensive maize agriculture, but large-scale terrace and irrigation systems were not built until Inca times.

New sites with Qotakalli pottery appear to represent changing settlement preferences—from areas offering visibility, natural defense, and access to herding and tuber lands, to areas suitable for a variety of lower-elevation agricultural crops. The proximity of small settlements to water resources may indicate the establishment of modest irrigation systems, but sites are not found in proximity to large-scale hydraulic works. An increased focus on irrigated fields could mean that crops requiring a more reliable water supply (like maize) were cultivated more frequently, but this cannot be demonstrated with survey evidence alone. Given that the lowest elevations in the Chit'apampa Basin are above the ideal limits for low-risk maize cultivation, it seems reasonable to expect that local irrigation systems supported crops other than maize in many locations.

It is possible that the EIP settlement shift represents a response to colder and drier conditions, which would depress the elevation limits for existing crop regimes and encourage reliance on channeled water from larger catchment areas instead of rainfall. Survey work throughout the Sacred Valley did not encounter evidence for new EIP/MH settlements associated with hydraulic agricultural infrastructure near the floor of the Vilcanota-Urubamba Valley, even in the Calca-Yanahuara study region. Settlement changes occurring in the Sacred Valley appear to reflect changing local production concerns—probably due to climate changes, regional patterns of intergroup cooperation and conflict, and the introduction of new crop strains or agricultural technologies through interaction with other groups in the Andean highlands. Excavations are needed to develop meaningful portraits of subsistence practices in the Formative, EIP, and MH.

Settlement Dispersal and Interpretation of Clustering

As discussed, EIP/MH settlement in the Sacred Valley is hierarchically flat and fairly dispersed, with no evidence of local centers that would provide political administration or defense above the village level. Despite the dispersed nature of the settlement pattern, clusters of hamlets and small villages can be identified in a handful of locations in the study region. The most significant of these is in the Chit'apampa Basin, where a clear disruption of Formative settlement patterns gave way to small villages and hamlets located on valley-bottom lands in close proximity to water (Fig. 7.4). Most of these sites have Araway pottery on the surface, suggesting continuity during the MH. This

Figure 7.4.

The upper Chit'apampa Basin, looking toward the Cuzco Valley. Numerous small EIP/MH sites were established in and around the valley-bottom lands of Huillcarpata, in the foreground, as larger Formative villages from lower in the basin were abandoned.

cluster of 23 sites in the lands of Ccorao, Qorimarka, Sequeracay, and Huillcarpata comprised more than 6 ha of occupational area and about half of all sites where the Qotakalli style was present in the Sacred Valley region. Although most of these are hamlets, 3 small villages of about a hectare in size (VS-082, VS-043, VS-055) were encountered. Because all of these sites were found in areas with modern agriculture and settlement, the original size of these sites could have been somewhat larger.

Two other areas with substantial Qotakalli pottery can be noted. Around modern Patabamba on the south rim of the Sacred Valley, 4 sites (VS-378, VS-379, VS-380, VS-381) indicate the presence of a small village and some outlying hamlets, a total occupation area of around 3 ha (Fig. 7.5). This settlement group

represents a rare case of settlement continuity from the Formative period, and the principal sites are all located above 3900 masl. The final site is located at Willkarayan (VS-130), located in the lower Chit'apampa Basin as it drops into the Sacred Valley (Fig. 7.6). This site, built on a low prominence, was about 1 ha in area, surrounded by concentric terrace walls that may have had a defensive function. Together with the Patabamba area sites, Willkarayan sites mark the limit of EIP/MH surface collections dominated by the Qotakalli style.

In the Sacred Valley, the Qotakalli style predominates at new EIP/MH sites as far as the southern rim of the valley. In terms of travel time, almost 90% of Qotakalli components appear at sites lying within a half-day (six hour) walk from the largest settlement

Figure 7.5.

The Patabamba area on the south rim of the Sacred Valley, located at almost 4000 masl. A cluster of Formative settlements has evidence of continued occupation into the EIP.

Figure 7.6. The lower Chit'apampa Basin, showing the large Formative settlements at Muyumuyupata and Raqchi. The EIP/MH site of Willkarayan is located at a strategic point as the basin descends to the Sacred Valley, and marks the limit of strong Qotakalli distribution in local EIP/MH collections.

clusters in the Cuzco Basin (Covey et al. 2013). The presence of local variants of Qotakalli and Araway, and the rare occurrence of other Middle Horizon styles (including Wari, Muyu Urqu, and an unidentified style that might originate in the Paucartambo region), suggests that these sites were established and occupied throughout the EIP/MH. The absence of distinct local styles in the Sacred Valley during the EIP/MH contrasts with some parts of the Cuzco region (e.g., Bauer 1989, 1999), suggesting links to the Cuzco Basin.

The EIP/MH sites in the Sacred Valley itself tend to be quite small, and are usually located 200–300 m above the valley floor, in areas with natural defense that are close to small streams. Qotakalli pottery is present at 5 sites in the Sacred Valley that are six to nine hours of travel time from the Cuzco Basin sites, but local imitations of Cuzco Basin styles appear to predominate at more distant settlements, and there were 20 sites where a "Middle Horizon" component was identified in the absence of Qotakalli or Araway pottery. Small settlement clusters are found in the lower Chongo Basin and in the Sacred Valley near Taray. These sites, as well as other sites along the Sacred Valley and its tributary valleys to the north (for example, near Calca and the Santuario de Huanca), tend to have small amounts of Qotakalli and Araway pottery, with larger components of local imitations. Only a modest population appears to have lived in the main valley and areas to the north during the EIP. Roughly two-thirds of

settled area for the EIP/MH (in cases where site size could be estimated) lies within 15 km of the largest contemporary Cuzco Basin sites (26.1 ha of a total of 39.9 ha).

Evidence for Mortuary Practices and Local Religion

Formative sites display a certain preference for occupation of prominent locations, at times using prominent outcrops for burial. Such practices do not appear to have continued in the EIP/MH. No particular mortuary patterns could be conclusively identified with EIP/MH ceramics, although excavation evidence suggests a continued pattern of individual inhumations with limited grave preparation and few accompanying goods (Andrushko 2007:67; Bélisle and Covey 2010:90–91). Given the absence of preserved architecture from this period, it is not surprising that no religious structures were registered for this time period. The mortuary evidence from local EIP/MH populations challenges McEwan's (2005a:158–60) assumption of an Inca-like practice of veneration of ancestral mummies and portable sacred objects, as well as his speculation that Wari colonists captured local mummies and held them hostage at Pikillacta to force local groups to submit to imperial dominance. No archaeological evidence for mummy curation or the use of portable sacred objects has been encountered in the Cuzco region to date.

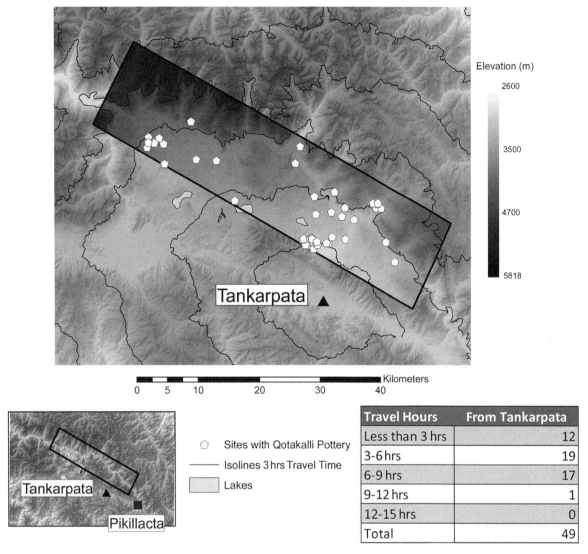

Travel Hours	From Tankarpata
Less than 3 hrs	12
3-6 hrs	19
6-9 hrs	17
9-12 hrs	1
12-15 hrs	0
Total	49

Legend:
⬠ Sites with Qotakalli Pottery
—— Isolines 3 hrs Travel Time
▨ Lakes

Figure 7.7. Distribution of Qotakalli components in the Sacred Valley, measured in terms of walking time from Tankarpata, a village in the Cuzco Basin. Courtesy of L. Tsesmeli.

Spatial Distribution of Ceramic Styles

The distribution of decorated ceramics in the EIP and MH offers valuable perspectives on the relationship between Sacred Valley populations and those of the Cuzco Basin and the area upstream where Wari populations established colonies after AD 600. As Figures 7.7 and 7.8 demonstrate, few decorated sherds of either style are found much beyond 20 km of the largest Cuzco Basin sites. Sites and decorated material clearly cluster closer to the Cuzco Basin, with approximately 60% of sites found within 15 km of the principal EIP/MH sites there—collections at these sites yielded 67% of all Qotakalli material (150/223), 63% of all Araway (153/241), and 73% of the overall EIP/MH sample (689/943). Although collection methods do not permit these figures to be considered as representative, the spatial tie to the Cuzco Basin—as opposed to the Lucre Basin or Huaro area—is apparent.

Prevalence of Decorated Ceramics within the Regional Hierarchy

The greater site count for EIP/MH components and smaller average site size suggest that decorated ceramics were widely available. Three changes from the earlier Formative period should be noted. First, Formative settlement hierarchies across the region suggest the presence of multiple local centers with a range of satellite settlements focusing on variable economies. In the EIP/MH, settlement hierarchies appear to be more restricted across the axis of valley-bottom farming areas. Second, decorated Formative styles (e.g., Chanapata) focused on low investments in burnishing, incising, and slipping, and vessel forms would not have required high levels of technical skill. By contrast, EIP/MH decorated pottery shows greater preparation of clays, more delicate vessel forms, and patterned polychrome designs—these

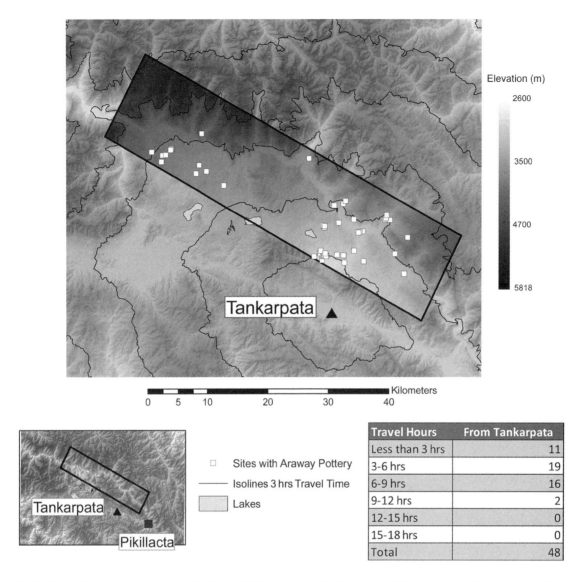

Travel Hours	From Tankarpata
Less than 3 hrs	11
3-6 hrs	19
6-9 hrs	16
9-12 hrs	2
12-15 hrs	0
15-18 hrs	0
Total	48

Figure 7.8. Distribution of Araway components in the Sacred Valley, measured in terms of walking time from Tankarpata, a village in the Cuzco Basin. Courtesy of L. Tsesmeli.

styles appear to have been produced at a much more restricted number of locations across the region. Finally, whereas decorated Formative pottery is found throughout the Cuzco region, not all parts of the region appear to have developed local EIP/MH styles. Qotakalli and Araway appear to have been produced in the Cuzco Basin, and the Ccoipa style was probably produced in the southern part of the Paruro area (Bauer 1999; Delgado et al. 2007; Montoya et al. 2003, 2009). The Xaquixaguana region and the Sacred Valley lack distinct local EIP/MH styles, with local imitations of Qotakalli and Araway representing the only apparent locally produced styles.

Summary of the Formative–EIP Settlement Transition

The distribution of the Qotakalli style in the Sacred Valley reveals some important characteristics about political and economic organization in the Cuzco region prior to Wari colonization. The strong distribution of Qotakalli style in areas close to the Cuzco Basin contrasts with Formative production and distribution patterns and occurs at the same time as substantial economic changes and alterations to local settlement locations and hierarchies. If such changes are interpreted as evidence for shared identity, close exchange relationships, or influence of

Cuzco Basin populations over their northern neighbors, then these relations were territorially circumscribed, as the distribution of the Qotakalli style drops off sharply beyond round-trip distances that could be traversed in a single day.

The shift away from inaccessible settlements on ridges and mountaintops to a more dispersed settlement pattern close to well-watered valley-bottom areas indicates important social changes among local populations in the Sacred Valley. New settlement locations close to the Cuzco Basin were selected for their agricultural potential rather than for visibility and defense, suggesting that ancient village locations lost some of their symbolic prominence or defensive relevance. This is not to say that defense was not a consideration during the EIP—as noted above, the hamlets and small villages to the north of the Vilcanota-Urubamba River tend to be located in less accessible locations. Although climate changes could have encouraged the transition away from Formative settlement patterns, the abandonment of long-established Formative villages, mountaintop shrines, and burial locations suggests that significant social and religious changes occurred at this time. The survey data do not permit a detailed evaluation of new ways of life, although they can be used to identify key sites for future excavation work.

Wari Colonization in the Cuzco Region and Archaeological Expectations for State Influence

The Cuzco region has been considered by many scholars to be the quintessential province of a Wari empire that dominated the Andean highlands during the MH (e.g., McEwan 1984, 1991). With the impressive administrative complex at Pikillacta in the Lucre Basin and what once appeared to be a significant urban area surrounding it, it was inferred that the Wari had conquered the region and imposed a direct imperial administration over the native population. This interpretation has begun to be revised and nuanced in recent years, with the publication of excavation results from Pikillacta (McEwan 2005) and the completion of new research in the Huaro area to the southeast of Pikillacta (e.g., Glowacki 2002). As Wari scholars seek more dynamic interpretations of the interactions between the Ayacucho region and other parts of the Andes (e.g., Jennings 2006, 2010), regional survey data offer an important dataset for assessing the impact of Wari colonization in the Cuzco region (Covey et al. 2013). The completion of several survey projects in the Cuzco region has identified more than 500 EIP/MH components, greatly improving the prospects for regional reconstructions of Wari administration and influence (see Covey et al. 2013; cf. McEwan 1984:185–90; Glowacki 1996:71–98).

As McEwan (1984:185) notes, the interpretation that the Wari state achieved a province-level administration of the Cuzco region raises the question of "the hinterland and satellite centers." In developing a regional archaeological test for Wari influence or administration, differing aspects of influence (e.g., political, social, economic, military, religious) and varying degrees of

Table 7.4. Regional indicators of Wari state influence.

Cultural Domain	Regional Manifestation
political	Evidence of regional hierarchies, strong Wari cultural affiliation at higher-order sites, changes in site distribution and clustering.
social	Changes in social hierarchies in household architecture and mortuary patterns, changes in local identities (stylistic developments).
religious	Presence of Wari religious architecture (e.g., D-shaped temples), disruption or Wari patronage of local ritual and mortuary practices.
economic	Distribution of Wari-managed goods (such as obsidian and fancy pottery), intensification of local agropastoral production, increased craft production.
military	Changes in defensive settlement, construction of Wari or local forts.

intensity should be taken into account (Table 7.4). The issue is not whether the Wari state attempted or achieved some form of provincial administration in the Cuzco region, but the ways that Wari people, institutions, ideas, and technology affected the populations living throughout the region over time. Ultimately, the most straightforward analysis of these changes comes from taking the overall regional picture prior to Wari colonization (discussed above) and comparing continuity and change relative to the changes occurring in the areas known to have strong Wari affiliation. To do so requires a brief discussion of the MH development of the Huaro area and the Lucre Basin.

Wari Sites in the Huaro Area

Around AD 600, Wari populations established new settlements in the Huaro area, located about 45 km to the southeast of Cuzco (Glowacki and McEwan 2001). Reconnaissance and survey work in this area have identified Wari cemeteries, administrative facilities, and residential sites, and excavation work has yielded evidence of a strong Wari cultural affiliation (Glowacki 1996:81–85, 2002; Zapata 1997). The initial Wari settlement of the area is closely affiliated with the site of Batan Urqu, a Formative site with a religious function that was also considered sacred in Inca times. Many of these sites have fancy pottery originating in the Ayacucho area, where the Wari capital was located. The Huaro area occupation would have allowed Wari settlers to monitor movement out of the Cuzco Valley and up the Sacred Valley in the direction of the Titicaca Basin, as well as to access passes descending to nearby lowland areas. It is unclear how large the Wari population of the Huaro area was at any given time, but Glowacki's (2002) work has demonstrated a continuous occupation lasting until the Late Intermediate period.

Pikillacta

Following the establishment of the Huaro colony, construction began around AD 600 on the massive site of Pikillacta, a complex of walled rectangular enclosures that was without precedent anywhere in the Andean highlands between the capital cities of the Wari and Tiwanaku states (Glowacki and McEwan 2001; McEwan 2005). This site was built in the Lucre Basin about 30 km to the southeast of Cuzco, or to judge from the existing Qotakalli distribution patterns, at the outer part of the region that had regular economic interactions with Cuzco Basin populations (Covey et al. 2013; cf. Jennings and Craig 2001). Several valley-bottom farming communities were already established in the Lucre Basin before AD 600 (e.g., Minaspata, Chokepukio, Mama Qolla), and the Wari state built the first planned enclosure at Pikillacta in an unpopulated location without easy access to a permanent water supply. The population of the Lucre Basin and nearby areas presumably participated directly in the Wari system and would have helped in the construction of new settlements, as well as major systems of agricultural terraces and irrigation canals (but see Covey et al. 2013).

Glowacki (2005a:123) has used Wari ceramics to date the initial construction at Pikillacta beginning around AD 600–700 and continuing into MH Epoch 2 (AD 700–800). Glowacki sees the construction as stalling before the completion of the complex, with parts of the site sealed off. As McEwan (2005b:72) notes, the initial site of Pikillacta—and the only part thought to be intensively occupied—was the 12 ha Sector 2 enclosure. The remainder of the site cost millions of worker-days, but was never used for the purposes for which it was constructed. Beyond Pikillacta, the Lucre Basin landscape was transformed through the construction of canals and agricultural terraces thought to have been established during the Wari occupation (Valencia Zegarra 2005). More than 48 km of canals are preserved in the Lucre Basin, and Valencia (2005:96) estimates that 572 ha of irrigable land could have been cultivated there in Wari times.

Overall, the Huaro area and Lucre Basin show strong Wari cultural affiliation. In terms of the cultural changes outlined above, the following represent some changes occurring in these areas during the MH:

Political: Wari administrative architecture was constructed in the area, although the attempt to complete Pikillacta and use it as an urban administrative center appears not to have succeeded. Local populations were presumably administered directly by Wari officials.

Social: Mortuary remains and domestic excavations suggest a social hierarchy that included at least Wari officials and colonists. Status was communicated in differential mortuary investments and the use of pottery and other craft goods from Ayacucho and other parts of the Andean highlands.

Religious: D-shaped temples have not been identified, but architectural preservation is not good at most sites. Mortuary patterns conform to Wari interment practices. The Wari cemetery at Batan Urqu was established near an existing religious center,

and the site of Mama Qolla in the Lucre Basin may also have had religious dimensions.

Economic: A focus on valley-bottom hydraulic agriculture is marked for the area, presumably using long canals and involving some amount of terrace construction. Although large-scale storage facilities might have been planned at Pikillacta, excavations suggest that they were not mobilized.

Military: Pikillacta was built with high walls, but existing MH villages do not show an emphasis on defense. Most residential sites are located near to valley-bottom fields that relied on irrigation systems that were not defended.

The general sense that emerges from the Huaro area and Lucre Basin is that the Wari occupation of these areas increased population densities and introduced new administrative hierarchies. Social inequality came to be measured using Wari status markers, and economic production patterns were transformed in ways seen in the Wari heartland and some other colonized areas. Wari religious influence is difficult to assess; real changes to militarism do not appear to have occurred. The construction of Pikillacta reveals an ambitious imperial project, but it is clear that this site was never occupied as a fully operational provincial capital.

Settlement Continuity and Change in the Sacred Valley, AD 600–1000

Based on different kinds of changes that took place in areas that are known to have been colonized by Wari populations, it is possible to look at the regional evidence from the MH in the Sacred Valley to assess whether similar transformations occurred in a valley with excellent resource availability and access to important routes to the lowlands.

Settlement Hierarchy

Wari populations clearly settled in the Huaro area and the Lucre Basin, transforming these areas by building administrative facilities and infrastructure for hydraulic agriculture, but the nearby Sacred Valley shows no evidence of Wari architecture—although it should be noted that no architecture dating before AD 1000 was identified on survey—and only two fragments of Wari-style ceramics. All sites with EIP/MH components received a second visit to ascertain the presence or absence of a Wari component, but the Sacred Valley survey collected only a single Wari fragment at two sites, compared with several hundred examples of other EIP/MH styles. The distribution of Wari-influenced Araway pottery overlaps substantially with that of Qotakalli, suggesting overall settlement continuity for most of the Middle Horizon (ca. AD 600–1000). No significant changes in settlement hierarchy can be discerned during this time, although the co-occurrence of small Araway components at large LIP sites suggests that the shift away from valley-bottom agriculture may have begun at the very end of the Middle Horizon (see Chapter 9 for a more detailed discussion).

Table 7.5. Ecological distribution of multicomponent sites with Araway pottery.

Multicomponents	Kichwa Sites	Suni Sites	Puna Sites
Qotakalli, MH, Araway	3	5	2
Qotakalli, MH, Araway, LIP	10	6	1
Araway, LIP	5	2	5

Regarding the latter point, Table 7.5 demonstrates how Araway distribution relates to that of other EIP/MH components. There is significant overlap between Qotakalli and Araway distributions (27/42 Araway sites), although there is evidence of some minor settlement changes taking place during the MH—probably later in the period—that included the establishment of new settlements that continued to be occupied during the LIP. These are found in all ecological zones, but it should be noted that sites in the puna zone tend to be larger villages, whereas new kichwa sites are of modest size. To the extent that Araway diverges from Qotakalli site distributions, it appears to represent a shift away from the kinds of settlements and economic resources promoted by the Wari state, which occurred around the time that the Wari colonies in Cuzco were failing.

Settlement Ecology

Araway site locations and field observations of contemporary environmental characteristics are comparable with Qotakalli settlements, with a slight apparent shift toward mountain and ridge site locations—as already discussed, this is explained by the presence of small components of Araway pottery at sizeable LIP sites.

Settlement Dispersal and Interpretation of Clustering

As noted above, Araway pottery is frequently found in the Sacred Valley among the clusters of small villages and hamlets nearest to the Cuzco Basin. There is substantial overlap with the distribution of Qotakalli pottery, although there are a few small villages where one style was collected but not the other. The co-occurrence of these two styles communicates a continuity of settlement and subsistence from the EIP through much of the MH, although the overlap between Araway and LIP ceramics suggests that by the end of the MH there were populations that were abandoning established agricultural villages in favor of new sites—the beginnings of the decentralized settlement pattern seen throughout the Sacred Valley until the Inca conquest of the Cuzco region.

Evidence for Mortuary Practices and Local Religion

No mortuary features or religious contexts were identified in association with Araway pottery. Excavation work may be necessary to make such identifications at sites in the Sacred Valley region.

Spatial Distribution of Ceramic Styles

In the Sacred Valley, Araway pottery is distributed in areas closest to the Cuzco Basin, and sites with the style do not reflect a significant settlement shift from Qotakalli patterns. Stratigraphic excavations have demonstrated that Araway and Qotakalli were produced and distributed simultaneously during the MH (Bauer and Jones 2003). As noted above, Araway is considered to be a Wari-influenced style, one that Glowacki (1996, 2005b) believes was produced in the Cuzco region using actual Wari vessels from Ayacucho as templates (cf. Covey et al. 2013). Although there are still questions surrounding the production of this style, the Sacred Valley survey data allow certain expectations regarding the distribution of decorated ceramics to be evaluated using regional data.

If Araway were produced at one or more Wari sites in the Cuzco region—most likely in the Huaro area or the Lucre Basin—and distributed through continuous regional exchange networks controlled by Wari throughout the region, then the distribution of Araway would be strongest around the Wari colonies and reflect the presence of an administrative hierarchy. At the very least, the distribution of Wari and Wari-influenced pottery (in this case, Araway) should decline with distance from each tier of the regional administrative hierarchy. Regional analysis of the distribution of Araway pottery confirms that Araway is less common in the Lucre Basin than it is in the Cuzco Basin and nearby areas, and it is not distributed hierarchically in a pattern suggesting lower-order Wari administrative facilities.

As noted above, the majority of Araway sherds are found in close proximity to the Cuzco Basin, rather than in areas in the Sacred Valley that are significantly closer to Pikillacta (Fig. 7.9). Only two Araway components in the Sacred Valley are found within a six-hour walk from Pikillacta, whereas all but four sites with the style are within a six-hour walk of the Cuzco Basin site of Tankarpata (Covey et al. 2013). Distribution patterns and the absence of a large Wari (or Araway) site in the valley suggest that most Araway pottery came into the area through interactions with the Cuzco Basin rather than the Wari colonies. Identifiable MH pottery was almost completely absent in the Sacred Valley below Calca (Covey, Aráoz Silva, and Bauer 2008; cf. Kendall 1994; Kosiba 2010).

Collections at the site of Wanka—which is located in the Sacred Valley within a six-hour walk from Pikillacta—offer an important contrast with sites in the Chit'apampa Basin and other areas close to the Cuzco Basin. Surface collections from two visits to the site yielded fragments of Qotakalli, Araway, and a possible local MH style, but no Wari pottery (see Covey 2006:74–75). This site has a religious significance of great antiquity, but no evidence of Wari influence during its MH occupation. The largest EIP/MH village in the Sacred Valley proper was a few kilometers downstream at VS-291, a 2 ha village located on a prominent point about 200 m above the valley floor, in a location

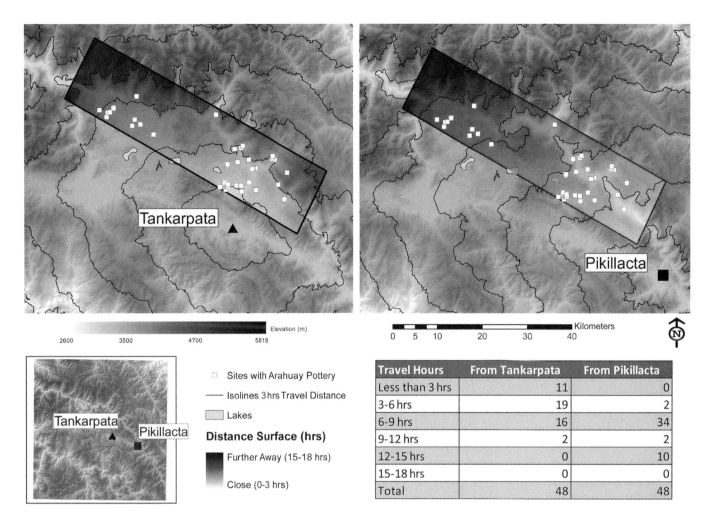

Travel Hours	From Tankarpata	From Pikillacta
Less than 3 hrs	11	0
3-6 hrs	19	2
6-9 hrs	16	34
9-12 hrs	2	2
12-15 hrs	0	10
15-18 hrs	0	0
Total	48	48

Figure 7.9. Distribution of Araway components in the Sacred Valley, comparing walking distances from Tankarpata in the Cuzco Basin (*left*), and Pikillacta, the large Wari installation in the Lucre Basin (*right*). Courtesy of L. Tsesmeli.

called Pillawara. Collections from this site included Qotakalli, Araway, and local MH pottery, but no Wari. Survey work along the Sacred Valley systematically investigated a region lying at an aerial distance of 12–60 km from Pikillacta (within about a ten- to thirty-hour round trip walking time) without encountering evidence of Wari architecture, hydraulic agricultural works, or significant amounts of Wari pottery. Sites in the area around Pisac lack Wari pottery, whereas those in the Cuzco Basin, which lies at a comparable travel time from Pikillacta, have small Wari components present at sites with much larger Qotakalli and Araway collections (Covey et al. 2013).

Prevalence of Decorated Ceramics within the Regional Hierarchy

Araway ceramics are not distributed as widely as the Qotakalli style in many parts of the Cuzco region, but in the Sacred Valley study region the two styles appear in similar quantities, at small villages and hamlets. As described above for Qotakalli, local imitations of Araway pottery are more common with distance from the Cuzco Basin.

Wari and the Sacred Valley during the Middle Horizon Period

Taking the pre-Wari and MH settlement data into account, it is possible to assess the impact of the Wari state on the Sacred Valley. In terms of political power, there is no evidence of an administrative center in the Sacred Valley, and no increase in settlement hierarchy is evident after AD 600. Qotakalli settlement clusters (small villages and hamlets) are found most densely in the area nearest to Cuzco Basin, and most of these continued to be settled during the MH. There appears to have been an erosion of regional stability in the later part of the MH, evidenced by the shift toward LIP settlement patterns at some sites. This suggests that to the extent that Wari administration was felt locally, it was in the disorder that the *failure* of an attempted provincial order brought to the Sacred Valley.

The regional data do not provide sufficient evidence to consider most changes that could have occurred in local social organization, but the continuity of EIP settlement patterns suggests that significant disruptions did not take place among the modest population of the Sacred Valley. The distribution of Wari-influenced ceramics shows that status markers emulating Wari material culture were in general use, at least among populations living closest to the Cuzco Basin. The persistence of the Qotakalli style suggests that Wari iconography and identity did not supplant existing local ones. Regional data do not offer specific evidence of Wari influence in local religious life—there are no sites with a strong Wari ceremonial assemblage found in the Sacred Valley.

The Wari state does not appear to have established economic control over the Sacred Valley, or to have developed new productive resources there. The shift to lower-elevation farming occurred in the Sacred Valley before Wari colonies were established, and there is no evidence of the introduction of canal and terrace construction prior to the final years of the LIP. During the MH, local populations maintained existing subsistence economies without significant evidence for population growth, production intensity, or reliance on centralized storage.

The persistence of EIP settlement patterns suggests that Wari colonization did not greatly alter the role of warfare among the modest populations of the Sacred Valley. The continuity of dispersed settlement from the EIP through much of the MH suggests that armed conflict was not a pressing concern for populations living near the Cuzco Basin, although many of the small settlements found within the Sacred Valley are found in less accessible locations. The Araway–LIP sites appear to represent an increasing concern for local self-sufficiency and defense at the end of the MH.

Conclusions

Although there is evidence for direct Wari administrative control in the Lucre Basin and Huaro area, there is none in the Sacred Valley, which would have been a logical area to annex and develop economically. Wari pottery is virtually absent at the MH sites in the Sacred Valley. Meanwhile, Araway, a Wari imitation produced by local potters, appears to have been distributed most commonly in areas closest to the Cuzco Basin, and is found rarely beyond a half-day's walk from the basin. The continuity of the Qotakalli style—which is distributed more widely, and found at sites in the areas colonized by Wari—suggests that local craft economies and iconography were not replaced by Wari, but were goods that were part of two-way exchanges between members of different groups. Wari's political influence is hard to discern beyond a few kilometers of the colonies, whereas its economic influence might have come from the ability of Wari colonists to acquire long-distance prestige goods for exchange. Local leaders could have been recruited by access to Wari pottery, obsidian, and other prestige items.

At the same time, Wari may have established its colonies and spread its influence through religious patronage, a sort of "soft power" that some scholars may have overestimated by applying an Inca model to ambiguous evidence. By underwriting some ceremonies, Wari colonists and state officials could offer a more elaborate ceremonial life, but this does not appear to have affected the local subsistence economy in the Sacred Valley. It is possible that a more intensive administrative policy, aimed at raising labor tribute and undercutting local elites, would have contributed to local resentment and led to the abandonment of Pikillacta and other MH sites. As discussed in Chapter 9, the abandonment of Wari's Cuzco colonies occurred at a time of increasing regional competition that ultimately led to the formation of the early Inca state.

References

Andrushko, Valerie A.
2007 The Bioarchaeology of Inca Imperialism in the Heartland: An Analysis of Prehistoric Burials from the Cuzco Region of Peru. PhD dissertation, Department of Anthropology, University of California, Santa Barbara.

Bauer, Brian S.
1989 Muyu Orqo y Ccoipa: Dos nuevos tipos de cerámica para la región del Cuzco. *Revista Andina* 7(2):537–42.
1999 Th*e Early Ceramics of the Inca Heartland*. Fieldiana Anthropology, n.s., 31. Chicago: Field Museum of Natural History.
2004 *Ancient Cuzco: Heartland of the Inca*. Austin: University of Texas Press.

Bauer, Brian S., and Bradford M. Jones
2003 *Early Intermediate and Middle Horizon Ceramic Styles of the Cuzco Valley*, pp. 1–65. Fieldiana Anthropology, n.s., 34. Chicago: Field Museum of Natural History.

Bauer, Brian S., Lucas C. Kellett, and Miriam Aráoz Silva
2010 *The Chanka: Archaeological Research in Andahuaylas (Apurímac), Peru*. University of California, Los Angeles: Cotsen Institute of Archaeology.

Bélisle, Véronique
2011 Ak'awillay: Wari State Expansion and Household Change in Cuzco, Peru (AD 600–1000). PhD dissertation, Department of Anthropology, University of Michigan, Ann Arbor.

Bélisle, Véronique, and R. Alan Covey
2010 Local settlement continuity and Wari impact in Middle Horizon Cusco. In *Beyond Wari Walls: Regional Perspectives on Middle Horizon Peru*, edited by J. Jennings, pp. 78–95. Albuquerque: University of New Mexico Press.

Covey, R. Alan
2006   *How the Incas Built Their Heartland: State Formation and the Innovation of Imperial Strategies in the Sacred Valley, Peru.* Ann Arbor: University of Michigan Press.

Covey, R. Alan, Miriam Aráoz Silva, and Brian S. Bauer
2008   Settlement patterns in the Yucay Valley and neighboring areas. In *Imperial Transformations in Sixteenth-Century Yucay, Peru*, edited by R. A. Covey and D. Amado González, pp. 3–17. Memoirs, no. 44. Ann Arbor: Museum of Anthropology, University of Michigan.

Covey, R. Alan, Brian S. Bauer, Véronique Bélisle, and Lia Tsesmeli
2013   Regional perspectives on Wari state influence in Cusco, Peru (c. AD 600–1000). *Journal of Anthropological Archaeology* 32(4):538–52.

Delgado, M., P. Olivera, E. Montoya, and A. Bustamante
2007   Building a bridge to the past: Archaeometry at the IPEN reactor. *Archaeometry* 49(2):403–12.

Glowacki, Mary
1996   The Wari Occupation of the Southern Highlands of Peru: A Ceramic Perspective from the Site of Pikillacta. PhD dissertation, Department of Anthropology, Brandeis University, Massachusetts.
2002   The Huaro archaeological site complex: Rethinking the Huari occupation of Cuzco. In *Andean Archaeology I: Variations in Sociopolitical Organization*, edited by W. H. Isbell and H. Silverman, pp. 267–85. New York: Kluwer Academic/Plenum Publishers.
2005a   Dating Pikillacta. In *Pikillacta: The Wari Empire in Cuzco*, edited by Gordon F. McEwan, pp. 115–24. Iowa City: University of Iowa Press.
2005b   Pottery from Pikillacta. In *Pikillacta: The Wari Empire in Cuzco*, edited by Gordon F. McEwan, pp. 101–14. Iowa City: University of Iowa Press.

Glowacki, Mary, and Gordon F. McEwan
2001   Pikillacta, Huaro, y la gran región del Cuzco: Nuevas interpretaciones de la ocupación wari de la sierra sur. *Boletín de Arqueología PUCP* 5:31–49.

Heggarty, Paul, and David G. Beresford-Jones
2010   Agriculture and language dispersals: Limitations, refinements, and an Andean exception? *Current Anthropology* 51(2):163–91.

Jennings, Justin
2006   Core, peripheries, and regional realities in Middle Horizon Peru. *Journal of Anthropological Archaeology* 20:479–502.

Jennings, Justin (editor)
2010   *Beyond Wari Walls: Regional Perspectives on Middle Horizon Peru.* Albuquerque: University of New Mexico Press.

Jennings, Justin, and Nathan Craig
2001   Polity-wide analysis and imperial political economy: The relationship between valley political complexity and administrative centers in the Wari empire of the central Andes. *Journal of Anthropological Archaeology* 20:479–502.

Kendall, Ann
1994   *Proyecto Arqueológico Cusichaca, Cusco: Investigaciones arqueológicas y de rehabilitación agrícola, tomo I.* Lima: Southern Peru Copper Corporation.

Kosiba, Steven B.
2010   Becoming Inka: The Transformation of Political Place and Practice during Inka State Formation (Cusco, Peru). PhD dissertation, Department of Anthropology, University of Chicago.

Lumbreras, Luis G.
1974   *The Peoples and Cultures of Ancient Peru*, translated by Betty J. Meggers. Washington, D.C.: Smithsonian Institution Press.

McEwan, Gordon F.
1984   The Middle Horizon in the Valley of Cuzco, Peru: The Impact of the Wari Occupation of Pikillacta in the Lucre Basin. PhD dissertation, Department of Anthropology, University of Texas.
1991   Investigations at the Pikillacta site: A provincial Huari center in the Valley of Cuzco. In *Huari Administrative Structure: Prehistoric Monumental Architecture and State Government*, edited by W. H. Isbell and G. F. McEwan, pp. 93–119. Washington, D.C.: Dumbarton Oaks Research Library and Collection.
2005a   Conclusion: The functions of Pikillacta. In *Pikillacta: The Wari Empire in Cuzco*, edited by Gordon F. McEwan, pp. 147–64. Iowa City: University of Iowa Press.
2005b   Pikillacta architecture and construction requirements. In *Pikillacta: The Wari Empire in Cuzco*, edited by Gordon F. McEwan, pp. 63–84. Iowa City: University of Iowa Press.
2010   Indicators of possible driving forces for the spread of Quechua and Aymara reflected in the archaeology of Cuzco. In *Archaeology and Language in the Andes: A Cross-Disciplinary Exploration of Prehistory*, edited by Paul Heggarty and David Beresford-Jones, pp. 247–63. New York: Oxford University Press.

McEwan, Gordon F. (editor)
2005   *Pikillacta: The Wari Empire in Cuzco.* Iowa City: University of Iowa Press.

Montoya, E., M. Glowacki, J. Zapata, and P. Mendoza
2009   Caracterización de cerámicos wari mediante análisis por activación neutrónica. *Revista de la Sociedad Química del Perú* 75(4):473–78.

Montoya, E., J. Zapata, P. Mendoza, and M. Glowacki
2003   Chemical Characterization of Archaeological Ceramics Using K0-Based Instrumental Neutron Activation Analysis: A Study in the Production and Distribution of Middle Horizon Pottery of Cuzco, Peru. Reporte Técnico presentado al Instituto Peruano de Energía Nuclear, Lima.

Schreiber, Katharina J.
1992   *Wari Imperialism in Middle Horizon Peru.* Anthropological Papers, no. 87. Ann Arbor: Museum of Anthropology, University of Michigan.

Valencia Zegarra, Alfredo
2005   Wari hydraulic works in the Lucre Basin. In *Pikillacta: The Wari Empire in Cuzco*, edited by Gordon F. McEwan, pp. 85–97. Iowa City: University of Iowa Press.

Vivanco, Cirilo, and Lidio M. Valdez
1993   Poblados Wari en la cuenca del Pampas-Qaracha, Ayacucho. *Gaceta Arqueológica Andina* 23:83–102.

Zapata Rodríguez, Julinho
1997   Arquitectura y contextos funerarios Wari en Batan Urqu, Cusco. *Boletín de Arqueología PUCP* 1:165–206.

PART IV

The Advent of the Inca State

Chapter 8: Late Intermediate Period Archaeology and Inca Rivals on the Xaquixaguana Plain

R. Alan Covey

Indigenous Andean chroniclers (Garcilaso de la Vega 1965 [1609]; Guaman Poma de Ayala 1980 [1615]) recount that when Manco Capac, the founding Inca ancestor, established himself in Cuzco, he had counterparts to the northwest and southeast who used the title *qhapaq* (king). Perhaps the most powerful of these was Tocay Capac, the ruler of the Ayarmaca people, a prominent group living in the Xaquixaguana study region that vied with the Incas for regional preeminence in the generations leading up to the first campaigns of imperial conquest. Inca rulers gradually attracted Ayarmaca allies and reduced them to tributary status, and a rebellion against Pachacutic Inca Yupanqui led to the destruction of the Ayarmaca homeland and the scattering of the remnant population across the Cuzco region (Covey 2006; Rostworowski 1970). In moving from the discussion of the prehistoric societies of Cuzco to the archaeology of the Late Intermediate period (LIP)—a somewhat arbitrary slice of time (ca. 1000–1400) that spans the decline of the Wari state and the rise of the Inca empire (Covey 2008a)—regional archaeology encounters a new interpretive counterpart in the archives and published chronicles written after the European invasion. Ethnohistoric descriptions of the LIP tell stories from the Inca perspective, combining myth, legend, and historical fact into overlapping narratives that were written to advance or challenge Spanish colonial rule. Rather than attempt the full synthesis of archaeological data and infor-

mation from hundreds of unpublished documents investigated in Hanan Cuzco research projects, this chapter describes the LIP settlement pattern data for the Xaquixaguana region (Fig. 8.1), and then turns to the documents for a brief discussion of how the two lines of evidence intersect.

The Transition to LIP Settlement Patterns in the Xaquixaguana Region

As has been noted in the preceding chapters on the Middle Horizon occupation in the Hanan Cuzco region, the Araway style has been recovered in small components at sites that remained or became large settlements after AD 1000. A brief comparison of two key sites, Ak'awillay (X-228) and X-032, offers perspectives on this overlap. Located near well-watered valley-bottom farmlands in the Anta area, Ak'awillay was the largest settlement in the Xaquixaguana region before Inca times, and Araway material appeared in intensive collection units representing about 4 ha of settlement. LIP pottery appeared in three-quarters of these units, whereas the overall LIP occupation of the site comprised 58 collection units (roughly 15 ha) in which 260 diagnostic fragments of LIP styles were recovered. In comparison, X-032 was a village site in the Maras area that lacks a significant Qotakalli

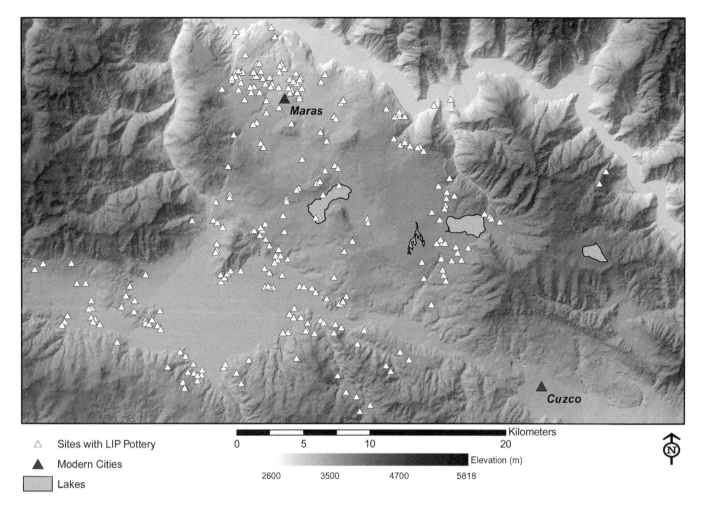

△ Sites with LIP Pottery
▲ Modern Cities
▨ Lakes

Kilometers
0   5   10   20

Elevation (m)
2600   3500   4700   5818

Figure 8.1. Map showing all LIP sites in the Xaquixaguana and Qoricocha study regions. Courtesy of L. Tsesmeli.

component. In total, 10 Araway sherds appeared in a handful of collection units, whereas the LIP component at this site constituted 146 diagnostic sherds found in 19 units (roughly 5 ha site area). X-032 is a mid-sized site in the Maras area LIP settlement hierarchy, and the nearby site of Yunkaray (X-019) yielded no Araway pottery in 81 intensive collection units (approximately 20 ha site area) containing 825 LIP diagnostic sherds. The intensive collection data from large sites in the Xaquixaguana region indicate that the transition from the Middle Horizon involved the establishment of new settlements and site hierarchies in some areas, as well as significant site-level changes at ancient villages like Ak'awillay. Given the local variations observed for the Xaquixaguana study region, this chapter discusses settlement at the level of contemporary district boundaries.

The relative dates provided by the Cuzco ceramic sequence suggest that settlement patterns that were more or less stable for several centuries during the EIP/MH began to change toward the end of the Middle Horizon, with the full development of new site hierarchies during the first centuries of the LIP. The survey data correspond with excavation evidence for the abandonment and

burning of key Wari sites in the colonized areas to the southeast of Cuzco (e.g., McEwan 1996), as well as developing climatic reconstructions for the period, which emphasize the onset of more arid and unpredictable precipitation patterns (see Chapter 2). The collapse of the Wari state does not seem to be a likely prime mover for the MH–LIP settlement transition, given the continuity of settlement patterns in the Cuzco Basin, where village settlements continued to favor alluvial terraces just above the valley floor (Bauer and Covey 2002). Climate change represents a better explanation for the patterns seen in the Cuzco region, and local precipitation and environmental characteristics would be expected to encourage subsistence responses ranging from hydraulic agriculture to broad-spectrum agropastoralism (Covey 2006). It is possible that the decline of some Wari sites dispersed population into other parts of the Cuzco region, although the continuity of settlement at Wari sites such as Chokepukio and Cotocotuyoc (Glowacki 2002; McEwan, Chatfield, and Gibaja 2002) suggests that the destruction of administrative facilities cannot alone account for the establishment of new settlements across the Hanan Cuzco region.

Chronological Ambiguities

Previous chapters have highlighted some of the challenges for comparing settlement pattern data between periods in the Cuzco sequences, as well as for deriving a representative discussion of subsistence and social practices at any given time during large, undifferentiated blocks of time. While shorter than the combined EIP/MH periods, the LIP is nevertheless a long period, and the large number of identified sites—295 in the Xaquixaguana and Qoricocha study regions—suggests that there were settlement changes occurring within the LIP that are not easily discernible based on our current knowledge of ceramic styles for the period. More excavation work must be done to subdivide the LIP sequence, not only for Killke, but for local styles in use at different times and places that are currently used to identify "LIP" occupation at survey sites.

LIP Settlement Patterns in the Maras Area

The Maras area did not have a large population during the EIP/MH, and work in the nearby Sacred Valley suggests an equally low profile population in the Calca-Yanahuara study region (Covey, Aráoz Silva, and Bauer 2008). Araway pottery was more common than Qotakalli at the 28 sites in the Maras district with EIP/MH components, with 58 fragments identified at 14 sites. As Bélisle has discussed (Chapter 6), these sites are small and scattered across *kichwa* zones in the area, with no evidence of settlement clustering or hierarchy.

The LIP settlement pattern in the Maras area reflects a significant departure from earlier periods, with increases in site counts, settled area, and regional hierarchy that are unlikely to be explained by natural increases in the local EIP/MH population (Fig. 8.2). XPAS survey crews encountered LIP pottery at 82 sites in the district of Maras, and excavations have identified a LIP component at Moray (X-095) (Quirita 2002), raising the total count to 83. LIP sites in Maras cover a cumulative area of 119 ha, a massive increase from the EIP/MH. This overall settlement area was generated using general collection size estimates at small sites, as well as the identification of LIP pottery in 372 intensive collection units at 21 large sites in the region. More than 7700 diagnostic LIP fragments were identified in the laboratory, including approximately 1900 sherds identified as Killke and 22 fragments identified as Lucre. Local LIP styles constituted the majority of the material collected at Maras area sites; excavation work has begun to clarify some of the stylistic parameters for Maras area LIP pottery (Haquehua and Maqque 1996; Maqque and Haquehua 1993; Quave 2012) (Fig. 8.3).

The large number of intensively collected sites in the Maras area reflects the high density of sites larger than a hectare, and the collection work effectively identifies a multi-tiered local settlement hierarchy (Fig. 8.4). There are 21 LIP village sites lying within an hour's walk of Yunkaray (X-019), the largest site in the area—a settlement system with a total area of at least 94

ha. Yunkaray is located on an undefended alluvial terrace at the center of the settlement system. At 20 ha, this site is roughly three times the size of the largest villages registered in the neighboring Sacred Valley (Chapter 9), and is of a scale comparable with the largest local centers in the Cuzco region during the LIP (Covey 2009:368, 2011). The second-tier sites surrounding Yunkaray are as large or larger than the largest villages in the Sacred Valley at this time (6–10 ha) (Chapter 9), and these sites all lie within about 2 km of Yunkaray. The main habitation centers are situated on alluvial terraces, and the intervening gullies provide frost-free kichwa lands that can be irrigated easily from the streams flowing through them. The XPAS survey observed the remains of a large complex of terraces (~50 ha) located just to the west of Yunkaray (Fig. 8.5). These fields are surrounded by sites with a virtually exclusive LIP occupation, and irrigation water could be brought to them with the construction of fairly modest canals. In addition to productive farmland, Yunkaray is located just 2 km from the salt pans discussed in Chapter 2, and approximately the same distance from Cheqoq (X-075), which has a quarry that has been used for centuries for construction materials.

A scatterplot of LIP site size and elevation (Fig. 8.6) shows that the LIP settlement system in the Maras area focuses on the kichwa zone, with easy access to nearby resources through small villages, hamlets, and perhaps seasonal occupations. Yunkaray lies in the middle of the most productive maize-producing elevations (3279 masl), whereas the second tier of settlements ranges across the kichwa zone. As Table 8.1 demonstrates, the largest LIP sites are found at the lowest elevation, although it is important to note that these are situated well above the valley bottom of the nearby Sacred Valley (Fig. 8.7), where settlements of this size were not encountered (Covey, Aráoz Silva, and Bauer 2008). The smallest sites are scattered across a wide range of elevations, which suggests direct access to ecozones ranging from high grassland to hot lower kichwa elevations. Site locations and the ecological spread of sites along the settlement hierarchy suggest the central control over productive resources in the immediate hinterland of Yunkaray, but not necessarily a centralized coordination of ecological complementarity.

The Maras area represents one of the most densely and hierarchically occupied parts of the Cuzco region during the LIP. Yunkaray is one of the largest local centers found anywhere in the Cuzco region, and unlike some of the other large valley-bottom sites (e.g., Chokepukio, Minaspata, Cotocotuyoc), it is surrounded by a dense network of lower-order settlements. Only the Cuzco Basin has yielded evidence for a similar rise in multi-tiered valley-bottom settlement during the LIP (e.g., Covey 2006). Yunkaray cannot be considered to be an urban center, but its immediate catchment includes agricultural terraces, salt pans, and quarries that would presumably be part of a more specialized and surplus-based economy than has been identified in many parts of the Cuzco region. Quave (2012) has excavated a pre-Inca storehouse at Cheqoq (X-075) that suggests some sort of centralized mobilization of staple surpluses during the LIP (see Covey, Quave, and Covey, forthcoming).

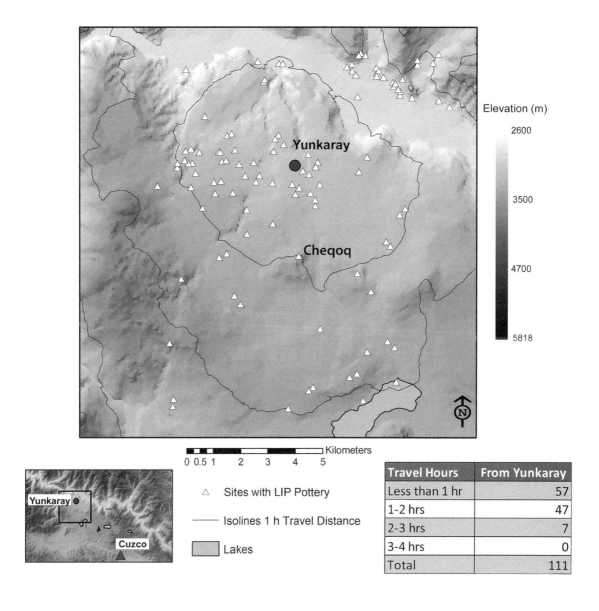

Travel Hours	From Yunkaray
Less than 1 hr	57
1-2 hrs	47
2-3 hrs	7
3-4 hrs	0
Total	111

Figure 8.2. Local LIP settlement system in the Maras area. Isolines show walking time from Yunkaray, the largest settlement. More than 100 LIP sites lie within a two-hour walk of the local center. Courtesy of L. Tsesmeli.

Figure 8.3.

Photograph of local LIP pottery excavated at Cheq'oq in the Maras area. Courtesy of Kylie E. Quave.

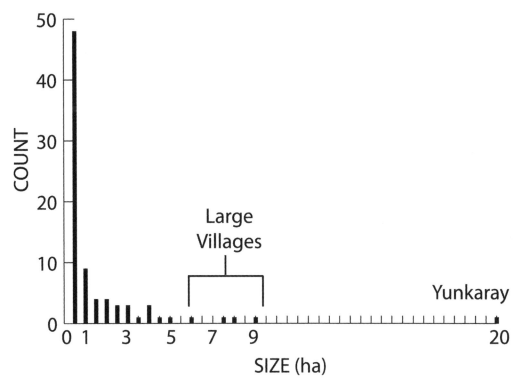

Figure 8.4. Site size hierarchy for LIP sites in the Maras area. The largest settlement in the area, Yunkaray is approximately three times the size of the largest LIP site in the Sacred Valley, and sits atop a multi-tier hierarchy that is highly localized.

Figure 8.5. Terraces near Yunkaray lie in close association to the system of nucleated and hierarchical LIP settlements.

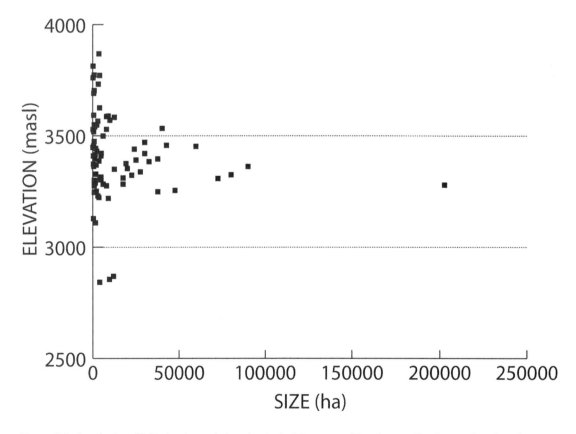

Figure 8.6. Scatterplot of LIP site size and elevation in the Maras area. Sites favor valley-bottom locations in proximity to a range of natural resources, including salt pans, quarries, and pastures.

Figure 8.7. View of the drop from the Maras area to the Sacred Valley near Urubamba.

Table 8.1. LIP site size and elevation in the Maras area.

Size Range (ha)	Count	Number of Hectares	Average Elevation* (masl)	Range (masl)
>10	1	20.3	3279	3279
5–10	4	30.3	3361	3308–3452
1–5	21	53.0	3377	2869–3584
<1	56	15.9	3421	2842–3869

*Average elevation calculations account for site size.

LIP Settlement Patterns in the Chinchero-Huayllabamba Area

Whereas the Maras area contained a cluster of small sites with Qotakalli and Araway components indicative of a modest EIP/ MH population, the districts of Chinchero and Huayllabamba show almost no occupation during that period in areas that lie somewhat closer to the Cuzco Valley. In total, there were only 3 sites in the Chinchero-Huayllabamba area with Qotakalli pottery, and just 3 with Araway—an estimated 5 ha of settled area during the EIP/MH. Given the proximity of these two districts to Cuzco, the paucity of EIP/MH components is noteworthy when

considering the abundant distribution of Cuzco Basin styles in the neighboring Chit'apampa Basin and Anta-Pucyura area.

This is probably due in part to the more marginal ecology of the area compared with other parts of the Xaquixaguana region. The Chinchero-Huayllabamba area is dominated by high rolling plains that can be used for tuber cultivation and herding today, depending on elevation, soil quality, and drainage. The district of Huayllabamba stretches into the Sacred Valley, where the village of Huayllabamba is found roughly a vertical kilometer below the high plain. For the purposes of discussion, the 2 LIP sites from Huayllabamba that lie within 300 vertical meters of the Sacred Valley floor have been trimmed from the overall data

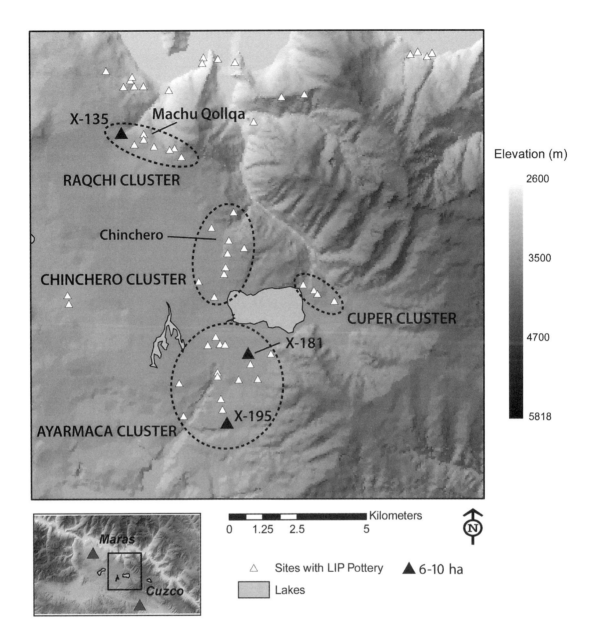

Figure 8.8. Map of LIP sites in the Chinchero-Huayllabamba area.

set and are considered in the discussion on the Sacred Valley (Chapter 9).

Like the Maras region, upland parts of the Chinchero-Huaylla-bamba area experienced major settlement changes during the LIP (Fig. 8.8). A total of 50 LIP sites appeared in the area, comprising an estimated 85 ha of site area. LIP sizes for Machu Qollqa [X-141] and Chinchero [X-151] were estimated based on survey visits and earlier excavation work (Alcina Franch 1976; Alcina Franch et al. 1976:31; Valencia 2004). XPAS crews conducted intensive collections at 13 sites, encountering LIP material in 205 units. The sample of LIP pottery from the area was smaller (1633

diagnostic fragments) than what was collected from the Maras area. It contained a greater proportion of Killke pottery from the Cuzco Basin (38%, $n = 622$), especially at sites with a large Inca imperial component. The remaining pottery was made up of local styles from the Chinchero area, material thought to originate in the Maras area (see Rivera Dorado 1971a, 1971b, 1972), and a few sherds of other Cuzco LIP styles, such as Lucre ($n = 4$).

The settlement hierarchy for the Chinchero-Huayllabamba area differs from that of Maras in two respects (Fig. 8.9). First, no single site occupies the apex of the regional settlement hierarchy or serves as a central place. There are a handful of large villages

Figure 8.9.

Site size hierarchy for the
Chinchero-Huayllabamba area.
Settlement in this area comprises
multiple clusters of small and
large villages.

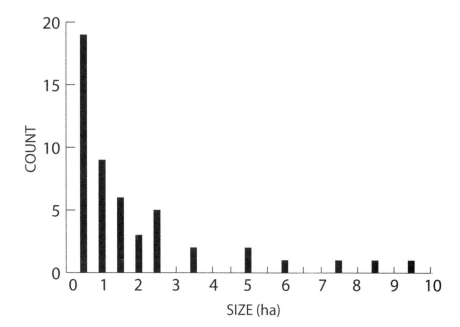

Table 8.2. LIP village clusters in the Chinchero-Huayllabamba area.

Area	Village Sites	Total Village Area (ha)	Distance to Next Cluster (km)
Raqchi	X-135 (Muqukancha), X-137, X-140, X-141 (Machu Qollqa), X-143	16.7	3
Chinchero	X-149, X-150 (Qerapata), X-151 (Chinchero), X-152, X-155, X-156 (Wankapata)	10.9	2.5–3
Ayarmaca*	X-181, X-182 (Minasmuq'u), X-183 (Hatun Qhawana), X-184, X-192, X-195 (Ayarmaka), X-197 (Tukukyapampa)	30.8	2.5
Cuper	X-157, X-163 (Misalpata)	6	3

*Site names differ from those given by Alcina Franch (1976) to three sites in the area: Cancha Cancha, Sipasuarcuna, and Chacamoco.

(6–10 ha) smaller in number and size than the second tier of sites in Maras, and no site approaches the size of Yunkaray. The larger villages are not found in proximity to each other, except in the case of a few clusters of large villages. This suggests that the regional settlement system is not as integrated or centrally coordinated as what has been described for the Maras area. The second key difference is the apparently more limited role that very small sites play in the regional hierarchy. Survey work in the Chinchero-Huayllabamba area identified 18 sites smaller than 5000 m², a total area of about 3.8 ha. In the Maras area, 47 small sites contained LIP ceramics, representing a total area of 9 ha. Overall, these characteristics make the Chinchero-Huayllabamba settlement pattern look less hierarchical at the regional level, and at the same time more nucleated at the level of villages and small clusters of communities.

Villages in the area often appear in clusters that create fairly densely populated areas surrounded by spaces with little LIP settlement. There are four noteworthy areas of village clustering:

Raqchi, Chinchero, Ayarmaca, and Cuper (Table 8.2). The largest of these, in the Ayarmaca area, is the most dispersed, consisting of several pairs of village sites located about 400–500 m apart. The largest sites (X-181 and X-195) are located the farthest from each other, more than 2 km apart. By comparison, the settlement cluster surrounding Yunkaray in the Maras area is four times larger, and more centralized.

LIP settlements in the Chinchero-Huayllabamba area favor the rolling plains, with 22 sites designated as *pampa*. Gentle valley sides were the next most common geomorphological designation (*n* = 9), followed by steep slopes (*n* = 7) and hilltops (*n* = 7). Village sites were found across these areas, suggesting that resource access was more important than defense for LIP communities. Site locations reflect proximity to permanent water sources, with an average distance of just over 200 m. The most common water sources were naturally occurring (streams, springs, lakes), and no sites were associated with canal constructions. This contrasts with the situation in Maras, where the average distance to water

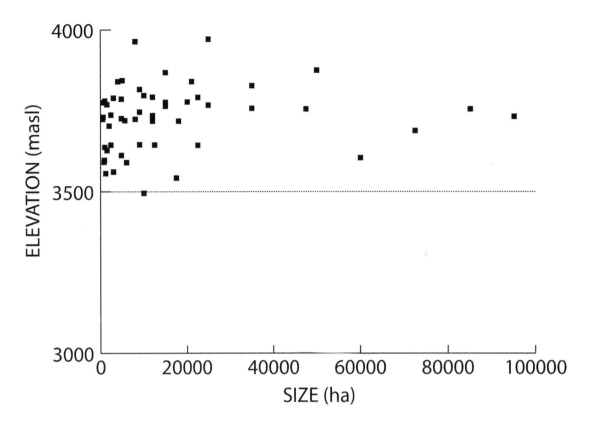

Figure 8.10. Scatterplot of LIP settlements in the Chinchero-Huayllabamba area. Except for sites in the nearby Sacred Valley, few sites are found below 3600 masl, and there is little settlement in the puna above 4000 masl.

was well over 400 m, and where a dozen sites were located close to canals. Site locations in the Chinchero-Huayllabamba area were frequently classified as tuber lands, and potatoes were under cultivation in the vicinity of 17 sites. Beans and tarwi were also common crops ($n = 11$), as were Old World cereals (barley [$n = 9$], wheat [$n = 19$]). The overall ecological picture of LIP settlement for the area is selection of sites with access to sources of drinking water and lands on which rainfall farming of *suni* crops can be conducted. Herding was probably an element of these upland economies, although the evidence for corrals in the nearby Qoricocha *puna* does not indicate large-scale LIP use. A scatterplot of settlement in upland parts of the area shows that very little settlement is to be found above 4000 masl (Fig. 8.10).

The reoccupation of symbolically powerful locales does not appear to have motivated settlement preference in the Chinchero-Huayllabamba area. Of the 12 sites with Formative components, 7 have LIP pottery, although in some cases this apparent overlap consists of very small components of one period or the other. The only instance where a cluster of LIP sites seems to have a large Formative precedent is in the vicinity of Lake Huaypo, at the margins of this area. This is not surprising, given the ritual significance of the local mountain, Cerro Huanacaure, in Inca times (Albórnoz 1989 [ca. 1582]). Other parts of the area appear to have

been resettled without a sense of reoccupying ancestral spaces, which seems to be true for most sites in the Maras area as well.

Overall, the picture of LIP settlement in upland parts of the Chinchero-Huayllabamba area is of transformative increases in settlement that are more modest, less hierarchical, and less centralized than those seen in the LIP settlement system in the Maras area. The presence of a distinctive ceramic style suggests that local people did not identify completely with their larger neighbors in Maras or Cuzco, although they appear to have had regular exchanges with these areas. The villages and village clusters in this area are not defended, although they may indicate a tendency to exploit local resources rather than to project broad networks of ecological complementarity.

LIP Settlement Patterns in the Xaquixaguana Valley

The southern part of the XPAS survey region differs from the Maras and Chinchero-Huayllabamba areas, and because of similarities in local LIP settlement patterns in the districts of Pucyura, Anta, Huarocondo, and Zurite, the entire area once known as the Xaquixaguana Valley can be considered as a single settlement system (Fig. 8.11). LIP pottery was present at 156 sites in the

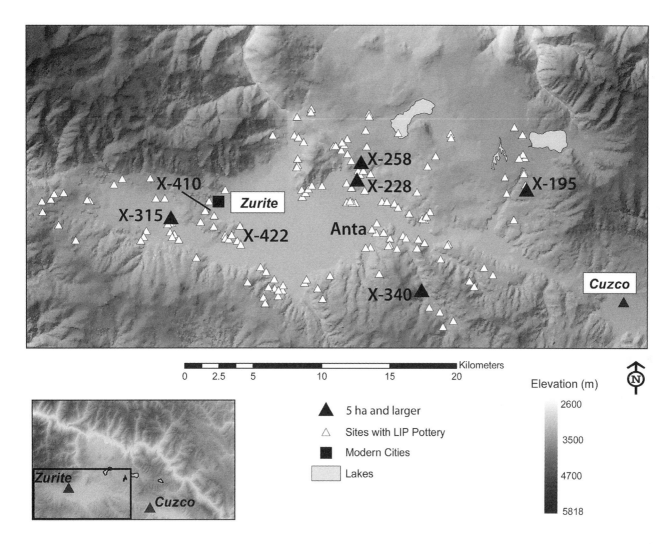

Figure 8.11. LIP sites in the Xaquixaguana Valley, which comprises parts of the districts of Pucyura, Anta, Huarocondo, and Zurite. Courtesy of L. Tsesmeli.

four districts comprising the Xaquixaguana Valley, a total site area estimated to be approximately 140 ha. The LIP collection consists of 3933 diagnostic fragments, of which about one-third (*n* = 1336) was classified as Killke. The remaining material consisted of local LIP styles, including 5 fragments of Lucre pottery identified in the laboratory. The prevalence of Killke pottery differs significantly between the districts of Pucyura and Anta (23%, 516/2260) and the districts of Huarocondo and Zurite (49%, 820/1673). Since the former area lies closer to the Cuzco Basin, the high percentage of Killke pottery in the Huarocondo-Zurite area suggests a closer relationship between the Incas and local populations beginning in the LIP, especially at sites in the Huarocondo area (Table 8.3).

Intensive collections at 20 large sites encountered LIP pottery in 229 standard units, but this area has multiple large sites that were not collected in this manner. Most of these are in the 1–2 ha range and estimating their sizes does not significantly

influence the regional settlement hierarchy, but the 3 largest—Qhakyaurqu (X-315), Tumibamba (X-410), and Tambo Real (X-422)—are large enough that the estimation of their sizes should be discussed. Qhakyaurqu is a large ceramic scatter that contains a sizeable LIP component, and its estimated 6 ha size seems reasonable based on the reconnaissance of the site during two visits (Fig. 8.12). Tumibamba and Tambo Real are low to medium density sites with surface pottery that is predominantly Inca—these are not large LIP sites, and their sizes have been estimated downward to reflect this. The modern town of Anta (X-384) may overlie a LIP settlement of unknown size, which was presumably the home of the group of the same name in Inca times and earlier. The footprint of the modern town is approximately 12 ha, suggesting that the site would not have been larger than Ak'awillay. Inca pottery was observed at the time of site registration, but it is likely that a village of a few hectares was present in LIP times.

Table 8.3. Killke components in Xaquixaguana valley districts.

District	LIP Fragments	Killke	Other LIP
Pucyura	122	15 (12.3%)	107
Anta	2138	501 (23.4%)	1637
Huarocondo	1223	700 (57.2%)	523
Zurite	450	120 (26.7%)	330

A histogram of site sizes in the Xaquixaguana Valley (Fig. 8.13) presents some similarities with the areas already discussed in this chapter. Like the Maras area, there is a large local center that sits atop a localized settlement hierarchy, located at the long-standing village site of Ak'awillay (X-228), which was almost 15 ha during the LIP. There are a dozen sites larger than a hectare lying within about an hour's walk of Ak'awillay. Villages found near the valley floor are all small (1–3 ha), whereas 3 of the largest sites are located in higher elevations to the north of Ak'awillay, where the kichwa transitions to the rolling suni lands of the Lake Huaypo area. These sites include Chullapunku (X-258; 8.5 ha), Rumikancha (X-268; 4.75 ha), and Muyu Urqu (X-256; 3.5 ha). In total, village settlements closest to Ak'awillay account for more than 45 ha—about half the size of the Maras settlement system, but significantly larger than the largest village cluster in the Chinchero-Huayllabamba area. Beyond a 4 km radius of Ak'awillay are small clusters of villages that are reminiscent of the settlement pattern in the Chinchero-Huayllabamba area. These tend to be modest in size—for example, the 7 small villages in the Tambo Real area cover an area of about 12 ha. In addition to small settlement clusters, XPAS research encountered large villages in more isolated areas that could monitor traffic between the Xaquixaguana Valley and nearby areas. Qhakyaurqu was the largest, but others include Antaq Urqu (X-340; 5 ha) on the route to Corca, and X-484 (4.5 ha) on the route to Mantocclla.

Overall, the settlement picture for the Xaquixaguana Valley suggests a relationship between site size and catchment area, with larger settlements located at the upper reaches of the kichwa or in strategic locations. As Figure 8.14 illustrates, smaller villages are found near the valley floor, and a large number of hamlets and other small sites can be found distributed across multiple ecological floors. The proportion and size of very small sites is comparable with the Maras area—there are 94 sites smaller than 5000 m² in the Xaquixaguana Valley, a total area of nearly 20 ha. This may reflect a lack of concern for defense, as well as a concomitant mobilization of ecological complementarity at a local level.

The Xaquixaguana Valley has a settlement pattern in the LIP that reflects its settlement history and long focus on valley-bottom farming. Approximately 30 sites with LIP pottery on the surface show evidence of EIP/MH settlement, and the site of Ak'awillay

continued to cast a shadow over local populations, even if it did not exercise formal control beyond a few kilometers.

Synthesizing Settlement Patterns and Ethnohistoric Descriptions of Early Inca Allies and Rivals

The XPAS survey focused on the archaeological test of a rich ethnohistoric record for Inca and Colonial settlement patterns. Colonial period documents identify a number of different named groups that lived in the XPAS region at the time of early Inca state formation and territorial expansion (see Bauer and Covey 2002; Covey 2006:209). Sources on the region were written for a range of purposes, including political consolidation (Toledo 1940 [1571]; Fornée 1965 [1586]), religious administration (Albórnoz 1989 [ca. 1582]; see Bauer and Barrionuevo 1998), colonial representation of native history (Cabello Balboa 1951 [1586]; Sarmiento de Gamboa 2007 [1572]), indigenous narration of the Inca past (Guaman Poma de Ayala 1980 [1615]; Pachacuti Yamqui Salcamaygua 1993 [17th c.]), and legal contestations over land and natural resources. In many cases, the identification of named groups on the XPAS landscape occurs in the context of describing Inca interactions with local groups. There are also sources that can help to associate these groups with particular places, although this usually requires the assumption that these groups were not significantly resettled in Inca or Colonial times.

Figure 8.15 shows the ethnohistorically-derived picture of pre-Inca settlement prior to the regional survey research (Covey 2003). Documentary sources distinguish two basic patterns in the groups living in the XPAS region: major rivals and ethnic allies. These correspond to the northern and southern parts of the region. In the north, the powerful Ayarmaca group is said to have rivaled the power of early Inca rulers until their destruction on the eve of imperial expansion; in the south, multiple groups occupying the Xaquixaguana Valley were Inca allies and marriage partners, and many groups received honorary Inca status in the imperial period.

The Ayarmaca

Inca origin stories and accounts of pre-imperial rulers place the Ayarmaca to the northwest of Cuzco, with several principal sites identified in the Maras area (see Covey 2006, 2008b; cf. Cahill 2002; Julien 2000). In the early Colonial period, people identified as Ayarmaca lived in and around the district of Chinchero and in the Cuzco Basin, a settlement pattern that reportedly developed following Inca conquest (Cahill 2002; Rostworowski 1970). References to the Ayarmacas prior to Inca annexation describe a powerful group under the centralized leadership of a kingly office (Tocay Capac) said to be the equivalent of early Inca paramounts. At the height of his power, Tocay Capac is said to have had well-established marriage alliances with elite families from groups living in the Sacred Valley and the Xaquixaguana Valley. As the Inca dynasty grew more powerful, former

Figure 8.12. View of Qhakyaurqu, a large LIP–Inca site located on a prominent hill that monitors traffic from the Xaquixaguana Valley toward the Apurímac Valley.

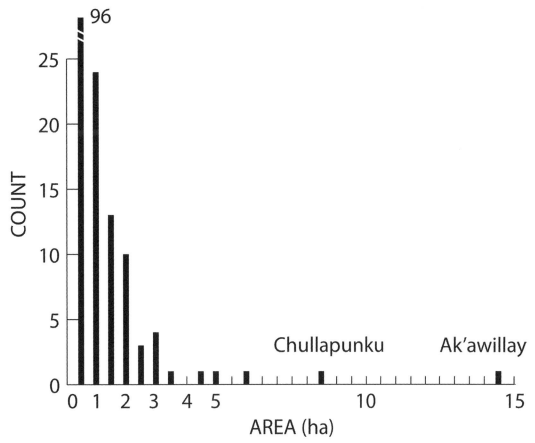

Figure 8.13. LIP site size hierarchy for the Xaquixaguana Valley. Ak'awillay remained the largest local center in the area, and most other villages were of a modest size.

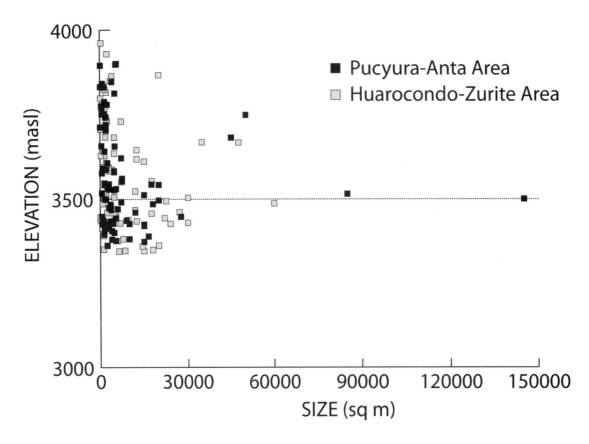

Figure 8.14. Scatterplot of site size and elevation for LIP sites in the Xaquixaguana Valley. The local center, Ak'awillay, occupies the transition between valley-bottom farmlands and the rolling plains that lie above the valley. Aside from a lower tier of upland villages near Ak'awillay, most sites favor alluvial terraces near the valley floor.

Ayarmaca subordinates established marriage alliances with Inca nobles, and the Ayarmacas became tribute-paying vassals of the growing Inca state.

The final fall of this group occurred just prior to the first campaigns of Inca imperial expansion. As Sarmiento de Gamboa (2007 [1572, chap. 34]) describes it:

> Near the Cuzco Valley is a nation of Indians called Ayarmacas, who had a proud and wealthy *sinchi* [war leader] named Tocay Capac. Neither he nor the Ayarmacas wanted to pay reverence to the Inca. Instead, they sought to ready their weapons against the Cuzcos, should they decide to turn against them. Knowing this, Inca Yupanqui called an assembly of his people and . . . they discussed what they must do. . . . And with the warriors thus gathered, they went against the Ayarmacas and their *sinchi*, and they fought each other in Guanancancha. Inca Yupanqui defeated them, and he destroyed the towns and killed almost all of the Ayarmacas.

The ethnohistoric descriptions of the Ayarmacas suggest a group with greater hierarchy than that of surrounding populations,

which should be associated with material culture indicating a broad regional influence to the north and west of Cuzco. Settlement patterns should demonstrate evidence for the disruption of areas most strongly associated with Ayarmaca political and economic power, with marked patterns of site abandonment in the imperial period.

Xaquixaguana Valley Groups

Whereas the northern part of the XPAS region is said to have been the dominion of a single powerful group, the early Inca population of the Xaquixaguana Valley lacked political cohesion or a shared identity. Ethnohistoric sources situate several small groups in the valley. Some of these, including the Anta, Huarocondo, Xaquixaguana, Equeco, Sanco, and Mayo, are identified in various sources as honorary Incas (see Bauer 1992:21–22; Covey 2006). Other communities, including Circa, Conchacalla, Casca, Ancahuasi, and Marco, appear to have a local identity, as opposed to populations from provincial regions that were settled

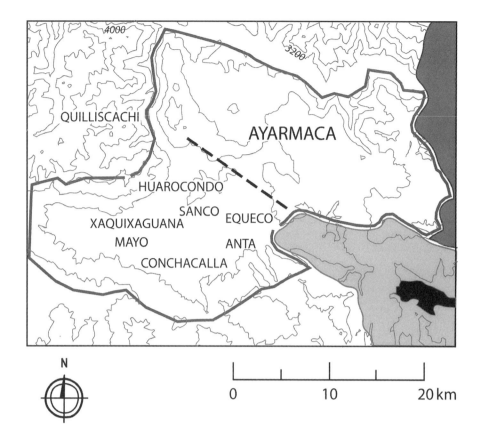

Figure 8.15. A schematic distinction of group distribution in the XPAS region prior to survey research. Adapted from the grant proposal presented to the National Science Foundation (Covey 2003).

in other towns in the Xaquixaguana Valley during Inca times. The Anta are probably the group with the greatest record of early interactions with the emerging Inca state, largely because this group was a former Ayarmaca vassal that sought out a marriage alliance with the sixth Inca ruler.

Narratives of pre-imperial Inca rulers do not permit a detailed reconstruction of the social and political organization of the Xaquixaguana Valley. The heterogeneity of the local population and its local diversity with regard to shrines (Albórnoz 1989 [ca. 1582]; see Bauer and Barrionuevo 1998) suggest a lack of central control over the valley before Inca annexation, as does the apparent absence of narratives of powerful rival rulers needing to be conquered. On the basis of this sketchy record, one would expect a local settlement pattern hierarchy with widespread villages lacking a sense of regional hierarchy or central authority, as well as perhaps numerous local substyles of LIP pottery. The apparent lack of military conflict with the Incas and the visibility of local groups in the early Colonial period would support expectations of local settlement continuity into the imperial period.

Assessment of the Ethnohistoric Model

XPAS survey work confirms and corrects some of the broad strokes of the ethnohistoric model. The settlement system identified in Maras demonstrates the presence of a major Inca rival that experienced major settlement reorganization prior to the development of the Inca imperial ceramic style (see Chapter 10). Stylistic variations between the Maras and Chinchero areas suggest some variations in local identity across the north part of the XPAS region that are not anticipated by ethnohistoric reconstructions of the Ayarmaca. In addition, settlement pattern data from the Chinchero-Huayllabamba area indicate economic organization that differs from what is seen in the Maras area. Even though the site of Yunkaray appears to have dominated a large and hierarchically-organized population, there is no reason to think that it was the capital of a polity with power that reached the Chinchero area. This suggests that the ethnohistoric accounts may not offer a complete picture of the local groups living to the northwest of Cuzco—for the Incas, identifying a recalcitrant rival king was sufficient justification for occupying and reorganizing the broader area.

The archaeological settlement patterns for the Xaquixaguana Valley partially validate ethnohistoric expectations. Assuming that the Anta people lived at the site of the same name during the LIP, it is likely that their village lies under the modern town of that name, which was established as a *reducción* town at the location of the Inca-era settlement of Anta. This means that the largest LIP site in the valley was Ak'awillay, and that the group it represents is not one that figures prominently in Inca narratives of military conquest or royal marriage alliances. In the early Colonial period, the Sanco and Equeco groups owned the lands where Ak'awillay and its larger satellite villages were located. Even though Ak'awillay approaches the size of the largest LIP site in the Maras area, its immediate hinterland is affiliated with three or four honorary Inca groups, suggesting a less hierarchical and unified administration of the valley.

As noted above, the Anta area has a lower proportion of Killke pottery in its LIP assemblage than is seen in the Huarocondo and Zurite area. Although this does not disprove Inca narratives of marriage alliances with nobles in the Anta area, it suggests that other groups living in the Xaquixaguana Valley acquired and consumed early Inca pottery on a more frequent basis. The survey work in the valley did not encounter multiple local ceramic styles that could be affiliated with specific locales, and the overall settlement pattern does not indicate the presence of discrete territories that can be tied to named groups. Overall, this suggests that the "ethnogenesis" described in the documentary record reflects Inca-era identity formation that became more fixed in the early Colonial period.

Summary

LIP settlement patterns in the XPAS region reveal varying degrees of settlement continuity, diversity in local subsistence economies, and significant ranges in local political complexity. These can be used to a certain degree alongside Inca narratives about ancestral actions in these regions, but the archaeological evidence also shows some ways that Inca informants fell short of a faithful narrative of life before state annexation. The XPAS region demonstrates that in the uncertain climate—political and environmental—of the LIP, local populations experimented with different ways to manage risk, to protect themselves from threats, and to resolve disputes in their growing communities. In some places these social strategies built on community traditions of the EIP/MH, but in others, new communities grew to unprecedented sizes or built their economies around novel mixes of herding and horticulture.

References Cited

Albórnoz, Cristóbal de
1989 [ca. 1582] Instrucción para descubrir todas las guacas del Piru y sus camayos y haziendas. In *Fábulas y mitos de los incas*, edited by Henrique Urbano and Pierre Duviols, pp. 161–98. Madrid: Historia 16.

Alcina Franch, José
1976 *Arqueología de Chinchero. 1. La arquitectura*. Madrid: Ministerio de Asuntos Exteriores.

Alcina Franch, José, Miguel Rivera, Jesús Galván, María Carmen García Palacios, Balbina Martínez-Caviro, Luis J. Ramos, and Tito Varela
1976 *Arqueología de Chinchero. 2. Cerámica y otros materiales*. Madrid: Ministerio de Asuntos Exteriores.

Bauer, Brian S.
1992 *The Development of the Inca State*. Austin: University of Texas Press.

Bauer, Brian S., and Wilton Barrionuevo Orosco
1998 Reconstructing Andean shrine systems: A test case from the Xaquixaguana (Anta) region of Cusco, Peru. *Andean Past* 5:73–87.

Bauer, Brian S., and R. Alan Covey
2002 Processes of state formation in the Inca heartland (Cuzco, Peru). *American Anthropologist* 104(3):846–64.

Cabello Balboa, Miguel
1951 [1586] *Miscelánea antártica, una historia del Perú antiguo*, edited by L. E. Valcárcel. Lima: Universidad Nacional Mayor de San Marcos, Instituto de Etnología.

Cahill, David
2002 The virgin and the Inca: An Incaic procession in the city of Cuzco in 1692. *Ethnohistory* 49(3):611–49.

Covey, R. Alan
2003 Territorial Expansion and Administrative Consolidation in the Inka Heartland, Cusco, Peru: The Xaquixaguana Plain Archaeological Survey. Grant proposal to the National Science Foundation, proposal BCS 0342381.
2006 *How the Incas Built Their Heartland: State Formation and the Innovation of Imperial Strategies in the Sacred Valley, Peru*. Ann Arbor: University of Michigan Press.
2008a Multiregional perspectives on the archaeology of the Andes during the Late Intermediate period (ca. AD 1000–1400). *Journal of Archaeological Research* 16(3):287–338.
2008b The Inca empire. In *The Handbook of South American Archaeology*, edited by Helaine Silverman and William H. Isbell, pp. 809–30. New York: Springer.

2009   Inka agricultural intensification in the imperial heartland and provinces. In *Andean Civilization: A Tribute to Michael E. Moseley*, edited by Joyce Marcus and Patrick Ryan Williams, pp. 361–73. University of California, Los Angeles: Cotsen Institute of Archaeology.

2011   Landscapes and languages of power in the Inca imperial heartland (Cuzco, Peru). *SAA Archaeological Record* 11(4):29–32, 47.

Covey, R. Alan, Miriam Aráoz Silva, and Brian S. Bauer
2008   Settlement patterns in the Yucay Valley and neighboring areas. In *Imperial Transformations in Sixteenth-Century Yucay, Peru*, edited by R. Alan Covey and Donato Amado González, pp. 3–17. Memoirs, no. 44. Ann Arbor: Museum of Anthropology, University of Michigan.

Covey, R. Alan, Kylie E. Quave, and Catherine E. Covey
forthcoming   Inca storage systems in the imperial heartland (Cusco, Peru): Risk management, economic growth, and political economy. In *Storage and Administration in Ancient Complex Societies*, edited by Linda Manzanilla and Mitchell Rothman.

Fornée, Niculoso de
1965 [1586]   *Breve relación de la tierra del corregimiento de Abancay, de que es corregidor Niculoso de Fornée*. Biblioteca de Autores Españoles 184:16–30. Madrid: Ediciones Atlas.

Garcilaso de la Vega, "El Inca"
1965 [1609]   Los comentarios reales de los incas. In *Obras Completas*, edited by Carmelo Sáenz de Santa María. Biblioteca de Autores Españoles, vol. 132–135. Madrid: Ediciones Atlas.

Glowacki, Mary
2002   The Huaro archaeological site complex: Rethinking the Huari occupation of Cuzco. In *Andean Archaeology I: Variations in Sociopolitical Organization*, edited by William H. Isbell and Helaine Silverman, pp. 267–85. New York: Kluwer Academic/ Plenum Publishers.

Guaman Poma de Ayala, Felipe
1980 [1615]   *El primer nueva corónica y buen gobierno*, edited by J. V. Murra and R. Adorno. Mexico City: Siglo Veintiuno.

Haquehua Huaman, Wilbert, and Rubén Maqque Azorsa
1996   Cerámica de Cueva Moqo-Maras. Tesis, Facultad de Ciencias Sociales, Universidad Nacional de San Antonio Abad del Cusco.

Julien, Catherine J.
2000   *Reading Inca History*. Iowa City: University of Iowa Press.

Maqque Azorsa, Rubén, and Wilbert Haquehua Huaman
1993   Prospección arqueológica de Cueva Moqo-Maras. Informe de prácticas preprofesionales. Facultad de Ciencias Sociales, Universidad Nacional de San Antonio Abad del Cusco.

McEwan, Gordon F.
1996   Archaeological investigations at Pikillacta, a Wari site in Peru. *Journal of Field Archaeology* 23(2):169–86.

McEwan, Gordon F., Melissa Chatfield, and Arminda Gibaja
2002   The archaeology of Inca origins: Excavations at Chokepuquio, Cuzco, Peru. In *Andean Archaeology I: Variations in Sociopolitical Organization*, edited by William H. Isbell and Helaine Silverman, pp. 287–301. New York: Kluwer Academic/ Plenum Press.

Pachacuti Yamqui Salcamaygua, Joan de Santa Cruz
1993 [17th c.]   *Relación de antigüedades deste reyno del Piru*, edited by Pierre Duviols and César Itier. Cusco: Centro de Estudios Rurales Andinos, "Bartolomé de Las Casas."

Quave, Kylie E.
2012   Labor and Domestic Economy on the Royal Estate in the Inka Imperial Heartland (Maras, Cuzco, Peru). PhD dissertation, Department of Anthropology, Southern Methodist University, Dallas.

Quirita, Rosa Alicia
2002   *Conjunto arqueológico de Moray*. Cuzco: Instituto Nacional de Cultura.

Rivera Dorado, Miguel
1971a   La cerámica killke y la arqueología de Cuzco (Perú). *Revista Española de Antropología Americana* 6:85–124.

1971b   Diseños decorativos en la cerámica killke. *Revista del Museo Nacional* 37:106–15.

1972   La cerámica de Cancha-Cancha, Cuzco, Peru. *Revista Dominicana de Arqueología y Antropología* 2(2–3):36–49.

Rostworowski, María
1970   Los Ayarmaca. *Revista del Museo Nacional* 36:58–101.

Sarmiento de Gamboa, Pedro de
2007 [1572]   *The History of the Incas*, translated and edited by Brian S. Bauer and Vania Smith. Austin: University of Texas Press.

Toledo, Francisco de
1940 [1571]   Información hecha por orden del Virrey Don Francisco de Toledo . . . Yucay, Marzo 19–Julio 2 de 1571. In *Don Francisco de Toledo, supremo organizador del Perú: Su vida, su obra (1515–1582). Tomo II: Sus informaciones sobre los incas (1570–1572)*, edited by Roberto Levillier, pp. 99–121. Buenos Aires: Espasa-Calpe.

Valencia Sosa, Amalia
2004   Informe Anual 2004 Restauración y Puesta en Valor del Sitio Arqueológico Camino Machuqollqa Comunidad Raqchi-Huaillabamba. Report submitted to the Instituto Nacional de Cultura, Cusco, Peru.

Chapter 9: Late Intermediate Period Settlement Patterns in the Sacred Valley and the Measure of Early Inca State Power

R. Alan Covey

Around AD 1000, the Sacred Valley entered a period of major settlement disruption that involved the reconfiguration of subsistence strategies, the production of new social hierarchies, and the reconceptualization of local landscapes. Similar processes have already been discussed for the Xaquixaguana region (Chapter 8), so this chapter follows a similar structure, presenting local settlement pattern data from the Sacred Valley Archaeological Project (SVAP) and the Calca-Yanahuara Archaeological Survey (PACY). Variations in patterns in the Chit'apampa Basin, the Sacred Valley proper, and the small basins lying to the north of the Vilcanota-Urubamba River indicate differences in local subsistence practices and social organization. The distribution of Killke pottery and Inca architecture at local Late Intermediate period (LIP) sites provides evidence for the reach of the early Inca state in the last years of the LIP. Once the settlement pattern data have been presented, discussion turns to the question of congruence with ethnohistoric descriptions of early Inca-era populations in the Sacred Valley.

The same chronological concerns voiced for the LIP in other chapters apply to the Sacred Valley; it is also important to note that site size estimates in that region are based on general collection data. Survey crews mapped several large LIP sites (Pukara

Pantillijlla, Markasunay, Qhapaqkancha, Ankasmarka), which presented the opportunity to assess size estimates at some of the largest settlements. Because it was logistically impractical to conduct intensive collections in the Sacred Valley, the sherd count from survey work is much lower than that of the Xaquixaguana region. SVAP and PACY research identified a comparable number of LIP sites ($n = 291$) to that of the Xaquixaguana and Qoricocha regions, but only about 4000 LIP diagnostics were collected and analyzed in the laboratory (Fig. 9.1).

The Onset of the LIP in the Sacred Valley

As discussed in Chapter 7, settlement pattern data indicate that the Sacred Valley was moderately populated before AD 1000, with an agrarian focus on valley-bottom lands that could be easily irrigated. The regional distribution of Cuzco Basin styles (Qotakalli and the Wari-influenced Araway) suggests that settlements lying to the south of the Vilcanota-Urubamba River had more regular contact with populations in the Cuzco Basin, whereas sites more distant show a more limited affiliation. The Wari colonization of the Lucre Basin did not lead to settlement

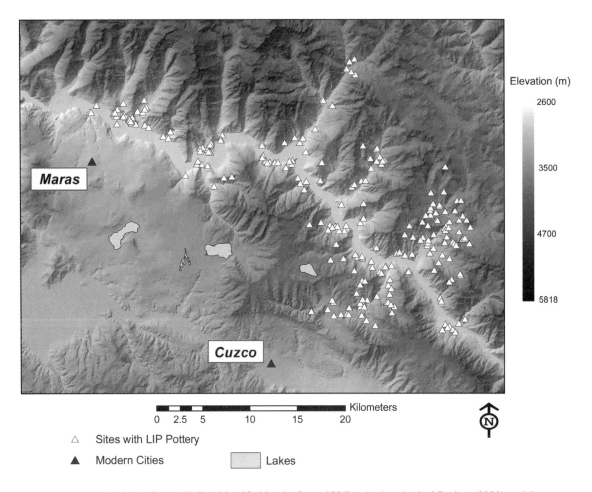

Figure 9.1. LIP sites in the Sacred Valley, identified by the Sacred Valley Archaeological Project (2000) and the Calca-Yanahuara Archaeological Project (2007). Courtesy of L. Tsesmeli.

changes in the Sacred Valley, and the overall Early Intermediate/ Middle Horizon (EIP/MH) settlement pattern appears to be fairly stable until the end of the first millennium.

By AD 1000, populations across the Cuzco region were undergoing variable degrees of social transformation that would culminate in the formation and expansion of the Inca state (Bauer and Covey 2002). Although the climate became more arid and unpredictable, many of the largest valley-bottom farming communities continued to work the same lands that they had for centuries. This is true for most of the larger villages in the Cuzco Basin, and for sites like Ak'awillay (Fig. 9.2). By contrast, some areas with excellent agricultural lands experienced notable population decline. Valley-bottom villages in the Oropesa Basin were abandoned in the LIP in favor of the site of Tipón, where the population built a monumental wall to enclose itself and its best farmland (Bauer and Covey 2002) (Fig. 9.3). In the Lucre Basin, construction halted at the Wari installation at Pikillacta and the site was abandoned and burned (McEwan 2005), although nearby valley-bottom sites such as Chokepukio and Minaspata

continued to be occupied (Dwyer 1971; McEwan, Chatfield, and Gibaja 2002) (Fig. 9.4).

Climate change and social upheaval contributed to the abandonment of valley-bottom farmlands and settlements in some areas, but it also stimulated new settlement and intensification projects, especially in the Maras area (Chapter 8) and parts of the Cuzco Basin (Bauer and Covey 2002). This suggests that in some parts of the region, reliance on agricultural surpluses served as an effective risk-management strategy, although one that would be expected to produce higher rates of population growth and resource stress (Covey 2006, 2009). This approach to subsistence stands in contrast to the prevailing local economies that developed in the central Andes following the collapse of the Wari and Tiwanaku states (Covey 2008, 2012). Intensification and surplus production were not the only way to deal with the risks of a fluctuating climate, and the LIP saw major settlement growth in areas amenable to a very different subsistence strategy: broad-spectrum agropastoralism (Covey 2011). Instead of emphasizing surplus production, these systems invested kin-based labor

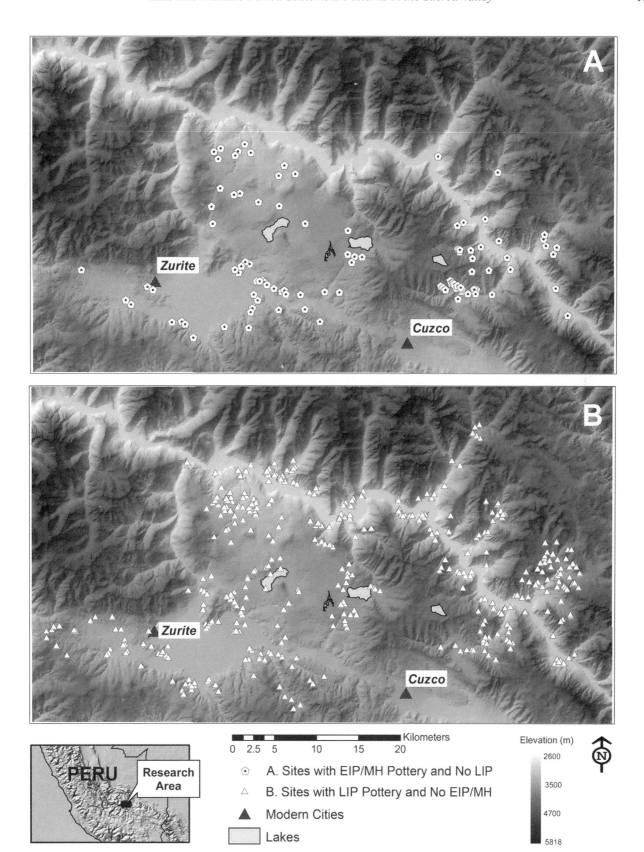

Figure 9.2. Areas experiencing abandonment and resettlement during the LIP. Valley-bottom farming and broad-spectrum agropastoralism appear to have been viable subsistence strategies, depending on local climate and social conditions. Courtesy of L. Tsesmeli.

Figure 9.3.

Photograph of a fortified
Inca complex within the
Tipón site. After AD 1000,
locals abandoned sites
located near productive
valley-bottom farmland,
moving to Tipón, where a
massive fortification wall
protected settlement, herd
animals, and well-watered
lands. The site reportedly
was one of the last
holdouts against the Incas.

Figure 9.4.

Shippee-Johnson
expedition photograph
of Minaspata, a large
valley-bottom site located
in the Lucre Basin to the
southeast of Cuzco. The
sprawling site covers some
15–20 ha, and represents
a continuous occupation
from the first millennium
BC through Inca times.
Courtesy of Department of
Library Services, American
Museum of Natural History
(neg. no. 334821).

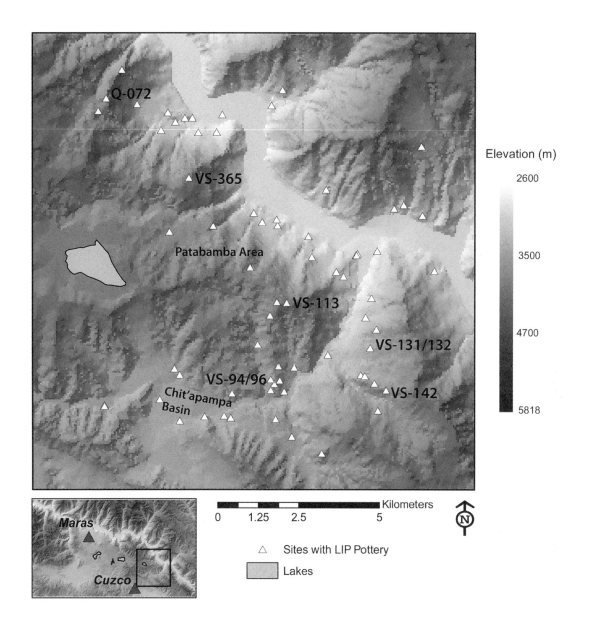

Figure 9.5. Map of LIP sites found to the south of the Vilcanota-Urubamba Valley (inset area only). Courtesy of L. Tsesmeli.

networks in producing diverse cultigens across a range of local microclimates, ensuring more modest surpluses while safeguarding against total crop failure (Covey 2006; see Zimmerer 1997).

The settlement patterns in the Sacred Valley suggest a shift to this subsistence strategy at the onset of the LIP, but with a gradual expansion into the area by valley-bottom farming societies from the Maras area and the Cuzco Basin. Generally, there is little continuity between Cuzco-dominated Middle Horizon styles and LIP settlements. In the SVAP region, 83.5% (183/224) of LIP sites have no EIP/MH component, and in the Calca-Yanahuara region, this figure was even lower owing to the virtual absence of identified EIP/MH diagnostics (1.5%, 1/67) (see Covey, Aráoz Silva, and Bauer 2008).

LIP Settlement Patterns in the Chit'apampa Basin

As discussed in Chapter 7, EIP/MH sites in the Chit'apampa Basin exhibited a strong stylistic affiliation with the neighboring Cuzco Basin, with no clear local settlement hierarchy. After AD 1000, the dispersed valley-bottom sites in the basin were abandoned in favor of larger, nucleated settlements that were frequently established on prominent ridges at a greater distance from Cuzco (Fig. 9.5). The largest of these is Raqchi (VS-94/96), which had been a major Formative site, although many LIP villages occupied locations that had never been previously occupied (Fig. 9.6). The timing of this shift appears to be at the very end of the Middle Horizon, indicated by the presence of

Figure 9.6. Photograph of lower Chit'apampa Basin. The LIP occupation at Raqchi (VS-94/96) resettled the site of an abandoned Formative village, a location with excellent visibility and defensive potential.

small components of Araway pottery at large LIP sites where no Qotakalli pottery was present.

The LIP settlement pattern for the Chit'apampa Basin exhibits a modest hierarchy that was absent during the EIP/MH (Fig. 9.7). A total of 61 sites in the Chit'apampa Basin and Patabamba area have a LIP component, representing a total area of approximately 60 ha. There are 3 village sites in the 6–7 ha range, although one of these (VS-109) appears to be primarily an Inca occupation with a small Killke component. The other 2 large villages, Raqchi and VS-131/132, are located in the lower Chit'apampa Basin at elevations of around 3800 masl, where rain-fed tuber lands and pastures are locally accessible. Other village sites lying to the south of the Vilcanota-Urubamba River are found in the lower basin and near the rim of the Sacred Valley, at high-elevation locations that have excellent visibility and lie close to herding and dry farming resources (Fig. 9.8). These include Qhapaqkan-cha (VS-365), Hatun Pukara (VS-113), and Wat'arayanpata (VS-142). The average elevation for the 15 Chit'apampa LIP sites larger than a hectare is 3843 masl, and no site larger than a hectare is found below 3600 m. Figure 9.9 illustrates the shift to higher elevations in Chit'apampa, showing a greater range of site elevations among smaller sites. This suggests that villages

managed horticulture and herding in distinct ways that were tailored to the resources of their immediate catchment areas, perhaps extending the breadth of their productive range through hamlets or seasonal occupations.

The shift to high village sites near the southern rim of the Sacred Valley was not restricted to the Chit'apampa Basin and Patabamba area. To the west of this area, high-elevation sites are isolated and fairly small, lying far from productive farmlands and major water sources. The Qoricocha survey identified Aylluq Tiyasqa (Q-072), a 1.8 ha village site located on a prominence at 4150 masl, about 3.5 km to the west of Qhapaqkancha. Farther to the west, the Calca-Yanahuara survey registered 2 sites along a high ridge on Cerro Sauceda (CY-143/144), an occupation of about a hectare that is about a vertical kilometer above the floor of the Sacred Valley across from Huayoccari. Similar sites were not identified along the southern rim of the Sacred Valley to the east of the Chit'apampa Basin due to the steep and rocky terrain of the upper valley slopes and the lack of reliable water sources.

Because of the strong link observed between the Chit'apampa Basin and the nearby Cuzco Basin during the EIP/MH, it is important to evaluate whether or not the new villages in the area appear to have had similar contacts. Because SVAP crews made

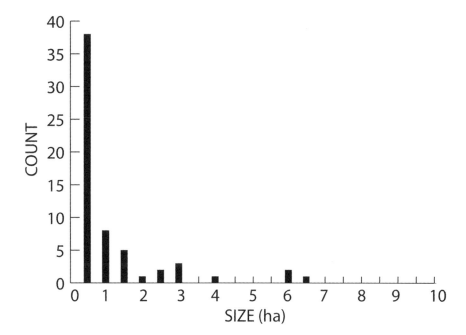

Figure 9.7.

LIP site size hierarchy for the Chit'apampa and nearby areas. A modest village hierarchy is present, although the largest sites are considerably smaller than contemporaneous villages in the neighboring Xaquixaguana region.

Figure 9.8.

Photograph of the Huata area in the lower Chit'apampa Basin. LIP villages in the area lie above 3800 masl, hundreds of meters above the floor of the nearby canyon that descends into the Sacred Valley.

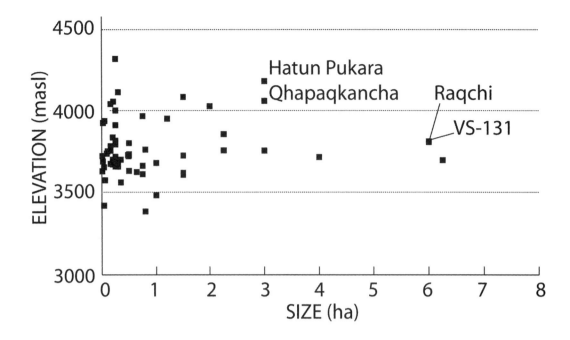

Figure 9.9. Scatterplot of size and elevation of LIP sites in the Chit'apampa Basin and nearby areas to the south of the Sacred Valley. Village sites favor higher elevations, with lower-order sites occupying a broader range of local microenvironments.

general collections at large sites, the sample of survey pottery cannot be considered representative, although it can be thought of as a series of small random samples that can be aggregated to develop some coarse-grained perspectives on pottery distributions. Overall, about 700 LIP sherds were collected at sites in the Chit'apampa area, and the sample contains a sizeable proportion of Killke material (48.7%, *n* = 344). Some of the prevalence of Killke pottery can be attributed to Inca expansion into the area later in the LIP (discussed below). The remaining material comprised local imitations of Killke and other LIP styles, including modest components of Lucre pottery (mostly restricted to the larger villages) and material thought to originate in the Chinchero and Maras areas. Notably, the local Cuyu style identified in the Chongo Basin appears to be absent at LIP sites in the Chit'apampa Basin.

The ceramic collections from villages in the Chit'apampa area suggest exchange relationships with populations living in the Cuzco Basin, but also with groups living within a day's journey along the southern rim of the Sacred Valley. Taken with changes in settlement locations and size hierarchies, it is reasonable to infer that local populations interacted with the emerging Inca state, but were not administered directly by a Cuzco Basin polity early in the LIP.

LIP Settlement Patterns along the Sacred Valley

The settlement pattern data from the Sacred Valley suggest that valley-bottom farming served as an effective risk-management strategy for only a small population during the LIP. In the SVAP survey region, the LIP site count for the Sacred Valley proper—areas found at an elevation within a few hundred meters of the valley floor—was comparable to that of the Chit'apampa Basin (*n* = 64), although the estimated total site area is significantly smaller, 29 ha (Fig. 9.10). The Calca-Yanahuara survey adds 64 LIP sites in the valley, with an estimated total area of about 35 ha. In the SVAP region, Killke pottery constituted 37.5% of the LIP assemblage (343/914), a figure that is markedly lower from what had been noted for the Chit'apampa area. The scatterplot of site size and elevation in the Sacred Valley (Fig. 9.11) shows that LIP sites favor areas close to the valley floor, which drops gently from about 2990–2840 masl along the surveyed section. Most sites are fairly small, and the villages tend to be located on prominent points close to permanent streams and side valleys. These could be single isolated settlements, or small clusters of villages and hamlets. For example, Lluk'urqu (VS-285) is a lone 1.2 ha site found near San Salvador (Fig. 9.12), whereas survey work around the communities of Quillhuay and Macay (across

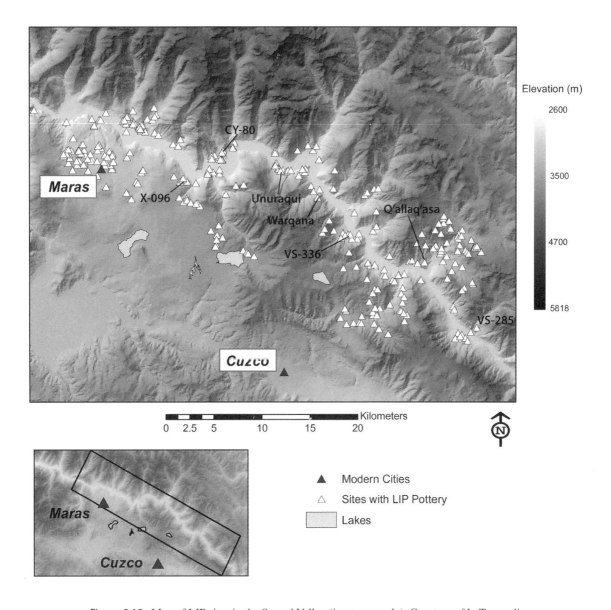

Figure 9.10. Map of LIP sites in the Sacred Valley (inset area only). Courtesy of L. Tsesmeli.

the river from Coya) encountered a 3 ha cluster of small sites, the largest of which was VS-336, a 1.2 ha site (Fig. 9.13).

Similar site configurations appeared in the Calca-Yanahuara study region. The largest cluster was found in the Unuraqui area; crews registered 9 LIP sites that covered about 7 ha of total area, including CY-46 (1.8 ha), Antaracay (CY-75/76/77; total area of 2.7 ha), and Tuqaqa Huayco (CY-86; 1.8 ha). In the Huayoccari area, CY-80 was a single 2.1 ha settlement on a ridge at 3279 masl, about 400 m above the valley floor (Fig. 9.14). The Xaquixaguana survey conducted intensive collections at Umaspata

(X-096), a 3 ha LIP settlement overlooking Huayllabamba with a dense ceramic scatter that yielded a modest Killke component (16.5%, 74/448) (Fig. 9.15). Overall, the LIP occupation of the Sacred Valley exhibits less hierarchy than do nearby areas, and the small villages appear to be situated to take advantage of permanent water sources and farmlands on and near the valley floor. Visibility and security might also have been considerations, although the large number of very small sites near the valley floor suggests that small-scale subsistence activity in the valley was a sufficiently safe enterprise during at least some times in the LIP.

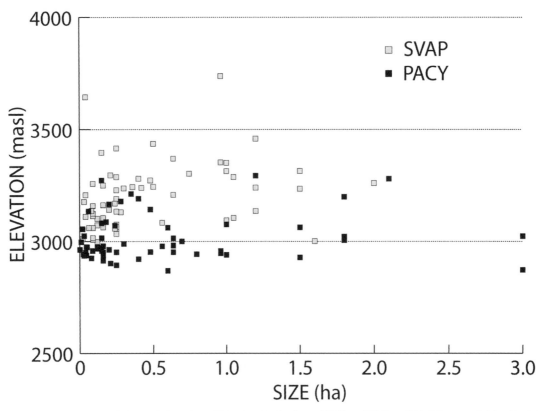

Figure 9.11. Scatterplot of size and elevation of LIP sites in the Sacred Valley. SVAP and PACY research identified 128 sites within a few hundred meters of the valley floor, most of which were of modest size.

Figure 9.12. Lluk'urqu (VS-285), a small LIP village located on a prominent point near San Salvador, close to a small stream that flows into the Vilcanota-Urubamba River.

Figure 9.13. View of the Sacred Valley near Quillhuay and Macay. The high-elevation site of Qhapaqkancha overlooks a cluster of small settlements situated around a prominent point a few hundred meters above the valley floor, including VS-336.

Figure 9.14. The ridgetop site of CY-80 overlooks the Huayoccari area in the lower Sacred Valley.

Figure 9.15. Umaspata (X-096), a LIP village site overlooking the Sacred Valley, with the town of Yucay in the background. The Inca occupation of this area focuses on a storage facility at the nearby site of Wayna Qollqa.

Figure 9.16. The Q'allaq'asa complex at Pisac—the architectural remains in the center of the photo—has evidence of LIP settlement. The terraces seen below and across the valley date to Inca times.

Special mention should be made of a limited number of locations where LIP settlements were developed into rural estates by Inca rulers and their families. At Pisac on the north side of the Sacred Valley, the Q'allaq'asa complex has evidence of an occupation commencing in the LIP, which is higher (3440 masl) and farther from the Sacred Valley than the sites just discussed (Fig. 9.16) (Yépez 1985). This site became part of the estate of Pachacutic Inca Yupanqui, who reportedly consolidated Inca rule over the area following an assassination plot by the local Cuyo population (Covey 2006). This ruler's father, Viracocha Inca, developed a royal retreat at Caquia Xaquixaguana, and Kendall and colleagues (1992) have identified LIP components at the nearby site of Warqana, which is located on a prominence about 750 m above the valley floor (Fig. 9.17). These sites are in many ways atypical of the LIP occupation of the Sacred Valley, and they seem to represent a downward shifting of Inca power from high-elevation sites located at a greater distance from the valley floor (see below).

LIP Settlement Patterns to the North of the Sacred Valley

The settlement pattern for the side valleys lying to the north of the Vilcanota-Urubamba River is similar to that of the Chit'apampa Basin and nearby high-elevation areas (Fig. 9.18). SVAP survey crews found 99 LIP sites in the northern side valleys, a total site area of about 104 ha. These figures are fairly comparable given the different sizes of the two areas. In the Calca-Yanahuara study region, the northern drainages were much more narrow and marginal, and there were few LIP sites found at a distance from the main valley. One site, CY-51, was found in the Pumahuaca Quebrada, a few kilometers from the valley. The site measured 5–6 ha and had the remains of perhaps 200 stone structures, but architectural collapse and dense vegetation made it impossible to determine the date of the site.

The site size hierarchy for the northern drainages (Fig. 9.19) would be similar to that of the Chit'apampa area if not for the site of Pukara Pantillijlla (VS-176), which grew to about 10 ha under

Figure 9.17. The site of Warqana is situated on a prominence and surrounded by irregular terraces. The valley-bottom town of Calca is in the background.

Inca influence during the late thirteenth and fourteenth centuries (Covey 2006). Excavations at the site (Covey, n.d.) indicate that the earlier LIP community was smaller, so that before Inca expansion north of the Sacred Valley, the largest communities were 6–7 ha. These include Muyuch'urqu (VS-157) in the upper Chongo Basin, and Markasunay (VS-353) in the Quebrada Carmen above Lamay. A third site (VS-350) in the Poques area of Quebrada Carmen has an Inca component of the same size as the LIP collection—it is likely that the site was smaller than 6 ha during the LIP. These "large" villages are small when compared with the local LIP centers in the Xaquixaguana region (Chapter 8), and are only slightly more extensive than the next group of villages in the 4–5 ha range. Spatially, the larger villages tend to cluster in the higher elevations in the Chongo Basin and Quebrada Carmen, where 21 sites of a hectare or larger are located. The total site area of this group is about 70 ha, making it much smaller and less hierarchical than settlement clusters in the Maras area and Xaquixaguana Valley. There are several village sites that lie outside this cluster in strategic locations, including Ancasmarca (VS-385) and Kaytumarka (VS-324) (Fig. 9.20).

The scatterplot of site size and elevation for the northern drainages (Fig. 9.21) reveals a focus on high-elevation locations for larger sites—the 26 sites of at least a hectare are found

at an average elevation of 3860 masl, and the largest sites tend to be found above 3900 masl. (By comparison, sites smaller than a hectare have an average elevation of 3754 masl.) Pukara Pantillijlla is situated on a prominent ridge that separates the upper and lower Chongo Basin, at an elevation that offers access to a tier of very high villages (4000–4300 masl), and a lower group of somewhat smaller villages situated in the *suni*. This settlement pattern is the ecological opposite of the Maras area, where the site size was inversely correlated with elevation. It should be noted that the high-elevation villages of the northern side valleys represent a clear break from EIP/MH patterns. There appears to be some reoccupation of sites that were used in Formative times (although not necessarily as population centers). Pukara Pantillijlla, Markasunay, and Apu Sompechu are 3 of the larger sites where a Formative component has been identified.

A few important distinctions can be drawn between the northern drainages and the Chit'apampa area. First, the percentage of Killke pottery is very low to the north of the Sacred Valley. Excluding the sites of Pukara Pantillijlla and Ankasmarka—2 settlements with a sizeable Inca component that were collected in a more intensive fashion than other sites in the region—the LIP assemblage from the northern side valleys contained only 10.3% Killke pottery (112/1186). The site of Muyuch'urqu (VS-

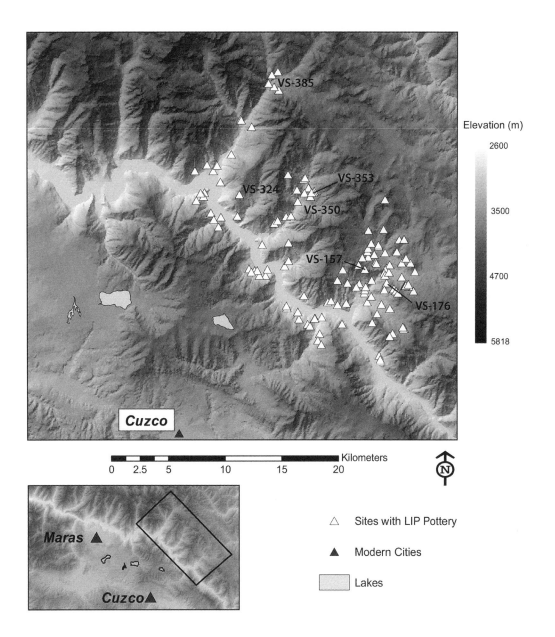

Figure 9.18. Map of LIP sites to the north of the Sacred Valley (inset area only). The largest LIP sites in the Sacred Valley appeared on high ridges in side valleys to the north of the valley. Courtesy of L. Tsesmeli.

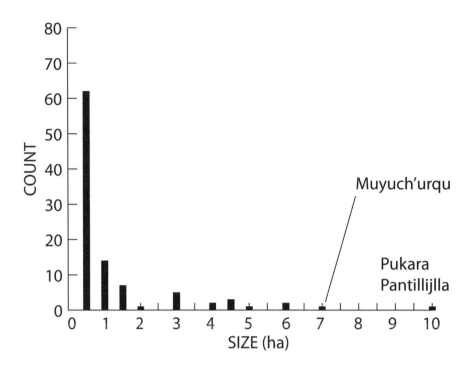

Figure 9.19. Site size hierarchy for the northern drainages of the SVAP region. Before the Inca expansion of Pukara Pantillijlla, there was a modest hierarchy with a few villages of 6–7 ha.

157) and a 3 ha satellite village (VS-156) yielded 109 fragments of LIP pottery, of which only 2 were identified as Killke. These sites had no Inca material in their surface collections. Whereas Cuzco Basin pottery was rare to the north of the Sacred Valley, a local ceramic style called Cuyo (Covey 2006) was encountered commonly in and around the Chongo Basin. This style represents about 20% of the decorated pottery collected from VS-156/157, but it is absent at sites to the south of the Sacred Valley, as well as in the Qochoc Valley above Calca. The presence of a local ceramic style and the absence of large amounts of material from the Cuzco Basin suggest that the Sacred Valley promoted cultural distance between groups living to the north and south. This interpretation is buttressed by the prevalence of above-ground mortuary structures near LIP villages in upper basin areas, a burial pattern not observed to the south of the Sacred Valley (Covey 2006). Freestanding mortuary structures are most common in the upper Chongo Basin, and mortuary practices and domestic architecture vary in other parts of the northern side valleys.

LIP Settlement and Pre-Inca Social Power in the Sacred Valley

Populations living in and around the Sacred Valley in the LIP engaged in a wide range of subsistence practices that were intended to reduce seasonal and interannual risks during a time of marked climatic fluctuation. Diversity appears to have played a role in all parts of the region, but the largest communities and most hierarchical settlement clusters favored elevations where horticulture and herding could be conducted locally. The largest cluster of villages is found in the upper Chongo Basin and the Quebrada Carmen, where a modest settlement hierarchy was present prior to Inca expansion into the area. The distribution of mortuary remains, local pottery, and domestic architecture suggests a shared identity within a few hours' walk of Muyuch'urqu, the largest village, but ideological power of local leaders would have been limited to a modest population living in a fairly constrained region. The resettlement of prominent places that had ancient (Formative) habitation and burials occurred to the south of the Sacred Valley (at Raqchi) and the north (at Markasunay and Pukara Pantillijlla), as well as at the site of Wat'a lying to the west of the Xaquixaguana region (Kosiba 2010). This suggests some broadly shared values regarding the conceptualization of sacred landscapes in upland areas (Covey 2011).

As discussed above, the distribution of ceramic styles indicates important patterns in the SVAP region that speak to Inca ideological and economic power in local communities. These perspectives can be enhanced by the presentation of paste and temper data from survey collections. SVAP personnel worked in the laboratory to identify each diagnostic LIP sherd based on paste and temper. The survey sample comprises 2780 sherds from about 150 sites across the study region, which are grouped among

Kaytumarka (VS-324)

Figure 9.20. The high-elevation site of Kaytumarka (VS-324) overlooks the Sacred Valley at Calca, and is isolated from the cluster of LIP villages in the upper Chongo Basin and Carmen Quebrada.

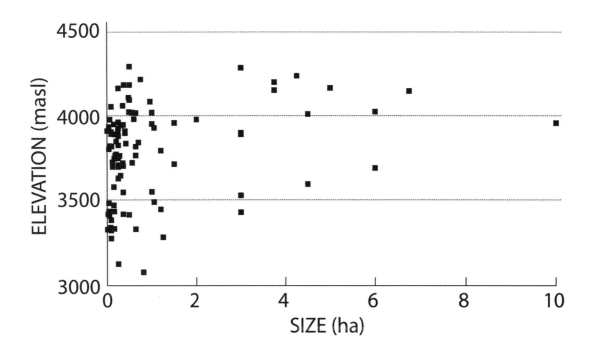

Figure 9.21. Scatterplot of site size and elevation for LIP settlements in the northern drainages of the SVAP region. The largest villages before Inca conquest are on high ridges, but the growth of Pukara Pantillijlla provided greater ecological integration of the Chongo Basin and nearby areas.

12 paste/temper categories (Table 9.1). Dividing the sample between areas to the south of the Sacred Valley (Chit'apampa and Patabamba areas), the main valley, and the northern drainages (Chongo, Carmen, and Qochoc) reveals clear differences in local assemblages.

Several pastes (1, 2, 4, 5, 6, and 7) were most common north of the Sacred Valley, less abundant within the valley, and even less common to the south of the valley. These pastes constitute more than 50% of the LIP pottery to the north of the Sacred Valley, 27.2% of the collection in the Sacred Valley, and just 14.1% of the assemblage to the south of the valley. There are two pastes (10 and 11) where the pattern is reversed—to the south of the valley, these comprise 40% of the LIP pottery, and they are less common in the valley (20.4%) and northern drainages (11.3%). Two additional pastes (8 and 9) have greatest proportionate representation in the valley (49.7%), and are less abundant to the north and south (35% and 44.8%, respectively). The large sample of Paste 9 might indicate pottery that was associated with Inca state expansion into the Sacred Valley, although this ware does not appear to be exclusively decorated with the Killke style (see Chapter 11).

In terms of economic power, the distribution of village sites suggests that local communities were situated to take advantage of a broad range of resources, but that the reach of local kin groups and community leaders would not be expected to encompass the complete range of crops and herd animals found in the study region. Villages on the rim of the valley might have practiced some form of ecological complementarity, and there are a few cases (Qhapaqkancha, Kaytumarka) where a larger village is located at the *suni/puna* transition, but close to smaller communities at lower elevations that could exploit *kichwa* lands. The settlement cluster in the upper Chongo Basin seems to unite the farming and herding resources of the uplands without a clear connection to kichwa resources in the Sacred Valley. This cluster is also situated in a way that would permit it to monitor movement from the Sacred Valley to lowland areas where chile peppers, coca, and other lowland products could be accessed. Monitoring the movement of caravans (or raiding groups from rival communities) is accentuated by site location in other areas as well, such as the siting of Raqchi and Ankasmarka. Overall, there does not appear to be centralized control over economic production, but rather, a fairly local emphasis on access to a wide range of resources.

Large LIP sites in the Sacred Valley occupy prominent locations, which could enhance local ideological and economic power. Such locations also reflect the military power of communities in the region, as these locations are inaccessible and have natural defenses from nearby cliffs and outcrops. There

Table 9.1. Counts and proportions of paste/temper categories in SVAP LIP collections.

Paste	South	%	Sacred Valley	%	North	%	Total
1	5	0.8	41	4.9	129	9.9	175
2	2	0.3	12	1.4	57	4.4	71
3	1	0.2	18	2.2	28	2.2	47
4	2	0.3	3	0.4	41	3.2	46
5	15	2.3	58	6.9	120	9.2	193
6	56	8.7	75	9.0	214	16.5	345
7	11	1.7	38	4.6	107	8.2	156
8	49	7.6	83	9.9	114	8.8	246
9	240	37.2	332	39.8	340	26.2	912
10	209	32.4	144	17.2	112	8.6	465
11	49	7.6	27	3.2	35	2.7	111
12	6	0.9	4	0.5	3	0.2	13
total	645	100.0	835	100.0	1300	100.0	2780

is evidence of formal construction of community defenses at some sites. Raqchi is protected on three sides by steep slopes and cliffs, and the approach from the fourth side was made less passable by the construction of ditches and embankments cut across the ridge. Muyuch'urqu is also protected by cliffs, and has two perimeter walls blocking the only easy access to the site. Other sites appear to have relied on their high elevation for protection, and some of the sites recorded during the survey reach elevations of 4300 masl, well above the most productive agricultural land. The investment in defensive works is modest when compared with other parts of the Andean highlands during the LIP, where recent scholarship suggests that the most elaborate of these constructions belong to the last years of the period (e.g., Arkush 2011; Bauer, Kellett, and Aráoz Silva 2010; Covey 2008). Communities in the Sacred Valley were probably not locked in internecine warfare throughout the LIP, which would help to explain the proliferation of small, undefended sites in many parts of the region.

This is not to say that conflict was absent, and there are indications that raiding might have affected people living in LIP villages. SVAP survey workers noted the presence of burnt wall daub when registering sites, evidence of burning of mud-plastered structures that is of unknown cause (see Covey 2006). This material has not been found in many other surveyed parts

of the Cuzco region, and it is not associated with periods other than the LIP. Burnt daub was identified at 28 LIP sites, and was widely scattered on the surface at several sites, including the villages of Raqchi, Hatun Pukara, Qhapaqkancha, Willkarayan (VS-130), Q'atakancha (VS-142/144), Muyuch'urqu, and Apu Sompechu. Less extensive amounts of burnt daub appeared at other villages and at smaller sites, suggesting that burning was not restricted to large settlements. It would be problematic to assume that all burnt daub reflects intentional burning by raiders, or that raiding and warfare were universal concerns in the valley during the LIP. If this valley shares a comparable developmental trajectory with other parts of the Andean highlands, it may be that violent conflict increased in the later part of the LIP, and that at least some of it was introduced by the expanding Inca state.

Evidence for Early Inca Influence in Local Communities

The chronological overlap between LIP and Inca pottery styles makes the assessment of early Inca expansion into the Sacred Valley difficult using purposive survey collections alone. Architectural remains that approximate the Inca canon offer a second line of evidence, although without radiocarbon dates for construction, it is an inferential leap to assume that divergence from the canon reflects an early construction date. With these caveats in mind, some general patterns regarding early Inca influence can be proposed for the Sacred Valley. The first is that groups living to the south of the Sacred Valley interacted more frequently with Inca populations in the Cuzco Basin than did groups living to the north. The Sacred Valley served as a conduit for some economic interactions, but also imposed a cultural divide, and groups to the north differed in many regards from the emerging Inca society. Groups living in the Chit'apampa and Patabamba areas were more susceptible to Inca power and influence before the emergence of a centralized state, although they do not appear to have been under Inca dominion until later in the LIP.

A second general observation is that Inca power and influence extended to the north of the Sacred Valley by establishing state political power in local communities, as indicated by elevated frequencies of Inca (including Killke) pottery and architecture. In the upper Chongo Basin, this seems to be a reasonable conclusion based on differences between the large village of Muyuch'urqu and the site of Pukara Pantillijlla. The latter site grew to an unprecedented size (10 ha) beginning in the late thirteenth century, has significant proportions of Killke and Inca pottery in surface collections and excavations, and has several buildings that conform to the Inca canon (Covey 2006, n.d.). Kendall's (1985) work at Ancasmarca identified a non-Inca LIP occupation of unknown size, which continued under Inca rule. The construction date of the rectangular Inca structures at the site is unknown. A third LIP site to the north of the Sacred Valley that appears to have an early Inca component is Markasunay, which has Inca-style structures dotted among circular domestic structures that remain at the site. A Killke component was present at the site along with local LIP pottery, but no Inca imperial pottery was collected, suggesting that the Inca architecture is from the late LIP.

To the south of the Sacred Valley, an intrusive Inca presence can be noted at some of the larger villages. Kendall, Early, and Sillar (1992) have documented the Inca reorganization of the LIP site of Warqana, which was used as a fort prior to the construction of the nearby Inca-era palace. Raqchi has a fort built in the Inca style, with an Inca ceramic component that is smaller than the LIP occupation. Qhapaqkancha has a rectangular platform associated with three Inca-style structures at a site that has a much larger collection of LIP pottery than Inca. Sherd counts from general surface collections cannot be used as a representative picture of occupation size, but if field assessments are accurate, these sites represent the Inca reorganization of space in strategic locations during the time when state ceramic and architectural styles were emerging. This would indicate the expression of different aspects of state power (military, political) intended to facilitate expansion into the Sacred Valley and beyond. Although excavation work is needed at these sites, it appears that Inca expansion into the Sacred Valley began in the late LIP, targeted specific existing upland villages, and established only a subset of the state's social power.

Synthesizing Archaeological and Documentary Evidence for the Sacred Valley

Archaeological settlement patterns in the Sacred Valley during the LIP identify settlement clusters and individual sites that have differing expressions of local identity (ceramic style, mortuary pattern, domestic architecture). This accords to a certain degree with ethnohistoric descriptions of the area in the generations prior to Inca imperial expansion (see Covey 2006). The diverse documentary record describes Inca interactions with a few groups living in the region, including the Huayllacans and Cuyos. Some chronicles also name multiple places that were conquered in early Inca campaigns.

The Huayllacans

The chronicles describe the Huayllacans as marriage partners of early Inca rulers who were eventually destroyed after proving themselves to be faithless allies and meddlesome kin (Covey 2006). Place names associated with the group are found in the Patabamba area on the southern rim of the Sacred Valley, and in the Sacred Valley itself near the community of Paullu. The site of Qhapaqkancha is the only LIP site of any significance in this area, and its Inca platform and buildings set it apart from contemporaneous sites in the vicinity. If Qhapaqkancha was the principal site of the Huayllacans, then this group appears to be a small cluster of villages spread across multiple environmental zones. The villages in the lower Chit'apampa Basin are larger and more numerous, but receive no mention in the documentary accounts of early Inca expansion.

The Cuyos

Descriptions of the Cuyos place the group to the north of the Sacred Valley, in the Chongo Basin (Covey 2006). This group was reportedly an early Inca conquest, and the Inca ruler who defeated them established a close relative to govern over the area as a new Inca province. The final destruction of the Cuyos occurred during the reign of Pachacutic Inca Yupanqui. When this ruler visited the Cuyo province after his liquidation of the Ayarmacas (see Chapter 8), he nearly lost his life in an assassination attempt that was blamed on the Cuyos. A campaign of retribution razed local settlements, decimated the Cuyo population, and justified the transformation of the area as a royal estate.

The archaeological settlement patterns in the upper Chongo Basin and nearby areas suggest a larger and slightly more hierarchical population than that living in other parts of the Sacred Valley region, and the Inca-influenced growth of Pukara Pantillijlla accords with the description of early administrative practices in the area. As an Inca "province," this area represents a small territory with limited economic surpluses, with a small population compared with the areas to the west and southeast of the Cuzco Basin.

Conquered Places and Civilized Spaces

In addition to the descriptions of the Huayllacans and Cuyos, the chronicles mention the conquest of specific places in the Sacred Valley during the early years of Inca territorial expansion, as well as the imperial-era intensification of valley-bottom lands that were reportedly unoccupied (e.g., Betanzos 1999 [1550s]). Multiple sources describe the conquest of isolated communities in the Sacred Valley that include Kaytumarka (Caytomarca), Caquia, Calca, Ancasmarca, Pillahuara, Choyca, and Yucay (Covey 2006; see Cabello Balboa 1951 [1586]; Cieza de León 1988 [ca. 1550]; Cobo 1964 [1653]; Murúa 1987 [1590]). To the extent that such places can be identified, they are associated with LIP communities found in or near the Sacred Valley itself (except for Ancasmarca). For example, the place today known as Pillahuara is the location of VS-291, a 2 ha LIP village; VS-285, a 1.2 ha site on a prominence called Lluk'urqu, is situated within a few hundred meters of a contemporary valley-bottom hamlet called Chuecacruz (Choyca). Descriptions of conquests tend to take the form of lists of communities defeated in campaigns that moved through the valley. Based on the settlement pattern for the main valley, accounts of isolated villages seem consistent with the archaeology, although they do make early Inca expansion claims seem appropriately modest.

Ethnohistoric descriptions of the Sacred Valley seem fairly accurate for the areas that played a part in the narratives of early Inca rulers, although there are many places and groups that did not receive mention by early Colonial period Inca informants. Accounts of local Sacred Valley populations promoted noble Inca interests in the valley, and the descriptions of local treachery should be taken as self-serving justifications for depriving autochthonous populations of their resources. Likewise, claims that parts of the Sacred Valley were uninhabited—especially in the Yucay and Urubamba areas—are obviously overstated, given the settlement evidence. Barren lands and lawless people both fell into the conceptual category of "wild" (*purum*), which justified Inca actions of civilization—conquest and intensification—that characterized the transformations occurring in the valley during the imperial period.

Summary

The Sacred Valley contains some of the most productive farmland in the Cuzco region, but its LIP occupation reflects an embrace of diversity-oriented subsistence practices. Populations in the valley organized as communities or modest clusters of villages that spread across ecozones to maintain a diverse set of resources that would not fail in hard times. Village locations favor broad resource access, visibility, and natural defense. The region shows limited evidence of Inca influence before the thirteenth century, with strategic nodes of Inca state power appearing in larger communities in the generations leading up to the imperial period. The successful emplacement of state officials in communities to the north of the Sacred Valley reflects the development of a centralized state in the Cuzco Basin. Once the region was reduced to state rule, the agrarian potential of the valley bottom could be developed by Inca rulers and their families.

References Cited

Arkush, Elizabeth N.
2011   *Hillforts of the Ancient Andes: Colla Warfare, Society, and Landscape*. Gainesville: University Press of Florida.

Bauer, Brian S., and R. Alan Covey
2002   Processes of state formation in the Inca heartland (Cuzco, Peru). *American Anthropologist* 104(3):846–64.

Bauer, Brian S., Lucas C. Kellett, and Miriam Aráoz Silva
2010   *The Chanka: Archaeological Research in Andahuaylas (Apurímac) Peru*. University of California, Los Angeles: Cotsen Institute of Archaeology.

Betanzos, Juan de
1999 [1550s]   *Suma y narración de los incas*. Cusco: Universidad Nacional de San Antonio Abad del Cusco.

Cabello Balboa, Miguel
1951 [1586]   *Miscelánea antártica, una historia del Perú antiguo*, edited by L. E. Valcárcel. Lima: Universidad Nacional Mayor de San Marcos, Instituto de Etnología.

Cieza de León, Pedro de
1988 [ca. 1550]   *El señorío de los incas*, edited by Manuel Ballesteros. Madrid: Historia 16.

Cobo, Bernabe
1964 [1653]   *Obras del P. Bernabé Cobo de la Compañía de Jesus, v. 2*, edited by P. Francisco Mateos. Biblioteca de Autores Españoles, 92. Madrid: Ediciones Atlas.

Covey, R. Alan
2006   *How the Incas Built Their Heartland: State Formation and the Innovation of Imperial Strategies in the Sacred Valley, Peru*. Ann Arbor: University of Michigan Press.
2008   Multiregional perspectives on the archaeology of the Andes during the Late Intermediate period (ca. AD 1000–1400). *Journal of Archaeological Research* 16(3):287–338.
2009   Inka agricultural intensification in the imperial heartland and provinces. In *Andean Civilization: A Tribute to Michael E. Moseley*, edited by Joyce Marcus and Patrick Ryan Williams, pp. 361–73. University of California, Los Angeles: Cotsen Institute of Archaeology.
2011   Landscapes and languages of power in the Inca imperial heartland (Cuzco, Peru). *SAA Archaeological Record* 11(4):29–32, 47.
2012   The development of society and status in the late prehistoric Titicaca Basin (circa AD 1000–1535). In *Advances in Titicaca Basin Archaeology–III*, edited by Alexei Vranich, Elizabeth A. Klarich, and Charles Stanish, pp. 299–310. Memoirs, no. 51. Ann Arbor: Museum of Anthropology, University of Michigan.

n.d.   A Multiscalar Investigation of Early Inka State Expansion. Manuscript in preparation.

Covey, R. Alan, Miriam Aráoz Silva, and Brian S. Bauer
2008   Settlement patterns in the Yucay Valley and neighboring areas. In *Imperial Transformations in Sixteenth-Century Yucay, Peru*, edited by R. Alan Covey and Donato Amado González, pp. 3–17. Memoirs, no. 44. Ann Arbor: Museum of Anthropology, University of Michigan.

Dwyer, Edward B.
1971   The Early Inca Occupation of the Valley of Cuzco, Peru. PhD dissertation, Department of Anthropology, University of California, Berkeley.

Kendall, Ann, Rob Early, and Bill Sillar
1992   Report on archaeological field season investigating early Inca architecture at Juchuy Coscco (Q'aqya Qhawana) and Warq'ana, Province of Calca, Dept. of Cuzco, Peru. In *Ancient America. Contributions to New World Archaeology*, edited by Nicholas J. Saunders, pp. 189–256. Oxbow Monograph 24. Oxford: Oxbow Books.

Kosiba, Steven B.
2010   Becoming Inka: The Transformation of Political Place and Practice during Inka State Formation (Cusco, Peru). PhD dissertation, Department of Anthropology, University of Chicago.

McEwan, Gordon F. (editor)
2005   *Pikillacta: The Wari Empire in Cuzco*. Iowa City: University of Iowa Press.

McEwan, Gordon F., Melissa Chatfield, and Arminda Gibaja
2002   The archaeology of Inca origins: Excavations at Chokepukio, Cuzco, Peru. In *Andean Archaeology I: Variations in Sociopolitical Organization*, edited by William H. Isbell and Helaine Silverman, pp. 287–301. New York: Kluwer Academic/Plenum Press.

Murúa, Martín de
1987 [1590]   *Historia general del Perú*. Madrid: Historia 16.

Yépez, Wilfredo
1985   Sub-proyecto puesto en valor de moumentos, Dirección de Patrimonio Cultural y Monumental, Obra Pisaq—Q'allaq'asa: Informe Annual—1985. Annual report to the Instituto Nacional de Cultura, Cusco.

Zimmerer, Karl S.
1997   *Changing Fortunes: Biodiversity and Peasant Livelihood in the Peruvian Andes*. Berkeley: University of California Press.

PART V

Imperial Transformations

Chapter 10: Local Populations, Royal Lineages, and State Entities in the Inca Occupation of the Xaquixaguana Plain

R. Alan Covey

A final tally of Inca sites in the Xaquixaguana regional survey numbered 166 sites, at which 2494 diagnostic sherds were collected in general grab samples and intensive collection units. The neighboring Qoricocha region yielded an additional 13 sites and 115 fragments of Inca pottery (Fig. 10.1). Several hundred additional "Inca-related" fragments were identified in the laboratory, but these are not used as the basis for stylistic presence or absence at any site. Although the number of Inca sherds collected seems substantial, it represents only about a quarter of the non-Killke Late Intermediate period (LIP) diagnostic count. The lower Inca site count in the Xaquixaguana region is comparable with results from the SVAP, but it contrasts with PACY data (Chapter 11)—the lower part of the Sacred Valley shows a slight increase in site count in Inca times. The decrease in site count from the LIP to Inca times reflects the opposite of the settlement trend seen in many other surveyed parts of the Cuzco region. In the Cuzco Basin, Bauer (2004:94) identified more than 850 Inca sites, reflecting a rise in the site count and total occupied area. To the south of Cuzco, Bauer's (1992:99) Paruro survey recorded an Inca site count (131) that was more than 50% greater than the number of LIP sites (85). Closer to the Xaquixaguana region, Kosiba's (2010) survey in the Wat'a and Ollantaytambo area recorded about twice as many Inca sites as LIP ones.

This raises some important interpretive questions. The first is how directly comparable Inca period settlement patterns are to the LIP, given that the two periods are not of equal duration. To the extent that LIP site locations changed within the 400-year period, site counts would be conflated, artificially augmenting population estimates before Inca times. The second, given the temporal overlap of LIP and Inca styles discussed in other chapters, is to what extent LIP pottery represents vernacular styles that persisted under Inca domination, and how accurately the presence of the Killke style represents Inca state expansion. This is an issue that would be relevant to all Cuzco region surveys, so it would not explain the observed differences in LIP–Inca site counts. A third question is to what degree Colonial and contemporary settlement obscures large Inca settlements in more intensively occupied areas.

These are important issues to reflect on, and this chapter begins by comparing the co-occurrence of LIP and Inca pottery, at the site level, as well as within intensive collection units. From there, some settlement pattern variations are explored at a subregional level, with a discussion of the Maras, Chinchero-Huayllabamba, and Pucyura-Anta areas. The Qoricocha *puna* receives special attention, as does the Huarocondo-Zurite area; the latter includes the first Inca way station (*tampu*) on the royal highway (Julien 2012), and contains the Ancahuasi area, where the pastures of Ichubamba are located. Following the presentation of settlement pattern data, a brief discussion of the documentary record of the region offers some inroads for integrating the two lines of evidence.

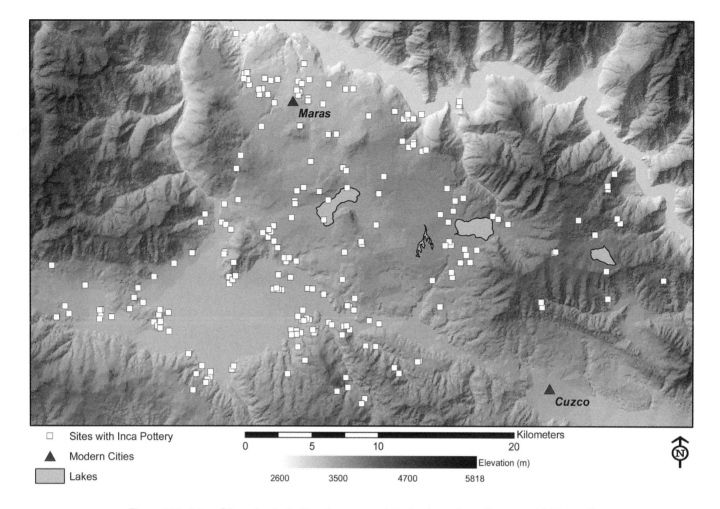

Figure 10.1. Map of Inca sites in the Xaquixaguana and Qoricocha regions. Courtesy of L. Tsesmeli.

Continuity and Change in the Fourteenth and Fifteenth Centuries

As discussed below, the majority of sites with Inca sherds have some component of LIP pottery present in surface collections. Only 42 Inca sites across the combined Xaquixaguana-Qoricocha region (less than a quarter of Inca sites) had no LIP component (9 additional Inca sites had a Killke component but not other LIP styles). The majority of these were small sites—only a handful were larger than one hectare, and those tended to be associated with Inca constructions, including terraces and corrals. By comparison, SVAP research encountered 50 sites that were single component Inca (and an additional 17 with Inca and Killke components). This represents one-third of all SVAP Inca sites, whereas downstream in the Sacred Valley the PACY project registered approximately 30 Inca sites with no LIP component whatsoever (of 75 Inca sites). Along the Sacred Valley, several single component Inca villages were identified, and the overall picture of the valley is one of greater discontinuity in the distri-

bution of LIP and Inca styles. This suggests that Xaquixaguana region sites were characterized by greater settlement continuity, greater social and geographic distribution of the Inca imperial style, or a combination of the two.

Given the transitional overlap between LIP and Inca styles, an additional measure of settlement continuity can be generated at a deeper time scale by assessing the proportion of sites that have components from the EIP/MH, LIP, and Inca. Table 10.1 presents these data for the different subregions of the Xaquixaguana region. The local variations can be compared with results from the two Sacred Valley surveys to illustrate how Inca imperial ceramics distribute across areas with more or less long-term settlement continuity. As the table shows, only a very limited subset of Inca sites reflects settlement continuity deep into the past, and there are local variations in the degree that Inca settlement practices diverge from those of the LIP. The presentation of site-level data obscures how local settlement hierarchies experienced continuity and change, which are discussed below in greater detail.

In terms of within-site correspondence of LIP and Inca pottery, the intensive collection database provides important data for consideration. Of the 982 intensive collection units, 245 contained Inca pottery. Only 71 contained Inca and Killke but no other LIP material, and only 44 contained Inca with no LIP component. To compare this with the distribution of LIP pottery, there were 611 units that contained LIP pottery but no Inca sherds. This suggests that Inca polychromes did not completely dominate the assemblage of the region during the period in which they were used, even though they are ubiquitous in the neighboring Cuzco Basin. The Inca style can be used as a temporal marker of imperial-era occupation, but perhaps not to reconstruct occupation sizes relative to LIP occupations in all parts of the Cuzco region.

Because LIP settlement in the Xaquixaguana region varied substantially at the local level (Chapter 8), the discussion of the Inca occupation of the region proceeds with the separate presentation of data from four distinct subregions: (1) Maras, (2) Chinchero-Huayllabamba, (3) Pucyura-Anta, and (4) Zurite-Huarocondo. Qoricocha results are summarized as a distinct dataset pertaining to the high-elevation survey.

Inca Settlement Patterns in the Maras Area

As discussed in Chapter 8, a nucleated and hierarchical settlement system covering well over 100 ha was present in Maras in LIP times, providing evidence of a major early Inca rival. The local LIP settlement pattern exhibits a marked absence of Inca material, and the growth of a large Inca settlement and storage depot at Cheqoq (X-075) and a nearby settlement (X-067) suggests that this pattern of discontinuity reflects settlement abandonment rather than limited contact with the Inca state or noble factions developing estates in the region. Quave's (2012) excavations at Cheqoq have encountered evidence of an Inca ceramic workshop at the site, which strengthens an argument that the absence of Inca pottery at Maras area sites can be explained by a temporal (rather than social) distance.

Of the 82 sites registered in the district of Maras with a LIP component, only 28 had any Inca material, representing a total site area of about 44 ha. This might seem like a considerable overlap, but sherd counts from intensive collections demonstrate that Inca material is rare at large LIP settlements.

Table 10.2 illustrates the settlement disruption in the Maras area in the LIP–Inca transition. Inca material was present in intensive collections at 12 sites (of 21 collected), a total of 64 units out of nearly 400. The Inca component at 9 of these sites was present in 3 units or fewer, representing very low percentages of the overall diagnostic collection.

Intensive collection data from the Maras district indicate the presence of a limited number of Inca villages, although it is difficult to reconstruct a complete settlement hierarchy owing to the unknown size of the Inca occupation that underlies parts of the modern town of Maras. The footprint of the contemporary town is greater than 40 ha, so it is possible that a community of

Table 10.1. Occupation depth of Inca sites in the Hanan Cuzco region.

Area	Inca Sites	With LIP	With LIP and EIP/MH
Maras	36	29 (81%)	9 (25%)
Chinchero-Huayllabamba	30	28 (93%)	4 (13%)
Qoricocha	13	1 (8%)	0 (0%)
Pucyura-Anta	57	41 (72%)	9 (16%)
Huarocondo-Zurite	44	38 (86%)	6 (14%)
SVAP (all)	150	100 (67%)	29 (19%)
PACY (all)	75	45 (60%)	1 (1%)

Table 10.2. Maras district sites with Inca material in intensive collections.

Site	Units with Inca	Killke	LIP	Inca
X-019	3/81	158	667	5
X-028	2/12	16	69	4
X-029	3/29	126	450	4
X-039	2/17	69	310	4
X-040	11/26	168	567	42
X-041	2/36	344	480	2
X-050	2/12	85	198	6
X-067	7/8	5	11	94
X-075	29/29	14	48	431
X-078	1/10	19	165	1
X-120	1/4	3	24	4
X-129	1/7	11	33	4

substantial size was present in Inca times. Of sites where intensive collections took place, only 3—X-040 (Yakasuqu), X-067, and X-075 (Cheqoq)—had an Inca component representing more than a hectare of settlement, and Yakasuqu represents a considerably smaller settlement in Inca times than the identified LIP occupation. Cheqoq and the associated village site at X-067 are the only sites in the Maras area where Inca pottery was more common than LIP.

Overall, the Maras area under Inca imperial rule appears to be dominated by Cheqoq, an impressive installation that was not a significant site during the LIP (Figs. 10.2, 10.3). Excavations at this site have encountered a large complex of long storehouses, as well as an extended residential area associated with a quarry, corrals, and a ceramic workshop (Quave 2012; see Guevara 2003, 2004) (Fig. 10.4). The Inca-era settlement covered 22 ha (Quave 2012:116), making Cheqoq slightly larger than the local LIP center at Yunkaray, and roughly equal to the combined size of all other Inca sites in the Maras area. The Inca settlement pattern lacks tiers of large and small villages, which were present in the

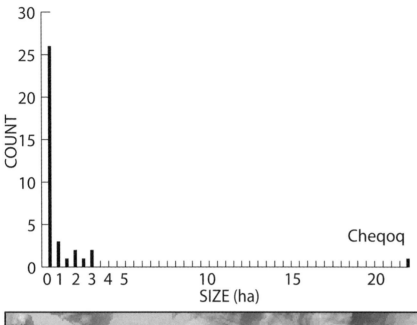

(*left*) Figure 10.2.
Site size hierarchy for known Inca sites in the Maras area. Cheqoq dominates the settlement system, although an Inca occupation under the contemporary town of Maras may have occupied a substantial area.

(*below left*) Figure 10.3.
Map of Inca sites in the Maras area. The growth of Cheqoq established a center of more than 20 ha that was linked to the royal estate of Huayna Capac in the Yucay Valley. Courtesy of L. Tsesmeli.

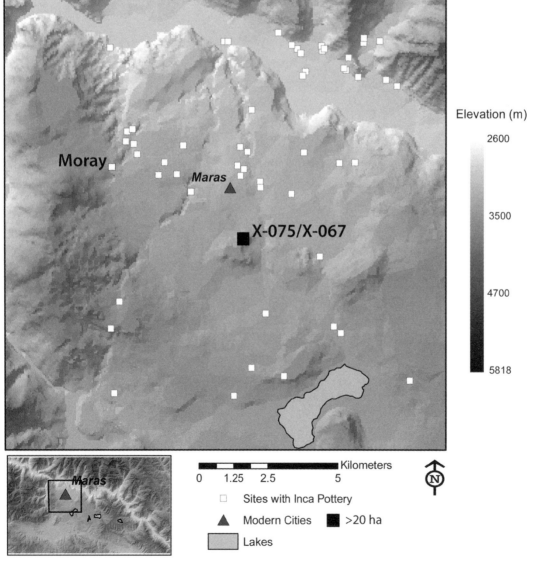

Figure 10.4. Cheqoq is the largest known Inca site in the Maras. The 22 ha site comprises a zone of storehouses, as well as a domestic sector associated with corrals and a ceramic workshop.

LIP. Below Cheqoq are a few small villages of a few hectares, although Maras might have been somewhat larger. Other than these sites, the region appears to be occupied by a dispersal of a few dozen hamlets and other small settlements. This reflects a significant reorganization of settlement in the region in which settled area dropped by about two-thirds and shifted away from the central management of valley-bottom farming. As the scatterplot of Inca settlement in the Maras area indicates (Fig. 10.5), Cheqoq is located at the *kichwa-suni* transition, whereas smaller settlements are situated at elevations where a broad range of economic activities could be conducted.

The monumental terrace complex at Moray has attracted the attention of researchers (e.g., Earls and Silverblatt 1981; Wright, Wright, and Valencia Zegarra 2012), and its settlement context should be discussed (Fig. 10.6). There is no large Inca habitation site in immediate proximity to the complex of sunken circular terraces, suggesting that Moray was not built for local subsistence activities. Colonial-era documents discussing toponyms in the area near Moray describe pasturelands and gardens (*moyas*) belonging to the Inca, and to the Sun. For example, a 1625 proceeding (AGI, Escribanía 506A: f. 3) refers to a 1558 petition by Pedro Ortiz de Urue that "collected an account that next to the town of Maras and Mullaca were some lands named Caquia and Quillillibamba, which were moyas and pastures where they herded the livestock of the Sun, and lands of Topa Inca Yupanqui, who was lord of this land."[1] A copy of this petition includes testimony by multiple indigenous informants, including noble Incas, all of whom confirmed this information. Other legal proceedings (e.g., AGN, Superior Gobierno, L1 C10 [1586]) include similar testimony about the use of Maras area lands for herding by the Inca nobility. Although such accounts were presented in order to buttress a Spaniard's petition to take over "vacant" lands to which contemporary communities had no claim, they help to explain the Inca-era depopulation of the area. After the local polity of the Maras area fell—apparently prior to the development of the imperial pottery style in the fourteenth century—population there was eventually reorganized under royal houses to herd and manage estate resources.

It is noteworthy that several of the communities that worked lands in the Maras area in the early Colonial period lived in or near the Sacred Valley estate facilities in the Urubamba and

---

1. "El capp[ita]n pedro ortiz de urue padre de los dichos mis partes presento en el cauildo justicia y regimiento dela ciudad del cuzco en veynte y tres de henero del año de cinquenta y ocho una peticion en que hizo relacion que junto al pueblo de maras y mullaca abia unas tierras que fueron moyas y pastos donde pastaban los ganados del sol y tierras de topa ynga yupangui señor [margin: caquia y quillibamba] que fue desta tierra nombradas caquia y quillillibamba."

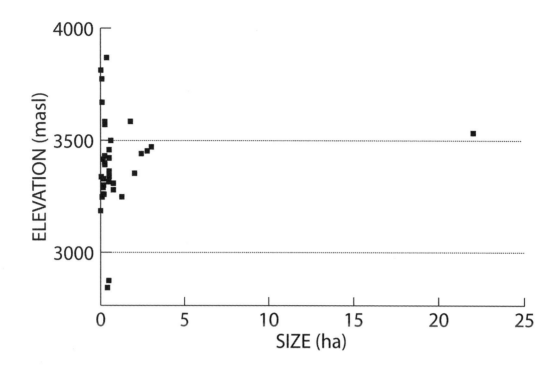

Figure 10.5. Scatterplot of site size and elevation for Inca sites in the Maras area. Cheqoq is situated at a location that is ideal for managing herding and stored food surpluses from nearby valley-bottom lands.

Yucay area, where there were numerous small retainer communities affiliated with the estate of the ruler Huayna Capac. The 1558 *visita* of Damián de la Bandera lists several named groups that were reduced into the communities of Cache, Yucay, and Urquillos (Villanueva Urteaga 1970:59–82). Cache, a community associated with the salt pans located just north of Maras, appears to have been a settlement of fewer than 150 households at the time (there were 2 local leaders who had 60–70 tributary males reporting to them), and the other groups resettled there (Guaro, Chauca, Paca) comprised 56–70 tributary males each. The total population of the new *reducción* was just under 600 individuals.

Inca Settlement Patterns in the Chinchero-Huayllabamba Area

The country estate of Tupa Inca Yupanqui dominated the imperial-era landscape of the Chinchero-Huayllabamba area (e.g., Betanzos 1999 [1550s]; Sarmiento de Gamboa 2007 [1572]). The remains of this ruler's palace and an associated town are found at Chinchero, where the history of archaeological restoration at the site precludes the collection of surface pottery (e.g., Alcina 1976; Alcina et al. 1976) (Fig. 10.7). It is difficult to estimate the

size of the Inca settlement at Chinchero, but it is almost certain that when the town was built in the late fifteenth century, it was by far the largest settlement in the area. XPAS survey work in the upland parts of the Chinchero-Huayllabamba area identified just 26 sites with Inca pottery on the surface,[2] the largest of which was Muqukancha (X-135), part of a cluster of LIP villages in the vicinity of Raqchi that continued to be occupied during Inca times. This group of settlements includes the storage facility at Machu Qollqa, which appears to have been expanded during the imperial period (Valencia 2004).

Overall, the Inca settlement pattern in the upland parts of the Chinchero-Huayllabamba area reflects continuity from LIP village clusters already discussed—only 2 small sites registered in the area appear to have been new Inca occupations (Fig. 10.8). More than half of LIP sites larger than a hectare have an Inca component, although it is found in fewer intensive collection units and in smaller quantities at every large site. LIP pottery appeared in 202 intensive collection units in the area (1218 sherds), whereas Inca pottery was recovered from 72 units (424

---

2. Four additional Inca sites were found in the Sacred Valley near the valley floor and have been excluded from this discussion.

Figure 10.6. Sunken circular terraces at Moray, built in Inca times. Colonial-era documents associate this area with private lands of Inca rulers and the cult of the Sun.

Figure 10.7. Photograph of ornamental terraces and monumental structures at Chinchero. The Colonial town behind the Inca ruins overlies an Inca-era settlement of unknown size.

sherds). Small sites reflect a similar pattern—almost all Inca sites smaller than a hectare (14/16) have LIP components, but Inca pottery is found at only about half of all small LIP sites. Excluding Chinchero, the total area of Inca settlement in the Chinchero-Huayllabamba uplands is about 27 ha, less than a third of the settled area identified for the LIP.

This pattern of stylistic distribution suggests either that the imperial period occupation of the area resulted in diminished populations at local villages, or that some pottery that is currently classified as "LIP" reflects local settlement after AD 1400. Local abandonment would be a plausible scenario based on chronicle accounts of the dispersal of Ayarmaca populations following the Inca conquest (Chapter 8), although the degree of Inca imperial settlement overlap would have to be explained. To the extent that some local LIP styles continued to be produced and used in the imperial period, XPAS collections suggest that Inca polychrome ceramics were used at most sites in the area, but not as the exclusive or dominant style.

This suggests that until the construction of Chinchero in the late 1400s, the Chinchero-Huayllabamba uplands were either sparsely populated or socially marginal within the developing Inca imperial heartland (or both). The new Inca town was built in a place that allowed it to manage the local production of suni lands, with direct access to kichwa lands belonging to Tupa Inca Yupanqui in the Sacred Valley at Urquillos (Rostworowski 1970). The scatterplot of Inca sites (Fig. 10.9) indicates a much more constrained elevation range than is seen for the LIP, perhaps reflecting the limited distribution of the imperial style rather than the subsistence strategies of the estate and surrounding villages of retainers and locals.

Inca Settlement Patterns in the Pucyura-Anta Area

The settlement data presented for the north part of the XPAS region suggest widespread site abandonment (Maras) and social marginalization (Chinchero-Huayllabamba) as the Incas consolidated control over the Cuzco region. In the late fifteenth and early sixteenth century, large sites (Cheqoq and Chinchero) established royal control over rural estate resources, including modest populations living in small villages and hamlets. By contrast, Inca settlement in the south part of the XPAS region was expected to be more continuous, owing to the reported presence of multiple honorary Inca groups living along a principal highway route connecting Cuzco to the province of Chinchaysuyu (Covey 2003). The apparent absence of major royal estate resources in the

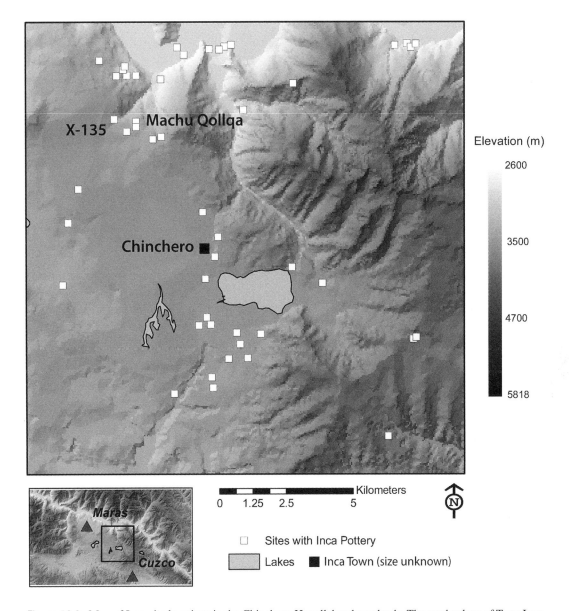

Figure 10.8. Map of Inca site locations in the Chinchero-Huayllabamba uplands. The rural palace of Tupa Inca Yupanqui at Chinchero dominates a modest system of local villages that were first settled in the LIP. Courtesy of L. Tsesmeli.

districts of Pucyura and Anta was expected to limit discontinuity in local subsistence and settlement patterns.

Overall, the Inca site count in the Pucyura-Anta area was larger (*n* = 57) than that of neighboring areas, almost as large as the entire north part of the XPAS region. Total site area was approximately 40 ha, a figure that excludes the Inca-era settlement of Anta, which underlies the modern town and is of unknown size (Fig. 10.10). These figures are nevertheless much lower than the LIP site count (*n* = 84) and total site size (73.7 ha, excluding Anta). Less than half of LIP sites have Inca pottery in their

collections, and the count of LIP sherds in survey collections (*n* = 2260) is significantly higher than that of Inca material (*n* = 796). This suggests either an overall depopulation of the area, or the continued use of local "LIP" pottery, with the Inca style reflecting distributions through administrative and elite networks.

Whereas single component Inca sites are rare in the north part of the XPAS region, survey work in the Pucyura-Anta area identified 15 sites with only Inca pottery, representing an area of almost 10 ha. Most of these were small sites, although the site of Rosasq'asa (X-303) was a village estimated at 6 ha that

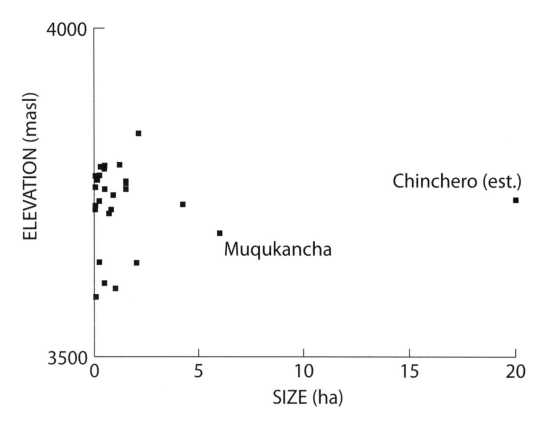

Figure 10.9. Scatterplot of sites with Inca pottery in the Chinchero-Huayllabamba area. The size of Chinchero is estimated at 20 ha, although it could be considerably larger or smaller.

is located at the valley floor where the modern town of Pucyura is now situated. A nearby 1.1 ha site (X-205) represents the other single component Inca site larger than a hectare. These new Inca villages are situated in undefended valley-bottom areas where there is evidence of new Inca terrace construction, and where the ethnohistoric record mentions the Inca resettlement of populations belonging to the resistant Ayarmaca group (Rostworowski 1970).

In the Anta area, the largest Inca sites were Ak'awillay (X-228) and Anta (X-384), which were large villages during the LIP. Intensive collections at Ak'awillay encountered Inca pottery in 27 units, representing a much smaller dispersal than the LIP scatter (58 units). As discussed in Chapter 8, the size of Anta after AD 1000 is uncertain, but satellite sites around the contemporary town suggest that there was a sizable community in LIP and Inca times. Anta was the residence of local elites claiming to be ancient marriage allies of Inca rulers (Covey 2006), and it became a Colonial reducción that absorbed population from the communities of Cazca, Cuzco, Equecco, and Tambo (Covey and Amado 2008 [1572 f. 443v–444]). The documentary evidence suggests that Anta was at least a large village in Inca times, although probably not a regional administrative center.

Assuming that Anta was a large village of 5–10 ha, the overall settlement pattern for the Pucyura-Anta area contrasts with the two areas already discussed (Fig. 10.11). New areas of Inca settlement emphasis are at the village level, comparable to the size of local LIP villages that continued to be settled in imperial times. There is no large royal estate facility, nor is there evidence of a state administrative center designed to coordinate settlement in the area. The scatterplot of site size and elevation (Fig. 10.12) suggests a shift toward valley-bottom agriculture. Village sites are located near the valley floor, whereas smaller sites are found across kichwa and suni lands nearby. LIP villages located in the uplands to the north of Ak'awillay and Pucyura either ceased to be important settlements, or were significantly less influenced by the distribution of Inca-style pottery.

Inca Settlement Patterns in the Huarocondo-Zurite Area

During the LIP, the western part of the Xaquixaguana Valley had clusters of small villages, but it lacked sites of the scale of Ak'awillay (Chapter 8). The Huarocondo district in particular yielded evidence of much higher proportions of Killke pottery

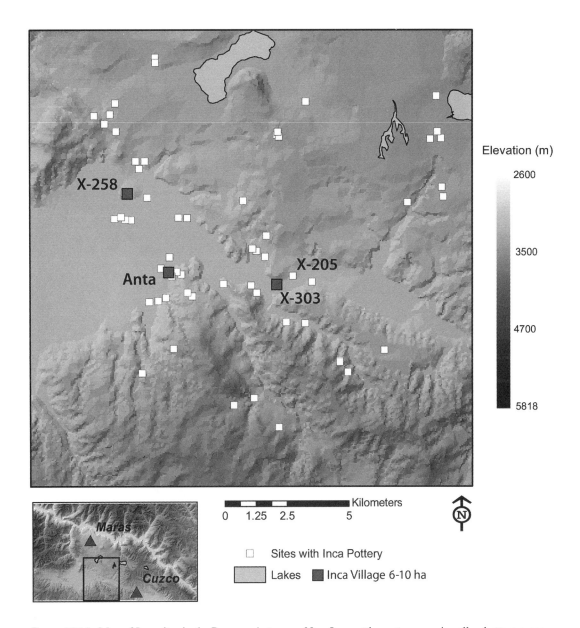

Figure 10.10. Map of Inca sites in the Pucyura-Anta area. New Inca settlements appear in valley-bottom areas around Pucyura, while the large villages at Anta and Ak'awillay (X-258) continued to be occupied. Courtesy of L. Tsesmeli.

than were observed in other parts of the XPAS region. In Inca times, the Huarocondo-Zurite area is known to have areas affiliated with the royal estates of Tupa Inca Yupanqui and Huayna Capac, and it was the location of the first way station on the royal road to Chinchaysuyu. As discussed below, parts of this area were also dedicated to the service of the Inca ruler and the cult of the Sun, particularly in the Ichubamba Valley, the drainage where the community of Ancahuasi is found today.

XPAS survey work encountered 44 sites with Inca pottery in the districts of Huarocondo and Zurite, a total of 359 fragments of the style (Fig. 10.13). This is a fairly small sample of Inca

pottery, due in part to the relatively modest Inca components at sites with intensive collections—only 30 intensive collection units placed at sites in the area yielded the style (compared with 75 for the LIP). A few small LIP villages (X-252, X-273, and X-454) have Inca distributions about the size of the LIP component, but these are villages of under 2 ha. The Inca component in the Huarocondo-Zurite suggests greater settlement continuity than has been observed in other parts of the Xaquixaguana region—53% of LIP sites (38/72) have an Inca component. Only 6 new Inca sites were identified, which consisted largely of small occupation areas.

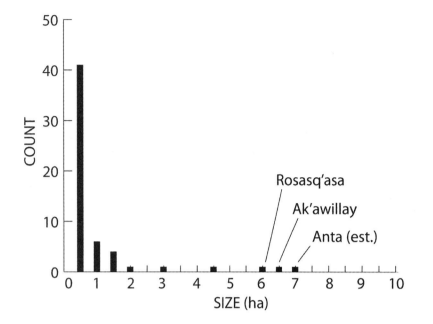

Figure 10.11.

Site size hierarchy for the Pucyura-Anta area in Inca times. No large royal estate installation or administrative center is present in this area, although new Inca settlements near Pucyura appear to be of a size comparable with local villages at Ak'awillay and Anta.

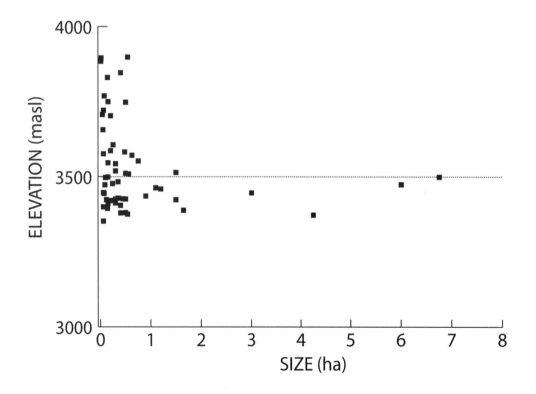

Figure 10.12.

Scatterplot of site size and elevation for Inca occupations in the Pucyura-Anta area. Larger settlements concentrate close to highly productive valley-bottom lands, with smaller sites extending into nearby suni areas.

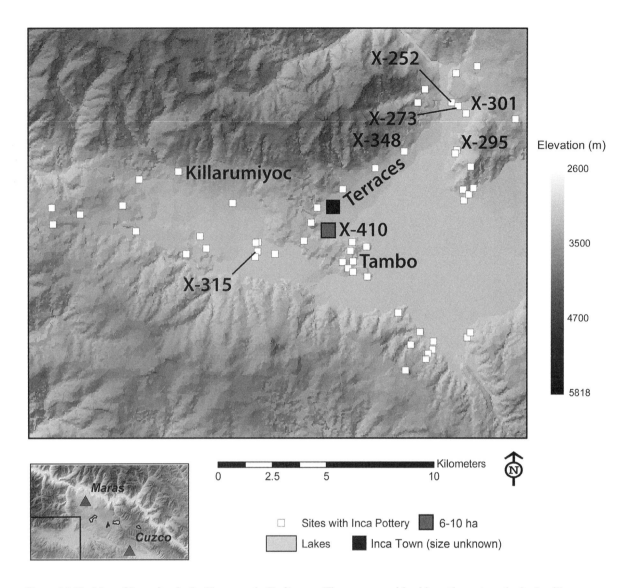

Figure 10.13. Map of Inca sites in the Huarocondo-Zurite area. There was considerable settlement continuity in villages around Huarocondo, but large-scale construction of new terraces near Zurite, where the Incas constructed a royal country palace and an imperial way station. Courtesy of L. Tsesmeli.

The settlement hierarchy for the Huarocondo-Zurite area (Fig. 10.14) differs slightly from that of the eastern part of the Xaquixaguana Valley. The largest site in the area, Tambo Real (X-422), was estimated to be 9 ha based on observations made during the initial registration of the site. Assuming that this size is accurate, the site is larger than other local villages, and it is associated with the remains of storehouses on the nearby hillside. This would make a strong candidate for the Xaquixaguana tampu, the first imperial way station on the Chinchaysuyu road (cf. Julien 2012). The nearby site of Tambokancha-Tumibamba (X-410) represents another large imperial-era site—XPAS size estimates for the site were 5 ha, but Farrington and Zapata (2003:59) state

that it is 8 ha. These sites lie approximately 2 km from each other and represent a royal/administrative nexus of imperial influence in the area. Below these sites are 3 or 4 villages in the 3–6 ha range, all of which have LIP pottery present alongside the Inca component. The largest of these was Qhakyaurqu (X-315), which might correspond to the village of a group called Circa (e.g., AGN, Tít. Prop., L18 C359 [1647]). This site and other villages are located at or near the valley floor, as are about a dozen other small settlements that are larger than a hectare. The Huarocondo area has several small villages with settlement that continues from the LIP, including X-348 (Plazapampa), X-295 (Umacalle), X-273 (Sector Belén), X-252, and X-301 (Rosaspampa). Sites

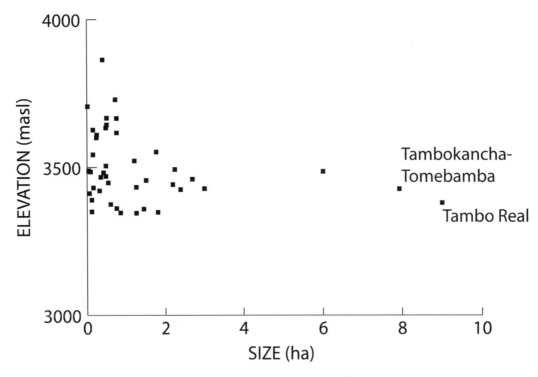

Figure 10.14. Scatterplot of site size and elevation for Inca sites in the Huarocondo-Zurite area. The large sites of Tambo Real and Tambokancha-Tomebamba reflect imperial transformations in the Zurite area.

smaller than a hectare cluster near the valley floor, as well as in higher-elevation locations more suitable for herding.

As mentioned already, the Xaquixaguana tampu was a manifestation of imperial infrastructure that changed economic practices in the region. The Zurite area also experienced large-scale agricultural intensification and the establishment of specialized herding. These enhancements appear to be associated with the development of royal estate resources in the area, as well as patronage of sites of sacred or symbolic significance. Colonial witnesses interviewed in the 1570s identified themselves as the descendants of servants of Inca Yupanqui (don Alonso Condor, a Sora from Pomaguanca) and Huayna Capac (Juan Apitauco, a Chachapoya from Lavanqui) (Toledo 1940a [1571], 1940b [1571]). Other sources identify a sumptuous palace belonging to Tupa Inca Yupanqui at Tambokancha, where Farrington and Zapata (2003) have excavated Inca architecture and encountered abundant examples of Inca material culture (Albórnoz 1989 [ca. 1582]; see Bauer and Barrionuevo 1998).

The construction of a country palace and imperial way station in the Tambo Real area was accompanied by other transformations to the local landscape around Zurite. The most obvious alteration is in the construction of some large terrace complexes, the largest of which (X-362) measures approximately 60 ha (Fig. 10.15). A smaller complex (X-379) immediately next to Zurite

measures 20 ha. Given the proximity of Zurite to major imperial-era agricultural infrastructure, the fact that it was a reducción town that received population from more than 5 surrounding Inca-era towns (Covey and Amado 2008 [1572 f. 443v–444]), and its large size in the 1570s relative to other Xaquixaguana settlements (Cook 1975 [1570s]), it is likely that there is a large Inca settlement under the modern town. The footprint of the Colonial town is about 20 ha, and that community represents the agglomeration of multiple groups, so the size of the Inca settlement would be expected to be somewhat smaller.

In addition to the construction of elaborate terrace groups and irrigation works, Julien (2012:159–62) asserts that later Inca rulers invested in reclaiming land on the swampy and periodically inundated valley floor in the western Xaquixaguana Valley. In the late sixteenth century, this area received enough runoff from its tributary rivers to form a seasonal lake, and the road that crossed the area was built on a causeway to protect it from flooding (Fornée 1965 [1586]:201, 203). Julien (2012:161) states that the drainage features (grids of simple canals) in use today "are evidence of a reclamation project designed to drain the pampa and reclaim arable land." It should be noted that such features are not associated with archaeological sites and are not mentioned in early Colonial period land disputes. Similar drainage features appear in other parts of the Cuzco region (Ancahuasi, Chit'apampa)

Figure 10.15. Inca terraces in the Zurite area added large new agricultural resources associated with royal estates and state infrastructure.

that are not associated with royal agricultural intensification projects. There is no reason to assume that these contemporary drainage patterns predate the mid-twentieth century.

As royal estate resources and state infrastructure developed in the Zurite area, the Ancahuasi area became a royal and sacred domain with limited population in the imperial period. Known as Ichubamba, the valley above the site of Qhakyaurqu contained only 5 small sites with Inca pottery in an area of roughly 60 km², a total site area of just over a hectare. In addition to these was Killarumiyoc (X-302), a 2.5 ha Inca site known for its carved rock outcrops (Figs. 10.16, 10.17), where previous archaeological consolidation precluded surface collections. Despite the fact that the Inca highway to Chinchaysuyu ran through Ichubamba, the area was not a focus of imperial settlement and economic intensification.

This might partly be due to the swampy character of the lands in this area, but Colonial documents indicate that the area was set apart for its sacred and symbolic significance to the Inca elite. Shrines of significance to the local Mayo people were found in this valley, as well as Inca carved rocks and places that memorialized a mythical battle against the Chancas that set Inca imperial expansion in motion (Albórnoz 1989 [ca. 1582]; see Bauer and Barrionuevo 1998). In 1572, Pedro Sánchez, a royal scribe, made a secret visit to the Xaquixaguana Valley to interview indigenous

leaders about shrines in the area (AGN, Tít. Prop., L18 C359 [1647]). Representatives of 10 communities testified (f. 21–21v) that Ichubamba and a nearby place called Episcara were moyas of the Sun. Episcara was located just to the west of Tambo Real, in the vicinity of Qhakyaurqu, and a different set of witnesses testified in 1588 that the nearby lands of Omotoro were a royal domain where a small number of miniature camelids were herded for the ruler (f. 38–38v). No commoner or elite person could enter, under penalty of death (f. 40v).

The settlement pattern for the Huarocondo-Zurite area shows some local variation that distinguishes it from the eastern part of the Xaquixaguana Valley. Whereas settlement in the Huarocondo area reflects continuous occupation of LIP villages at somewhat smaller sizes, the Inca sites in the Zurite area show evidence of site growth in a fairly restricted area that contained an imperial way station, a royal country palace, new agricultural terraces and storehouses, and lands set aside for the Inca and the cult of the Sun. Beyond Zurite, there is very little evidence of Inca occupation as one ascends to the Vilcaconga Pass and begins the descent to the Apurímac River. The cluster of sites around Zurite seems like a rough counterpart of the imperial-era centers constructed at Chinchero and Cheqoq in the final decades of Inca rule, although there appears to be greater continuity in local settlement than was observed around the latter site.

Figure 10.16. Photograph of the carved rock at Killarumiyoc, an Inca site in the Ichubamba Valley near contemporary Ancahuasi.

Figure 10.17. Carved rock outcrop near Killarumiyoc.

Inca Sites in the Qoricocha Puna

During the LIP, several high-elevation sites located on the southern rim of the Sacred Valley would have had access to the puna lands of the Qoricocha Basin (Chapter 9), but survey of the area did not encounter any evidence of permanent settlements in the area before Inca times. The Inca occupation of the Qoricocha puna was limited to 13 sites, none of which was a new village. About half of the sites with Inca pottery were corral complexes, which suggests an imperial-era intensification of herding in the area. Corrals are found in all parts of the puna, with some larger complexes located along an Inca road that connects Cuzco to the Sacred Valley by way of the royal Inca estate at Huchuy Cuzco (Fig. 10.18). At the pass that marks the descent to the Sacred Valley, the road passes a pair of boundary markers that are faced with Inca masonry, which had a small sample of imperial ceramic fragments scattered on the surface (Fig. 10.19).

The documentary record for the Qoricocha area is not detailed, but the association of Inca corrals with royal lineages and the Sun cult can be noted in numerous chronicles, and for many other parts of the Xaquixaguana region. Rostworowski (1962) has published a document from the 1550s by descendants of Tupa Inca Yupanqui who claim lands in the Qoricocha area, although the authenticity of the document has been questioned. During the Qoricocha survey, a 3 ha corral complex (Q-120) was registered above 4300 masl near a seasonal lagoon in a high side valley about 2.5 km above Huchuy Cuzco, the estate of Viracocha Inca (Fig. 10.20). Although no diagnostic pottery appeared on the surface, Inca-style masonry was observed in the corral construction (Fig. 10.21). The proximity to the royal estate and the use of fine stone work in a remote facility suggest a special affiliation.

During the imperial period, the Qoricocha puna came to be used more intensively than in the LIP, despite the general settlement shift away from high-elevation villages. The pasture resources in this area are modest compared with other parts of the Inca empire known for herding societies, and the scale of corral construction does not indicate a major transformation of the regional economy. Rather, the increase in herding appears to be an activity associated with noble and ritual life.

Overview of Xaquixaguana Settlement Patterns

Inca pottery appears in smaller quantities than LIP styles, and at fewer sites across the Xaquixaguana region. This suggests either that there was a substantial decline in the size and number of settlements during the imperial period, or that imperial polychromes do not represent the full extent of settlement in the region. Excavation work at important LIP sites would clarify some of the chronological issues that currently remain unresolved, and compositional analysis of local LIP and Inca pottery would provide important evidence on the production and distribution of pottery in the region. For the present, the imperial style can be considered as an imperfect temporal marker that also speaks

to some issues of the rural influence of Inca nobles and state institutions.

Inca expansion in the Xaquixaguana region introduced sweeping change to some areas, whereas the Incas built atop existing settlement and subsistence systems in others and gradually transformed strategic parts of the region. This is to say not only that Inca impact varied across the region, but that the refashioning of the region as part of an imperial heartland was a process that occurred over several generations and was still underway at the time of the European invasion. If we exclude large Inca sites that were reportedly built in the final decades before the European invasion, the local settlement systems show differing degrees of continuity and change, with the Maras, Pucyura, and Zurite areas exhibiting the strongest evidence for significant departures from local LIP site locations. These areas do not reflect identical treatment under Inca rule—community sizes differ, as does the degree of investment to intensify local agricultural production. Chinchero-Huayllabamba, Anta, and Huarocondo exhibit considerable continuity at the village level, but with differing degrees of evidence for local settlement hierarchies.

Regional Archaeology and Regional Ethnohistory in the Xaquixaguana Region

The challenge of reconstructing Inca settlement using regional survey data is compounded by the enormous quantity of documentary sources pertaining to the Xaquixaguana region in Inca and early Colonial times. The documents purport to do things that survey archaeology cannot hope to accomplish—identifying the identities and motivations of individuals and groups that shaped social power in the region over time. The full consideration of the documentary record for this region lies well beyond the scope of this chapter, but some important observations can be made regarding the transformation of the region in terms of population levels, social identities, institutional organization, and symbolic interpretation of the changing landscape.

Population Levels

When discussing settlement pattern evidence, the size of Inca population is a relative one that returns to the question of how the total distribution area of the imperial style compares with earlier periods. This is a question that can also be discussed in terms of population figures coming from early Colonial census data and other sources. Estimates of Inca-era population are rare, but a 1647 copy of a 1588 proceeding in the Xaquixaguana Valley preserves testimony by "the oldest and most ancient who could be found in the town of Zurite" regarding a few Inca-era communities (AGN, Tít. Prop., L18 C359). The witnesses state (f. 40) that the Circa group numbered 800 in Inca times, whereas the Mayo group was the same size, and the people of Tomebamba numbered 500, along with a group of *yanakuna* that numbered 500. The population of this part of the Zurite area comprised 2600

Figure 10.18. Photograph of Mallkikancha (Q-001), a corral complex in the Qoricocha puna with Inca-style pottery on the surface.

Figure 10.19. A group of three boundary markers at the pass where the Inca road from Cuzco begins its descent to the Sacred Valley. The foundations of the two flanking monuments are faced with Inca-style masonry.

Figure 10.20. Q-120, a corral complex found high above the estate of Viracocha Inca at Huchuy Cuzco.

Figure 10.21. Inca masonry blocks reused in contemporary corrals at Q-120.

Table 10.3. Xaquixaguana region population figures from the late sixteenth century.

Town	Description	Population*		Source
Maras	reducción of local communities and estate workers	1262	[240]	Cook 1975; Levillier 1921
Chinchero, Cupirpongo, Tambococha, Amantuy	upland royal estate and three communities	1342	[274]	Levillier 1921; cf. Cook 1975
Collas of Cupiz	yanakuna near Chinchero	74	[10]	Cook 1975
Xacxaguana**	Inca way station	638	[210]	Cook 1975
Alpasondor	one or more local communities	137	[26]	Cook 1975
Puquiura	reducción community	1304	[246]	Levillier 1921
Anta, Huarocondo, Zurite	three reducción communities	3877	[615]	Cook 1975; Levillier 1921
Pomaguanca, Ancahuasi	two communities	1883	[348]	Levillier 1921
Pampaconga	local community	397	[70]	Cook 1975

*Male tributaries are listed in brackets.
**Figures provided by Cook (1975: xxxv) from Vázquez de Espinosa.

"Indians," possibly male tributaries (given that Spanish officials at that time tended to enumerate population on the basis of this subset of population).

The Inca population of four groups living in the area of Zurite can be compared to the size of the indigenous population as recorded by census documents from the 1570s. Table 10.3 shows total population figures (male tributaries are listed in brackets) from documents prepared by the viceroys Francisco de Toledo and Martín Enríquez. Although there was considerable demographic change in the region following the European invasion (e.g., Covey, Childs, and Kippen 2011), there were well over 10,000 indigenous people living in the XPAS region a generation later, and it is reasonable to expect that Inca-era settlement was at least of comparable size. A rough comparison of the reducción communities in Maras, Chinchero, and the Xaquixaguana Valley suggests much smaller populations in the north part of the region than in the south. Teasing apart community size prior to Spanish resettlement is difficult, but the figures offered for the early reducciones in the Maras and Yucay area (Villanueva Urteaga 1970) suggest very modest community sizes in that area, especially for groups not native to the area.

Social Identities

Archaeological settlement patterns register the distribution of artifact styles that represent a particular time period, but they do not tell us who was using these artifacts. The documentary record for the Xaquixaguana region reveals a multiplicity of named groups living in the region prior to Inca expansion, as well as communities of different ethnic identities and social statuses. In the early Colonial period, the Xaquixaguana region was occupied by populations who considered themselves to be native to the area (e.g., Anta, Huaro, Circa, Equecco, Sanco, Mayo, Quilliscache, Ayarmaca), individuals who identified themselves as Incas from

Cuzco, and people from provincial groups who were brought to Cuzco by Inca rulers (e.g., Wanka, Cañari, Sora, Chachapoya, Collas, Canas) (see Covey and Amado 2008; Toledo 1940a [1571], 1940b [1571]). Some communities appear to have been multiethnic, reflecting the presence of multiple social statuses in places associated with royal estates and state institutions.

As the Incas extended their control over the Xaquixaguana region, they resettled some local populations in other parts of the Cuzco region and in strategic provincial settings. Inca elites and colonists from Cuzco settled in some communities, and rulers introduced large numbers of provincial populations (Covey 2006). Provincials were resettled in the region as rotational labor specialists (mitmaqkuna) and permanently relocated artisans (kamayuqkuna) and royal servants (yanakuna) (Covey 2009, 2013). While some lived in established communities, others were placed in small new communities associated with the productive resources to which their labor was applied.

Given the apparent decline of settlement in the Inca period in the Xaquixaguana region, it is worth noting that some Cuzco groups migrated within the Cuzco region in Inca times (Covey and Elson 2007). For example, the tabulation of male yanakuna in the Yucay Valley in the late 1560s includes more than 20 men from Xaquixaguana (Covey and Amado 2008). Almost all were too young to have migrated there in Inca times, but the population movement suggests that construction of large terrace complexes in certain parts of the Cuzco region encouraged the resettlement of populations from other parts of the region.

Royal Estates and Imperial Institutions

Documentary sources identify several parts of the Xaquixaguana region where Colonial period witnesses identified lands, labor, corrals, and other resources belonging to the rural estates of multiple Inca rulers. The documents permit us to identify some perspectives on the labor force of royal estates, as well as facilities lying outside well-preserved monumental complexes, such as those seen in the Sacred Valley. Settlement pattern data can contribute to the study of royal estates, although excavation work is needed to clarify their role in the development of the Inca imperial heartland. For example, the excavation of a ceramic workshop at Cheqoq (Quave 2012), a site with explicit royal affiliations in the documentary record, speaks to the economic and ideological role of the estate system in the production and distribution of the Inca style.

As more work is done to understand how royal estates grew within particular rural contexts, a second important avenue for studying the institutional transformation of the Xaquixaguana region is the role of the road system in connecting state installations and in functioning to administer tributary populations. The Xaquixaguana tampu represents one of only a few "state" installations intended to connect the Cuzco region with the provinces, and it is important to consider how way stations, storage facilities, planned colonist communities, and other sites enhanced networks of social power that might be considered to belong to the state rather than to the Inca nobility. In the Xaquixaguana region, more work can be done to model settlement patterns with regard to the highway network and the distribution of way stations, but horizontal excavations are also needed.

Sacred Landscapes and Imperial Rule

The Colonial documentary record permits the consideration of how Inca-era populations experienced the landscapes of the Xaquixaguana region. The full treatment of the known ethnohistoric corpus has the potential to address aspects of local sacred landscapes, and the ways that Inca royals and agents of the Sun cult appropriated or transformed them. The documents are fragmentary and biased in different ways, but they identify local shrines, Inca sacred places and ritual circuits, and places that were expropriated from local landscapes as royal or sacred domains. Excavations at Tambokancha-Tomebamba by Farrington and Zapata (2003) demonstrate the potential for developing excavation programs that build off regional studies of the sacred landscape (e.g., Bauer and Barrionuevo 1998). Such work needs to be accompanied by problem-based excavations of households and mortuary features to build a broader view of ritual activity in Inca times.

The archaeology of the Inca occupation of the Xaquixaguana region offers valuable insights, but raises many questions for future study. At present, the full synthesis of archaeological data and known ethnohistoric records for the region is still not possible, but the survey work delimits a number of productive avenues for future research. The general description of settlement pattern data also makes it possible to conduct broader regional comparisons of Inca settlement patterns and how they maintained or diverged from those of earlier times.

References Cited
Archival Documents

Archivo General de Indias (AGI), Escribanía 506A
1625   Juan Enríquez de Borja, Marqués de Oropesa con el fiscal y Luis de Orúe y consortes, hacendados de San Francisco de Maras en el valle de Yucay, sobre restitución de unas tierras.

Archivo General de la Nación (AGN), Superior Gobierno, Legajo 1, Cuaderno 10
1586   Testimonio de las diligencias que se practicaron en el pueblo de Maras, en el Cuzco, por el Licenciado Dn. Gallen de Torres, Teniente de la Corregidor de la ciudad del Cuzco, sobre la propiedad de unas tierras que fueron pastos y moyas del Inca, las cuales pretendia los Padres de la Compañía de Jesús de esa ciudad.

Archivo General de la Nación (AGN), Títulos de Propiedad, Legajo 18, Cuaderno 359
1647   Títulos de la estancia de Ipiscara o Episcara en el valle de Jaquijahuana, provincia de Abancay, jurisdicción de la ciudad del Cuzco . . .

Published Sources

Albórnoz, Cristóbal de
1989 [ca. 1582]   Instrucción para descubrir todas las guacas del Piru y sus camayos y haziendas. In *Fábulas y mitos de los incas*, edited by Henrique Urbano and Pierre Duviols, pp. 161–98. Madrid: Historia 16.

Alcina Franch, José
1976   *Arqueología de Chinchero. 1. La arquitectura*. Madrid: Ministerio de Asuntos Exteriores.

Alcina Franch, José, Miguel Rivera, Jesús Galván, María Carmen García Palacios, Balbina Martínez-Caviro, Luis J. Ramos, and Tito Varela
1976   *Arqueología de Chinchero. 2. Cerámica y otros materiales*. Madrid: Ministerio de Asuntos Exteriores.

Bauer, Brian S.
1992   *The Development of the Inca State*. Austin: University of Texas Press.
2004   *Ancient Cuzco: Heartland of the Inca*. Austin: University of Texas Press.

Bauer, Brian S., and Wilton Barrionuevo Orosco
1998   Reconstructing Andean shrine systems: A test case from the Xaquixaguana (Anta) region of Cusco, Peru. *Andean Past* 5:73–87.

Betanzos, Juan de
1999 [1550s]   *Suma y narración de los incas*. Cusco: Universidad Nacional de San Antonio Abad del Cusco.

Cook, Noble David
1975 [1570s]   *Tasa de la visita general de Francisco de Toledo*. Lima: Universidad Nacional Mayor de San Marcos.

Covey, R. Alan
2003   Territorial Expansion and Administrative Consolidation in
       the Inka Heartland, Cusco, Peru: The Xaquixaguana Plain
       Archaeological Survey. Grant proposal to the National
       Science Foundation, proposal BCS 0342381.
2006   *How the Incas Built Their Heartland: State Formation and the
       Innovation of Imperial Strategies in the Sacred Valley, Peru.*
       Ann Arbor: University of Michigan Press.
2009   Domestic life and craft specialization in Inka Cusco and its
       rural hinterland. In *Domestic Life in Prehispanic Capitals: A
       Study of Specialization, Hierarchy, and Ethnicity*, edited by
       Linda R. Manzanilla and Claude Chapdelaine, pp. 223–34.
       Memoirs, no. 46. Ann Arbor: Museum of Anthropology,
       University of Michigan.
2013   Binding the imperial whole: The transition from capital to
       province in the Inka imperial heartland. In *Empires and
       Diversity: On the Crossroads of Archaeology, Anthropology,
       and History,* edited by Gregory Areshian, pp. 208–230.
       University of California, Los Angeles: Cotsen Institute of
       Archaeology.

Covey, R. Alan, and Donato Amado González (editors)
2008   *Imperial Transformations in Sixteenth-Century Yucay, Peru.*
       Memoirs, no. 44. Ann Arbor: Museum of Anthropology,
       University of Michigan.

Covey, R. Alan, Geoff Childs, and Rebecca Kippen
2011   Dynamics of indigenous demographic fluctuations: Lessons
       from sixteenth-century Cusco, Peru. *Current Anthropology*
       52(3):335–60.

Covey, R. Alan, and Christina M. Elson
2007   Ethnicity, demography, and estate management in sixteenth-
       century Yucay (Cusco, Peru). *Ethnohistory* 54(2):303–35.

Earls, John, and Irene Silverblatt
1981   Sobre la instrumentación de la cosmología Inca en el sitio
       arqueológico de Moray. In *La tecnología en el mundo andino*,
       edited by Heather Lechtman and Ana María Soldi, 443–73.
       Mexico City: UNAM.

Farrington, Ian S., and Julinho Zapata
2003   Nuevos cánones de arquitectura inka: Investigaciones en
       el sito de Tambokancha-Tumibamba, Jaquijahuaua, Cuzco.
       Boletín de Arqueología PUCP 7:57–77.

Fornée, Niculoso de
1965 [1586]   *Breve relación de la tierra del corregimiento de
              Abancay, de que es corregidor Niculoso de Fornée.* Biblioteca
              de Autores Españoles 184:16–30. Madrid: Ediciones Atlas.

Guevara Carazas, Luis
2003   Restauración y Puesta en Valor Conjunto Arqueológico
       Cheqoq-Maras, Informe Anual Preliminar 2003. Report sub-
       mitted to the Instituto Nacional de Cultura, Cusco, Peru.
2004   Informe Final de Investigación Arqueológica 2004: Conjunto
       Arqueológico Qolqas de Cheqoq-Maras Cusco. Report sub-
       mitted to the Instituto Nacional de Cultura, Cusco, Peru.

Julien, Catherine J.
2012   The Chinchaysuyu road and the definition of an imperial
       landscape. In *Highways, Byways, and Road Systems in the*

Pre-Modern World, edited by Susan E. Alcock, John Bodel,
and Richard J. A. Talbert, pp. 147–67. Malden, MA: Wiley-
Blackwell.

Kosiba, Steven B.
2010   Becoming Inka: The Transformation of Political Place and
       Practice during Inka State Formation (Cusco, Peru). PhD dis-
       sertation, Department of Anthropology, University of Chicago.

Levillier, Roberto (editor)
1921 [1583]   Relación hecha por el Virrey D. Martín Enríquez de
              los oficios que se proveen en la gobernación de los reinos y
              provincias del Perú (1583). In *Gobernantes del Perú: Cartas y
              papeles: Siglo XVI: Documentos del Archivo de Indias*, tomo
              IX. Madrid: Sucesores de Rivadeneyra.

Quave, Kylie E.
2012   Labor and Domestic Economy on the Royal Estate in the Inka
       Imperial Heartland (Maras, Cuzco, Peru). PhD dissertation,
       Department of Anthropology, Southern Methodist University,
       Dallas.

Rostworowski, María
1962   Nuevos datos sobre tenencia de tierras reales en el incario.
       Revista del Museo Nacional 21:130–94.
1970   Los Ayarmaca. *Revista del Museo Nacional* 36:58–101.

Sarmiento de Gamboa, Pedro de
2007 [1572]   *The History of the Incas*, translated and edited by Brian
              S. Bauer and Vania Smith. Austin: University of Texas Press.

Toledo, Francisco de
1940a [1571]   Información hecha por orden del Virrey Don
               Francisco de Toledo . . . Yucay, Marzo 19–Julio 2 de 1571.
               In *Don Francisco de Toledo, supremo organizador del Perú:
               Su vida, su obra (1515–1582). Tomo II: Sus informaciones
               sobre los incas (1570–1572)*, edited by Roberto Levillier, pp.
               99–121. Buenos Aires: Espasa-Calpe.
1940b [1571]   Información comenzada en el Valle de Yucay . . .
               Junio 2–Septiembre 6 de 1571. In *Don Francisco de Toledo,
               supremo organizador del Perú: Su vida, su obra (1515–1582).
               Tomo II: Sus informaciones sobre los incas (1570–1572)*,
               edited by Roberto Levillier, pp. 122–77. Buenos Aires:
               Espasa-Calpe.

Valencia Sosa, Amalia
2004   Informe Anual 2004 Restauración y Puesta en Valor del Sitio
       Arqueológico Camino Machuqollqa Comunidad Raqchi-
       Huaillabamba. Report submitted to the Instituto Nacional de
       Cultura, Cusco, Peru.

Villanueva Urteaga, Horacio
1970   Documento sobre Yucay en el siglo XVI. *Revista del Archivo
       Histórico de Cuzco* 13:1–148.

Wright, Kenneth R., Ruth M. Wright, and Alfredo Valencia Zegarra
2012   *Moray: Inca Engineering Mystery*. Reston, VA: ASCE Press.

Chapter 11: Inca Imperial Settlement Patterns in the Sacred Valley

R. Alan Covey

The Vilcanota-Urubamba Valley received its popular name—the Sacred Valley of the Incas—because of the remains of monumental constructions linked ethnohistorically to multiple rulers of the Inca dynasty. In recent decades, archaeological research has focused on the study of the surviving Inca monuments, including Quispiwanka (Niles 1999), Yucay (Niles 1999; Valencia 1982), Urcon (Candia 2008), Calca (Niles 1988), Huchuy Cuzco (Kendall, Early, and Sillar 1992), and Pisac (Angeles Vargas 1970; Kaulicke et al. 2003; Yépez 1985) (see Niles 2004). To varying degrees, scholars have also explored the documentary record for such sites (e.g., Farrington 1995; Rowe 1997; Rostworowski 1970; Villanueva Urteaga 1970). Although the study of the Inca occupation of the Sacred Valley has focused on monumental sites, some excavations have investigated side valleys and high-elevation sites such as Ankasmarka (Kendall 1985) and Pukara Pantillijlla (Dwyer 1971).

This chapter presents the settlement patterns collected by the Sacred Valley Archaeological Project (SVAP) and the Calca-Yanahuara Archaeological Project (PACY), which offer a dataset that provides new perspectives on the Inca transformation of the valley. To make strong comparisons with the Xaquixaguana region (Chapter 10), the discussion first presents overall data from the two projects in the valley, and then evaluates the settlement patterns for the three principal parts of the region—areas to the south of the Sacred Valley, the valley proper, and the side valleys lying to the north of the valley. Following the presentation of data, broad themes related to the Inca occupation of the valley are considered.

Inca Settlement in the Sacred Valley

Survey crews collected Inca pottery at 225 sites in the two survey projects in the Sacred Valley (Fig. 11.1). SVAP research accounted for 150 sites, and PACY for the remaining 75. The site count for the SVAP region represents 67% (150/224) of the number of sites registered for the Late Intermediate period (LIP), whereas the PACY region showed a slight increase (10%) in the number of Inca sites, from 68 in the LIP. The comparison of LIP and Inca sherd counts is not appropriate in the Sacred Valley, given that intensive collections were not carried out at larger sites in this region. The overall continuity of settlement from the LIP into Inca times differs in the two Sacred Valley study regions. Less than half of the LIP sites in the SVAP region (44.6%, 100/224) had Inca components, whereas two-thirds (66.2%, 45/68) of LIP sites in the PACY region yielded examples

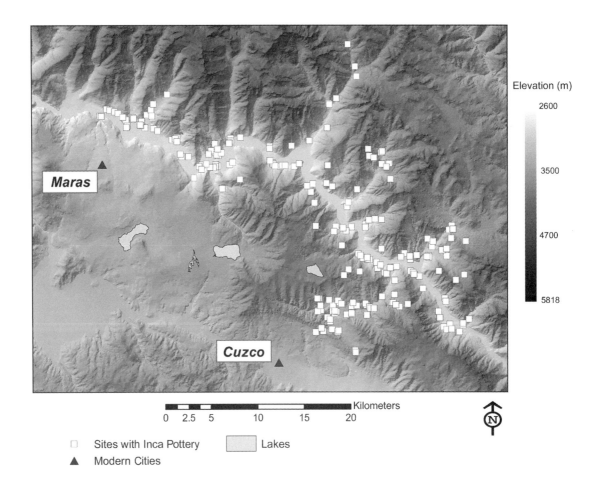

Figure 11.1. Map of Inca sites in the Sacred Valley, registered by the Sacred Valley Archaeological Project (2000) and the Calca-Yanahuara Archaeological Project (2007). Courtesy of L. Tsesmeli.

of the imperial style. Table 11.1 places these figures in comparison with subregions in the XPAS study region, showing variations in the proportion of LIP sites with Inca components, the percentage of single component Inca sites, and the percentage of sites with Killke pottery and no other LIP or Inca component. The Sacred Valley projects both show higher rates of new Inca settlement than any Xaquixaguana area, but they vary in terms of continuity from LIP times. As discussed below, proximity to Cuzco and Inca promotion of valley-bottom agriculture account for these differences.

Table 11.1. Variations in co-occurrence of LIP, Inca, and Killke components.

Area	LIP Sites with Inca	Inca Sites with No LIP	Killke Sites with No LIP
SVAP	100/224 (45%)	50/150 (33%)	17/224 (8%)
PACY	45/68 (66%)	30/75 (40%)	N/A
Maras	28/86 (33%)	9/35 (26%)	2/86 (2%)
Chinchero-Huayllabamba	28/52 (54%)	2/30 (7%)	3/52 (6%)
Xaquixaguana Valley	79/156 (51%)	22/101 (22%)	4/156 (3%)

Note: Data have not been trimmed to account for elevation, so there are minor differences in site counts from figures presented in Chapter 10. Killke pottery was not differentiated from other LIP styles in the laboratory analysis of the PACY project.

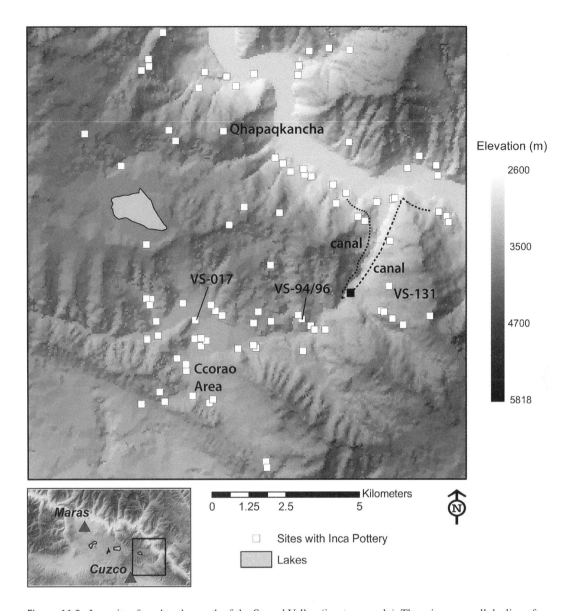

Figure 11.2. Inca sites found to the south of the Sacred Valley (inset area only). There is an overall decline of settlement at most high-elevation LIP villages, with a shift in settlement to small sites near the Cuzco Basin and low-elevation sites near new canal systems feeding terraces in the Sacred Valley. Courtesy of L. Tsesmeli.

Inca Settlement Patterns to the South of the Sacred Valley

SVAP survey crews registered 51 sites with Inca pottery in the Chit'apampa Basin and nearby areas of the south rim of the Sacred Valley, including Patabamba (Fig. 11.2). The Inca site count is lower than the LIP ($n = 61$) and represents a considerable discontinuity between the two periods. Twenty-two Inca sites lack any LIP component, and an additional 9 sites had Inca and Killke but no other LIP material. The total site area for the Inca period is approximately 40 ha, which is about two-thirds of the estimated area for the LIP. This is in part because some of the high-elevation villages—such as Raqchi (VS-94/96), Qhapaqkancha, and Hatun

Pukara—appear to have experienced a decline in occupation by the imperial period. Villages located closer to the Sacred Valley—especially in the Huancalle area, where the canal outtakes for two major Inca irrigation systems are located—demonstrate greater settlement continuity, and the largest village in this area is VS-131 (a second site called Raqchi), which is located above 3800 masl. As the scatterplot of site size and elevation demonstrates (Figs. 11.3, 11.4), Inca components are present in villages that continue to occupy the *suni-puna* transition, although there are new settlements that favor lower elevations.

These tend to be found in two areas—in the upper Chit'apampa Basin in places with easy access from the Cuzco Basin, and in

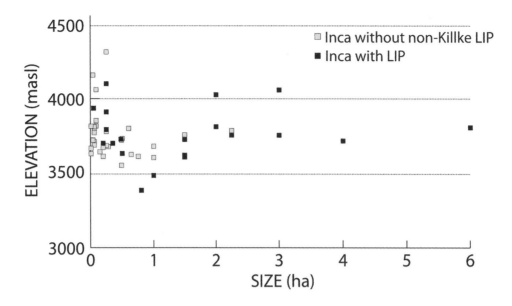

Figure 11.3. Scatterplot of site size and elevation for Inca sites to the south of the Sacred Valley. Many LIP communities in the suni continued to be occupied, but there is a shift to lands close to Cuzco and close to the valley-bottom facilities constructed in the Sacred Valley.

Figure 11.4. Photograph of the Ccorao area in the upper Chit'apampa Basin. The photograph shows the highway from Cuzco to Pisac as it crosses into the Cuzco Basin—survey work here encountered a series of small, dispersed single component Inca sites.

Figure 11.5. The south slope of the Sacred Valley, facing the Inca site of Pisac. The parallel lines are relict canals originating in the lower Chit'apampa Basin, which brought water for terraces on the lower valley slopes.

the lower Chit'apampa Basin in places in proximity to new irrigation infrastructure. With regard to the former, survey work in the Ccorao area encountered a series of small, dispersed single component Inca scatters just across the ridge from the Cuzco Basin. Although some covered areas of a hectare or more, the scatters were almost all of low density, suggesting a repeated and ephemeral occupation of the area, perhaps on a seasonal basis. This settlement pattern is comparable with Inca site distributions in the Cuzco Basin, where Bauer (2004) identified more than 850 sites, including large numbers of small and dispersed single component scatters. These small sites might represent opportunistic exploitation of resources lying within easy travel of villages in the Cuzco Basin—such sites were not typically encountered beyond the Ccorao area.

Moving through the Chit'apampa Basin toward the Sacred Valley, there is evidence of Inca-era reorganization of subsistence and settlement in the lower elevations of the basin. A small storage complex at Qollqarakay (VS-017) was built on a low prominence overlooking the Huillcarpata area, where there is evidence of agricultural terrace construction and several small

Inca sites. The valley floor in this area lies at around 3600 masl, making these lands best suited for crops other than maize.

The evidence for subsistence intensification and settlement change is substantially greater in the lower part of the Chit'apampa Basin, beginning in the area of Huancalle, where the outtakes for two major Inca canals are located. One of these carried water more than 5 km to terraces on the lower slopes of the Sacred Valley across from Pisac (Fig. 11.5), and the other waters terraces in the Taray area, about 3 km away. New Inca sites appear along these canal systems—typically small settlements (discussed in the following section)—but the LIP settlements in the Huancalle area also appear to have continuous settlement into the imperial period.

Inca settlement to the south of the Sacred Valley reveals state intervention in local subsistence production in some areas, but also evidence that local villages took advantage of nearby resources to meet their subsistence needs. There is a degree of continuity at some local LIP villages, although the large number of new Inca sites in the area suggests a social order distinct from the early LIP.

Inca Settlement Patterns in the Sacred Valley

In the Sacred Valley, there is much greater evidence of Inca transformation of land, water, and labor resources, which were marshaled to pursue surplus production that could support noble houses and the growing city of Cuzco (Covey 2006; Covey, Aráoz Silva, and Bauer 2008). The Inca site count for the main valley totals 130 sites: 55 in the SVAP region and 75 in the PACY region (Fig. 11.6). This figure is comparable with the LIP site count for the valley—64 LIP sites were registered in the SVAP part (11 of them with only Killke material), and 68 in the PACY part. Forty-six Inca sites in the Sacred Valley contained no LIP component, and most of these new imperial-era sites lie in the lower part of the study region (30/46 were registered by PACY research). These figures exclude sites with known Inca occupations where survey crews were unable to collect pottery because of contemporary occupation or designation as monumental archaeological zones. Such sites include the Colonial towns of the valley—San Salvador, Pisac, Coya, Lamay, Calca, Huayllabamba, Yucay, and Urubamba—several of which are known to have been established as *reducciones* at the location of existing communities. For example, the reducción of Pisac brought population from 9 existing communities (Quillhuay, Caquia Xaquixaguana, Coya, Paullu, Tankarpata, Patawaylla, Tuqsan, Paulo Wayllakalla, and Chuquibamba) to an existing settlement (Covey and Amado 2008 [1572: f. 444–444v]).

Although it is impossible to verify with survey data, the footprint of the larger Colonial towns suggests possible Inca-era settlement sizes of 10 ha or larger, whereas the smaller towns probably represent settlements of more modest size. Associated royal palace complexes represent additional occupied areas beyond the settlement of tributary or retainer populations. For example, the footprint of the modern town of Pisac is more than 10 ha, and the elite complexes of the archaeological site of the same name add several additional hectares of associated settlement. Calca and Urubamba represent 2 other potentially large Inca towns associated with royal palaces (Castillo and Jurado 1996; Farrington 1995; Niles 1988, 1999). Even excluding Inca palaces and towns of unknown size, the total area of lower-order Inca sites is about 70 ha in the Sacred Valley, and it is possible that the larger sites could double that figure.

Figure 11.7 presents a scatterplot of site size and elevation for sites of verified size in the Sacred Valley where Inca pottery was collected (this excludes royal palaces). Although both study regions favor *kichwa* elevations in the valley, there are slight contrasts between the SVAP and PACY regions in terms of site distributions. SVAP sites show a broader range of elevations, in part because of the establishment of sites above canal systems bringing water to the lower slopes and valley bottom. Also, this part of the valley has more LIP village sites located on prominent points not far from the valley floor, and almost all of these communities continued to be occupied in the imperial period. The PACY region shows a much greater concentration of settlements on the valley floor itself, including many small occupations found

on or near monumental terrace complexes. To a certain degree, the practice of settling directly on the valley floor might be a late imperial settlement pattern—it is associated with the palaces of the very last rulers, Huayna Capac (Quispiwanka) and Huascar (Calca), whereas earlier rulers built palaces several hundred meters above the valley floor (Covey 2006).

Overall, the Sacred Valley exhibits a massive investment in the construction of rural palaces and agricultural infrastructure (discussed below). The upper tiers of the settlement hierarchy are difficult to reconstruct archaeologically, but there is reason to view the settlement system as a series of country palaces belonging to different royal lineages, some of which were associated with large villages and towns located near improved valley-bottom agricultural infrastructure. Existing local villages in the valley do not appear to have been abandoned, but new populations settled in new communities, many of them very small and directly associated with Inca irrigation canals and agricultural terraces.

Inca Settlement Patterns to the North of the Sacred Valley

The Inca impact to the north of the Sacred Valley differed in the two survey regions. The PACY region contained little evidence of LIP settlement in the small quebradas draining into the Vilcanota-Urubamba River, and many of the larger ones became hunting grounds and pleasure lands associated with the royal estate of Huayna Capac at Yucay (Niles 1999; Covey, Aráoz Silva, and Bauer 2008). The northern drainages in the SVAP region were much more substantial in terms of LIP settlement, with 99 sites covering a total area of more than 100 ha (Chapter 9). Survey work in this area encountered a much more modest occupation associated with Inca pottery—44 sites, which represent less than 60 ha of total site area (Fig. 11.8). Two-thirds of the LIP sites in the northern drainages (67/99) have no Inca component, suggesting widespread site abandonment in the transition to the imperial period. As discussed in Chapter 9, several of the larger LIP sites showed evidence of Inca architecture and pottery, most notably Markasunay, Ankasmarka, and Pukara Pantillijlla. The latter 2 sites have excavation dates that indicate occupation continuing into the imperial period (Covey 2006; Kendall 1985), although grass in wall plasters in some structures at Pukara Pantillijlla returned earlier dates, possibly suggesting that some parts of the site were abandoned during the imperial period. Several of the larger LIP villages in high-elevation areas show little or no evidence of Inca period occupation (Fig. 11.9). Most of the continuing village occupations are found in suni elevations, either at the transition to the puna (3800–4000 masl) or the transition to the kichwa (3400–3600 masl) (Fig. 11.10). The location of Pukara Pantillijlla suggests that early Inca administration focused on maximizing administrative oversight of diverse local subsistence systems, rather than a direct management of specialized herding or valley-bottom farming.

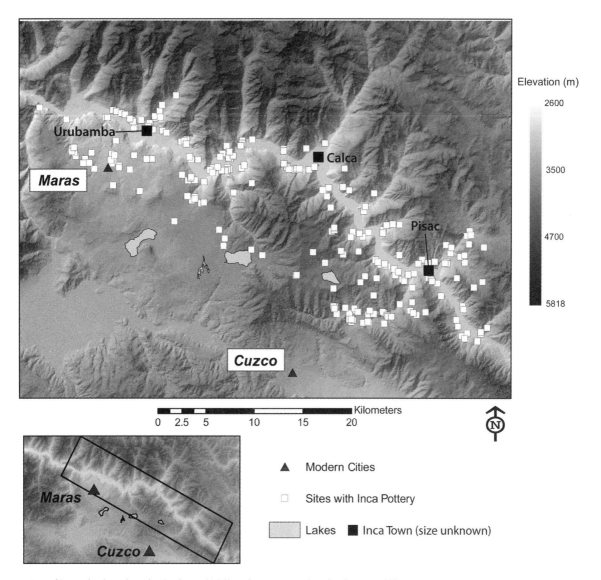

Figure 11.6. Map of Inca site locations in the Sacred Valley (inset area only). Settlement shifted to the valley bottom, where Inca nobles developed new agricultural lands, built country palaces, and settled new towns. Outside estate-related towns like Pisac and Calca, the typical Inca settlement was small and closely associated with new agricultural infrastructure. Courtesy of L. Tsesmeli.

Figure 11.7.

Scatterplot of site size and elevation for Inca sites in the Sacred Valley. SVAP Inca sites (*black*) show somewhat more elevation variation than PACY sites (*gray*), but both regions show an emphasis on kichwa zone settlement close to valley-bottom agricultural resources.

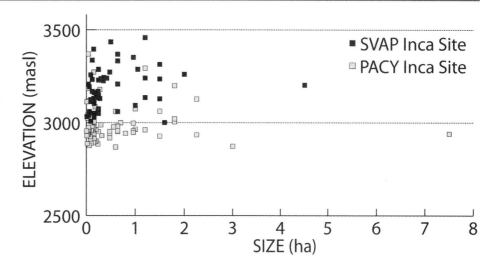

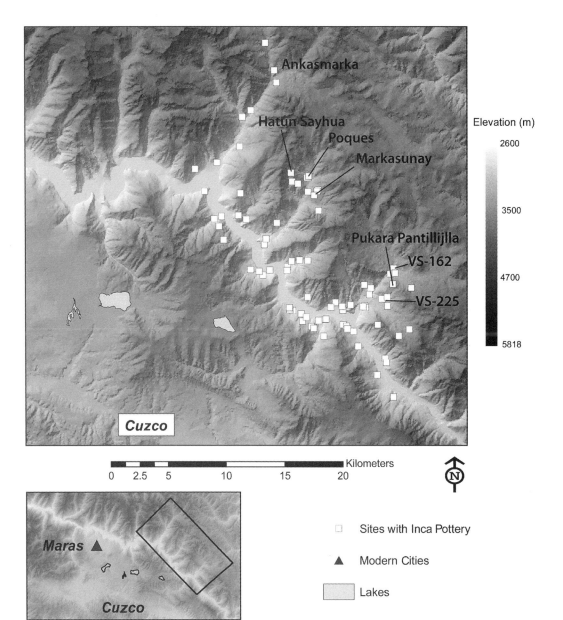

Figure 11.8.

Map of Inca site locations
to the north of the Sacred
Valley (inset area only).
Lower basin areas show
evidence of agricultural
intensification and
new site construction,
whereas many upper basin
communities show little or
no evidence of Inca period
occupation. Courtesy of L.
Tsesmeli.

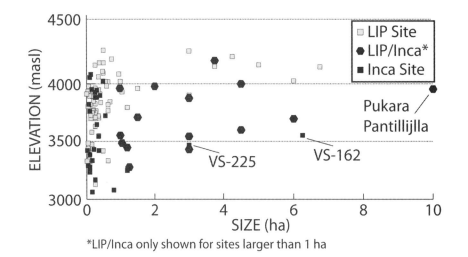

Figure 11.9.

Scatterplot of LIP and
Inca site size and elevation
in the drainages to the
north of the Sacred Valley.
Many upper basin villages
were abandoned, whereas
suni villages exhibit
more continuity into the
Inca period. New Inca
sites tend to be found in
the lower basins, close
to new Inca production
infrastructure.

Figure 11.10. Photograph of VS-217, a small village in the lower Chongo Basin. The site was first occupied in the LIP, but shows evidence of continued settlement as Inca administration shifted from Pukara Pantillijlla to Pisac (shown in the background).

Twelve Inca sites to the north of the Sacred Valley were new occupations, representing about 12 ha of settlement in previously uninhabited areas. Half of these were in the lower Chongo Basin, between Pukara Pantillijlla and Pisac, where 2 new village sites were established at VS-162 and VS-225. New Inca sites were also registered in the Carmen Quebrada, in the mid-valley area near Poques, where there is Inca terrace construction, as well as new farming and herding settlements (see below). The average elevation of new Inca sites was below 3500 masl, and almost all are situated near new Inca agricultural infrastructure in the kichwa zone. This shift downward might reflect the transition in Inca administrative focus toward specialized valley-bottom farming (and to a lesser degree, high-elevation herding).

As with areas to the south of the Sacred Valley, the northern drainages show evidence of Inca intensification projects in areas where new valley-bottom lands could be developed, and there is a marked abandonment of larger villages situated at high elevation. This is not to say that the herding zone was depopulated, but rather that the herding that took place in the imperial period probably occurred under the supervision of a few sites with a direct Inca presence, such as Ankasmarka, Hatun Sayhua, and Pukara

Pantillijlla. It is likely that the distribution of Inca pottery in these upland areas underrepresents the population in imperial times, and that some sites that appear to be largely depopulated simply did not acquire and use imperial polychromes on a regular basis.

Summary of Inca Settlement in the Sacred Valley

Settlement pattern data from SVAP and PACY research indicate three specific settlement trajectories in the Sacred Valley in Inca times, which are strongly influenced by ecological differences and proximity to Cuzco. To the south of the valley, there is a downward shift as many high-elevation sites diminished in size or were abandoned, with evidence of Inca intensification projects in valley-bottom areas below about 3600 masl. The higher Inca site count and larger number of new sites can be attributed to subsistence strategies of populations living in the Cuzco Basin, as well as the establishment of new settlements around improved agricultural infrastructure. In the Sacred Valley, there is greater continuity in local settlement, but also a significantly more pronounced Inca investment in land reclamation and intensification projects that are associated with the establishment of new sites and growth of large villages and towns associated with royal estates. The northern drainages exhibit some of the same patterns seen to the south of the valley—abandonment of high villages and shifts toward Inca facilities in the lower valley areas—but there seems to be less Inca pottery in local contexts, with the exception of a few strategic sites that continued to be occupied, presumably to monitor local labor and the movement of caravans between the Inca heartland and nearby lowland areas where coca and other resources were available.

Synthesizing Archaeological and Ethnohistoric Resources

On the basis of the settlement pattern data, it is possible to turn to some thematic issues regarding local settlements and Inca strategies in the Sacred Valley. These include ecology and risk management, changes in cultural identity, and the role of the royal estate system in building sources of social power that facilitated the expansion and administration of imperial provinces. As discussed in the previous chapter, the documentary record permits us to develop interpretations that would not be feasible on the basis of the settlement pattern data alone.

Ecology and Risk Management

Current perspectives on subsistence practices and risk management strategies for pre-Inca and Inca populations in the Sacred Valley are based primarily on environmental observations regarding the elevation of site locations. From these data, inferences are made based on the assumption that most subsistence activities occurred within a fairly localized catchment area, and that current climatic and environmental conditions are at least fairly comparable with those of the past. Chapter 2 discusses some of the problems with making such assumptions, and a considerable amount of additional excavation and laboratory work will be needed in order to test and clarify current interpretations. We do not have paleobotanical or biogeochemical evidence for reconstructing subsistence practices in the region, and the household archaeology that has been conducted to date has not yet contributed actively to these issues.

In general, LIP village locations in and near the Sacred Valley reflect a diverse set of local catchment characteristics, during a time of lower and more unpredictable precipitation than in Inca times. The largest settlements favor prominent points that were probably found in the puna or the transition from dry-farming lands to high pastures. Smaller villages are found in the lower farming ecozones, including the warm kichwa lands in the Sacred Valley. These settlements are not associated with infrastructure for intensive agriculture; sites with good architectural preservation appear to have storage structures integrated within the household (Covey 2006; Kendall 1985). The lower part of the Sacred Valley offers better evidence for the construction of formal storage complexes outside domestic contexts, and excavations

at Machu Qollqa and Cheqoq demonstrate that these practices began in the LIP (Covey, Quave, and Covey, forthcoming). On the basis of settlement location and the apparent absence of agricultural infrastructure and community-level storage, it is reasonable to interpret local subsistence practices as widely variable and oriented toward the fairly localized exploitation of a wide range of agropastoral resources. Site sizes and the overall absence of monumental construction suggest that these systems were successful at maintaining populations that grew at a fairly modest rate, but there is little evidence of large-scale surpluses that would accentuate social inequality or facilities designed to integrate region-wide populations. Even defensive works at the largest sites tend to be quite modest when compared with other parts of the Andean highlands at this time (e.g., Arkush 2011).

The distribution of Inca pottery in the Sacred Valley indicates a downward settlement shift in regional settlement, which suggests a new ecological focus that is associated with large-scale construction projects underwritten by the Inca nobility and state institutions (Covey 2006). Whereas the large LIP sites were located at an average elevation of over 3900 masl, Inca sites of one hectare or larger were found much lower, at an average elevation of 3588 masl. Small Inca sites had the lowest average elevation for any group of sites found on the survey (3479 masl), and Inca settlement as a whole was located lower than for any other period (3515 masl). This shift would be even more dramatic if the large ridgetop sites with small Inca components were excluded.

Inca period sites as a whole reflect a shift toward maize production on improved lands at the valley bottom, and settlement in this period also indicates more intensive land use, including reliance on irrigation canals for agricultural production. Inca period sites are closer than LIP settlements to permanent water. Morphologically, SVAP Inca sites were found more frequently on valley slopes (36% of all designations, or 85/237), with a smaller component of sites located on the valley bottom or in agricultural lands (17%, or 41/237). Land use designations for Inca sites indicate proximity to hillside zones (*loma*, 34%, or 35/103), but valley-bottom lands are settled more frequently (45%, or 46/103) than suni and puna lands (21%, or 22/103). This evidence, combined with field observations, reveals that Inca villages tend to be located just above irrigation canals and terrace complexes, with many small (possibly temporary) sites established in upper valley dry-farming areas (Fig. 11.11). The Inca pattern in the SVAP region displays a concern with minimizing settlement in irrigated areas and providing easy access to hillside fields and high pastures. Thirty Inca sites had a canal as their nearest water source, indicating a shift to locations that were more dependent on centrally managed infrastructure for their water and agricultural resources. The association of 28 Killke sites with irrigation canals suggests that this process of development and dependency began in the LIP and continued into the imperial period.

Along the Calca-Yanahuara stretch of the valley, Inca settlements favored the valley floor, with an average elevation of 3003 masl. This represents a slight downward shift from LIP

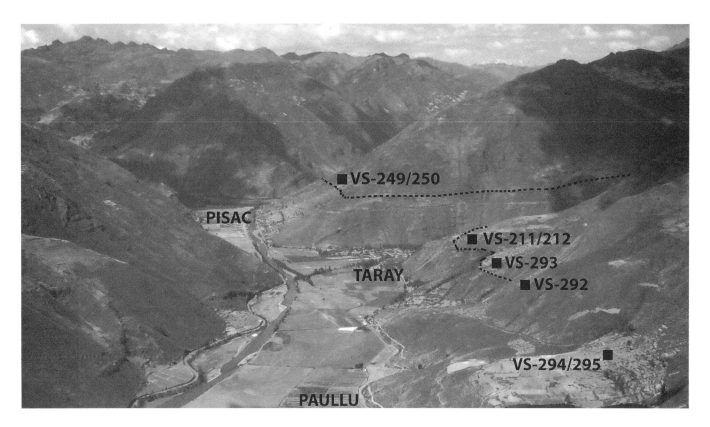

Figure 11.11. A photograph of the Sacred Valley near Pisac. Dashed lines show the route of irrigation canals originating in the Chit'apampa Basin, and several of the Inca-era sites located just above the canals are shown. These tended to be small settlements.

times, and only 4 sites above 3200 masl had any Inca pottery (a total of 11 fragments). Compared with the SVAP region, the Inca occupation of the Calca-Yanahuara region favors the valley floor itself, especially in the Urubamba and Yucay areas where the valley bottom is wide and intensively terraced (Fig. 11.12). As discussed previously, the LIP settlement pattern in the Calca-Yanahuara region does not generally focus on prominent high-elevation locations in the northern tributary valleys. This is probably because such valleys are narrower and steeper in the lower part of the Sacred Valley, with lower elevation thresholds for marginal conditions.

The most significant change in the economic organization of the Sacred Valley was the transformation of valley-bottom lands for intensive agriculture, which focused particularly on the cultivation of maize. This occurred over the span of several generations, affecting particular stretches of the valley, especially the confluences of tributary rivers with the Vilcanota-Urubamba River (Farrington 1983). Land improvement occurred on the valley floor and lower slopes and involved symbolically important changes to land and water. At the valley floor, the canalization of waterways in the confluence area reduced seasonal flooding, bringing order to the risks associated with the flowing-together (*tinku*) of the rivers. As canals were built, rock and fill were

brought to the area to fill in low-lying spaces and establish hundreds of hectares of flat, well-drained agricultural terraces. The arid lower slopes of the valley were subject to drought or erosion, depending on the intensity of seasonal rains, and in many areas water was channeled away from tributary rivers, carried several kilometers in some cases to hillside terraces that would improve soil retention. The diversion of water from its sources created resources that could sustain new kin groups and communities living in and around a new landscape dominated by the Inca nobility (Covey 2011). Rostworowski (1962) has published a 1559 document from the Coya area that describes how the transformation of previously barren lands granted the Inca ruler who invested the labor the authority to rename and reallocate new fields, often at the expense of autochthonous communities. It is important to note that this process of landscape development did not affect all parts of the valley equally. There are still stretches of river that meander and lack evidence for hydraulic infrastructure for agriculture (Fig. 11.13).

Inca elites laid claim to more than just the areas where their labor projects tamed the Vilcanota-Urubamba River and brought water to its lower slopes. As discussed already, several small terrace and canalization projects have been identified in the transverse valleys draining into the river—in the Chit'apampa

Figure 11.12. Inca terracing at Poron (CY-6) in the Yanahuara area developed available water sources to intensify valley-bottom agriculture. Construction created an estimated 32 ha of irrigated terraces, and multiple sherd scatters on the terraces suggest that some Inca populations lived on the terraces.

Basin near Huillcarpata, the Chongo Basin near Amaro, the Carmen Quebrada near Poques, and in the lower part of the Qochoc Valley. These projects would have been more likely to expropriate fields used by local populations. Terrace construction is also prominent in the areas surrounding Inca country palaces. In addition to valley-bottom terraces with explicit royal affiliation (e.g., Covey, Aráoz Silva, and Bauer 2008), estate construction sometimes included significant modification of the hillsides near palaces through the construction of terraces that were not all fed by irrigation canals (Figs. 11.14, 11.15). In many instances, the energy invested to shape the hillside could not expect to be recovered during the lifetime of the ruling couple laying claim to the lands—this suggests that such constructions represent investments of wealth to make an ideological statement about ownership (cf. Kaulicke et al. 2003).

In addition to new water and land resources, Inca rule marked the landscape of the Sacred Valley through the construction of complexes of storehouses of varying size and architecture (Covey, Quave, and Covey, forthcoming). Survey teams registered storage architecture at close to 20 sites in the Sacred Valley and Calca-Yanahuara regions, although it is difficult to treat this sample as complete or representative of the imperial period. Some complexes of storehouses conform to architectural patterns seen in provincial regions (e.g., LeVine 1992), but many are built in a distinct architectural style that is strongly tied to the imperial heartland (see Protzen 1993). Most storage architecture is placed in prominent and visible locations close to the valley floor. The architecture and location of storage facilities suggests that the Inca focused on kichwa agriculture for the surplus production of crops like maize, a distinct risk-reduction strategy that could be mobilized for elite and state projects (military campaigns, new construction, ceremonies) in good years. A shift toward maize as the fundamental Inca foodstuff also represents a recentering and homogenization of subsistence and diet in the Sacred Valley and in areas supported by its staples.

The intensive Inca use of prime valley-bottom lands required the political integration and development of both sides of the Sacred Valley, which could be achieved only by a state-level polity (Covey 2006). Following the annexation/incorporation of the drainages to the north of the Sacred Valley, Inca rulers began to develop the valley bottom, constructing huge new terrace groups that were fed by canals originating several kilometers away. Some

Figure 11.13. The Sacred Valley below Calca illustrates the differential effects of Inca river canalization and terrace construction. On the right side, the valley bottom was terraced and dominated by the Inca site of Urcon (center of photograph), whereas local LIP villages on the left side continued to occupy communities near the unimproved lands of Chimbacalca and Unuraqui.

Figure 11.14.

Hillside terraces on the
approach to Viracocha's
estate at Huchuy Cuzco.
While visually impressive,
these terraces created a
very limited amount of new
cultivation space.

Figure 11.15.

Hillside terraces at Pisac
reshaped lands that were
not productive before Inca
times, but did not create the
kind of large, well-watered
expanses of frost-free land
that projects at the valley
bottom brought into use.

projects are likely to have involved the full subordination of lo-cal groups, who were moved away from areas where they could maintain economic and political autonomy. The ethnohistoric documents suggest that some of these groups continued to live in the area, while others were dispossessed of their lands and resettled elsewhere (Covey 2006).

Evidence of Economic Specialization in the State Production System

As agriculture in the Sacred Valley was being transformed into a more intensive valley-bottom cultivation of a few impor-tant staples, there is some evidence that the herding component of the Inca economy was specialized under state management. The site of Hatun Sayhua (VS-310), a 3.75 ha village located on a ridge in the Carmen Quebrada at 4200 masl, offers evidence of economic specialization. Prior to the period of Inca domina-tion, the largest upper valley settlement was the 6 ha village of Markasunay (VS-353), situated on a prominent ridge across the valley from Hatun Sayhua at an elevation of about 4000 masl. The spread of Inca control may have initially involved some sort of local administration at Markasunay, given the presence of rectangular Inca-style structures at the site, although excava-tions are needed to clarify this.

Over time, the focus of settlement in the upper valley shifted from Markasunay as 2 new Inca sites were established. One of these, Hatun Sayhua, was built well above agricultural lands in an area where high-elevation puna areas could be easily accessed. Several areas with corrals were found around 4200 masl, as well as a number of looted mortuary monuments (VS-307, VS-308, VS-309) that had a few fragments of local Late Intermediate period pottery, but mostly Killke and Inca. This suggests the expansion of a small existing site, or the establishment of a new site under Inca domination, possibly settled with local Poques people to herd for the state.

As a new village grew in the high puna grasslands, a second village (VS-350) was established at the valley floor in the mid-valley area (around 3700 masl). This new site was about 6 ha in size and today shows the remains of more than 60 circular or semi-circular structures, as well as a complex of rectangular Inca-style buildings. Agricultural production in the mid-valley intensified with the construction of new stone-faced terraces that were fed by new irrigation canals. As was observed at Hatun Sayhua, the pottery found on the surface had some local LIP sherds, but was mostly Killke and Inca. More than 100 simple cliff inhumations were observed around VS-350, as well as the remains of some mortuary structures (VS-326, VS-327, VS-347, VS-349). It is possible that this represents an Inca administrative resettlement of nonlocal population in a new valley-bottom community. Overall, the Inca sites in the Poques area suggest a state resettlement of local populations, intensification of resources, and management of specialized production.

A second possible case of specialized herding might include the large village site of Ankasmarka (VS-385), located at about 4000 masl in the Qochoc Valley above Calca. This site has the remains of about 300 circular and irregular structures, as well as 3 or 4 rectangular ones. Surface pottery indicates that the site was settled under Inca control at the end of the LIP, although its population might have declined in imperial times. Other sites in the small basin where Ankasmarka is situated (e.g., Machaqwayniyuq [VS-369], a 1 ha site with evidence of mortuary remains) show evidence of LIP occupation with no Inca surface material, which could indicate settlement shifts accompanying an Inca reorganization of local herding groups.

Social Identities and State Relationships in the Sacred Valley in Inca Times

As noted in Chapter 10, the documentary record offers distinct advantages for discussing who lived in particular parts of the Cuzco region in Inca times, and how many people might have populated the imperial heartland. Given the constraints discussed above in making accurate estimates of the largest Inca towns at the valley bottom, it is worth presenting early Colonial census data from some of the reducción communities in the Sacred Valley. Population counts from the 1570s, the time of the Tole-dan reducciones, indicate large numbers of people living in or resettled into sites that appear to have been associated with royal estates or large Inca towns, and although these data are imprecise windows into Inca-era site sizes, they attest to the considerable population present in and around the valley floor after a genera-tion of migration and demographic decline (see Covey, Childs, and Kippen 2011). As Table 11.2 shows, early Colonial towns associated with valley-bottom estates had tributary populations numbering in the low thousands a generation after the European invasion, numbers that presumably omit the noble Inca and re-tainer (*yana*) population of these communities (e.g., Covey and Amado 2008; Rostworowski 1990). There were sizeable com-munities settled in other parts of the valley bottom, as well as in side valleys. Smaller population counts at places like Lamay may be misleading—there were supposedly 500 Wanka households living in the community in the early Colonial period, as well as an *ayllu* of Cuzco Inca identity (Covey 2009). The identification of a few small villages in upvalley locations (e.g., Pampallacta, which might refer to the community of Ankasmarka) suggests that some local populations continued to reside there in Inca times. The total population count for these twelve *repartimientos* approaches 20,000, a figure that excludes many of the Colonial communities that are known for the Sacred Valley, and which represents major declines from Inca times.

Even though some significant ambiguities remain regarding the Sacred Valley settlement hierarchy, a few important observa-tions can be made. First is that if the large reducción settlements are excluded, valley-bottom sites with Inca pottery are of fairly modest size. As Table 11.3 demonstrates, Sacred Valley Inca sites found below about 3200 masl tend to be quite small, with few sites larger than a hectare. A few hundred meters above the valley floor—frequently along the line of Inca canals, or just

Table 11.2. Early Colonial population counts for repartimientos in the Sacred Valley region.

Town	Location	Census Data (1570s–1580s)	Source
Yucay and Urubamba	valley floor estate	3433	Cook 1975; Levillier 1921
Calca	valley floor estate	3340	Cook 1975
Pisac	valley floor estate	2246	Levillier 1921
San Salvador	valley floor town?	1492	Levillier 1921
Urcon	valley floor town	1802	Cook 1975
Lamay	valley floor town	253	Cook 1975
Oma and Taray	valley floor town	1222	Cook 1975
Caquia Xaquixaguana, Paullu, and Quilloay	upvalley estate communities	2044	Cook 1975; Levillier 1921
Matinga	upvalley town	160	Cook 1975
Puquises	upvalley town	1147	Cook 1975
Guatauma	upvalley town	220	Cook 1975
Pampallacta	upvalley town	1279	Cook 1975

Sources: Cook 1975 [1570s]: xxxv; Levillier 1921 [1583]:166–67.

Table 11.3. Inca sites located at low elevations in the Sacred Valley.

Elevation Range (masl)	Site Count	Average Size (ha)
below 3100	15	0.38
3100–3199	15	0.33
3200–3299	23	0.70
3300–3399	9	0.56

above terrace complexes—there are more sites, including several small villages (see below for a specific case). These results are consistent with descriptions of large royal estate complexes—some of them associated with sizeable settlements—surrounded by numerous small communities that were occupied by labor specialists and servants of the royal lineages that owned the improved farmlands at the valley floor.

The Calca-Yanahuara survey data indicate a greater prevalence of valley-bottom settlement, with more than two-thirds of Inca sites found below 3000 masl (52/75). These were predominantly modest scatters with an average size much smaller than a hectare. Some of these were associated with large valley-bottom terrace complexes, such as Poron (CY-6: 32 ha) and Luisayoq (CY-107: 20 ha). The documentary descriptions of this part of the Sacred Valley (Covey and Amado 2008; Rostworowski 1970, 1990; Villanueva Urteaga 1970) suggest that later generations of royal estate construction favored the valley floor as a place for royal retreats (see Niles 1999, 2004).

Inca settlements in and around the Sacred Valley preserved some of the local social diversity that developed during the

LIP, and there were local groups that are described as receiving honorary Inca status (e.g., Poques), whereas others are described as being destroyed after proving to be unfaithful kin or rebellious subjects (e.g., Huayllacans, Cuyos) (Covey 2006). As Inca rulers reshaped the Sacred Valley, they brought new populations to the valley, including settlers from Cuzco, labor colonists (*mitmaqkuna*) from provincial regions, and retainers (*yanakuna*) taken from tributary communities (e.g., Covey 2006, 2013; Covey and Elson 2007).

During the early Colonial period, the communities of Lamay, Coya, Pisac, and Calca had descent groups named Cuzco Ayllu, suggesting that part of the Inca resettlement program in the SVAP area consisted of encouraging or requiring populations from Cuzco to resettle in the valley. This part of the valley also had residents belonging to the descent groups of Yahuar Huaccac, Viracocha Inca, and Pachacutic Inca Yupanqui, who lived around the estate communities in the valley (Covey 2013). Inca nobles also lived in the lower part of the Sacred Valley, where numerous individuals owned land worked by retainers in the Yucay area (Covey and Amado 2008).

Laboring alongside Inca commoners and nobles were rotations of labor colonists who engaged in large-scale construction projects and worked some of the new valley-bottom lands. The chronicler Juan de Betanzos (1999 [1550s]) offers a particularly detailed account of the land reclamation project in the Yucay Valley, which involved more than 100,000 temporary provincial workers, most of whom returned to their homes after new royal domains had been created (cf. Covey and Amado 2008). Given that a group of 500 Wanka mitmaqkuna lived in Lamay permanently enough that the town had a Guanca Ayllu during the Colonial period, it seems likely that some labor colonists occupied specific communities or state facilities for longer periods of time and engaged in agricultural labor in the valley.

The final group of Inca-era inhabitants of the Sacred Valley comprises individuals bound to the Inca nobility or the state religion—a labor force that included yanakuna and *mamakuna*, retainers of the Inca who often had special skills and came from diverse parts of the empire. The Yucay estate had agricultural specialists, stonemasons, and other *kamayuqkuna* (those specialized in something), and these people constructed houses, special fields, and gardens for the Inca ruler and his family (Covey and Amado 2008). Testimony pertaining to the Pisac estate indicates that herders and cloth-making specialists (*qumpikamayuq*) from the Colla of the Titicaca Basin were resettled by the Inca to create valuable cloth that was used as gifts to loyal subjects (Covey 2006). In addition, the chronicles suggest that the Inca imperial agricultural production in the valley changed as well. Higher-status foodstuffs like chili peppers were supposedly cultivated at the valley bottom, along with exotic foods. It is possible that maize production was transformed from the production of maize races that would be good for storage and transport to varieties that would be good for making *aqha* (maize beer) for ceremonial use.

The documentary evidence for Inca populations in the Sacred Valley suggests that there was a large population with varying degrees of obligation to the royal estates that grew sequentially in the valley. Estates and retainers are much more prominent in the Sacred Valley than in the Xaquixaguana region, and the resources controlled by royal lineages probably contributed to funding state institutions. More work is needed to establish an archaeological database that can contribute to interpretations of noble and political networks in the Inca imperial heartland.

As discussed in Chapter 10, the imperial system of roads and way stations represents an important network of state infrastructure that links the imperial heartland to provincial regions. The principal route to Chinchaysuyu passed through the Xaquixaguana Valley, where the first way station was located. No such installation has been identified in the Sacred Valley. Short stretches of Inca road have been observed around Ñawpa Taray, Huchuy Cuzco, Qhapaqkancha, and Ankasmarka, but these seem to be minor routes leading from Cuzco to the Sacred Valley and from the Sacred Valley to the lowlands beyond. Survey work encountered two possible way stations (*tampu*) near Ankasmarka (VS-276) and Pukara Pantillijlla (VS-176). Both consisted of a small patio group (*kancha*) built in the Inca style, located at the confluence of upper basin streams. Given this location and the fact that these sites are at varying distances from the nearest Inca site, it is also possible that they are of a ritual nature and do not represent infrastructure. Based on the documentary record, the Amazonian slope was not accessed from Cuzco by way of a single highway, and many of the valleys neighboring the Sacred Valley had a strong affiliation with royal lineages that established coca lands there (Covey 2006).

Despite some of the ambiguities that remain in the survey data, regional settlement patterns demonstrate that the Inca occupation of the Sacred Valley was one of the most profound social and economic transformations achieved by the empire, and it offers some important contrasts with the local portraits of continuity and change discussed for the Xaquixaguana region. The settlement pattern data offer some important insights into the nature and timing of the imperial transformation, although they leave significant lacunae that demand more intensive attention through problem-oriented excavations.

References Cited

Angeles Vargas, Victor A.
1970   *P'isaq: Gran metropoli inca*. Lima: Industrial Gráfica.

Arkush, Elizabeth N.
2011   *Hillforts of the Ancient Andes: Colla Warfare, Society, and Landscape*. Gainesville: University Press of Florida.

Bauer, Brian S.
2004   *Ancient Cuzco: Heartland of the Inca*. Austin: University of Texas Press.

Betanzos, Juan de
1999 [1550s]   *Suma y narración de los incas*. Cusco: Universidad Nacional de San Antonio Abad del Cusco.

Candia, Maritza Rosa
2008   La ocupación inka en Urqo-Calca: Una visión de su función y abandono a través de un contexto ritual. *Saqsaywaman* 8:72–84.

Castillo Tecsi, Tula, and Katy M. Jurado Chamorro
1996   El centro prehispánico de Calca. Thesis, Facultad de Ciencias Sociales, Universidad Nacional de San Antonio Abad del Cusco.

Cook, Noble David (editor)
1975   *Tasa de la visita general de Francisco de Toledo*. Lima: Universidad Nacional Mayor de San Marcos.

Covey, R. Alan
2006   *How the Incas Built Their Heartland: State Formation and the Innovation of Imperial Strategies in the Sacred Valley, Peru*. Ann Arbor: University of Michigan Press.

2009   Domestic life and craft specialization in Inka Cusco and its rural hinterland. In *Domestic Life in Prehispanic Capitals: A Study of Specialization, Hierarchy, and Ethnicity*, edited by Linda R. Manzanilla and Claude Chapdelaine, pp. 223–34. Memoirs, no. 46. Ann Arbor: Museum of Anthropology, University of Michigan.

2011   Landscapes and languages of power in the Inca imperial heartland (Cuzco, Peru). *SAA Archaeological Record* 11(4):29–32, 47.

2013   Binding the imperial whole: The transition from capital to province in the Inka imperial heartland. In *Empires and Diversity: On the Crossroads of Archaeology, Anthropology, and History,* edited by Gregory Areshian, pp. 208–30. University of California, Los Angeles: Cotsen Institute of Archaeology.

Covey, R. Alan, and Donato Amado González (editors)
2008   *Imperial Transformations in Sixteenth-Century Yucay, Peru.* Memoirs, no. 44. Ann Arbor: Museum of Anthropology, University of Michigan.

Covey, R. Alan, Miriam Aráoz Silva, and Brian S. Bauer
2008   Settlement patterns in the Yucay Valley and neighboring areas. In *Imperial Transformations in Sixteenth-Century Yucay, Peru*, edited by R. Alan Covey and Donato Amado González, pp. 3–17. Memoirs, no. 44. Ann Arbor: Museum of Anthropology, University of Michigan.

Covey, R. Alan, Geoff Childs, and Rebecca Kippen
2011   Dynamics of indigenous demographic fluctuations: Lessons from sixteenth-century Cuzco, Peru. *Current Anthropology* 52(3):335–60.

Covey, R. Alan, and Christina M. Elson
2007   Ethnicity, demography, and estate management in sixteenth-century Yucay (Cuzco, Peru). *Ethnohistory* 54(2):303–35.

Covey, R. Alan, Kylie E. Quave, and Catherine E. Covey
forthcoming   Inca storage systems in the imperial heartland (Cuzco, Peru): Risk management, economic growth, and political economy. In *Storage and Administration in Ancient Complex Societies*, edited by Linda Manzanilla and Mitchell Rothman.

Dwyer, Edward B.
1971   The Early Inca Occupation of the Valley of Cuzco, Peru. PhD dissertation, Department of Anthropology, University of California, Berkeley.

Farrington, Ian S.
1983   Prehistoric intensive agriculture: Preliminary notes on river canalization in the Sacred Valley of the Incas. In *Drained Field Agriculture in Central and South America*, edited by J. P. Darch, pp. 221–35. BAR International Series 189. Oxford: British Archaeological Reports.

1995   The mummy, estate, and palace of Inca Huayna Capac at Quispeguanca. *Tawantinsuyu* 1:55–65.

Kaulicke, Peter, Ryujiro Kondo, Tetsuya Kusuda, and Julinho Zapata
2003   Agua, ancestros y arqueología del paisaje. *Boletín de Arqueología PUCP* 7:27–56.

Kendall, Ann
1985   *Aspects of Inca Architecture: Description, Function and Chronology*, pts. 1 and 2. BAR International Series 242. Oxford: British Archaeological Reports.

Kendall, Ann, Rob Early, and Bill Sillar
1992   Report on archaeological field season investigating early Inca architecture at Juchuy Coscco (Q'aqya Qhawana) and Warq'ana, Province of Calca, Dept. of Cuzco, Peru. In *Ancient America. Contributions to New World Archaeology*, edited by Nicholas J. Saunders, pp. 189–256. Oxbow Monograph 24. Oxford: Oxbow Books.

Levillier, Roberto (editor)
1921 [1583]   Relación hecha por el Virrey D. Martín Enríquez de los oficios que se proveen en la gobernación de los reinos y provincias del Perú (1583). In *Gobernantes del Perú: Cartas y papeles: Siglo XVI: Documentos del Archivo de Indias*, tomo IX, pp. 114–230. Madrid: Sucesores de Rivadeneyra.

LeVine, Terry Y. (editor)
1992   *Inca Storage Systems*. Norman: University of Oklahoma Press.

Niles, Susan A.
1988   Looking for "lost" Inca palaces. *Expedition* 30(3):56–64.
1999   *The Shape of Inca History. Narrative and Architecture in an Andean Empire*. Iowa City: University of Iowa Press.
2004   The nature of Inca royal estates. In *Machu Picchu: Unveiling the Mystery of the Incas*, edited by Richard L. Burger and Lucy C. Salazar. New Haven, CT: Yale University Press.

Protzen, Jean-Pierre
1993   *Inca Architecture and Construction at Ollantaytambo*. New York: Oxford University Press.

Rostworowski, María
1962   Nuevos datos sobre tenencia de tierras reales en el incario. *Revista del Museo Nacional* 21:130–94.
1970   El repartimiento de doña Beatriz Coya, en el valle de Yucay. *Historia y Cultura* 4:153–268.
1990   La visita de Urcos de 1572, un kipu pueblerino. *Historia y Cultura* 20:295–317.

Rowe, John H.
1997   Las tierras reales de los incas. In *Arqueología, Antropología e Historia en los Andes. Homenaje a María Rostworowski*, edited by Rafael Varón Gabai and Javier Flores Espinoza, pp. 277–87. Lima: Insituto de Estudios Peruanos.

Valencia Zegarra, Alfredo I.
1982   Complejo arqueológico de Yucay. In *Arqueología del Cuzco*, edited by Halo Oberti, pp. 65–81. Cuzco: INC.

Villanueva Urteaga, Horacio H.
1970   Documento sobre Yucay en el siglo XVI. *Revista del Archivo Histórico del Cuzco* 13:1–148.

Yépez, Wilfredo
1985   Sub-proyecto puesto en valor de moumentos, Dirección de Patrimonio Cultural y Monumental, Obra Pisaq—Q'allaq'asa: Informe Annual—1985. Annual report to the Instituto Nacional de Cultura, Cusco.

Chapter 12: Reconstructing Colonial Migration and Resettlement in the Cuzco Region

Kylie E. Quave

The Cuzco region underwent two major imperial transformations from AD 1400 to 1600 as the Incas built their heartland and Spaniards reduced the region to a province of their own empire. As the heartland of Tawantinsuyu until the 1530s, Cuzco experienced social and economic reorganization at the local and regional levels through the introduction of Inca sociopolitical structures, economic strategies, and ideological institutions. The European invasion disrupted Inca imperial practices in the Cuzco region, and it was only after decades of civil war and economic upheaval that Spanish Colonial institutions were eventually implemented among indigenous communities. With the arrival of new European populations, the evolution of Andean sociopolitical hierarchies, and the reconstitution of the Cuzco economy, native populations voluntarily migrated and were forcibly moved throughout and beyond the former heartland of Tawantinsuyu. At the same time, population numbers saw gradual and punctuated change with the introduction of diseases and new labor practices, as well as civil wars (e.g., Covey, Childs, and Kippen 2011; Wightman 1990).

Recent systematic archaeological surveys have documented more than 1500 Inca sites across the Cuzco region and many more from earlier periods (Bauer 1996, 2004; Covey 2006; Covey, Bélisle, and Davis 2006; Covey, Aráoz Silva, and Bauer 2008). These surveys were designed to identify and reconstruct

pre-Columbian state development; the research plans were not particularly intended to locate and understand Colonial settlement, and only later projects (the Xaquixaguana, Qoricocha, and Calca-Yanahuara surveys [Covey, Aráoz Silva, and Bauer 2008]) systematically registered and collected post-Conquest materials. Research on the Colonial period in Cuzco faces more methodological challenges than that on earlier periods, especially considering the rapidly changing indigenous and Spanish migration and settlement patterns in the first decades after conquest.

The Xaquixaguana and Qoricocha surveys identified 132 sites with a Colonial component. Continuities and shifts in the post-Conquest landscape are relevant to comprehending the implementation of imperial policies and local responses at the settlement level in a former imperial capital. Analysis of these sites at the regional level, with consideration of social and economic factors potentially influencing migration and settlement, indicates that there was an overall movement of populations from the *reducciones* to *haciendas* (landed estates) or to smaller hamlets and seasonal *estancias*. The migration from reducciones (Spanish-administered planned and nucleated towns to which indigenous tribute-paying populations were relocated) to haciendas and rural hamlets seems to be an effort to seek relief from tribute demands on the part of some native populations. While peasant populations moved away from reducciones, Spanish and native elites moved into lands that were reassigned by the Crown for sale or as *mercedes* (grants), lands that were reassigned from native farming communities. The consequent regional settlement patterns around Cuzco reflect the expected distribution of early Colonial sites based on the ethnohistoric record, showing initial sixteenth-century aggregation, then dispersal into smaller communities, and ongoing migration toward haciendas and other havens that are more expansive in size, where natives sought protection from Spanish administrative exploitation.

This analysis focuses on determining whether there are significant differences in the ecological strategies of settlement systems between the Inca and Colonial periods (i.e., elevation and distance to water), and evaluating the reoccupation or continued occupation of pre-Inca and Inca sites in the Colonial period. This study establishes that ecological and social factors each play a role in shaping Colonial settlement patterns, which contributes to a more comprehensive understanding of the processes underlying settlement pattern disruption and continuation. This latter issue provides insight into the migration of native populations in the Cuzco region during the Colonial period, as a response to Spanish rule and to the strains of changing demographics and tribute demands. Survey data can provide a more synchronic view of the overall diversity of economic and social strategies employed, although future research would be needed to refine chronology and develop more detailed perspectives on variations across the region.

Demographic Transitions and Migrations in Spanish Colonial Cuzco

A number of social, political, economic, and demographic changes contributed to the changes in settlement patterns after the arrival of Spaniards in the Cuzco region. Many of these can be attributed to the external force of Colonial policies and subsequent internal responses (and even the Spanish reactions to those alterations). Political strife during the initial shock of the Conquest, the Inca rebellion, and Spanish civil wars all contributed to significant interregional migrations during the period (see Hemming 1970). Old World diseases and hard mining labor requirements also led to ongoing bouts of population loss among natives (Cook 1981, 1992; Joralemon 1982). These processes were compounded by the number of indigenous persons fleeing tribute obligations, placing additional strain on the functioning of the Spanish bureaucracy (Wightman 1990). The Cuzco region experienced an overall absolute decline in indigenous populations (Cook 1982) along with rapid geographic shifts under forced resettlement and subsequent demographic shuffling (see Covey, Childs, and Kippen 2011). In the earliest decades of these transitions, the archaeological record is more difficult to recover and reconstruct; indigenous persons settled down in new locales for brief periods and were slow to incorporate European material culture. However, over the length of the Colonial period (politically bracketed as 1542–1824),

archaeological survey data can provide a sense of the changes seen in the ethnohistoric record.

From early on in the Colonial period, Spanish institutions and policies strained native populations in Cuzco. Tributary labor grants (*encomiendas* and *repartimientos*) and land grants (haciendas) were bestowed upon conquistadors, Spanish administrators, elite Incas, and religious orders, reorganizing economic structures among indigenous tribute-payers (see Lockhart 1969, 1991; Burns 1999). Crown policies indirectly allowed for harsh *encomendero* practices and excessive labor demands (Yeager 1995) and likely led to increased migration away from early encomienda grants. Native repartimientos were governed by *corregidores de indios* through their *kurakas* (indigenous local officials) after 1565, yet life in the *corregimientos* was difficult and corregidores ignored royal decrees and laws designed to protect indigenous people from fiscal and labor abuses (Rowe 1957). The *mita* (labor tax) demands under repartimientos, especially in mines and coca fields, sometimes moved thousands of people away from their homes periodically, led to labor-related deaths, and then caused many people to choose not to return home after the mita period (Cole 1985; Julien 1998; Rowe 1957; Stern 1982; Yeager 1995). The economic pressures of mita requirements propelled a trend of unsanctioned migration through the Colonial period.

A dramatic shift in settlement patterns in Cuzco and the rest of Peru occurred during the office of Viceroy Francisco de Toledo who, between 1570 and 1589, imposed a massive resettlement program of reducciones (Levillier 1940; Salles and Noejovich 2008), which transferred populations away from their native villages and lands to planned, nucleated towns that were centrally administered. Reducciones were intended to facilitate Colonial administration, Catholic missions, and access to native labor, as well as to free up land elsewhere for Crown grants to Spaniards. While meant to manage the settlement of native populations, reducciones instead exacerbated native migration after the 1570s. Families were moved farther from their fields and pastures; they lost access to productive tracts and saw lands reclassified by Crown officials, all while experiencing increasing tribute demands on their households.

Settlement patterns in the rural hinterland of Cuzco also changed as a result of the Spanish Crown's management of land sales. Philip II required revenue in the late sixteenth century and ordered the sale of public lands not in use by indigenous populations. Two royal *cédulas* dictated the *repartos* carried out in the 1590s under the Marqués de Cañete. In 1631, Philip IV ordered another survey of land holdings and the sale of lands without titles. Two additional surveys occurred by 1694. Many more lands were transferred to Spanish or native elite ownership as a result, often as mercedes. Those series of *visitas* (administrative visits) recorded demographic information, as well as land tenure, and served as the basis for the Crown's *tasa* (tax) assessments. With each administrative review, more land titles were transferred to Colonial elites, which contributed to the development of the hacienda system (Amado González 1999:38).

At the same time, land usage by native communities was formalized through the resulting *composiciones de tierras*, which helped in the designation of tribute requirements by *ayllu* (see Rowe 1957). In some communities, there was not enough land over time; in others, especially where populations declined from disease and migration, lands went unused and could be transferred to Spaniards after the ongoing *revisitas*. The paucity of sufficient productive land in more densely settled communities led to complaints from local kurakas and *retasas* to reassess requirements. When the Crown's response was insufficient to alleviate the tribute burden, some indigenous households elected to migrate elsewhere and become landless and were thus excluded from regular tribute requirements. Migrants transferred their production efforts from the repartimientos to work on hacienda lands in many cases.

Under Colonial policies, persons residing in a town where they were not originally registered as landowning residents (*originarios*) were considered *forasteros*. Forasteros were not generally required to pay tribute, but they also were not generally landowners. The growing number of registered forasteros (found through labor contracts, censuses, and parish records) reflects the dramatic shifts in settlement taking place in the Cuzco region (Wightman 1990). Ann Wightman, studying Colonial migration up to 1720, estimated that half the bishopric of Cuzco was composed of forasteros (1990:7), whereas John Rowe proposed that by 1775, 38 percent of the population was migrant (1957:180). One major effect of such large-scale migration was that hacienda labor pools were augmented while lands were abandoned in indigenous communities and were transferred to Crown holdings. Moving to the hacienda entailed sacrificing one's home and land, but also meant alleviation from onerous tribute. Wightman cited an example from the Xaquixaguana region, in which the natives of Maras requested a revisita in 1597 due to unusually heavy tribute burdens; the reassessment was not granted (1990:18), an outcome that probably aggravated flight from towns such as Maras.

By the 1680s, the severity of migration around Cuzco reached a tipping point. The Crown sought a solution to the massive flight from reducciones. The Duque de Palata attempted to reverse the Toledan reforms and curb the number of those avoiding tasa and mita obligations, as he declared that indigenous people be defined by current residence rather than original documented residence (Wightman 1990:30–36). Palata returned migrants to the Crown's pool of tributaries. Overall tribute burdens were reduced and made more flexible with consideration to changing local demographics (see Cole 1984). After the plague of 1720, a 1723 revisita aimed once again to find an appropriate response to the numbers of forasteros in Cuzco. Accordingly, officials differentiated between forasteros who owned land (and therefore had economic resources and could contribute to the tasa) and those who did not (Wightman 1990:43). Two hundred years after the conquest, these later transitions were designed to ease some of the pressure on originario and migrant populations to pay tribute and serve as laborers for the Crown while the growing hacienda

system continued to draw taxpayers out of the repartimientos to work for wages on behalf of native and Spanish elites.

As indigenous populations dwindled and fluctuated due to demographic and political changes, Spanish officials struggled to collect tribute as native communities faced similar challenges. Over the decades after Viceroy Toledo's reforms, the reducción policy proved ineffective at stabilizing native populations. Although the resettlement program freed up lands to be sold and reallocated by the Crown, it exacerbated other problems. As populations declined in Cuzco over the long term, indigenous communities shrank or moved toward smaller hamlets and seasonal high-elevation settlements, while haciendas also grew at the expense of tribute systems. Widespread, ongoing migration in the region makes settlement archaeology relatively difficult given that people moved often and frequently broke with ayllu organization. The Colonial period lacks a consistently observable pattern, except in the primacy of reducciones, many of which cannot be studied archaeologically. With the above historical context taken into consideration, the systematically identified sites in Xaquixaguana provide a framework for tracing land use in the Colonial period.

Research Questions

The first question to consider is whether or not there were significant differences in the ecological strategies of settlement in the Inca and Colonial periods, which will enable us to determine which forces—ecological, social, or a combination of the two—drove Colonial period settlement. Analysis considers the availability of fresh water and site elevation, the latter taken as a rough proxy for the type of ecological productivity around sites. In the Colonial period, fields and pastures were often used differently than they were prior to the introduction of European crops and animals (Covey, Childs, and Kippen 2011:345–46), which should have an influence on the ecological strategies of Colonial settlements in contrast with those prior to the conquest. If no significant ecological relationships are found, then settlement patterns may be better explained by social factors or some combination of the two processes. Several patterns emerge in exploring the data, but it is also evident that some ecological factors did not change significantly.

The second issue is a question of reoccupation patterns. If Late Intermediate period (LIP) sites were significantly associated with Colonial occupation, it may represent a return to pre-Inca ayllu lands by local indigenous populations. In this scenario, it would seem that the imposition of Inca rule did not erase the memory of former production and social patterns on the landscape of the imperial heartland. Similarly, if Colonial sites were continuously occupied from the Inca period, then it would appear that native populations returned to their Inca villages after resettlement into Spanish reducción towns. This pattern would suggest that the Inca empire was relatively successful in altering the social and economic landscape and in reconstituting kin associations in a manner complementary to their aims at the local level in the heartland (see Rowe 1982). This return to Inca lands could also mean that the ecological strategies of the Late Horizon were favored in reconstructing local agricultural and pastoral economic regimes, a logical pattern since there was more climatic similarity from the late Inca to Colonial periods than for the LIP compared to the Colonial period (Chepstow-Lusty, Bauer, and Frogley 2004). If, on the other hand, there were no significant correlations of Colonial sites with LIP or Inca settlement, one may conclude that there was a diversity of social and ecological strategies functioning at highly localized levels that are not easily detected through survey alone.

Study Methods

The intensively and systematically surveyed Xaquixaguana and Qoricocha regions include a variety of ecological zones that should demonstrate the strategies employed in settlement and resettlement in the Colonial period, but the regions also illustrate how post-Inca ayllus may have re-ordered themselves according to earlier land tenure patterns. The XPAS survey region is divided into the modern districts of Anta, Pucyura, Huarocondo, Zurite, Chinchero, Maras, and Huayllabamba, which are also Colonial reducciones and provide a useful framework for assessing reducción-centered settlement patterns over time. Because site locations were identified by contemporary district location, which, in turn, is based to some degree on the location of Toledan reducciones, these districts are used as shorthand for the populations living in and around the Colonial reducciones.

Colonial sites in Cuzco are difficult to identify and there are challenges in evaluating their extension, period of occupation, and use. While the XPAS survey followed a systematic methodology of 50-meter intervals to locate sites, modern urbanism outside Cuzco obscures some of the largest Colonial settlements, especially many reducciones (e.g., Maras, Pucyura, and Huarocondo). Many sites with an identified Colonial component were occupied earlier in time and/or intermittently over the Colonial period, with the Colonial period often represented by a small quantity of sherds. A sort of palimpsest effect is a concern at sites where intensive, systematic surface collections were not taken.[1]

The region analyzed in this study is not meant to be representative of changes in the Viceroyalty of Peru in general or even the Cuzco region. Rather, it consists of three main areas representing diverse pre-Colonial and Colonial patterns. The Xaquixaguana or Anta Plain is a large valley especially suitable for maize farming, while the relatively higher elevations around Maras and Chinchero represent former Inca royal estate lands devoted to herding and multiple mid- and high-elevation crops. In contrast, the Qoricocha *puna* east of Chinchero contains high

grasslands that are ideal for camelid herding, as well as the limited cultivation of bitter potatoes. Registered elevations for all Xaquixaguana and Qoricocha Colonial sites range from 2850 to 4350 meters above sea level. The XPAS region includes areas transformed by Inca estate development, as well as important Colonial encomiendas later on (Alcina Franch 1970; Rostworowski 1970; Villanueva Urteaga 1971; Niles 1999; Nair 2003; Covey and Amado González 2008).

Following the methodology set by Parsons and Hastings for full-coverage pedestrian survey (Parsons, Hastings, and Matos M. 2000), "sites" were identified by the presence of artifacts, architecture, or both (see Chapter 1). All architecture was considered a site, even without associated artifacts, but more than 5 artifacts per 2500 m^2 were required to constitute a site in the absence of architecture. Diagnostic Colonial artifacts (*majolica* pottery) were found in low densities at identified sites (between 1 and 35 sherds). This may indicate that very small non-village sites were overlooked in survey, although the survey team was able to find a large quantity of sites under one hectare ($n = 87$). "Grab samples" of diagnostic surface artifacts were collected at all sites and systematic, intensive collections in 50 m^2 units were made at sites larger than a hectare. A 2 percent sample was taken at these larger sites and all diagnostic materials collected from these surface units.[2]

As a "grab sample" (non-systematic collection) of representative diagnostic artifacts was taken from the surface of each site under one hectare (the majority of the Colonial sample, or 76.5 percent), there are also challenges in identifying site extension for those sites not included in the intensive collections. The biases in interpreting Colonial settlement patterns in the XPAS region thus have the greatest impacts on the continually-inhabited large reducciones. The survey identified many small habitation and nondomestic sites, but the sparse distribution of diagnostic Colonial artifacts indicates that it is possible that the smallest sites were not identified (as would be the case in any period).

Diagnostic Colonial artifacts for the survey included a glazed pottery type introduced by Europeans called majolica (or *mayólica*). This ware type is a wheel-thrown, tin-glazed pottery, but particular glazing techniques and styles vary (Ferrándiz Castro 2009). In addition to glazed wares, pottery that was produced using Inca technology but with Colonial-style iconography may be used to identify Colonial settlement. However, it was not found in this study (Stastny 1986).

Majolica from Triana in Seville, Spain, has been identified in at least 1 Ecuadorian site using instrumental neutron activation analysis (INAA) (Jamieson and Hancock 2004). INAA and visual studies at Cuenca and elsewhere have indicated a more local source within the Viceroyalty. Panama Vieja, a major port town that served Peru until 1671, was a manufacturing center for majolica and is often identified as the origin of early Colo-

---

1. There were 132 sites with a Colonial component, and intensive, systematic surface collections were taken at 31 of those.

2. Nearly 1000 intensive collection units were made in the XPAS survey. Of those, Colonial material appeared in just 89 units (less than 10 percent) at 31 sites.

nial glazed wares in the Andes (Jamieson 2001; Jamieson and Hancock 2004; Lister and Lister 1974). After that time, majolica was no longer manufactured in Panama, and it is unclear when majolica production began in the Cuzco region.[3] However, in 1588, Spanish authorities established a roof tile factory in the parish of San Sebastián in Cuzco, so producers might have produced majolica vessels there as well (Acevedo 1986).

In the earliest decades after the conquest, majolica may have been used only by the elite since it was initially imported from Spain and Panama Vieja. However, widespread distribution of the ware type in the XPAS survey area suggests it was eventually consumed by a variety of households in terms of both social status and ethnic identity (Fig. 12.1). It would not have been prevalent enough in indigenous *tributario* households to be an accurate temporal marker in the earliest period, leaving a void in the identifiable Colonial record. However, beginning with the 1570s, we can at least identify settlement patterns through the reducción locations; after migration from these settlements, majolica consumption appears to be more widely distributed and serves as a diagnostic for the post-reducción dispersal back into the countryside and toward haciendas.

Both discontinuities and continuities in ceramic consumption present challenges to reconstructing high-resolution chronologies around rural Cuzco. First, glazed pottery was probably not widely used in rural Cuzco during the earliest decades after the conquest, rendering some of the earliest settlements invisible to regional survey programs. Second, settlements throughout the Colonial period continued to consume indigenous (Inca and utilitarian) ceramic wares in addition to European types. There are some chronological changes in the colors that were used for majolica glazes in Cuzco that could elucidate the diachronic transitions (Acevedo 1986:25). However, a second, more focused analysis of the ceramic assemblage would be necessary to detect any patterns, as only the general ware type was recorded in initial analyses.

Distribution of Colonial Settlements

Over time in the Colonial period, some local populations moved from the reducciones to haciendas or to smaller hamlets in rural Cuzco, using estancias seasonally, especially small high-elevation stations like those seen in the Qoricocha puna region of the survey. Departing from the obligatory reducción settlement, they either connected themselves to hacenderos to avoid the tasa or lived in dispersed small villages or hamlets while avoiding the tasa altogether or as tributary populations who periodically assembled for administrative functions. These processes create the conditions for "the cultural entanglements of colonial encounters [that] produce new kinds of societies that are the product of both colonizer and colonized but controlled entirely by neither" (Wernke 2013:6). The archaeological outcomes of those processes can be recovered and analyzed in the present survey region (Fig. 12.2).

As seen especially in the high-elevation Qoricocha puna sites in the XPAS region, the Colonial period brought a proliferation of estancias. In many cases, small Colonial settlements appear to be seasonal camps for camelid or other herding, often represented by the presence of corrals in association with decorated Colonial pottery. These facilities were not located near permanent water, though there are some *qochas* that fill with water during the rainy season (Fig. 12.3). Estancias did not emerge as a dominant mode of settlement as a direct result of Spanish policies, as herding was not a part of Toledan-era tasa requirements (Covey and Yager 2005). However, there appears to be a new economic trend toward transhumance and high-elevation pasturing of native and European animals.

Survey work in the Xaquixaguana and Qoricocha regions identified 132 sites with a Colonial component. Most of those are smaller than a hectare and the larger sites (where intensive

Figure 12.1. Examples of Colonial artifacts excavated at Cheqoq. Glazed wares can be used to document settlement patterns developing in the generations following the European invasion.

---

3. Production began in Lima by the seventeenth century (Jamieson and Hancock 2004:580).

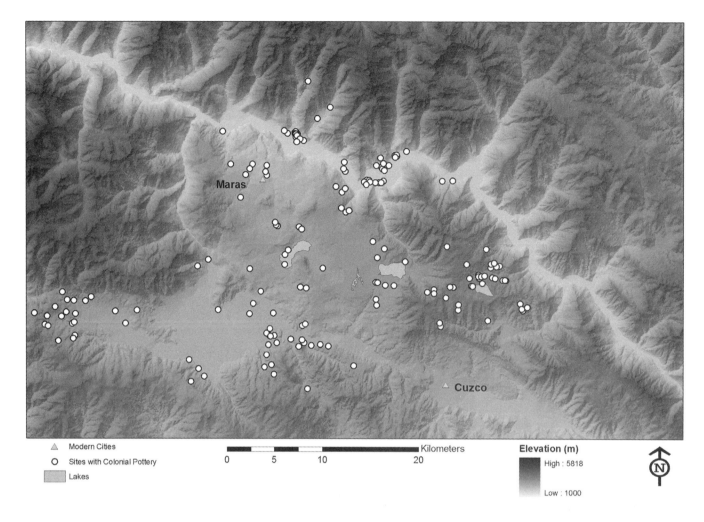

(*above*) Figure 12.2.
Map of XPAS sites with
glazed Colonial pottery
present on the surface.
Sacred Valley survey
projects did not record
Colonial sites systematically.
Note that the map excludes
reducción towns where
Spanish administrators
congregated indigenous
populations in the 1570s.
Courtesy of L. Tsesmeli.

(*left*) Figure 12.3.
Small corral group in the
Qoricocha puna, associated
with a seasonally inundated
pool.

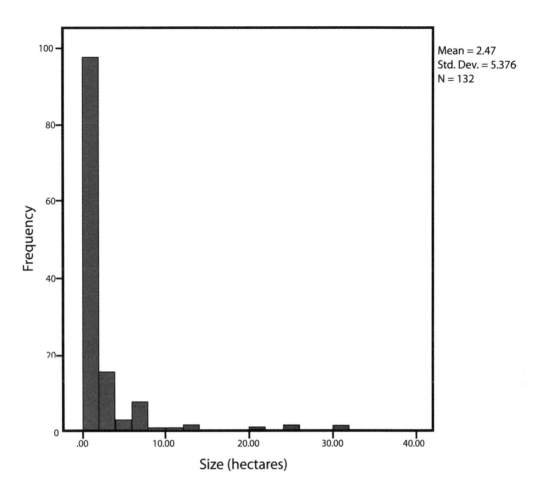

Figure 12.4. Histogram of site size estimates for Colonial sites in the XPAS region.

collections were conducted) usually contain only a minor Colonial component (Fig. 12.4). Some of the largest settlements in the Colonial period were presumably the reducción towns established in the 1570s by Viceroy Toledo; several of those are today obscured by modern settlement, including the towns of Pucyura, Anta, Huarocondo, Zurite, Chinchero, and Maras. These are not included in the survey data because they could not be registered using the project field methodology—reconciling site size estimates using surface collection data from these towns would be problematic and surface collections are not feasible. Other settlement types in the Colonial period include haciendas, hamlets, and estancias.

Some survey districts appear to have more dispersed or more nucleated settlements (Fig. 12.2). Huayllabamba, Pucyura, and Zurite appear to have more nucleated district settlement patterns, for instance. These reducciones are located in geographically circumscribed areas: Zurite and Pucyura abut the Xaquixaguana valley wall, which ascends rapidly to an impassable, uninhabitable area. The Huayllabamba district is directly adjacent to the Sacred Valley survey region, with part of the district within the

Calca-Yanahuara area (Covey 2006; Covey, Aráoz Silva, and Bauer 2008) and causing underrepresentation of the district in a district-focused analysis of XPAS data. In contrast, Anta and Huarocondo are the nuclei of more geographically extensive and dispersed districts and Maras and Chinchero are located on relatively open plains.

Thirty-one of the intensively collected XPAS sites had at least 1 Colonial sherd collected as a diagnostic for laboratory analysis (Fig. 12.5). Twenty of those intensively collected sites produced at least 2 Colonial sherds (29 percent of intensively collected Colonial sites). However, only 1 percent of decorated sherds from intensive collections at sites with a Colonial component were Colonial diagnostics. Overall, the intensively collected sites had low densities and ubiquities of Colonial diagnostics, which indicate that sites were probably less extensive during the Colonial period (Table 12.1).

While the preceding observations deal with the distribution and extent of sites in the Colonial period, it is also useful to see general district-by-district changes in the quantity of new Colonial settlements versus the quantity of settlements occupied

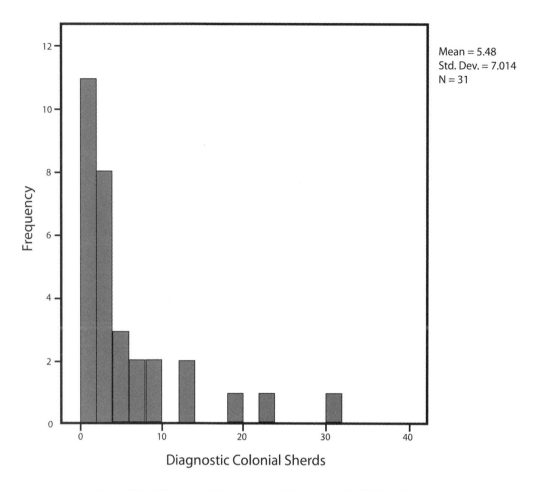

Figure 12.5. Histogram of Colonial sherd frequencies in XPAS collections.

in the Inca period and then abandoned. Comparison of these frequencies should indicate relative dispersal and nucleation between one period and the next between districts. There were significantly different numbers of sites by district between the Inca (no Colonial occupation) and Colonial (no Inca occupation) periods overall: $G(df = 6, n = 194) = 72.59, p = .000$.

The G test and Freeman-Tukey deviates show that on the Qoricocha puna, especially, there were significantly more sites established in the Colonial period than before (Table 12.2); this observation is discussed in greater detail below with regard to the ecological implications of that change in settlement strategies. There were significantly fewer newly-settled Colonial sites in the Huarocondo, Maras, and Anta districts.[4] This difference may be attributed to a lack of dispersal from within the reducción and/ or a relatively stable settlement trend (a lower level of migration within the district in general). Perhaps indigenous populations remained within the reducción because prehispanic settlement

was also relatively nucleated and travel to agricultural fields was not so onerous. All districts except Qoricocha had the expected number of settlements in the Inca period (all were relatively similar); Qoricocha had significantly fewer Inca sites, while Anta had significantly more. Changes in quantities of sites from the Inca to Colonial periods may indicate changing ecological strategies or intensification of small-scale sites and seasonally occupied estancias in regions with greater numbers through time. Data exploration with correspondence analysis, discussed below, contextualizes some of the differences seen in Table 12.2, as sites in particular survey districts were more strongly associated with Inca versus pre-Inca settlement patterns.

Ecological Strategies: Elevation and Distance to Permanent Water

The ecological impacts on settlement strategies within the Colonial period and through a trans-conquest view can be evaluated using site elevation (Fig. 12.6) and distance to a permanent

---

4. Huayllabamba was removed from the sample used for this test because there were no newly-settled Colonial sites.

Table 12.1. Diagnostic Colonial pottery at intensively collected XPAS sites.

Site	District	Overall Site Size (ha)	Colonial Sherd Count	Ubiquity of Colonial Sherds
X-019	Maras (m)	12.5	30	.17
X-028	Maras	1.12	3	.08
X-029	Maras	4.5	2	.03
X-040	Maras	7.5	1	.04
X-042	Maras	6.5	1	.03
X-050	Maras	3.6	5	.25
X-051	Maras	1.92	8	.6
X-075	Maras	24	9	.14
X-120	Maras	1.5	2	.5
X-129	Maras	3.75	12	.71
X-135	Huayllabamba (w)	7.5	19	.29
X-137	Huayllabamba	6	2	.1
X-150	Chinchero (c)	1.08	3	.14
X-152	Chinchero	3	3	.23
X-156	Chinchero	6	4	.2
X-157	Chinchero	5	1	.08
X-173	Anta (a)	20	1	.05
X-181	Chinchero	2	6	.13
X-183	Chinchero	5	1	.04
X-184	Chinchero	7.5	4	.18
X-195	Chinchero	10	1	.02
X-222	Anta	1.3	1	.2
X-228	Anta	12	1	.01
X-244	Anta	3	22	.41
X-258	Anta	30	1	.03
X-274	Pucyura (p)	3	3	.33
X-328	Huarocondo (h)	9	2	.33
X-331	Anta	3	1	.06
X-354	Anta	3	7	.31
X-384	Anta	31.5	13	.15
X-454	Zurite (z)	3	1	.11

Table 12.2. Observed site frequencies by district and period, with Freeman-Tukey deviates in parentheses (significant at the p < .05 level).

District	Colonial, No Inca		Inca, No Colonial	
Anta	1	(-3.18)	31	(1.29)
Chinchero	4	(-.64)	20	(.44)
Huarocondo	2	(-1.53)	20	(.8)
Maras	2	(-2.62)	32	(1.17)
Pucyura	2	(-1.1)	16	(.64)
Qoricocha	25	(4.67)	5	(-4.93)
Zurite	10	(.71)	24	(-.34)

water source (Table 12.3). Site-elevation patterns are used as proxies for changes in land use on the regional scale, since vertical shifts correspond with changing land use patterns in the past, while the absence of a permanent water source suggests a more seasonal or specialized use of a particular settlement.

There is a trend toward high-elevation settlements in the Colonial period, particularly due to the newly-established Qoricocha settlements (Fig. 12.7). A one-way between-groups analysis of variance in SPSS 19 was used to compare site elevations by period of occupation. The sites were divided into three discrete groups: (1) Colonial sites: mean = 3934, sd = 234.6, n = 46; (2) Inca sites without Colonial occupations: mean = 3551, sd = 221.8, n = 154; and (3) sites occupied in both periods: mean = 3639, sd = 353.8, n = 33. With equal variances not assumed, there was a statistically significant difference in elevation for the three groups: Brown-Forsythe (2, 60.776) = 30.923, p = .000. The effect size using eta squared was .27, which indicated large differences between the groups (Cohen 1988:284–87). Post-hoc comparisons using the Games-Howell test showed that the means for Colonial only and Inca only elevations were significantly different from each other (p = .000), as well as the means of Colonial only and

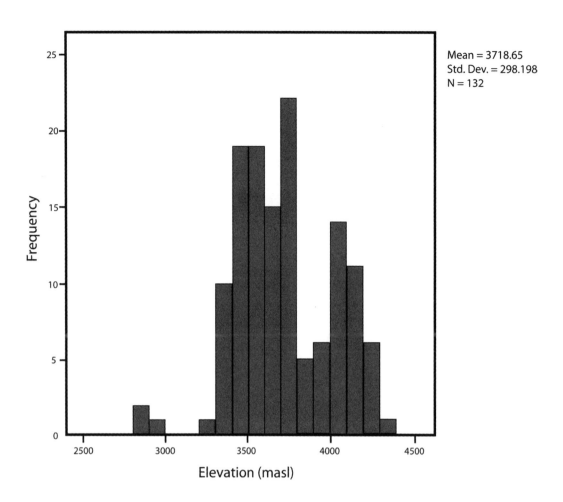

Figure 12.6. Histogram showing the frequency of Colonial sites identified at different elevations in the XPAS region.

Table 12.3. Descriptive statistics for site size, elevation, and distance to water by district.

District	Size (ha)			Elevation (m)			Distance to Water (× 100 m)		
	Mean	SD	SE	Mean	SD	SE	Mean	SD	SE
Anta	5.00	9.57	2.04	3547	141.8	30.2	1.00	.93	.20
Chinchero	2.30	2.84	.59	3815	280.2	58.4	2.22	2.13	.44
Huarocondo	1.86	3.51	1.43	3573	221.1	90.3	2.00	2.45	1.00
Huayllabamba	2.43	3.39	1.38	3856	323.2	132	5.17	3.25	1.33
Maras	3.77	6.12	1.08	3730	407.6	72.1	2.86	2.45	.43
Pucyura	.68	1.00	.32	3540	125.3	39.6	2.10	2.96	.94
Qoricocha	.21	.37	.11	4071	155.8	47.0	1.27	1.01	.30
Zurite	.36	.64	.14	3679	132.1	28.2	1.77	2.91	.62

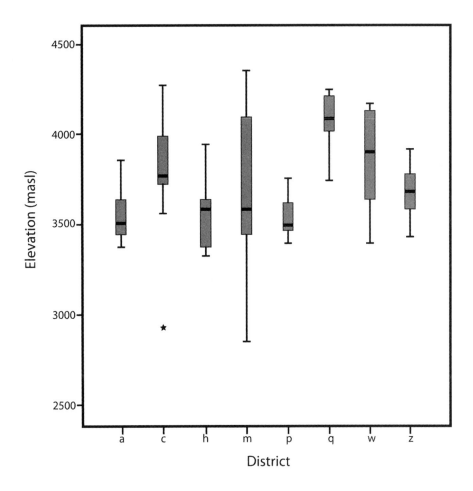

Figure 12.7. Boxplot of Colonial site elevations by district in the XPAS study region (see Table 12.1 for districts).

Inca–Colonial site elevations (p = .000). However, the means of Inca only and Inca–Colonial sites were not significantly different (p = .369) (Fig. 12.8).

The high-altitude puna zone (3800–4150 masl) that became a focus of Colonial occupation is linked to herding economies and low agricultural productivity; it experienced a marked Colonial establishment of estancias. Estancias with corrals have a major impact on this change, as 31 of 50 Qoricocha sites newly occupied in the Colonial period have corrals remaining on the surface. Local populations utilized previously uninhabited spaces for production of wool and meat on the puna. Another element to consider in evaluating elevation in the Colonial period is that 38 of 144 Qoricocha sites (or 38 of 64 sites that include non-architectural surface remains such as majolica pottery) had a Colonial component, representing 38 out of 132 total Colonial sites or 29 percent of total Colonial sites. In other words, the generally higher elevation of the Qoricocha puna pulls the mean site elevation upward when comparing means of all survey sites

and Colonial sites. There is a trend toward Qoricocha that did not exist before, which represents a significant economic shift on its own in the Colonial period. Native populations may have taken advantage of economic possibilities in seasonal herding at high elevation, an activity that was not directly linked to the tribute requirements of the tasa.

There is a significant change toward high-elevation herding in the Colonial period that is an outcome of departure from the reducciones and migration to other settlement types. However, although there appears to be a movement toward sites nearer to water in the Colonial period (Figs. 12.9, 12.10), a one-way between-groups analysis of variance using SPSS 19 indicates that there are not statistically significant differences in mean distance to water between Inca sites, Colonial sites, and sites occupied in both periods: $F(2, 230)$ = .158, p = .854. On the regional scale, strategies of access to water did not necessarily change from the Inca to the Colonial periods, at least not at sites outside the reducciones.

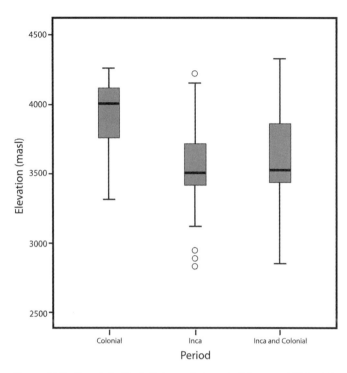

Figure 12.8. Boxplot of Late Intermediate period, Inca, and Colonial site elevations in the XPAS study region.

Figure 12.9. Boxplot of distance to permanent water sources for Inca and Colonial sites in the XPAS region.

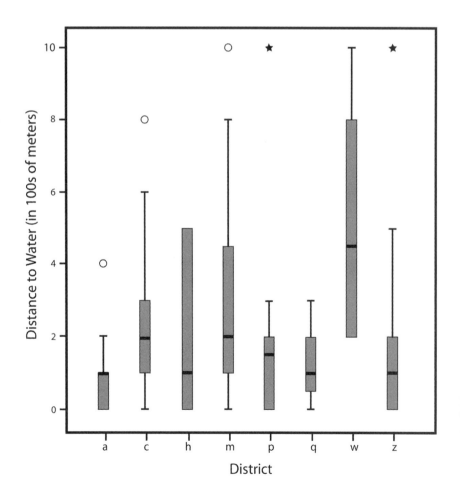

Figure 12.10.

Boxplot of distance to permanent water for Colonial sites in the XPAS region, by district (see Table 12.1 for districts).

Changes in household and community economies are evident in the trans-conquest view, and may be explained by Colonial tax requirements linked to farming that may have encouraged local populations to use the puna for herding. Many lands formerly used for camelids were devoted to cultivation in the Colonial period and the appearance of seasonal high-altitude settlements could be related to that shift. On the other hand, it does not appear that settlement strategies in relation to water access changed much. Increasing settlement in Qoricocha was not linked to water availability either; perhaps the puna was settled mostly during seasonally wet periods when small qochas would provide fresh water.

Social Influences on Migration and Resettlement (Dis)Continuities

As populations dispersed throughout the Xaquixaguana region following the reducción resettlement program, they might have returned to lands occupied within the Inca period or to lands occupied prior to Inca consolidation and resettlement policies. While the survey data cannot indicate whether descendants of a particular village returned to the pre-conquest settlements of their ancestors, there are some correlation and exploratory methods that may aid in finding similarities in the settlement patterns from one period to the next. Additionally, we cannot reconstruct the impetus for return to pre-Colonial settlements: did people migrate to the lands that their ancestors occupied in the Inca or pre-Inca periods in order to be closer to shrines and familiar toponyms? Was migration due to a return to a particular ecological strategy that just happened to coincide with previous periods? Or did people migrate to old settlements in order to reuse building materials, hydraulic systems, storehouses, and the like? The patterns and relationships suggested by the similarity coefficients and correspondence analysis in this section of the results are preliminary and suggest that excavations of targeted sites in the XPAS region are warranted in order to elucidate some of these issues.

Brainerd-Robinson similarity coefficients (BR) and correspondence analysis (CA) are exploratory methods used to seek patterns in the Colonial landscape. The objectives are to understand how similar diagnostic pottery assemblages from individual sites are to each other (BR) and to explore the continuity or discontinuity of Colonial settlement and LIP and Inca settlement (CA). Using the systematic surface collections from 31 Colonial sites, Brainerd-Robinson similarity coefficients were calculated with Keith Kintigh's Tools for Quantitative Archaeology DIST program (Table 12.4). The coefficients of similarity are calculated on a scale from 0 to 200, with 200 representing the strongest correlations and 0 representing no correlation (see Cowgill 1990). Similarity coefficients quantify the relatedness of pairs of sites based on the frequencies of diagnostic pottery types (frequencies of Formative, Middle Horizon, LIP, Late Horizon, and Colonial pottery at intensively collected Colonial sites). These coefficients can be compared with the membership lists provisionally generated through the correspondence analysis below.

Correspondence analysis was performed on two data sets: the intensively collected Colonial sites ($n = 31$), and the grab-sampled corpus of all sites with a Colonial occupation ($n = 132$). The first group is biased since it only includes sites over one hectare in the survey region and does not include any Qoricocha sites. However, it does provide a view of the Colonial patterns of resettlement and migration in the largest sites other than reducciones. On the other hand, the larger group of sites is limited since the diagnostic artifacts were not systematically sampled. However, correspondence analysis has been used successfully with a combination of frequency and presence/absence data, as performed here (see Beh 2004; Clouse 1999).

As a multivariate exploratory method, CA uses a two-way contingency table and chi square test of independence to generate a graphical representation of two-dimensional relationships; a significant chi square statistic indicates that the variables are dependent on each other and related. Correspondence analysis tends to even out variations in frequencies and instead focus on relationships between contexts (Wells 2006:35–36). Once dependence of sites and diagnostic pottery types is established with the chi square test, CA is used in a way similar to principal components analysis (Bølviken, Helskog, and Helskog 1982). Cases that are more similar appear more proximate to each other on a bivariate scatterplot of dimensions (similar to components) generated through CA, with each axis representing a dimension with a measured percentage of inertia in the model. Correspondence analysis was performed using JMP 9.

Correspondence Analysis of Intensively Collected Colonial Sites

Analysis of intensively collected Colonial sites showed significant departure from independence between sites and ceramic types (grouped as Formative, Middle Horizon [MH], LIP, Killke, Inca-related, Inca, and Colonial): $\chi^2 = 12492$, $df = 180$, $p < .0001$. Correspondence analysis provided dimensions that could be plotted to find clusters joining sites and pottery types together (Fig. 12.11). Four main clusters appear through visual inspection; these indicate that sites most strongly pulled by the Colonial pottery type are found closest (and thus, most related) to a cluster pulled by the Inca pottery variable and a cluster pulled by a combination of LIP, Killke, and Inca-related (Table 12.5). In other words, sites that are most closely associated with Colonial pottery have assemblages most similar to other Colonial sites closely associated with Inca and LIP/Killke/Inca-related styles. Some districts had Colonial sites more strongly associated with particular periods; for example, many of the earliest villages in Anta were reoccupied in the Colonial period, while many LIP sites in Maras were reoccupied in the Colonial period. Sites that were favorable to early village dwellers in Cuzco on the Anta Plain were apparently useful in the Colonial economy as well. Two of the 6 sites in this group were continuously occupied throughout the sequence of ceramic-producing societies in Cuzco, including Ayllu Tumibamba (X-454) and Ak'awillay (X-228).

Table 12.4. Brainerd-Robinson Similarity Matrix, demonstrating which intensively collected Colonial sites are most similar to each other.

	X019	X028	X029	X040	X042	X050	X051	X075	X120	X129	X135	X137	X150	X152	X156	X157	X173	X181	X183	X184	X195	X222	X228	X244	X258	X274	X328	X331	X354	X384
X028	183																													
X029	193	177																												
X040	188	189	187																											
X042	191	174	197	185																										
X050	196	182	195	189	192																									
X051	138	137	131	131	132	134																								
X075	32	48	28	40	26	33	29																							
X120	137	150	130	142	128	134	143	52																						
X129	150	166	143	156	141	148	169	50	153																					
X135	121	136	114	126	111	119	118	110	137	140																				
X137	111	128	107	120	105	112	107	120	126	129	189																			
X150	75	92	70	83	68	75	72	155	91	94	154	163																		
X152	181	191	174	186	172	180	145	42	150	169	132	122	87																	
X156	180	191	174	185	171	178	143	46	153	167	133	122	87	196																
X157	129	146	127	140	124	131	126	100	144	148	186	180	143	140	141															
X173	73	72	72	71	70	73	71	33	71	73	73	73	71	73	76	73														
X181	181	184	174	178	172	179	147	36	155	155	125	114	79	186	185	133	73													
X183	193	185	192	194	190	195	132	35	137	151	121	115	78	182	181	135	72	73												
X184	196	180	189	184	190	192	142	29	137	149	118	107	72	180	179	126	71	178	190											
X195	144	161	143	155	140	146	132	85	145	162	164	127	170	155	155	184	72	181	190	151										
X222	55	68	52	65	51	56	55	50	77	68	69	68	69	65	69	68	60	62	60	53	67									
X228	38	52	37	50	36	39	42	48	98	52	53	52	52	49	52	52	55	55	45	36	52	52								
X244	32	48	25	37	23	30	41	183	50	63	110	117	154	50	49	97	26	36	32	30	82	42	161							
X258	193	179	197	190	195	197	132	31	132	145	116	109	72	177	175	129	71	71	194	190	145	55	134	40						
X274	12	11	6	5	4	8	9	13	16	11	11	8	10	11	15	7	11	11	5	9	5	5	12	10	27					
X328	172	189	166	178	163	171	142	54	153	173	145	134	99	188	188	153	73	178	174	171	167	68	52	59	59	11				
X331	42	58	36	49	34	41	46	72	98	60	82	79	81	52	53	78	37	59	44	40	77	57	94	70	39	65	10			
X354	59	74	52	64	50	56	60	169	80	57	138	144	181	71	73	67	53	67	59	59	108	72	57	94	108	83	13	85		
X384	195	184	189	188	186	192	142	32	32	155	122	111	76	186	185	183	67	183	190	194	144	62	92	57	36	60	11	177	42	
X454	65	81	60	72	58	65	68	99	126	83	126	125	126	75	79	81	93	81	67	63	116	105	105	92	126	126	42	87	122	65

Table 12.5. Membership assigned from correspondence analysis of intensively collected Colonial sites.

Group Membership	Pottery Type and Sites	District
1	Formative Middle Horizon	
	X-173	Anta
	X.222	Anta
	X-228	Anta
	X-274	Pucyura
	X-331	Anta
	X-454	Zurite
2	LIP Killke Inca-related	
	X-019	Maras
	X-028	Maras
	X-029	Maras
	X-040	Maras
	X-042	Maras
	X-050	Maras
	X-051	Maras
	X-120	Maras
	X-129	Maras
	X-152	Chinchero
	X-156	Chinchero
	X-181	Chinchero
	X-258	Anta
	X-328	Huarocondo
	X-384	Anta
3	Inca	
	X-075	Maras
	X-150	Chinchero
	X-244	Anta
	X-354	Anta
4	Colonial	
	X-135	Huayllabamba
	X-137	Huayllabamba
	X-157	Chinchero
	X-195	Chinchero

Note: Pottery type membership shows which periods are most closely associated with the Colonial period occupation of a particular Colonial site. Group 4, with its Colonial-style membership, contains sites whose assemblages look more like each other than those with assemblages most closely associated with other styles.

In the Maras district, most of these larger sites have a major LIP component and a very minor Colonial ceramic presence, with little to no Inca occupation. Perhaps large LIP settlements became hamlets later in the Colonial period. More Colonial sites (in the sample of 31 intensively collected sites over one hectare) show LIP–Colonial continuity rather than Inca–Colonial continuity or new Colonial settlement. This "Colonial" group (Group 4) includes 2 sites each from Huayllabamba and Chinchero, which were all continuously occupied throughout the LIP, Inca, and Colonial periods. They are relatively large sites ranging from 7 to 15 ha, and are associated with both Killke and local LIP pottery types. This cluster includes the settlement of Ayarmaca in Chinchero (X-195), one of the supposed resettlement locations of the Ayarmaca ethnic group under Inca rule (Sarmiento de Gamboa 2007 [1572]). Huayllabamba and Chinchero thus appear to be locations of more continuous settlement in relation to other districts.

These exploratory results suggest that the data are too coarse-grained to make any definitive statements about resettlement connecting to Inca or pre-Inca ancestral lands in the Colonial period. Future research should further investigate Colonial sites at the intra-settlement level, especially through excavation and examination of the available ethnohistoric documents.

Correspondence Analysis of All Colonial Sites

Analysis of resettlement with the intensively collected sites only offered insight into relationships between the largest Colonial sites. Correspondence analysis of all Colonial sites (including those not intensively collected, $n = 132$) is not ideal since it combines systematic sampling with convenience sampling, but it does provide complementary results on settlement strategies in the whole region. Overall comparison of sites by pottery style frequencies (again, using Formative, Middle Horizon, LIP, Killke, Inca-related, Inca, and Colonial) found significant evidence for the dependence of the variables site and pottery style: $\chi^2 = 20879.42$, $df = 786$, $p < .0001$. A bivariate scatterplot of dimensions 1 and 3 for CA of all Colonial sites revealed three possible clusters of sites that covary with (1) Formative and Middle Horizon styles, (2) Inca styles, and (3) LIP and Colonial styles (Fig. 12.12).

The first cluster is pulled by Colonial sites coinciding with strong Formative and Middle Horizon signatures in the surface assemblage (Table 12.6). Only some districts are represented and this is the smallest group. The second cluster, more associated with Inca to Colonial continuities, is made up of sites from all districts except Huarocondo. The largest group, that which covaries with both Colonial and LIP and Inca-related pottery types, contains most of the Qoricocha sites, as well as many from Zurite and some from all other districts. The appearance of Qoricocha sites clustered with the LIP/Colonial group is misleading. There are no reoccupied LIP to Colonial sites in Qoricocha, and there is only one Inca-related site that also has Colonial material on the surface within the Qoricocha district. In general, some of the sites in the Colonial/LIP group have ceramics from only one period or the other. One important change occurs in the grouping created through CA when all sites are analyzed: all sites associated with Colonial occupation for the intensive collections change to the Inca group (they were all sites with occupations in all three major periods). There appears to be more association between Colonial and LIP/Killke/Inca-related material when all sites are included compared to the intensive collection CA in which Colonial-associated sites appear equidistant from the Inca and LIP/Killke/Inca-related pulls of the other groups.

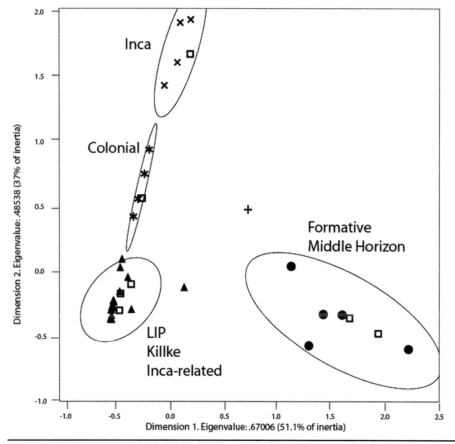

Figure 12.11.

Bivariate plot of dimensions 1 and 2 from correspondence analysis of intensively collected XPAS sites. Ninety-five percent confidence ellipses are around apparent groups. Squares represent the pottery type variables, while the other symbols differentiate between clustered groups of sites (see Table 12.5) (unclear group membership represented by "+").

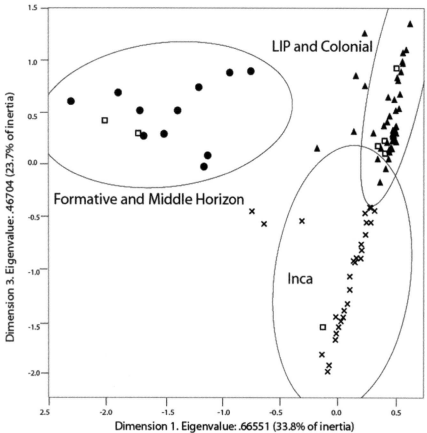

Figure 12.12.

Bivariate plot of dimensions 1 and 3 from correspondence analysis of all Colonial XPAS sites. Ninety-five percent confidence ellipses are around apparent groups. Squares represent the pottery type variables (labeled for each cluster), while the other symbols differentiate between groups of sites (see Table 12.6). The Colonial and LIP group also includes the pottery styles Killke and Inca-related.

Table 12.6. Apparent group clusters from correspondence analysis of all Colonial sites when dimensions 1 and 3 are plotted (Fig. 12.12).

Group Membership	District	Sites
Formative, Middle Horizon	Anta	X-173, X-222, X-228, X-234, X-331, X-425
	Chinchero	X-179
	Pucyura	X-213, X-274, X-286
	Zurite	X-338
Inca	Anta	X-244, X-354, X-373, X-375, X-383, X-386, X-389, X-463, X-473
	Chinchero	X-150, X-157, X-195, X-342
	Huayllabamba	X-097, X-135, X-137
	Maras	X-075, X-108, X-237
	Pucyura	X-210, X-352
	Qoricocha	Q-003, Q-029, Q-112, Q-113, Q-142
	Zurite	X-399, X-454
Colonial, LIP, Killke, Inca-related	Anta	X-258, X-341, X-384, X-395, X-416, X-467
	Chinchero	X-146, X-152, X-156, X-169, X-181, X-183, X-184, X-197, X-232, X-241
	Huarocondo	X-167, X-260, X-278, X-328
	Huayllabamba	X-099
	Maras	X-19, X-28, X-29, X-40, X-42, X-50, X-51, X-65, X-66, X-74, X-120, X-129
	Pucyura	X-276, X-283, X-292, X-319, X-350
	Qoricocha	Q-002, Q-005, Q-007, Q-010, Q-017, Q-020, Q-021, Q-025, Q-026, Q-034, Q-035, Q-037, Q-038, Q-040, Q-042, Q-043, Q-044, Q-055, Q-056, Q-058, Q-062, Q-069, Q-073, Q-078, Q-080, Q-081, Q-082, Q-083, Q-086, Q-087, Q-092, Q-093, Q-094
	Zurite	X-289, X-306, X-309, X-360, X-371, X-380, X-381, X-396, X-411, X-413, X-421, X-426, X-427, X-430, X-431, X-432, X-459, X-462, X-465

Conclusions

There are several confounding variables to address: possible continued use of Inca and even pre-Inca pottery, the lack of reducción site data for comparing site size in different periods, and the palimpsest that characterizes surface artifacts recovered in survey from multicomponent sites. Despite these limitations, there are some significant differences within certain districts and between certain periods. These preliminary results demonstrate some suggestive patterns that warrant horizontal excavation to address temporality, site function, and household demography and economies.

These survey data provide information for exploring ecological, social, economic, and political relationships over time and space in the Cuzco region. Follow-up studies can contribute to multiple lines of evidence for identifying and understanding Colonial settlement patterns and the histories of individual sites. In the XPAS region, Covey recently completed a toponym survey designed to identify Quechua and early Colonial place names in order to link ethnohistorical records with archaeological data, an approach that has been used effectively in other regions (e.g.,

Pendergast, Jones, and Graham 1993; Wernke 2007, 2013). While Colonial administrative records such as censuses and tribute assessments may be incomplete or biased, joining multiple archival and ethnohistoric sources with systematic survey of the region may promote a more cohesive reconstruction of the impacts of Spanish imperialism. Ongoing archival research will contribute to understanding the broader picture of how the Inca heartland was transformed for a second time under a new imperial government.

Comparison of a few attributes of the data reveals that there were some significant differences in population dispersals from the Inca to Colonial periods. After the reducción policy was enacted, populations transitioned toward higher elevations, perhaps seasonally, as they escaped the hardships of Crown policies or continued as tributaries in marginal areas such as the Qoricocha puna. The Qoricocha district experienced major seasonal exploitation under the influence of the Spanish administrative system, in the form of small specialized settlements. Architectural evidence indicates that herding was a major draw to higher altitudes there. Evaluation of social influences on resettlement after the Toledan reducción program is less clear. Some districts saw more continuity in Inca to Colonial settlement, which would be expected due to the chronological proximity and climatic similarities between the two periods. In other districts, however, new Colonial settlements were more associated with pre-Inca sites.

One way to advance with these results is by horizontal excavations at sites, in conjunction with toponym and ethnohistoric data. The Xaquixaguana Regional Toponym Survey (directed by Alan Covey) has already collected place names in the XPAS region for such a purpose, and subsequent excavations at these historically recognized sites would complement the regional trends culled from survey data. An appropriate subsequent project would be to return to sites smaller than one hectare with Colonial occupation to do intensive systematic collections. A sampling strategy of 10 percent of the surface would permit investigators to assess the intensity of occupation and make more secure assessments of the history of occupation. If test excavations within reducción towns become a feasible option, this could further resolve chronological issues and explain, in part, how Spaniards selected sites for the Toledan reducciones of the 1570s. Understanding the distribution and character of these sites will assist students of the Cuzco Colonial period in evaluating the top-down edicts and bottom-up responses under a European colonial power. Colonial Cuzco is a particularly interesting case as the upheaval of Inca rule was still part of collective memory when the Spaniards conquered the region and began an assault on native economies, religion, and social structure.

Acknowledgments

I would like to thank Sunday Eiselt for teaching me the quantitative and exploratory methods used in the analyses. Drafts of this paper were read by Sunday Eiselt and Alan Covey, who provided useful suggestions.

References

Acevedo, S.
1986   *Trayectoría de la cerámica vidriada en el Perú. Vidriados y mayólica del Perú*, edited by F. Stastny and S. Acevedo, pp. 19–29. Lima: Universidad Nacional Mayor de San Marcos.

Alcina Franch, J.
1970   Excavaciones en Chinchero (Cuzco): Temporadas 1968 y 1969. *Revista Española de Antropología Americana* 5:99–121.

Amado González, D.
1999   Introducción al estudio histórico de los títulos de la Hacienda de Punchaopuquio, Curahuasi-Cusco. *Revista del Archivo Departamental del Cusco* 14:25–43.

Bauer, B. S.
1996   *The Development of the Inca State*. Austin: University of Texas Press.
2004   *Ancient Cuzco: Heartland of the Inca*. Austin: University of Texas.

Bauer, B. S., and R. A. Covey
2002   Processes of state formation in the Inca heartland (Cuzco, Peru). *American Anthropologist* 104(3):846–64.

Beh, E. J.
2004   Simple correspondence analysis: A bibliographic overview. *International Statistical Review* 72(2):257–84.

Bølviken, E., E. Helskog, and H. Helskog
1982   Correspondence analysis: An alternative to principal components. *World Archaeology* 14(1):41–60.

Burns, K.
1999   *Colonial Habits: Convents and the Spiritual Economy of Cuzco, Peru*. Durham: Duke University Press.

Chepstow-Lusty, A., B. S. Bauer, and M. Frogley
2004   Human impact and environmental history of the Cuzco region. In *Ancient Cuzco: Heartland of the Inca*, edited by B. S. Bauer, pp. 23–29. Austin: University of Texas Press.

Clouse, R. A.
1999   Interpreting archaeological data through correspondence analysis. *Historical Archaeology* 33(2):90–107.

Cohen, J. W.
1988   *Statistical Power Analysis for the Behavioral Sciences*, 2nd ed. Hillsdale, NJ: Lawrence Erlbaum Associates.

Cole, J. A.
1984   Viceregal persistence versus Indian mobility: The impact of the Duque de la Palata's reform program on Alto Per, 1681–1692. *Latin American Research Review* 19(1):37–56.
1985   *The Potosí Mita, 1573–1700: Compulsory Indian Labor in the Andes*. Stanford: Stanford University Press.

Cook, N. D.
1981   *Demographic Collapse: Indian Peru, 1520–1620*. Cambridge: Cambridge University Press.
1982   Population data for Indian Peru: Sixteenth and seventeenth centuries. *Hispanic American Historical Review* 62(1):73–120.
1992   Impact of disease in the sixteenth-century Andean world. In *Disease and Demography in the Americas*, edited by J. W. Verano and D. H. Ubelaker, pp. 207–14. Washington, D.C.: Smithsonian Institution Press.

Covey, R. A.
2006   *How the Incas Built Their Heartland: State Formation and the Innovation of Imperial Strategies in the Sacred Valley, Peru*. Ann Arbor: University of Michigan Press.

Covey, R. A., and D. Amado González
2008   *Imperial Transformations in Sixteenth-Century Yucay, Peru*. Memoirs, no. 44. Ann Arbor: Museum of Anthropology, University of Michigan.

Covey, R. A., M. Aráoz Silva, and B. S. Bauer
2008   Settlement patterns in the Yucay Valley and neighboring areas. In *Imperial Transformations in Sixteenth-Century Yucay, Peru*, edited by R. A. Covey and D. Amado González, pp. 3–17. Memoirs, no. 44. Ann Arbor: Museum of Anthropology, University of Michigan.

Covey, R. A., V. Bélisle, and A. R. Davis
2006   Variations in Late Intermediate Period Group Interaction in the Cusco Region (Peru). Presented at the 72nd meeting of the Society for American Archaeology, Austin, Texas.

Covey, R. A., G. Childs, and R. Kippen
2011   Dynamics of indigenous demographic fluctuations: Lessons from sixteenth-century Cusco, Peru. *Current Anthropology* 52(3):335–60.

Covey, R. A., and K. Yager
2005   Herding Practices in Cusco, Peru: Evaluating the Inka-Colonial Transition. Presented at the 70th meeting of the Society for American Archaeology, Salt Lake City, Utah.

Cowgill, G. L.
1990   Why Pearson's r is not a good similarity coefficient for comparing collections. *American Antiquity* 55(3):512–21.

Ferrándiz Castro, I. A.
2009   Cerámica colonial. *Saqsaywaman* 9:253–59.

Hemming, J.
1970   *The Conquest of the Incas*. San Diego: Harcourt.

Jamieson, R. W.
2001   Majolica in the early colonial Andes: The role of Panamanian wares. *Latin American Antiquity* 12(1):45–58.

Jamieson, R. W., and R. G. V. Hancock
2004   Neutron activation analysis of colonial ceramics from southern highland Ecuador. *Archaeometry* 46(4):569–83.

Joralemon, D.
1982   New World depopulation and the case of disease. *Journal of Anthropological Research* 38(1):108–27.

Julien, C. J.
1998   Coca production on the Inca frontier: The Yungas of Chuquioma. *Andean Past* 5:129–60.

Levillier, R.
1940   *Don Francisco de Toledo, Supremo Organizador del Peru: Su Vida, Su Obra (1515–1582), Tomo II: Sus Informaciones sobre los Incas*. Buenos Aires: Espasa-Calpe, S.A.

Lister, F. C., and R. H. Lister
1974   Maiolica in colonial Spanish America. *Historical Archaeology* 8:17–52.

Lockhart, J.
1969   Encomienda and hacienda: The evolution of the great estate in the Spanish Indies. *The Hispanic American Historical Review* 49(3):411–29.
1991   Trunk lines and feeder lines: The Spanish reaction to American resources. In *Transatlantic Encounters: Europeans and Andeans in the Sixteenth Century*, edited by K. J. Andrien and R. Adorno, pp. 90–120. Berkeley: University of California Press.

Nair, S.
2003   *Of Remembrance and Forgetting: The Architecture of Chinchero, Peru from Thupa 'Inka to the Spanish Occupation*. Berkeley: University of California.

Niles, S. A.
1999   *The Shape of Inca History: Narrative and Architecture in an Andean Empire*. Iowa City: University of Iowa Press.

Parsons, J. R., C. M. Hastings, and R. Matos M.
2000   *Prehispanic Settlement Patterns in the Upper Mantaro and Tarma Drainages, Junín, Peru, Volume 1: The Tarama-Chinchaycocha Region, Part 1*. Memoirs, no. 34. Ann Arbor: Museum of Anthropology, University of Michigan.

Pendergast, D. M., G. D. Jones, and E. Graham
1993   Locating Maya Lowlands Spanish colonial towns: A case study from Belize. *Latin American Antiquity* 4(1):59–73.

Rostworowski, M.
1970   El repartimiento de doña Beatriz Coya en el Valle de Yucay. *Historia y Cultura* 4:153–268.

Rowe, J. H.
1955   El movimiento nacional inca del siglo XVIII. *Revista Universitaria* XLIII(107):17–47.
1957   The Incas under Spanish colonial institutions. *The Hispanic American Historical Review* 37(2):155–99.
1982   Inca policies and institutions relating to the cultural unification of the empire. In *The Inca and Aztec States, 1400–1800*, edited by G. A. Collier, R. Rosaldo, and J. D. Wirth, pp. 93–118. New York: Academic Press.

Salles, E. C., and H. O. Noejovich (editors)
2008   *La "Visita general" y el proyecto de gobernalidad del virrey Toledo*, tomo I, vol. I. Lima, Peru: Universidad de San Martín de Porres Instituto de Gobierno.

Sarmiento de Gamboa, P.
2007 [1572]   *The History of the Incas*. Austin: University of Texas Press.

Stastny, F.
1986   Iconografía Inca en Mayólicas Coloniales. In *Vidriados y mayólica del Perú*, edited by F. Stastny and S. Acevedo, pp. 7–18. Lima: Universidad Nacional Mayor de San Marcos.

Stastny, F., and S. Acevedo (editors)
1986   *Vidriados y mayólica del Perú*. Lima: Universidad Nacional Mayor de San Marcos.

Stern, S. J.
1982   *Peru's Indian Peoples and the Challenge of Spanish Conquest: Huamanga to 1640*. Madison: University of Wisconsin Press.

Villanueva Urteaga, H.
1971   Documentos sobre Yucay, siglo XVI. *Revista del Archivo Histórico del Cuzco* 13:1–148.

Wells, E. C.
2006   *From Hohokam to O'odham: The Protohistoric Occupation
        of the Middle Gila River Valley, Central Arizona.* Sacaton,
        Arizona: Gila River Indian Community Cultural Resource
        Management Program.

Wernke, S. A.
2007   Negotiating community and landscape in the Peruvian Andes:
        A transconquest view. *American Anthropologist* 109(1):130–52.
2013   *Negotiated Settlements: Andean Communities and Landscapes
        under Inka and Spanish Colonialism.* Gainesville: University
        Press of Florida.

Wightman, A. M.
1990   *Indigenous Migration and Social Change: The Forasteros of
        Cuzco, 1570–1720.* Durham: Duke University Press.

Yeager, T. J.
1995   Encomienda or slavery? The Spanish Crown's choice of
        labor organization in sixteenth-century Spanish America. *The
        Journal of Economic History* 55(4):842–59.